S0-BDT-401

SHORTCUT KEYS

Reshape Points/ Crop Bitmap	Ctrl-click button 1	Snap Mode	Ctrl-N
Restore	Alt-F5	Step Rotate	F8
Rotate	Shift-Ctrl-F8	Symbol ID	F12
Save	Ctrl-S	Text	Ctrl-T
Select	Shift-F3	Undo	Alt-Backspace (or Esc if button 1 is still held)
Select All	F2		
Show Controls	Ctrl-K	Unsmooth	Shift-F6
Size	Alt-F8	View Previous	Ctrl-V
Smooth	F6	Zoom	Ctrl-Z

SLIDESHOW SHORTCUT KEYS

Add a Slide	Ctrl-A	Next Slide	right arrow key (or button 2)
Begin Show	Ctrl-B	Paste	Shift-Ins
Blend	Ctrl-L	Pause the Show	F2
Close SlideShow	Alt-F4	Predraw	Ctrl-P
Copy	Ctrl-Ins	Previous Slide	left arrow key (or button 1)
Cut	Shift-Del		
Delete Slide Name	Del	Replace (no special effect)	Ctrl-R
Deselect All	Ctrl-F2	Save Script	Ctrl-S
Duration	Ctrl-D	Select All	F2
Fade	Ctrl-F	Stop the Show	Esc
Jump to Slide	type the slide number and press Enter	Undo	Alt-Backspace
Laser	Ctrl-E	Wipe	Ctrl-W
Move Highlight	arrow keys		

Computer users are not all alike.
Neither are SYBEX books.

We know our customers have a variety of needs. They've told us so. And because we've listened, we've developed several distinct types of books to meet the needs of each of our customers. What are you looking for in computer help?

If you're looking for the basics, try the **ABC's** series. You'll find short, unintimidating tutorials and helpful illustrations. For a more visual approach, select **Teach Yourself**, featuring screen-by-screen illustrations of how to use your latest software purchase.

Mastering and **Understanding** titles offer you a step-by-step introduction, plus an in-depth examination of intermediate-level features, to use as you progress.

Our **Up & Running** series is designed for computer-literate consumers who want a no-nonsense overview of new programs. Just 20 basic lessons, and you're on your way.

We also publish two types of reference books. Our **Instant References** provide quick access to each of a program's commands and functions. SYBEX **Encyclopedias** and **Desktop References** provide a *comprehensive reference* and explanation of all of the commands, features and functions of the subject software.

Sometimes a subject requires a special treatment that our standard series don't provide. So you'll find we have titles like **Advanced Techniques, Handbooks, Tips & Tricks,** and others that are specifically tailored to satisfy a unique need.

We carefully select our authors for their in-depth understanding of the software they're writing about, as well as their ability to write clearly and communicate effectively. Each manuscript is thoroughly reviewed by our technical staff to ensure its complete accuracy. Our production department makes sure it's easy to use. All of this adds up to the highest quality books available, consistently appearing on best-seller charts worldwide.

You'll find SYBEX publishes a variety of books on every popular software package. Looking for computer help? Help Yourself to SYBEX.

For a complete catalog of our publications:

SYBEX Inc.
2021 Challenger Drive, Alameda, CA 94501
Tel: (510) 523-8233/(800) 227-2346 Telex: 336311
Fax: (510) 523-2373

SYBEX is committed to using natural resources wisely to preserve and improve our environment. As a leader in the computer book publishing industry, we are aware that over 40% of America's solid waste is paper. This is why we have been printing the text of books like this one on recycled paper since 1982.

This year our use of recycled paper will result in the saving of more than 15,300 trees. We will lower air pollution effluents by 54,000 pounds, save 6,300,000 gallons of water, and reduce landfill by 2,700 cubic yards.

In choosing a SYBEX book you are not only making a choice for the best in skills and information, you are also choosing to enhance the quality of life for all of us.

Mastering Micrografx Designer

MASTERING
MICROGRAFX® DESIGNER™ 3.1

SECOND EDITION

Peter Kent

SYBEX®

San Francisco • Paris • Düsseldorf • Soest

Acquisitions Editor: Dianne King
Editor: Doug Robert
Technical Editor: Charlie Russel
Word Processors: Ann Dunn, Susan Trybull
Book Designer: Eleanor Ramos
Chapter Art: Suzanne Albertson
Screen Graphics: Cuong Le, Delia Brown
Typesetter: Elizabeth Newman
Proofreader/Production Assistant: Rhonda M. Holmes
Indexer: Ted Laux
Cover Designer: Thomas Ingalls + Associates
Cover Photographer: Mark Johann

SYBEX is a registered trademark of SYBEX, Inc.

TRADEMARKS: SYBEX has attempted throughout this book to distinguish proprietary trademarks from descriptive terms by following the capitalization style used by the manufacturer.

SYBEX is not affiliated with any manufacturer.

Every effort has been made to supply complete and accurate information. However, SYBEX assumes no responsibility for its use, nor for any infringement of the intellectual property rights of third parties which would result from such use.

First edition copyright ©1990 SYBEX Inc.

Copyright ©1992 SYBFX Inc., 2021 Challenger Drive, Alameda, CA 94501. World rights reserved. No part of this publication may be stored in a retrieval system, transmitted, or reproduced in any way, including but not limited to photocopy, photograph, magnetic or other record, without the prior agreement and written permission of the publisher.

Library of Congress Card Number: 91-66646
ISBN: 0-7821-1003-7
Manufactured in the United States of America
10 9 8 7 6 5 4 3 2 1

To Debbie, for looking after Nicholas,
and Nicholas, for letting me work—most of the time.
I owe y'all a trip to the dolphins.

At SYBEX I would like to thank Acquisitions Editor Dianne King for listening to my ideas and suggesting several of her own; Doug Robert, whose red pencil cut the manuscript down to size and brought some order to the final product; Dave Clark for helping me understand the wonders of ''snapshotting'' Windows; the various people whose names I never learned who were involved in the typesetting, art, and layout processes; and a special thanks to the proofreader who illustrated the galleys with anatomical sketches to indicate bottom-heavy headings.

At Micrografx I would like to thank everyone in technical support for answering what at times must have seemed like picky questions; the members of the design team—Amir Hessami, Brian McGlasson, Dave Mahafey, Brad Merkle, Joe Mills, Dylan Greiner, and Steve Emmons—who gave me more detailed explanations of various features; and Todd Fulks, who was especially helpful and patient.

I would also like to thank Slidemasters and MAGICorp for assisting with the section on TeleGrafx, and DFI for lending me an HS3000 Handy Scanner.

CONTENTS AT A GLANCE

TABLE OF CONTENTS

INTRODUCTION

$\mathbf{M}$icrografx Designer is one of the best illustration programs available for IBM PCs and compatibles. Designer produces high-quality vector-based images, it has a "user interface" that rivals that of Apple Macintosh programs (it has been described as a cure for "Mac envy"), it has won numerous awards, including the PC Magazine Award for Technical Excellence, and it was voted Editor's Choice by *PC Magazine.*

Designer lets you draw your own pictures, edit pictures scanned into your computer, or use commercial clip art. In fact, Designer even provides you with a large clip art library at no extra cost. But Designer doesn't stop there. It allows you to print or plot your work, of course, but unlike most illustration software it includes a special onscreen slide-show feature, and is even able to transmit your work across telephone lines to a print shop.

VERSIONS COVERED
AND SYSTEM REQUIREMENTS

This book covers all the features in versions 3.0 through 3.1. Micrografx Designer 3.0 had a release date of February 22, 1990. Micrografx released version 3.01 soon after 3.0—it is dated April 30, 1990—in order to provide full compatibility with Microsoft Windows 3.0. The new version also included new memory managers for 286 machines, and fixed a number of bugs that were in the original 3.0 version. Another minor upgrade, 3.02, was released some time later, and version 3.1 was released with a date of April 29, 1991. (If you want to know what date your software was released, watch the logo panel displayed when you open Designer, or select the Help | About command to see a dialog box with information about the program.)

Designer 3.1 has some important changes. The program is faster. Working with text, for example, which was a real problem with 3.0 and was slightly improved in 3.01 and 3.02, is much faster in 3.1. Gradients, object masks, and symbol fills are now much quicker, as are opening and saving files. There are some new features, also:

- Adobe Type Manager fonts can now be converted to curves.

- You can now bend lines of text to conform with a curve—for example, you can place text around a circle.

- You can blend two objects into each other.

- You can control the kerning of text (the spacing between letters and words).

- Wide lines can now be dotted or dashed—previously only the hairline could be anything but a solid line.

- *Hairline* now appears as an option in the lines menu.

- There is a new Batch Print window that lets you print several .DRW files at the same time, without opening them first.

- You can now import two more image formats: Adobe Illustrator and WordPerfect Graphics.

- 3.1 supports 256-color video boards.

- You can now make color separations of color bitmaps.

There are a few other notable features as well: you can create "square gradients," there is a new word-wrap command that controls the Paragraph settings, point sizes may now be specified in European didot points, bitmap display and printing has been improved, and you can edit the WIN.INI file to correct color and to remove undercolor.

You can use Designer on any AT-class IBM-compatible PC—a 286, 386SX, 386, or 486. The program requires at least 512K of RAM, although Micrografx recommends at least 640K, and more than that would help. (If you want to run Designer in Windows/386 or fully use Windows 3.0 you will need at least 2Mb of RAM.) You must have a hard-disk drive, and of course at least one floppy-disk drive. You will need a graphics card and monitor, and a mouse or another type of pointing device is recommended; it's not essential, but using Designer without a mouse is a bit like painting wearing boxing gloves—it's slow and awkward.

You also need DOS version 3.0 or higher. And Designer runs in Windows, so you need Windows 3.0, or Windows/386 or /286 (version 2.0 or later). **Version 3.1 will only run under Windows 3.0.** For more information on the configuration required, see Appendix A, "Installing Designer."

WHAT THIS BOOK COVERS

This book covers all the features of versions 3.0 through 3.1. You may wish to read the book from beginning to end, following the suggested tutorials to learn by practical example.

The first ten chapters present the basics of using Designer:

- Chapter 1 is an introduction to graphics programs in general and a discussion of what Designer can do for you.

- Chapter 2 explains the basic tools used by Designer. Microsoft Windows users will be familiar with most of these tools—such things as menu bars, dialog boxes, the pointer, scroll bars, and so on. Designer's tools, such as the rulers and grid, status line, and the drawing area, are also explained.

- Chapter 3 describes importing and using clip art, and simple editing procedures such as moving, rotating, and copying. It also explains how to use art that is in a file format different from Designer's .DRW format, and how to trace the image in order to convert it into a .DRW picture.

- Chapter 4 explains more techniques for modifying your imported art with colors and patterns, and how to use the clipboard.

- Chapter 5 teaches you to draw your own art using Designer's drawing tools.

- Chapter 6 explains the ways you can adjust line characteristics, such as colors, widths, joins, and ends. You will also learn about drawing with calligraphic lines.

- Chapter 7 describes how you can combine individual objects into more complicated pictures, using Designer's combine and connect commands.

- Chapter 8 introduces you to the text features, from selecting fonts and typing in the text, to adding colors and reshaping characters.

- Chapter 9 explains how to reshape objects using Designer's Reshape Points and Reshape Béziers tools—these tools give you absolute control over the final shape of any object.

- Chapter 10 shows you the basic methods used to produce your art on a printer or plotter.

The next six chapters offer more advanced techniques:

- Chapter 11 explains Designer's drawing aids, such as the rulers and grids, dimensions, layers, and arrays.

- Chapter 12 describes more advanced editing techniques such as aligning objects, using snap modes, selecting objects using symbol names (or IDs), and using the Array command to duplicate objects.

- Chapter 13 provides more information on using colors—how to mix your own colors, how to work with palettes, and how to label colors.

- Chapter 14 describes printing in more detail—the special illustration-layout tools, dual-spot separations, process-color separations, and using print files, for example.

- Chapter 15 introduces you to techniques used to produce slides, and shows you how to use TeleGrafx, Designer's telecommunications application.

- Chapter 16 explains how to use SlideShow, Designer's onscreen-presentation application for art produced in Designer. If you have the necessary hardware, you can also use this feature to produce a videotape presentation.

Appendix A describes how to install Designer, and tells you which clip art files you should install so that you can do the exercises in the first part of the book.

Appendix B shows how to use Help commands to get the latest information about Designer and quick answers to questions about the commands.

Appendix C helps you customize Designer, showing you the methods used to change the screen colors, to adjust the mouse and keyboard operation, and to change system defaults.

Appendix D explains how to import other graphics formats into Designer, and how to convert .DRW images into formats that can be used by other programs.

CONVENTIONS USED IN THIS BOOK

The following conventions are used throughout this book:

- **menu option names**   As a form of shorthand I will often refer to a menu option by preceding its name with the name of the menu. For example, you may see "select File | Save As" instead of "select the Save As option in the File menu."

- **clicking with the mouse**   Again, as a form of shorthand, I will often use the term "click on" instead of saying "use the mouse to move the pointer to the...and press the mouse button."

- **mouse instructions**   The instructions for using a mouse are in the main text. I will generally use the term "the mouse button" to mean button 1, the dominant button. I only use the terms "button 1" and "button 2" when necessary to be absolutely clear about which button should be pressed. (Although most programs use the left button as the dominant one, Designer lets you swap the buttons so the right one is dominant. This helps left-handed people, allowing them to use the mouse with the left hand. If you would like to change buttons before you begin, refer to Appendix C. You may find it easier to do this after reading Chapter 2, where you will learn the basic techniques for selecting commands.)

- **keyboard instructions**   The instructions for using the keyboard in place of the mouse appear after the mouse instructions, under a "Using the Keyboard" heading. In later chapters, when you have learned all the basic techniques, we will describe the mouse operations only, unless the keyboard operation is unusual.

- **keyboard shortcuts**   Designer has keyboard shortcuts that you can use to select commands more rapidly than you could using the menus. These shortcuts are included in parentheses in the main text, and they are listed on the inside front cover of the book.

- **icons**   When I refer to a commonly used tool, perhaps telling you to click on the tool in the tool box, the tool's icon is displayed in the margin.

- **key notations**   Most special keys are referred to by the name printed on the key. Sometimes we will call the four cursor-movement keys on the right side of the keyboard (↑, ↓, ←, and →) the arrow keys. The key labelled Enter or Return is referred to as ↵.

- **3.1** Most of the features and techniques covered in this book are the same for all versions 3.0 and higher. Where a technique is applicable only to version 3.1, the discussion will be flagged by the "3.1" tag in the margin.

You are ready to begin producing works of art with Micrografx Designer. Start with Chapter 1 if you want an overview of graphics programs. If you haven't yet installed Designer continue to Appendix A; otherwise go on to Chapter 2. Even if you have used Microsoft Windows for a while, read Chapter 2—it contains information on tools used by Designer, as well as standard Windows tools.

PART I

Learning the Basics

1

Understanding Illustration Software

Before you begin learning about Micrografx Designer you may want to learn a little about graphics software in general. This section is an introduction to the world of graphics, describing the different types of graphics programs, how they store their pictures, and what they can do for you.

TYPES OF GRAPHICS SOFTWARE

You purchased Designer because you needed an *illustration* program, one that will let you draw more sophisticated pictures than a simple *paint* program. But what are the actual differences between these two types of programs, and what other types of drawing packages are available?

PAINT PROGRAMS

Paint programs are simple drawing packages that produce *bitmapped* images. Bit mapping is explained later in this chapter; all you need to know right now is that bitmapped images have certain problems. Most important, they are difficult to enlarge or shrink without deforming the image, and the resolution of the final image is dependent on the resolution of the device used to draw the picture. In other words, if you use a low-resolution graphics board your image will always be a low-resolution image, regardless of the resolution of the printer or plotter you use to draw the final picture. Nevertheless, paint programs have their uses; you can make rough sketches and draw *freehand* (using a device such as a mouse or light pen in place of a paintbrush), and you can use them to touch up *scanned* images. In fact one of the most popular graphics programs is a paint program, PC Paintbrush.

ILLUSTRATION AND DESIGN PROGRAMS

Illustration programs have a distinct advantage over paint programs—their images are *vector-based*, which means they can be increased in size without changing shape, and the quality of the output depends on the output device, not the device used to draw the picture. In other words, even if you use a low-resolution graphics card to draw the image, you can still get a high-quality picture if you use a high-resolution printer or plotter. The best illustration packages, such as Micrografx Designer, provide special tools to help you draw and edit curves, to let you import bitmapped images and turn them into vector-based images, to produce camera-ready separations and slides, and so on.

CADD PROGRAMS

CADD (Computer-Aided Design and Drafting) programs are used in architecture, engineering, and technical design to produce technical drawings. These programs are rapidly replacing the drafter's drawing board, and their features, such as vector-based images, 3-D views, and object shading, are giving industry a more efficient way of getting ideas onto paper. You may have heard of CADD packages such as DesignCAD 3-D, AutoCAD, and Generic CAD.

PRESENTATION PROGRAMS

Presentation graphics are used to spice up business presentations. These programs produce professional looking graphs and charts in minutes, using data entered or imported from a spreadsheet or database. Two of the best known presentation packages are Harvard Graphics and Freelance Plus; these and the other top programs not only produce charts but also let the user import clip art to embellish the finished product. Some of the more advanced presentation programs let you produce *desktop presentations*, which are "slide shows" on a computer screen.

ANIMATION PROGRAMS

After producing beautiful pictures the obvious next step for the graphics software industry was to make those images move—and that is what animation software does. Packages such as PC Storyboard Plus and VCN Concorde link still images in sequence to produce a moving presentation that can be shown on a computer monitor or recorded on video tape. They let you "fade" or "wipe" between images and import images from other programs.

OTHER SOFTWARE PROGRAMS

The graphics programs just described are the most important and most common programs available, but are by no means the only way computers use graphics. *Clip art*—illustrations created by professional artists and sold copyright-free so that you can include them in your own work—is available for electronic art just as it is for paper art. *File conversion* programs, such as Micrografx's XPort, convert images from one format to another, allowing you to take a picture created in one program and use it with another. *Screen capture* programs, such as IMCAP, Hotshot, and Snap, take "snapshots" of whatever is on your monitor's screen, storing them as files for later editing and use. *Desktop publishing* and even many *word processing* programs can import pictures from graphics programs to be used as illustrations in newsletters and books. Still other graphics programs edit photographs or produce flow charts, organization charts, and forms. If you can imagine a use for computer graphics, there is probably a program to do it—or soon will be.

WHY PRODUCE ELECTRONIC ART INSTEAD OF PAPER ART?

So what's the use of electronic art? Why shouldn't you use paper instead? Just as the electronic spreadsheet makes accounting faster and more accurate, or word processing programs allow you to produce text more accurately and more rapidly, so too electronic art brings many advantages.

WHAT CAN DESIGNER DO FOR YOU?

You can produce art much faster on a computer than on paper. This may not be important to a budding Picasso or David Hockney, but to a business or graphic artist time is money, so speed pays. Furthermore, you can store images for security. If a graphic artist's office burned down, thousands of hours worth of paper could be lost, but if that artist used a computer (and saved backup tapes or disks at another location), he or she could be back in business the next day. Moreover, stored images are not only a form of insurance, but can become part of your future work; frequently used pictures, such as logos or drawings of a product's components, can be stored and used over and over again. Unlike a drafter working with paper, who will probably make a photocopy of one of these images to paste into a new drawing, you can "drop" the image into your new drawing in seconds, and then change its size, shape, or orientation at will.

Computer art makes editing a picture easy. Designer lets you quickly and easily enlarge or reduce pictures, modify their shapes, change individual parts' colors or shading, and delete, duplicate, replace, or move individual components. What could take hours on paper can take minutes or even seconds on a computer. In effect, Designer lets you "preview" a picture: instead of knowing exactly how you want the picture to look before you start, you can begin with a general idea and gradually build, changing the parts you don't like. You can try different shades, colors, or combinations of images, knowing that you can quickly change what doesn't look quite right.

WHAT DESIGNER CAN'T DO FOR YOU

Neither Micrografx Designer nor any other illustration package can make you an artist. "Art" demands more than technique; it demands an eye for what seems to "fit" or "work," for example, and it requires the ability to draw pictures with the correct proportions. After all, Micrografx can't tell you if the wheels on your car are too small, or if the eyes on your horse are too close together.

Designer cannot give you the talent of an artist, but it can help you produce professional results, especially when you start with professionally produced source material by using clip art and scanned images.

VECTOR-BASED GRAPHICS VERSUS BITMAPPED GRAPHICS

As you have already learned, Micrografx draws vector-based graphics, which are superior, in many ways, to bitmapped graphics. What does that mean? Let's start at the beginning, with bitmapped graphics.

BITMAPPED GRAPHICS

Your monitor's screen is made up of thousands of dots, or *pixels*. Your computer produces bitmapped pictures by filling specific pixels with color.

In order to draw a line, for example, the computer fills the pixels that lie on the path of the line.

In a bitmapped image, each pixel's location and color is recorded as a unique "bit" of information in a graphics file. If you take a bitmapped picture that was produced on a system with a coarse resolution, and display or print it on a system with high resolution, the image's resolution remains the same; the computer colors the *same pixels* the original line covered. Suppose the original line was one pixel wide, and the resolution of the output device is four times greater; that is, for every one pixel on the first device, the second device has four. That means that for every pixel the line covered on the old device four pixels are now covered. As you can see in Figure 1.1, the end result is that the line looks just the same, just as coarse. The computer cannot adjust the line's resolution, because it has no way to know which pixels *shouldn't* be colored.

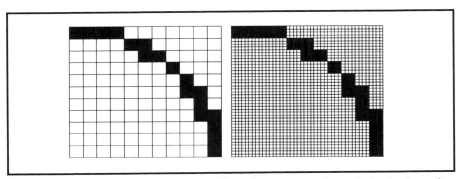

Figure 1.1: Bitmapped images: Changing the number of pixels doesn't change the resolution

For this reason, a bitmapped image doesn't change shape or size very well; most paint programs allow only very limited size adjustments because of this. Think of a program producing bitmapped images as a "dumb" program—it knows whether or not to color a pixel, and what color to use, but it doesn't know what the picture is.

VECTOR-BASED GRAPHICS

Programs that produce vector-based graphics (also known as *object-based* graphics) are "smarter" than bitmapped images. They store a series of instructions that tell the computer *how* to build a picture, rather than which pixels to fill in. Thus, the computer knows what the picture *is*, rather than just which spaces the picture covers. These instructions explain, using mathematical equations, where each line must go. Because the stored picture is made up of equations rather than instructions explaining which spaces must be colored, the picture quality improves when the picture is displayed, printed, or plotted on a device with a higher resolution; the computer fills only in as many pixels as is necessary to draw the picture. In Figure 1.2 you can see how the picture in Figure 1.1 would look if it were a vector-based image: only the necessary pixels would be covered, so as the output device's resolution increased, so too would the line's resolution. This "smart" program knows what the finished product should look like, so it can adjust accordingly. For the same reason, you can change the picture's size, without any distortion of the image.

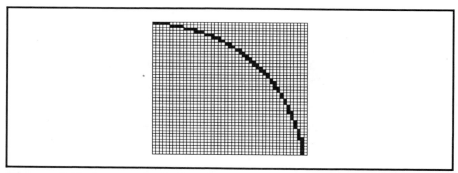

Figure 1.2: A vector-based image increases in resolution when you use a higher resolution output device.

Although Designer produces vector-based art, this doesn't mean you have to throw away all the art you produced with a bit-mapping program. You can still import some types of bitmapped images into Designer and incorporate them into your art. And you can even use Designer's Autotrace feature to convert them to vector-based art.

WHICH FILE FORMATS CAN YOU USE?

There are many different types of computer graphics formats. You can usually determine the file format by looking at the file's *extension*, the letters that appear after the period in a DOS file name. For example, a file called CAR.PCX is in .PCX format. When Designer draws an image it stores it in Micrografx DRAW format, using the extension, .DRW. Designer allows you to use other formats, though. You can *import* (bring into Designer) the following file types:

`3.1`

.AI	Adobe Illustrator files
.CGM	Computer Graphics Metafile—used by Pagemaker and Ventura Publisher
.DRW	Micrografx Designer files. This format is also used by Micrografx Draw Plus.
.DXF	Data Exchange File, produced by Autodesk for Auto-CAD, and supported by most CADD programs

`3.1`

.EPS	Encapsulated PostScript versions of Adobe Illustrator files
.GEM	Graphics Environment Manager, produced by GEM Desktop and used by many other programs, such as Ventura Publisher
.GRF	Micrografx Graph files, produced by Graph Plus
.PCT	Macintosh .PICT files
.PCX	Paint program files, such as PC Paintbrush. This is a bitmap format.
.PIC	Micrografx Picture files. This format was used by earlier Micrografx programs such as In*a*Vision. Compatible with many desktop publishing and presentation programs
.TIF	Tag Image File Format (TIFF), produced by scanners. This is a bitmap format.
.TXT	ANSI Text files
.WMF	Windows Metafile Format, developed for use in Microsoft Windows applications

`3.1`

.WPG	WordPerfect Graphics files

You can also *export* images; that is, you can save a Micrografx Designer image in a different format so that you can use the picture in another program.

You can *save* images in most of the formats that you can import. (The exceptions are the .GRF and .TXT formats.) You can also save in the following formats:

.EPS   Encapsulated Postscript, used to export images to desktop publishing programs such as PageMaker, Ventura Publisher, and IBM Interleaf Publisher. This is a combination bit-mapped and vector-based image.

.HP   Hewlett-Packard Graphics Language (HPGL), supported by most desktop publishing, CADD, and presentation programs

.PS   PostScript format

If you have formats that are not listed here, you may still be able to use the art by printing it using the program with which it was produced, scanning that image into your computer, importing the image into Designer, and using Designer's Autotrace feature to convert it into a .DRW image.

Now that you have learned a little about graphics programs, move ahead to Appendix A and install Designer, or to Chapter 2 to familiarize yourself with the basic tools used by Designer.

2

Getting
to Know
Designer

Because Microsoft Windows provides most of the basic tools used by Designer, you may already be familiar with much of the information in this chapter. Still, you should scan through this section, because some of the information relates specifically to Designer.

As you read this chapter experiment with the techniques described. Play with the program until you get a feel for it. Open a few menus, play with dialog boxes, and so on. This chapter doesn't have any step-by-step exercises, but if you follow the descriptions in the text, by the time you move on to Chapter 3 you should have learned all the basic skills you need. These are techniques that are used throughout Designer; so try to get comfortable with them before you continue.

AVOIDING MEMORY PROBLEMS

Graphics programs need a lot of memory. Even if you have lots of expanded or extended memory, you can still run into problems. If your computer is a 386, with lots of RAM, and you are using Designer 3.01 or later with Windows 3.0, you will be able to run other applications while you run Designer, and will rarely run into problems. But if you have a slow machine with little available RAM, if you are using an earlier version of Windows, if you have less than 1Mb of RAM, or even if you are using Windows 3.0 with lots of RAM but are running Designer 3.0, Designer can be very slow.

If you have pre-3.1 Designer and a pre-3.0 version of Windows, you can let Designer take over Windows' memory management functions, allowing Designer to run more efficiently, by using the /n switch when starting Designer from DOS, as discussed in Appendix A. If you don't use the /n switch, not only will some operations be slow, but some file-format translations may be impossible—Designer simply won't let you use the translators.

Strange things can happen when Designer gets low on memory, and art may even get "trashed"; you can reduce these problems by running Designer on its own whenever possible, and saving your work frequently. In fact, Micrografx recommends that you run Designer on its own.

When you are using Designer alone, the /n switch shouldn't cause any problems. However, some users have reported problems when they are running other Windows applications at the same time: the system might run very slowly, or it might become incapable of certain operations, such as printing. If you have any problems, try opening Windows without the /n switch, or try closing an application to get around the bottleneck, opening it again when you have finished the operation that caused the memory problem.

If you have to run other applications at the same time, give Designer enough time to redraw its window entirely when switching back to Designer from another application. If you don't do this—for example, if you select an option as soon as the menu bar appears—you may lock up the system. Pressing Esc may clear it, but at times you will have to reset your computer.

STARTING DESIGNER

How you start Designer depends on which versions of Windows and Designer you are using. Note that you cannot use Designer 3.1 with pre-3.0 or runtime Windows. If you have never used Windows before, some of these instructions (like double-clicking or selecting file names) may be unfamiliar to you. If this is the case, you should read the ''Hardware Tools'' section of this chapter before proceeding.

USING WINDOWS 3.0

1. If you have Designer 3.01 or later, start Windows as you would normally. If you have Designer 3.0, start Windows with the /r switch; type win/r and press ↵.

2. Double-click on the Designer icon in the Windows Applications window. (This is one of the easiest ways to open an application, but Windows actually has several other ways to open applications; see your Windows documentation for more information.)

USING PRE-3.0 VERSIONS OF WINDOWS

1. Open Windows using the DOS /n switch. For example, if you are using Windows/386, type win386 /n and press ↵.

2. Select Special | Change Directory, then type the path name of the directory in which you placed the Designer files. Press ↵.

3. Select the file named DESIGNER.EXE by using the arrow keys to select it and pressing ⏎, or pointing to the file with the mouse and double-clicking. Your computer begins running Designer.

USING RUNTIME WINDOWS

1. Get to the DOS C:> prompt.

2. If you used the the default directory name provided during setup, type **cd\designer** and press ⏎. If you chose another directory name, type that instead of **designer**.

3. Type **designer /n** and press ⏎. Your computer begins running Designer.

GETTING TO KNOW DESIGNER'S SCREEN

When you start Designer, you see a large, blank drawing area, bordered by various tools and bars, the main parts or components of Designer's screen:

- **Control-menu bar**   The place on which you click with the mouse to select the Control menu. This menu relates to Windows itself, and it is common to all programs operating under Windows.

- **title bar**   Displays the name of the program (Designer) and the name of the file in which you are working

- **size boxes**   Used to change the size of the window

- **menu bar**   The place on which you click with the mouse to select one of Designer's menus

- **scroll bars**   Used to display different parts of Designer's drawing area

- **tool box**   A box containing Designer's drawing tools and commands

- **status line**   Displays information about how the program is operating

- **rulers** Help you position your drawing and draw to scale

- **drawing area** The largest part of the window; the space in which you produce your art

- **pointer** A graphics "cursor" that indicates the part of the drawing area in which you are working. The pointer changes shape depending on the tool or command you are using; it changes to an arrow whenever you move it out of the drawing area.

These components are shown in Figure 2.1.

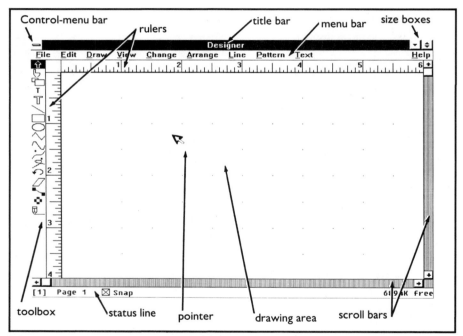

Figure 2.1: The main parts of Designer's screen

One of the main components of Designer's screen does not appear until the window is reduced from full-screen size. This is the window *border*, which is used to change the size and position of the window. You will learn more about this and the other "software" components after we learn how to use the essential "hardware" components.

THE HARDWARE TOOLS

To interact with Designer, you can use the keyboard or you can use a pointing device of some kind, usually a mouse. If you are using Designer for anything more than play, you will find that not having a mouse is very limiting, like painting a picture by telling someone else where to put the paint. Not only is it easier to learn how to work with menus and dialog boxes using a pointing device, but such a device also gets you closer to the art, letting you use your hands almost like they were holding a pencil or a paintbrush.

This doesn't mean you won't use the keyboard, though. In fact, as you get to know Designer and understand how all the commands work, you will find that it is often faster to use the keyboard than a mouse to select menu options, and you will use *keyboard shortcuts* for the commands that you use most frequently. You will still use the mouse for the commands you use only occasionally, though (because you won't remember all the shortcuts), and you will still use the mouse to move around in the dialog boxes.

THE MOUSE AND
OTHER POINTING DEVICES

You can use a number of devices for moving the pointer on your screen.

- **mouse**   The most popular pointing device is the mouse. Moving the mouse across your desk moves the pointer on the screen. Move the mouse to the left, and the pointer moves to the left; move the mouse forward, and the pointer moves up the screen; move the mouse diagonally, and the pointer moves diagonally across the screen.

- **trackball**   The trackball looks like an upturned mouse (a dead mouse, perhaps?). It has a large ball that you roll with your fingers or the palm of your hand, with essentially the same effect as moving a mouse in the same direction.

- **digitizing pad**   You may also want to try a digitizing pad, a large plastic rectangle that is used with an instrument often called a ''pen'' (but which is sometimes a mouselike object). The pad can sense where the pen is at any moment, so moving the pen to the top left part of the pad moves the screen's pointer to the top left of the screen. The digitizing pad can thus be used to trace art onto your computer, by placing the art on the pad and tracing around the picture with the pen.

- **light pen** This is an instrument that senses pulses of light transmitted to your screen by a special board installed in your computer; when you press the pen against the screen the pen transmits a message back to the computer, which calculates its position. To move the screen's pointer you just move the tip of the pen to a different place on the screen and press.

All these devices have buttons that you use to send commands to Designer. Designer uses two buttons; if your device has three buttons you will not use the center one.

You can use any type of pointing device that is supported by Windows. However, throughout this book I will use the term *mouse* simply because it's easier to write than "pointing device." It doesn't matter what type of device you are using, the technique is pretty much the same: you use the device to move the pointer, and you press the device's button(s) to select items. So, if you are using a non-mouse device, follow the mouse instructions.

These are the basic terms used for mouse operations:

point	Move the mouse until the tip of the onscreen pointer is resting on the area of the screen or the item that you want to select.
press	Press and hold the mouse button.
click	Press and release the mouse button.
click on	Point the mouse to the desired item and click.
drag	Move the mouse while you are pressing the mouse button.
double-click	Rapidly click the mouse button twice.

Most programs use one of the mouse buttons more than the other, and it is usual for computer programs to use the left button of a mouse for most operations, because that is the button that your index finger rests on if you are right-handed. That may seem unfair to lefties, so in the interest of equal opportunity, I offer (in Appendix C) instructions for changing the buttons so you can use the right button instead. Micrografx refers to the "dominant" button, whether it is the left or the right button, as *button 1*, and to the other button (initially the right button) as *button 2*. Throughout this book, I will identify the relevant button only when it might be necessary to avoid confusion; where I don't identify which button to click or press, you may assume I mean button 1.

THE KEYBOARD

Throughout Designer's menus and dialog boxes you will see names of commands and options with one letter underlined. You can use the keyboard to select these items by pressing Alt and typing the underlined letter. For example, to select Pattern | Color, first press Alt and type *P*. Designer displays the Pattern menu. Then type *C*, and Designer displays the Color dialog box. The inside covers of this book list all the keyboard shortcuts, and I will also mention them in the text when applicable. They can save you a lot of time. I recommend that you put them to use at every opportunity so that you find it easier to memorize those you run into frequently.

You can also duplicate mouse actions with the keyboard. These operations are explained as needed throughout the book. The main things to remember are that, in general, the space bar duplicates the mouse's button 1, and the arrow keys duplicate the mouse's movement—that is, you use the arrow keys to move the pointer.

As useful as the keyboard can be, you really need a pointing device as well if you are going to use Designer much at all. But if you have to work without one, it is a good idea to adjust the *keyboard speed*. This is the rate at which the keyboard repeats characters when you hold a key down. If this speed is too low, some operations will be all but impossible with the keyboard—moving objects, for example. If you don't have a mouse, go ahead and read this chapter and experiment with Designer's tools, but then go to Appendix C to find out how to change the keyboard speed. When you have done that, continue with Chapter 3.

THE SOFTWARE TOOLS

You will use the keyboard and some form of pointing device—your "hardware tools"—to get to the symbols and words on your screen—Designer's "software tools." There are a number of different software tools used by Designer:

- the pointer
- scroll bars
- menus
- dialog boxes
- the toolbox
- the status line
- scroll boxes
- size boxes

USING THE POINTER

The pointer is the graphics equivalent of a word processing program's cursor; the pointer indicates where you are working. Whenever it is in one of the border areas it shows what operation you are selecting—you may be pointing to a menu or to the scroll bar, for example—and whenever it is in the drawing area it shows where you are drawing. Outside the drawing area the pointer is an arrow, but inside the drawing area the pointer's shape depends on what sort of command you are using. For example, if you are using the Zoom command the pointer is in the shape of a hand pointing with a finger, but while you are using a drawing tool the pointer is in the shape of a pencil. Immediately to the right of the pointer Designer displays a small icon that shows what tool you are using; if you are using the Square tool, for example, the pointer is a pencil with a small square next to it. Figure 2.2 shows several different pointers.

You can abort pointer operations by pressing the Esc key. If you are using the Zoom tool to zoom in on an area, for example, or a drawing tool to draw an object, or the Block Select tool to select several objects, pressing Esc stops the operation. For instance, if the drawing tool is in mid-drawing, the drawing disappears. The tool remains selected, though, so you can begin again.

Using the Mouse   It's very simple using the pointer with a mouse: Simply move the mouse to move the pointer. Moving the mouse forward moves the pointer up, moving the mouse to the right moves the pointer to the right, and so on. Moving the pointer out of the drawing area enables you to select menu

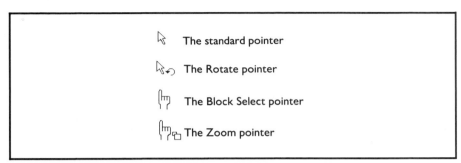

The standard pointer

The Rotate pointer

The Block Select pointer

The Zoom pointer

Figure 2.2: Various pointers

items or commands. Just use the mouse to point at the desired menu, then click or press the mouse button (button 1) to select the item you want.

Using the Keyboard   Using the keyboard to control the pointer is slow and awkward, but if necessary you can move the pointer in the drawing area by pressing the arrow keys, and you can simulate the action of the mouse's button 1 by pressing the space bar. Adjusting the keyboard speed might make things a little easier for you if you have to use the keyboard to move the pointer. Information for adjusting this speed is given in Appendix C.

You cannot use the arrows to move the pointer out of the drawing area. However, Designer provides a special cursor for keyboard users. Pressing Tab moves control from the pointer to this special cursor. The first time you press Tab the cursor appears in the ruler. Pressing Tab again moves the cursor into the toolbox, where you can use the arrow keys to select a drawing tool. Pressing Tab once more moves the cursor into the status line, where you can adjust the location of the pointer, change to another overlay, and change the Snap mode (all of this will be explained in the section on the status line later in this chapter). When you have finished in the status line, pressing Tab again moves control back to the pointer, where you can draw or perform other operations using the tool you selected. Pressing Shift-Tab, incidentally, moves the cursor in the opposite direction.

A Shortcut Method for Moving Objects

There is a special method for moving whatever you have drawn with the pointer. For example, if you are using a drawing tool, or using the Block Select tool to drag a dotted-line box (a ''rubber band'') around objects you want to select, you are either dragging the mouse while pressing button 1 or you are moving the pointer with the arrow keys while pressing the space bar. If you are using the mouse, press button 2 without releasing button 1, and the drawing or rubber band "freezes." While still holding both buttons, move the mouse: the drawing or rubber band changes position in the drawing area, without changing size. If you now release button 2 you can continue drawing or proceed to change the size of the rubber band.

If you are using the keyboard, you can freeze pointer operations in much the same way. While holding the space bar down, press *2* on your keyboard's character keypad (*not* on the numeric keypad), and then release it. The operation freezes—if you are drawing a square, for example, you can then drag the square, without its size changing. However, unlike the mouse method, this method does not return you to your previous operation. When you release the space bar the operation ends.

A Shortcut Method for Selecting Objects

Designer has a special feature that lets you select an object with the pointer even when you are already using one of the tools, such as a drawing tool or the zoom tool. It consists of quickly clicking on the object—but very quickly.

Suppose you have already selected one of the drawing tools when you find an object you want to move. You could select the arrow in the top of the toolbox (thus deselecting the drawing tool you were using), point to the object, and press the mouse button while moving the mouse to drag the object. But there is no need to deselect the drawing tool first. Instead, just point at the object you want to move, click very quickly to select it (the pointer turns into an arrow), then press and hold the button and move ("drag") the mouse. To change the arrow pointer back to the drawing tool, just click quickly in any blank space within the drawing area.

The speed at which you click is determined by the double-click speed you have set for the mouse; this speed is set in the Windows Control Panel, as explained in Appendix C. As long as you press and release (click) the mouse button at the double-click speed or faster, Designer changes the pointer to an arrow. (On the other hand, you must hold the button down longer than the double-click speed if you want to *draw* an object with a drawing tool you have already selected.)

There are a couple of important exceptions to the use of this shortcut. If you select the Text tool (the tool that allows you to type words into the drawing area) or the Trace tool (the one that traces bitmapped images) you cannot use the mouse button to select an object. As soon as you press the button with one of these tools selected, Designer assumes you want to type text or trace the image. Versions earlier than Designer 3.0 did not work like this, but Micrografx changed it because so many people had trouble making the text bar appear.

The pointer shortcut works for keyboard use as well: To select an object, quickly tap the space bar.

USING THE DRAWING AREA

Because most printers cannot print all the way to the edge of the paper, showing the printed page's full dimensions on screen can be misleading. Designer's drawing area shows only the area in which you can actually draw or position images; the unusable margins or blank borders are not shown. (This is why the default size of a page, 7 inches by 10 inches, is smaller than you might expect—it is actually the default *drawing area* of the page. You will learn in Chapter 11 how to adjust this size to allow even more effective use of your printer.)

When you draw or position an image that spans pages, Designer ensures that none of the image is lost for reason of printer margins. You are free to draw anywhere in the drawing area, which is enormous, really. The default drawing area is 54 pages, 7 inches by 10 inches each, arranged 6 by 9, as shown in Figure 2.3. When you are drawing, Designer's window can display only a small amount of this enormous area, so you need some way to move from one part to another. The mouse and two window scroll bars (one on the right side of the window and one across the bottom) do the trick best.

NOTE
You can't use the scroll bars if you don't have a mouse or another kind of pointing device; you have to use the Home, End, PgUp, PgDn, and arrow keys instead, as detailed in the next section. (Or enter a new page number or pointer coordinate in the status line— to be discussed in Chapter 11—and press ←⏎.)

Using the Window Scroll Bars to Move within the Drawing Area

Point to one of the black arrows, press the mouse button, and the window moves in the direction of the arrow. For example, if you press the arrow at the bottom of the *vertical* scroll bar the window moves *down*

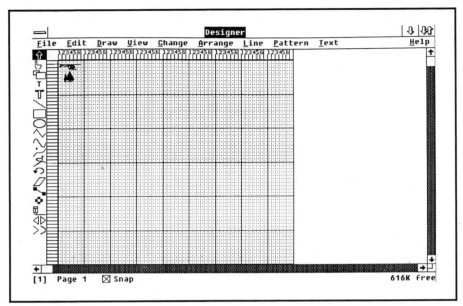

Figure 2.3: Designer's default drawing area

the drawing area, displaying the pages lower down. If you press the arrow at the right of the *horizontal* scroll bar, the window moves *across* the drawing area, displaying the pages to the right.

As the pages scroll you will notice that the small light-colored box (the *scroll box*) inside the bar moves also. The position of the scroll box along the scroll bar shows the position of the window relative to the overall depth or width of the drawing area. When the window is showing the middle page in the drawing area, the scroll box is in the middle of the bar; when the window is at the top of the drawing area, the box is at the top of the bar.

You can also use the scroll boxes to move the window to another part of the drawing area. Point at the box and press the mouse button, drag the box along the bar until it is in the approximate area you want, and release. Designer displays the area corresponding to the box's position.

One last way to use the scroll bars is to click on the bar itself; the scroll box moves toward where you clicked on the bar, and the drawing area "jumps" to the next window. By clicking on the bar several times you can scroll through the drawing area screen by screen, which not only gives you a more complete image of the drawing area but is sometimes faster than pointing at and dragging the arrow.

Using the Keyboard
to Move within the Drawing Area

The following list contains the keyboard pointer-movement commands. Snap to Rulers, explained more fully in Chapter 11, helps you align objects by limiting their movement to the ruler increments. With Snap to Rulers off, the pointer moves in small but undefined jumps. (Turn Snap to Rulers on and off by clicking on the Snap box in the status line.)

GENERAL:

Press	To Move
End	to the bottom left of the screen
Home	to the top right of the screen
PgUp	up one screen
PgDn	down one screen
Ctrl-PgUp	to the left one screen
Ctrl-PgDn	to the right one screen

WITH SNAP TO RULERS ON:

Press	To Move
down arrow	one ruler increment down
up arrow	one ruler increment up
left arrow	one ruler increment to the left
right arrow	one ruler increment to the right
Shift-Home	diagonally, one ruler increment to the left and one up
Shift-End	diagonally, one ruler increment to the left and one down
Shift-PgUp	diagonally, one ruler increment to the right and one up
Shift-PgDn	diagonally, one ruler increment to the right and one down

WITH SNAP TO RULERS OFF:

Press	To Move
down arrow	a small space down
up arrow	a small space up
left arrow	a small space to the left
right arrow	a small space to the right
Shift-Home	diagonally, a small space to the left and one up
Shift-End	diagonally, a small space to the left and one down
Shift-PgUp	diagonally, a small space to the right and one up
Shift-PgDn	diagonally, a small space to the right and one down

USING MENUS

NOTE

Throughout this book I have used a shorthand style of Menuname |
Commandname to identify commands. For example, ''select
File | Exit'' means select the Exit command from the File menu.

Designer lists all of its commands in menus. You can use commands by
selecting them from the menus, or, in some cases, by using a keyboard shortcut.

Notice that the menu names in the menu bar have one letter underlined. To open a menu using the keyboard, press the Alt key and then type
the underlined letter. For example, press Alt and type *F* to open the File
menu. (The Control menu—which is more a Windows menu than a
Designer menu—is indicated by a bar across the upper left corner of the
screen. If you want to open the Control menu, press Alt and then the space
bar.) The menu, a list of commands, drops down from the menu bar. Figure 2.4 shows the menu bar with the File menu selected. Once the menu is
open you can use the arrow keys to move up and down the list; when the
highlight rests on the command you want to select, press ⏎. Or just type
the letter that is underlined in the command name—there is no need to press
Alt first. (Also, once one menu is open you can use the right arrow or left
arrow keys to move to the next menu.)

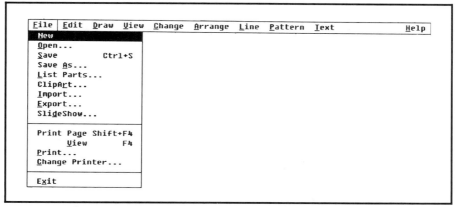

Figure 2.4: The File menu, showing the New option highlighted

There are two easy methods for selecting from menus using a mouse. The first involves clicking: click on the name of the menu (or on the Control-menu bar) to open the menu, then click again on the command you want. The second involves dragging: point to the menu name, and press and hold the mouse button until the menu drops down; then, still holding the button, move the pointer to the command you want, and release the button.

Some commands have not only an underlined letter, but also a shortcut key or key sequence, which is displayed within the menu, to the right of the command. You can use these shortcuts to actually bypass the menu. For example, once you use the Print Page command (in the Edit menu) enough times that you remember the shortcut sitting next to it is Shift-F4, you can print a page without having to open the Edit menu.

You may notice that some of the commands in a menu are dim, or *ghosted*. This means that you can't use the command at that time. If you don't have any objects selected, for example, and you look at the Edit menu, you will see that the Cut command is ghosted, because Designer doesn't know what to cut. Selecting commands followed by three periods, as in "Wide Style...," displays a dialog box, which is a sort of mini window that provides you with related options and information.

USING DIALOG BOXES

Sometimes when you select a command from a menu, Designer displays a *dialog box*. This is a box that contains a message or asks for information, which you input by typing or by selecting options. For example, in Figure 2.5 you can select various Save options (Screen Color, Background Style, etc.), and type a Smoothness value. Notice that the box has a cursor that indicates the area of the box in which you are working; the cursor takes the form of a dotted line (around Large in the Handle Size group, in this case) or a highlight (if it is in a text box). Dialog boxes typically have their own Control-menu bar that calls forth more options that let you size and move the box itself.

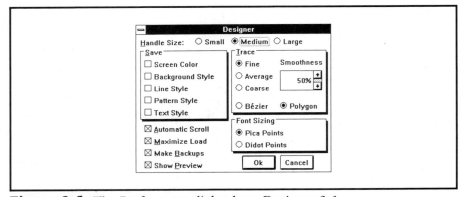

Figure 2.5: The Preferences dialog box, Designer 3.1

Using the Mouse: General   You can use the mouse to move the cursor within the dialog box by pointing and clicking. You can close a dialog box, canceling any instructions you have entered within it, by double-clicking on the Control-menu bar in the top left corner.

Using the Keyboard: General   To move the cursor with the keyboard, press Tab enough times to get to the item or group of items you want. (Pressing Shift-Tab moves the cursor in reverse.) You can also move the cursor directly to an item by pressing and holding Alt and typing the appropriate underlined letter. For example, in Figure 2.5 you can press Alt-T to move to the Trace options.

Checkboxes

The squares next to certain items, as in the Save group and in the group below that in Figure 2.5, are known as *checkboxes*. You select (or deselect, depending on their status) checkbox options by pointing to the square and clicking, or by pressing Tab to move the cursor to the square and pressing the space bar. Checkboxes are like on/off switches: the procedure is the same whether you are selecting or deselecting the option. (This type of feature is generically called a *toggle switch,* or simply a *toggle.*) You will know by the appearance of an X in the square that a checkbox is selected.

Option Buttons

The small circles in Figure 2.5 are called *option buttons.* Option buttons denote alternatives—unlike checkboxes, which allow you to select as many items as are available, option buttons allow you to select only one from any group. Options are grouped together, and the one that is selected displays a black dot inside the circle. In Figure 2.5, the options Fine, Average, and Coarse are in one group, and Bézier and Polygon are in the other; you could select, for example, Polygon and Coarse, but not Coarse and Fine.

Using the Mouse   Select the option you want by clicking on the circle next to it; a black dot appears inside that circle, and disappears from the circle it was in previously.

Using the Keyboard   Press Tab or Shift-Tab to move the cursor to the group of options you want, press the arrow keys to position the cursor in the circle next to the option you want, and press the space bar to select the option.

Text Boxes

Information you type, such as a file name or a number, goes into a *text box.* Figure 2.6 shows an example of a dialog box with a text box for entering a file name. Point to the box and click, or press Tab to move the cursor to the box. If you begin typing while existing text is highlighted, the old text is replaced by the new. However, you can also use the arrow keys to move around in existing text so that you can edit it, using Backspace to delete characters (and simply typing in the new ones). Pressing Home moves the cursor to the beginning of the text, and pressing End moves it to the end.

List Boxes

List boxes are used to display lists (as you may have guessed), often in alphabetical or numerical order, that may be too numerous to fit in the

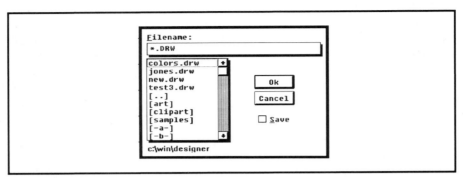

Figure 2.6: The Open File dialog box

dialog box. File names, for example, are displayed in list boxes, as in Figure 2.6. Note the scroll bar on the right side. If the list is too long to fit in the box you can use this bar to scroll through the list in much the same way that you use a window scroll bar to scroll through the drawing area.

Some list boxes are designed to show only one item at a time. An example of this can be seen in the Preferences dialog box (which was shown in Figure 2.5): although you could use the Smoothness box to select any number from 0 to 100 percent, there is only one number shown. If you wish, you can click on one of the arrows until the value you want is displayed, but it is sometimes easier to use this kind of list box as a *text box*, simply typing in the information you need.

Scrolling with the Mouse   Click on the down arrow; the list scrolls up, displaying entries lower down in the list. Or, point to the scroll box inside the scroll bar, press the mouse button, and drag the box down the scroll bar. When you release the button Designer displays the portion of the list corresponding to the relative position along the scroll bar at which you left the scroll box. This is especially useful in very long lists.

To actually select from the list, double-click on the item you want, or click on it once and then click on the OK button (a *command button*, the topic of the next section). For example, if you want to open a file you can double-click on the file name, or click once and then click on the OK button. In either case the file is opened.

Scrolling with the Keyboard   You can also use the keyboard to scroll and to select from the list. Press Tab until the cursor sits on the list box's scroll bar, and then press the up or down arrow key to scroll the list. To select items within the list, press Shift-Tab to get back into the list, then use the arrow keys, PgUp, or PgDn to move the highlight to the item you want. (Pressing End moves the highlight to the bottom of the list, and Home moves it to the top of the list.) If you know the name of the item you are looking for, you can type the first letter of the item to move directly to the section of the list that contains items starting with that letter. Once the item is highlighted, press the space bar to select it, and then press ↵ (the equivalent of clicking on the OK command button).

Command Buttons

Command buttons are rectangles with rounded corners, generally used to close the dialog box when you have finished using it. Most boxes have a button labeled "OK," which you click on to tell Designer that you have read its message or that you want to make the selected changes, and most also have a Cancel button that lets you close the box without making changes.

Using a mouse, you select the command button you want by simply clicking on it. Using the keyboard, you press ↵ to select the button that has a bold outline (usually the OK button), or press Esc to select the Cancel button. If there are buttons other than OK or Cancel, press the Tab key until the dialog box's cursor rests on the button you want, and then press ↵.

The Save Checkbox

Many dialog boxes, such as the Open File dialog in Figure 2.6, have a Save checkbox. You can use this box to change Designer's *defaults*. In this case selecting Save ensures that the next time you use Designer—even if you have turned off your computer in the meantime—the Open File dialog box will display the directory that was displayed the last time you closed the box.

Using the Keyboard in
Dialog Boxes: A Summary

The following summarizes how the keyboard works in a dialog box:

GENERAL:

Tab	Moves the cursor to the next area of the box
Shift-Tab	Moves the cursor to the previous area of the box

GENERAL:

Alt-	Pressing Alt in combination with a letter moves the cursor to the option that displays that letter underlined
arrow keys	Move the cursor between options
space bar	Selects the option on which the cursor is resting

IN TEXT BOXES:

arrow keys	Move the text cursor
Home	Moves the cursor to the beginning of the text
End	Moves the cursor to the end of the text
Backspace	Erases the letter to the left of the cursor

IN LIST BOXES:

arrow keys	Move the highlight up and down the list
PgUp and PgDn	Move the highlight up and down the list
Home	Highlights the first item in the list
End	Highlights the last item in the list

USING THE TOOLBOX

The toolbox duplicates menu commands. For example, if you want to select the square drawing tool, you can either select it from the toolbox or select Square from the Draw menu. Any command that can be chosen from a menu can be displayed in the toolbox; you will learn later how to add commands to the toolbox. The toolbox in Figure 2.7 shows the default toolbox, the one that Designer displays the first time you open it, with two extra tools added to the bottom.

Using the Mouse   The toolbox makes life easier for mouse users. Instead of using the mouse or keyboard to select a command or a tool from a menu, you can just point at the command's icon in the toolbox and click.

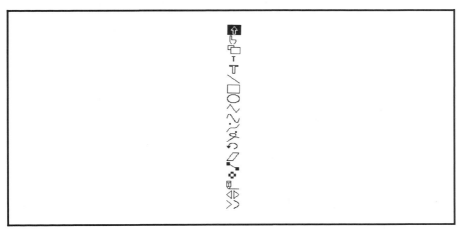

Figure 2.7: One of Designer's Toolboxes

Using the Keyboard   If you don't have a mouse you can still use the toolbox (though you may find the menus easier). Move the cursor into the toolbox by pressing Tab. Then use the arrow keys to move the cursor up and down the box. When the tool you want is highlighted, press the space bar to select it, then press Tab again enough times to move control back to the pointer.

USING THE RULERS

The rulers can help you position your pointer correctly, to ensure you draw with the correct proportions. The Rulers | Grid command in the View menu lets you modify the rulers, changing the increments and the scale. You can also make Designer display guides in the rulers as an additional aid—a dotted line displays in each ruler, showing the exact horizontal and vertical position of the pointer. You can use these guides to line up the pointer and draw accurately. You can turn the guides on and off using the Show Position option in the Rulers | Grid dialog box, or, if you have a mouse, by clicking in the corner between the two rulers. (Similarly, you can press Tab until the keyboard cursor appears in the corner between the rulers and then press the space bar. Then press Tab several times to move control back to the pointer.)

USING THE STATUS LINE

The status line displays helpful information. You can use the Status command in the View menu to choose the type of information you want to see:

- pointer coordinates, showing the pointer position in the drawing area, measured in coordinates per unit (inch or centimeter); the default is 480 per inch, so if the coordinates say "(480,960)," the pointer is 1 inch into the drawing area horizontally, and 2 inches down

- name or number of the layer displayed in the window

- number of the page displayed in the window

- Snap to Rulers mode (on or off)

- dimensions of the selected object

- amount of memory available to Designer

You can modify some of these directly in the status line: the pointer coordinates (the pointer moves to the coordinates you enter), the layer name or number (Designer displays the layer you enter), and the Snap mode.

Using the Mouse   To modify the pointer coordinates or layer number, point to the number you want to change, and click. Edit the number by using the arrow, Home, and End keys to move the cursor within the number, and type a new one. Press ◄┘ when you have finished changing the number. To change the Snap to Ruler mode, simply click on the Snap checkbox.

Using the Keyboard   Press Tab to move the cursor into the status line and between the items (as explained previously), then press the space bar to select an item (or type a new value where applicable).

CHANGING THE SIZE
AND POSITION OF WINDOWS

If you have used a windows-type program before you know how useful windows can be. You can use full-size windows, and jump to another screen when you need to, or you can use smaller windows, and have more

than one window on your screen at a time. You can move windows around
the screen, and change their sizes, and even turn them into icons so that you
can put them out of the way while you don't need them.

When you first open Designer the window is full size, or maximized,
covering the entire screen. You can change the size using the size boxes or
the Control menu. Figure 2.8 shows a screen with an open Designer window, a Designer icon, and the Windows 3.0 Program Manager icon.

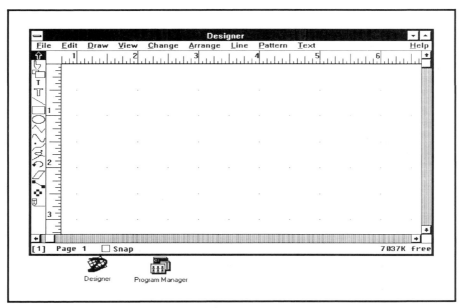

Figure 2.8: Window with icons

USING THE SIZE BOXES

The size boxes (in the upper right corner) let you modify the size of the
window. When you first open Designer the window is full size, and
the rightmost size box has two small triangles in it, one pointing up and one
pointing down. Clicking on this box reduces the window a little bit, by rais-
ing the bottom border and exposing the background underneath. This
allows you to see if you have any windows reduced to icon size; if you do,
they will be in this space at the bottom of the screen. At the same time, the
downward-pointing triangle in the rightmost size box disappears. In fact,

anytime the window is not full size, the box in the corner displays only one triangle, pointing up. Clicking on this box enlarges the window to full size, covering the entire screen, and the downward-pointing triangle returns.

NOTE

In pre-3.0 versions of Windows the small triangles in the size boxes are replaced by arrows.

If at some point you adjust the window size by dragging the borders (explained in the next section), and at a later point you maximize it, clicking on the rightmost size box will immediately reduce the window from full size to the size you had it before you maximized it.

Clicking on the box with the single downward-pointing triangle, the one next to the corner box, will reduce the window to icon size. The icon, a small picture of Designer's logo, is placed at the bottom of the screen. (If another window is in the way, however, you will not be able to see the icon.)

USING THE BORDERS

If you have a mouse you can modify a window's size, or move it, quite easily. (Note, however, that these techniques work only on windows that are not full size; that is, they work only when you can see the window's *borders*.) To resize a window, move the pointer to the window's border. (You will notice that the pointer changes to a double-arrow pointer.) Press the mouse button and drag the pointer to change the size of the window: If the pointer is on a side, you can move the side in and out; if the pointer is on a corner, you can move the two adjacent sides at once. Release the button when you have the window the size you want.

To move a window, point to the *title bar* at the top of the window and press the mouse button. Drag the mouse, and the window moves with the pointer. Release the button when the window is where you want it.

USING THE CONTROL MENU

The Control menu, shown in Figure 2.9, is common to all programs written for Microsoft Windows. (Designer has added one command, Add Window, to enable people using the runtime version of Windows to open multiple windows.) The Control menu lets you move the window, change

Figure 2.9: The Control menu

its size, change it into an icon, and restore it (change it from icon size to window size). Select the Control menu by clicking on the Control-menu bar in the top left corner of the window, or by pressing Alt followed by the space bar. If the window you want to move or resize has already been reduced to icon size, simply click on the icon itself to display the Control menu. (Dialog boxes also use the Control menu—or sometimes a shorter version of it—to move, size, and close the dialog box.)

These are the Control menu commands:

Restore	Changes the window back to the size it was before you reduced it to an icon or enlarged it to full size
Move	Lets you use the keyboard to move the window. Select this command and the pointer changes into a four-arrow pointer, signifying that you can use the arrow keys to move the window. Press ← to finish. (This option is not available if your window is full size, because, after all, where would you move it?)
Size	Lets you use the keyboard to change the size of the window by moving the top and right borders. Select this command and the pointer changes into a four-arrow pointer. Press the up arrow key to move the top border up, the down arrow key to move the top border down, the left arrow key to move the right border in, and the right arrow key to move the right border out. Press ← to finish. This option is not available if your window is full size, filling your screen.

Minimize	Changes the window to an icon at the bottom of your screen
Maximize	When you first open Designer the window is full size. Selecting Maximize at this point raises the bottom border, exposing the background screen (and any icons) underneath.
Close (Alt-F4)	Closes the window, ending the Designer session
Switch To (Ctrl-Esc)	Switches to Task List, a Windows dialog box that allows you to switch to other Windows applications and arrange the windows and icons. This option does not appear in the Control menu unless you are using Windows 3.0.
Add Window	Opens another Designer Window, so that you can work on another file

MOVING FROM ONE WINDOW TO ANOTHER

If you have several windows on your screen you can use the mouse, the size boxes, and the Control menu to move them and change their sizes; but how do you move from one window to another? There are a couple of keyboard commands to do this. Both Alt-Tab and Alt-Esc select the next window. These two commands are similar in many ways, but they have significant differences.

Pressing Tab while you press and hold Alt displays the *title bar* of the last window you had open. (If the window has been reduced to an icon, a small title bar is displayed under it.) If you continue pressing Tab while holding Alt, you can display one title bar after another. When the title bar belonging to the window you want to see is displayed, release the keys to select that window. The window will move in front of the other windows, if necessary. If you select an icon, the icon is enlarged into a window.

Pressing Esc while you press and hold Alt displays each *window* in sequence. This is a much slower method, because it doesn't just display the title bar. (If you select an icon, however, the icon is *not* enlarged into a window when you release Alt.) For this reason, this method is most suitable when you have only two windows open, or when you are changing back and forth between only two of the open windows.

Another way to select a window, if a portion of the window is visible on the screen, is simply to point at the window and click the mouse button. Designer changes that window to the active window, and moves it to the front.

USING THE ICONS

Reducing windows to icons is a handy method of keeping windows out of the way when you don't need them for a while. You can keep your screen uncluttered, yet you can quickly restore the windows when needed. The information that is in a window when you reduce it to an icon remains in the window, and is undisturbed by the reducing and restoring process.

Windows places icons at the bottom of the screen close to the left corner; if that part of the screen is covered by a window you won't be able to see the icon, but it's there nevertheless.

If you can see the icon you can use the mouse to select it. Click on the icon once to display its title bar and Control menu. Double-click to restore the icon to window size.

If you can't see the icon you can either use the mouse to move the obstructing windows out of the way, and then click on the icon, or you can use the Alt-Tab or Alt-Esc methods to select it. Pressing Tab, several times if necessary, while pressing and holding Alt will eventually display the title bar of the icon you want—the title bar displays even if the icon is underneath a window. When you release Tab, the icon turns into a window. Or, if you don't want to open the icon, press Esc while you press and hold Alt. The icon, as well as its title bar, displays over the window. When you release Alt, the icon remains displayed over the window, and appears thus until you click with the mouse in another window or use the Alt-Tab or Alt-Esc command again.

Moving Icons with the Mouse   You can move the icons around if you want by pointing to the icon, pressing the mouse button, and dragging. Release the button when the icon is where you want it.

Moving Icons with the Keyboard   Or use the Alt-Esc method to select the icon, then Alt-space to select the Control menu, and type *M* to use the Move command. Then press the arrow keys to move the icon. Press ←┘ when it is in position.

A SUMMARY OF SIZING AND MOVING COMMANDS

Operation	Using the Keyboard	Using the Mouse
Maximize the window	Control | Maximize	Click on the right-most size box or double-click on the title bar
Reduce the window's size	Control | Restore	Click on the right-most size box or double-click on the title bar
Change the window's size	Control | Size and the arrow keys	Drag the border
Reduce to an icon	Control | Minimize	Click on the leftmost size box
Display an icon's Control menu	Alt-Esc until the title bar is selected, then Alt-space	Click on the icon
Change an icon to its previous size	Control | Restore	Click on the icon twice
Move to another window	Control | Switch To (with Windows 3.0), Alt-Tab, or Alt-Esc	Click on the inactive window (if you can see it)
Move the window	Control | Move and arrow keys	Drag the title bar
Move an icon	Alt-Spacebar to select the Control menu, then Control | Move and the arrow keys	Alt-Esc until visible, then drag the icon

CLOSING DESIGNER

There are several ways to close Designer when you are finished working:

- Select Close from the Control menu

- Double-click on the Control-menu bar

- Select File | Exit

- Press Alt-F4

These commands close only the window you are working in; if you have more than one Designer window open you will have to close each one before the program terminates.

If you try to close Designer before you save your work, a dialog box will ask if you want to save the file before terminating the program. You can select Yes to save the file before closing, No to close the file without saving, and Cancel to return to the window without saving or closing.

If you have played with these features for a while, you should be comfortable with them; at least you know where to turn when the need arises. Now let's move on to Chapter 3 to begin work with Designer.

3

Using
Clip Art and
Imported Art

The best way to get a feel for Designer is to experiment with some of the free clip art that Micrografx provides. In this chapter you will learn how to select and display clip art, how to modify it, how to import art saved in other file formats, and how to trace bitmapped images to turn them into a vector-based image that Designer can work with.

Designer includes over 1700 pieces of clip art, stored in compressed files on the floppy disks. Unlike earlier versions of Designer, the current version does not let you use the sample clip art directly from the disks; you must install on your hard disk the ones you want to use. Before beginning this chapter, make sure that you have loaded the following files: BKGRN01D.DRW, TRANS01D.DRW, TRANS02D.DRW, and TRANS03D.DRW. (See Appendix A for information on installing these files.)

You should also set the Show Preview feature to *off*; this will speed things along when Designer needs to redraw a file. First, click on the View menu and then on the Show Preview option; if there is a checkmark in the menu next to Show Preview, the option is turned on. Select the option to toggle the option off. You will learn more about this command later in this chapter.

OPENING A CLIP ART FILE

If you allowed Designer's installation program to decide where to put the clip art, it is now in a subdirectory called CLIPART inside a subdirectory called DESIGNER, which is inside the windows directory (probably called WIN386, WIN286, or WINDOWS).

Select File | ClipArt to see a list of files:

1. Click on File in the menu bar.
2. Click on ClipArt... in the menu.

KEYBOARD
Press and hold Alt, and type *F*. Then type *R*.

Designer displays the ClipArt dialog box with the Open File dialog box in front of it, as shown in Figure 3.1.

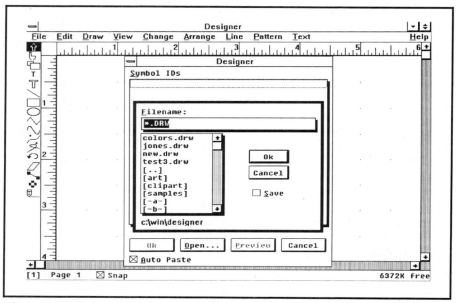

Figure 3.1: The Open File dialog box in front of the ClipArt dialog box

A QUICK LESSON ON DIRECTORIES

Those of you who are new to personal computing may need an introduction to directories before we go any further.

When you have a lot of different documents it's hard to keep track of what they all are. If you want to save documents you probably don't want to just take them all and throw them in a file drawer; instead you would probably want to organize them into folders and put the folders in the drawer. A *directory* is something like a folder; DOS lets you build directories in which you can save files in an organized manner.

DOS also lets you build *subdirectories*, directories within directories. This helps you to subdivide your information further, making it even easier to manage. Directories and subdirectories are arranged hierarchically. The first, or *root* directory, contains all the directories below it in what is called a directory "tree." Each directory in the tree may have a number of subdirectories, in which you may save numerous files.

You can describe a file, directory, or subdirectory position in this tree using a *path name*, which comprises the disk name, the name of the directory (and subdirectories if there are any), and file name, all divided by backslashes. For example, the path name C:\WIN386\DESIGNER\CLIPART\TRANS09D-.DRW refers to a file called TRANS09D.DRW which is in the CLIPART subdirectory, which is in the DESIGNER subdirectory, which is in the WIN386 directory, which is on disk C:.

Designer's Open File dialog box lets you move up and down this directory "tree," displaying the files from one directory at a time.

SELECTING A CLIP ART FILE

The Open File dialog box displays disk names, directory names, and file names. Disk names are shown as single letters between hyphens, in brackets; for example, [-C-] is the disk in drive C:. Clicking on one of these disk names displays the directory tree on that disk. The directory names are also in brackets, with [..] representing the root directory of the current disk drive. Click on this to move to the point from which the tree branches out, so that you can move to other "branches" (directories).

Try moving around in this tree by double-clicking on disk and directory names (but don't click on any file names yet—the ones showing a single period one, two, or three characters from the right) or by pressing Tab to move the highlight to the first entry in the list box. Press the down arrow key until the highlight rests on the name you want to select, then press ⏎. The list box displays the contents of the selected directory. (Unfortunately you may not be able to see the "highlight" when it first moves into the list box. It may be displayed as a dotted line around the first entry, or it may not display at all; however, when you press the down arrow key it will turn into a highlight again.)

Experiment with this Open File dialog box: select a directory name to see what files and directories it has; select the root directory to move up the directory tree; select other directories to see other branches. Or select a disk drive name to see what files and directories are contained by the disk in that drive.

When there are too many files and directories to display in the list box, you can scroll them into the box. Click on or press the down arrow in the scroll bar, or drag the scroll box to the bottom of the scroll bar.

KEYBOARD

Press End to move the highlight down the list, or use the arrow keys to scroll down the list.

In your experimenting you will probably notice the *path name* just underneath the list box. This shows you which directory is being highlighted in the list box, and also lets you select a directory on a branch further up the tree. Suppose, for example, the path name C:\WIN386\DESIGNER-\CLIPART is displayed. Everything displayed inside the list box is from the CLIPART subdirectory. You could list the contents of all the directories on the WIN386 branch by double-clicking on WIN386. Notice also the Save checkbox under the command buttons. If you select Save, then every time you use the File | ClipArt command Designer will redisplay the Open File dialog box open to the directory you were working in the last time.

Previewing the File

Designer lets you preview clip art before you select it, so you can make sure you have the correct picture. When you have finished experimenting with the list box, use it to display the contents of the CLIPART directory. Then follow this procedure:

1. Select the file called TRANS01D.DRW by double-clicking on it, or by clicking on it and then clicking on the OK command button.

KEYBOARD

Select the file name and then press ←┘.

---

2. The Open File dialog box disappears and the ClipArt dialog box lists the Symbol IDs (the names) of the pictures in the file, as shown in Figure 3.2. Select Helicopter03 and then click on the Preview command button (*do not double-click!*).

3. The ClipArt dialog box displays the helicopter. Even though you turned Show Preview off (at the beginning of the chapter), Designer still displays the clip art as shown in Figure 3.3. Press a key or mouse button, and Designer removes the picture.

KEYBOARD

Press Alt-S to move the cursor to the list and then use the arrow keys to highlight Helicopter03. Press Tab three times to move the cursor to the Preview command button, and press ↵.

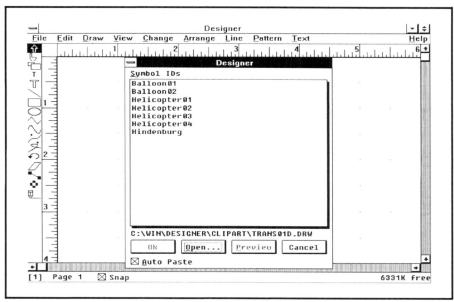

Figure 3.2: The ClipArt dialog box

Loading the File

Now you are going to place the helicopter into the drawing area:

1. Make sure that Auto Paste is selected (that there is an X inside the checkbox). If there is no X, click on the checkbox.

KEYBOARD

Use Tab to move to Auto Paste, and the space bar to select it. Then use Tab to move to OK and press ↵.

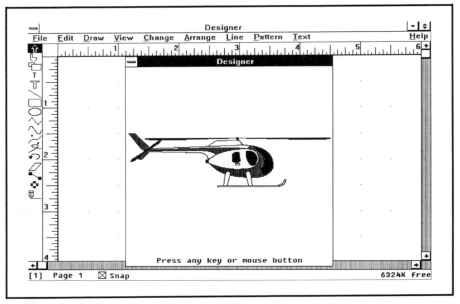

Figure 3.3: Previewing Helicopter03

2. With Helicopter03 highlighted, select the OK button. Designer removes the dialog box and draws the helicopter—but only its outlines—in the middle of the drawing area.

3. Now select the ClipArt dialog box again (File | ClipArt); Designer displays the same Symbol IDs. Click on Open... to see the list of files again.

4. Double-click on TRANS02D.DRW, and, when Designer displays the Symbol IDs, turn off Auto Paste.

5. Double-click on Sailboat02 (or select it and then click on the OK command button). The dialog box disappears, and the pointer turns into a cross; because you turned Auto Paste off Designer doesn't immediately draw the sailboat. Instead, it gives you time to move to another part of the drawing area first.

6. Use the scroll bar on the right side of the window to move the drawing area down one screen, to the area immediately below the helicopter. Then position the pointer in the middle of the window, and press and hold the mouse button. Designer displays the hourglass icon

momentarily, then draws a dotted-line box and the sailboat in the box. You can release the mouse button as soon as you see the hourglass or dotted-line box.

KEYBOARD

Move the pointer below the helicopter by using the arrow keys or the PgDn key. When the pointer is in position, press and hold the space bar.

That last step is something Micrografx's technical support line gets a lot of calls about. Remember, don't just press the mouse button (or the space bar) and release. You must actually hold it down until you see the hourglass or dotted-line box.

Viewing the Entire Drawing Area

1. Select View | View All Pages and you will see a view of the entire drawing area, with the helicopter and boat in the top left corner (Page 1 in the drawing area), as shown in Figure 3.4.

2. Now go back to the ClipArt dialog box (File | ClipArt). Select the Open... command button and the Open File dialog box is displayed again.

3. Select the file called BKGRN01D.DRW and then select the OK command button. Designer removes the Open File dialog box and displays the one Symbol ID in this file; "Mountain scene."

4. Double-click on the ID, position the pointer (a cross shape) in the middle of the page to the right of the helicopter and the boat, and press and hold the mouse button for a couple of seconds. Designer places the mountain scene into the drawing area.

5. Select View | View Used Pages. Designer changes the view to display enough pages to allow you to see all the pictures you placed; because the mountain scene takes space across three pages, the view shows a full three pages (see Figure 3.5).

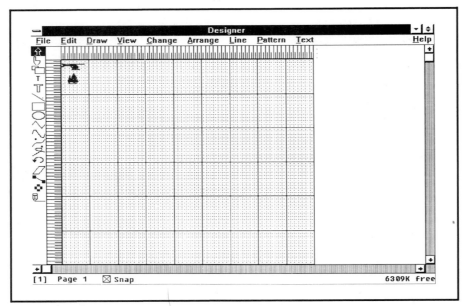

Figure 3.4: The view after using View | View All Pages

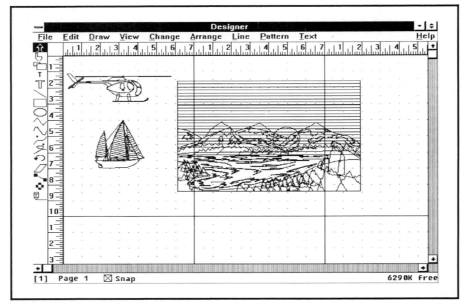

Figure 3.5: The clip art displayed with View | View Used Pages

RELATED VIEW COMMANDS:

View | View
Actual Size

Displays the selected object, actual size, in the middle of the screen

View | View Page

Displays the page containing the selected object, actual size, against the left and top borders. If no object is displayed, Designer looks to see which page occupies the top left corner of the drawing area, and displays that page's actual size against the left and top borders. It doesn't matter how much of the page first appears in the top left corner—if only a tiny corner of page 6 appears there, for example, Page 6 is the page that will be displayed after you choose this command.

View | View
All Pages

Displays the entire drawing area

View | View
Used Pages

Displays the pages that contain drawings

View | View
Previous (Ctrl-V)

Returns to the previous views in reverse order. You can go back to as many as 16 previous views.

Viewing the File
As It Will Look When Printed

Now that you've loaded the pictures you'll be working with, let's see what they actually look like. Remember at the beginning of this chapter I had you set Show Preview off? That was because when Show Preview is on, Designer draws the files you load with all the detail included, as they would be printed, and this can take time. Turning Show Preview off changes the drawings into ''wire frames''; no patterns, color, or special line ends are shown, and all the line widths are changed to the default width. This makes the drawings redraw (display) much faster, so it is useful when you are moving or importing drawings, or when you are drawing outlines of objects and are not yet concerned with colors and patterns. It is also useful when you want to select components that you can't see because they are at the back of a drawing, hidden by a color or pattern. How you set Show Preview will not affect the way the picture looks when you print it, and you can toggle it from on to off or off to on at any time, and as many times as you want, merely by selecting the Show Preview checkbox.

Try it now. Select View | Show Preview, and Designer changes the drawings, adding the colors and patterns (or *fills*). The boat doesn't look much different because it doesn't have color or fill anyway, but the helicopter and mountain scene look very different, as you can see in Figure 3.6.

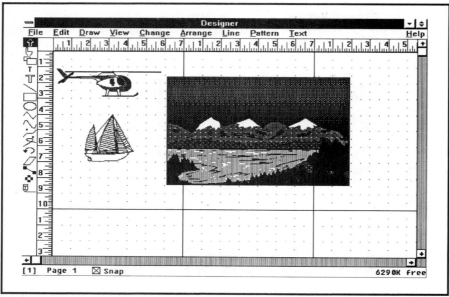

Figure 3.6: The clip art after setting View | Show Preview on

BEFORE GOING ANY FURTHER: HOW TO SAVE YOUR WORK

Every now and then you should save your work. Don't wait until you have finished, especially if you are working on a complicated picture, because if a memory crunch, power outage, hardware problem, or software bug crashes your system, you will lose everything you've done in that session. If you've never used Windows before you may not realize how often these things can happen—and they always seem to happen when you're working on something important!

If you have Windows 3.0 you should have fewer problems, but no version is immune to crashing. Get into the habit of saving your work every time you leave your desk, before you load clip art or other formats, and whenever you're otherwise just staring into space.

1. Select File | Save (Keyboard Shortcut: Ctrl-S). Because you haven't yet given this file a name, Designer automatically prompts you for one.

2. Notice the checkbox labelled Backup. If there is an X inside the box Designer will automatically make a backup file, with the file extension .BAK. Clicking on this box toggles the Backup feature on and off. Making a backup ensures that you can always go back to the previous version of the file. If you make changes to a file and then save the file, but later realize that you made a mistake making those changes, you can open the backup file (and use File | Save As to change the file extension from .BAK to the format you are currently using).

KEYBOARD

Press and hold Alt and type *B* to toggle Backup on and off.

---

3. If you created a directory named ART to store your work (as suggested in the installation procedure), type c:\win386\designer\art-\file1.drw (substituting as needed the correct Windows and Designer directory names for the system you are using) and press ←. Otherwise, to save your work in the directory displayed at the bottom of the dialog box, just type file1 and press ←. You can also use the path name at the bottom of the dialog box to select a directory further up the tree; just click on the name of the directory you want to use. See Figure 3.7 for an example of the Save dialog box.

NOTE

When you type long path names into the Save dialog box's text box, the text scrolls out of the box to the left. Don't worry, Designer still knows the text is there.

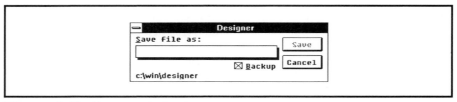

Figure 3.7: The Save dialog box

As you may have noticed, File | Save and File | Save As are rather different commands. The following should help you to remember the differences between the two:

- **File | Save (Ctrl-S)**   If you have been working on a previously named file, this command will *change* that file to reflect any changes you have made to it. Unless you have toggled Backup on, you will lose the previous version of the file when you use Save. If the file you are working on has not previously been named (i.e., you are creating a brand new file), Designer displays a dialog box that lets you enter a name and path.

- **File | Save As**   By using this command to give your file a different name from what it had, you can save the current (changed) version without disturbing the original version. The name should be different from any other file; otherwise you will replace the file that already has that name. This command displays the Filename dialog box; enter a name and a path and click on OK, and Designer creates a new file with that name. When you resume working, you are working in the new file (and the new name is displayed in the title bar).

WORKING WITH OBJECTS

Now that you have the clip art on your computer's screen, you can modify the objects; you can change their size and proportions, move them, make copies, rotate them, slant them, and even flip them around.

HOW TO CHANGE AN OBJECT'S SIZE

You are going to add the boat and helicopter to the mountain scene, so we need to reduce them.

1. Click on the helicopter. A box comprising eight small black squares (called *handles*) appears around the picture; one in each corner and one on each side, as you saw when you first displayed each drawing.

KEYBOARD

Move the pointer to the helicopter using the arrow keys, and then press the space bar.

You can use the handles to reduce or increase the size of the picture. Dragging one of the corner handles in or out reduces or enlarges the whole picture proportionally (that is, all the dimensions change to the same extent), and dragging a handle on one of the sides will stretch or compress the picture in the corresponding direction (for example, moving the handle on the bottom side toward the center of the box will reduce the picture's height only; the width remains the same).

2. Move the pointer until it is on one of the corner handles. The pointer turns into a double-headed arrow, with one arrowhead pointing to the center of the box, and the other pointing away from the box.

KEYBOARD

Move the pointer over the handle using the arrow keys.

---

3. Press the mouse button and drag the pointer toward the center of the box; Designer replaces the helicopter with a dotted-line box, which it then reduces in size as you move the mouse.

4. Release the mouse button when the picture is about half the original size. Figure 3.8 shows what the helicopter looks like while you are doing this.

KEYBOARD

Hold the space bar while moving the pointer inward using the arrow keys. Release the space bar when the picture is the correct size.

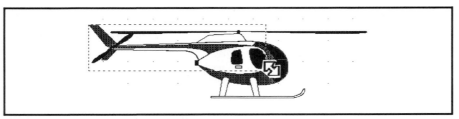

Figure 3.8: Reducing the helicopter

Now let's reduce the sailboat. Select the sailboat and, using the same techniques, move the handle on the bottom side toward the center until the box is about two thirds of its original height. Notice that the sailboat is not only smaller, but has changed shape: it is the same length but it is not as tall. Now use one of the corner squares to reduce the overall size of this shorter boat until it looks about the size of one of the white-tipped peaks in the mountain scene.

HOW TO MOVE OBJECTS

Moving the pictures couldn't be easier. Point to the center of the helicopter, press and hold the mouse button, and drag the picture until it is in the mountain scene, above the mountain peaks. Figure 3.9 shows how Designer displays a dotted-line box while you are moving the image. When you release the button, Designer draws the helicopter—and then it disappears behind the sky! This happens because you imported the mountain scene after the helicopter. When you draw or import objects, Designer assumes, unless you direct it otherwise, that the most recent object goes in front of the one preceding it. In other words, it assumes you start with the background and place foreground objects in order, from back to front.

KEYBOARD

If you don't have a mouse, you might try to use the arrow keys to move the pointer while you hold down the space bar. Unless the keyboard speed is on a fast setting, however, this is very difficult to do. As an alternative, you can use the Cut and Paste method, described later in this chapter. (Refer to Appendix C for information on setting the keyboard speed.)

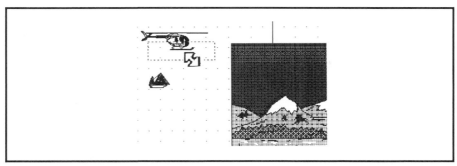

Figure 3.9: Moving the helicopter

By the way, there are two variations to moving objects with the mouse. If you point, press and hold the mouse button, and quickly drag the object, Designer displays the dotted-line box. But if you point, press and hold the mouse button, and wait a second or so before dragging the object, Designer displays an outline of the object as it moves it. This can be useful when you are trying to position an object correctly, though it can also be slow—the object seems to lag behind the pointer.

Also, if you want to be really precise about where you place an object, it might actually be easier to turn off Snap (in the status line) and use the keyboard method to move the object.

Moving an Object to the Front

Designer has added the helicopter to the mountain scene, but has placed it behind the other objects in the scene. Don't despair, though. As long as the helicopter is still selected (as long as you can still see the black squares), you can easily move the helicopter to the front. Just select Arrange-| Move to Front (Keyboard Shortcut: Shift-F9), and Designer displays the helicopter hovering in the sky.

But suppose you've moved the mouse and pressed a button and the boxes around the helicopter have disappeared. How can you get the helicopter back?

The easiest way is to turn off View | Show Preview. The outline of the object is then visible. Click on it twice: the first click selects the top object, the second selects the next layer down (the helicopter). Each time you click, Designer deselects the object from the previous layer and selects the next object below. If the helicopter were another layer or two deep, you would simply click again for each layer.

**Edit | Block
Select**

The drawback to the View | Show Preview method is that it takes time for Designer to redraw the object. If you have a good idea of the object's position, you can use another method to save the redrawing time. Either select Edit | Block Select (Keyboard Shortcut: Ctrl-B), or click on the Block Select tool in the toolbox (the second from the top, the one that looks like a hand with a pointing finger).

The pointer changes into a hand shape. Move the pointer until it is just above and to the left of the mountain scene, and press the mouse button. Drag the mouse diagonally down and to the right, across the mountain scene; you will see a dotted-line square being dragged out by the pointer. Once this square covers the area the helicopter is in, release the mouse button. (Don't entirely cover the mountain scene with the square, though, or you will select that instead.) The squares around the helicopter appear again; press Shift-F9 to move it to the front.

KEYBOARD

Select Edit | Block Select, press and hold the space bar, and move the pointer with the arrow keys.

RELATED SELECT COMMANDS:

Edit	Block Select (Ctrl-B)	Lets you select objects with the block-select tool
Edit	Select... (Shift-F3)	Lets you select objects by specifying a Symbol ID and criteria
Edit	Select All (F2)	Selects all the objects in the drawing area

Now let's move the boat. Select the boat, select the Arrange | Move to Front command, then move the boat, releasing the mouse button when the boat is somewhere in the lake. This time the Move to Front command ensures that Designer doesn't hide the boat behind other objects.

Using Cut and Paste

Another way to move objects—using the Edit | Cut and Edit | Paste commands—is useful if you want to move an object to another part of the drawing area or to another window. It is especially useful if you don't have a mouse. The procedure is simple. Select the object and then select Edit | Cut; Designer moves the object to the Windows *clipboard*. Move the pointer to where you want to place the object and select Edit | Paste. Then press and hold the mouse button to paste the new object onto the drawing area. (Keyboard Shortcuts: Cut = Shift-Ins, Paste = Shift-Ins.)

NOTE

Before Windows 3.0, you could not use the clipboard to hold images or files larger than 64K. The current version offers a greater clipboard capacity.

You can also use this method to move objects from one Designer file to another. Open the window that contains the art you want to move, then use the Control menu's Add Window command to open the window in which you want to put the art. Cut the object, and Designer loads it into the clipboard. Move to the other window (using Alt-Tab, for example), and place a copy of the object into the second window. (You don't have to select Edit-| Paste, because Designer automatically selects the Paste tool for you.)

NOTE

When using the numeric keypad for these commands, make sure the NumLock (numeric lock) key is not turned on!

RELATED MOVE AND COPY COMMANDS:

Edit | Cut (Shift-Del)	Removes the selected object and puts it in the clipboard
Edit | Copy (Ctrl-Ins)	Puts a copy of the selected object into the clipboard
Edit | Paste (Shift-Ins)	Copies the contents of the clipboard into the drawing area
Edit | Delete (Del)	Deletes the selected object
Edit | Replace	Replaces a selected object with the contents of the clipboard

HOW TO COPY OBJECTS

Making a copy of the picture is easy, too. Point at the boat, press and hold Shift, press and hold the mouse button, and drag the dotted-line box an inch or two across the lake. Release Shift and the mouse button, and Designer draws the new picture. Figure 3.10 shows what the pointer looks like when you are duplicating an object. Incidentally, if you need to move the picture to a position that is in a straight line above, below, or to the side of the original, use Ctrl (instead of Shift) with the mouse button.

KEYBOARD

Select the boat, press the space bar and Shift at the same time, move the pointer with the arrow keys, and release the space bar and Shift. This can be very slow and cumbersome, so make sure you have a fast keyboard-speed setting, or use the Copy and Paste method instead.

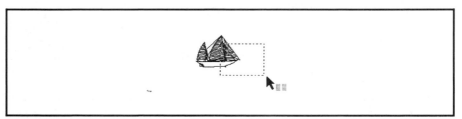

Figure 3.10: Copying the boat

There is a Duplicate menu command (Arrange | Duplicate), by the way, but you will probably never use it. Its only benefit is that you don't need to hold Shift while you move the pointer. And if you want to make sure the copy is on the same vertical or horizontal line as the original, you still have to hold down Ctrl.

Using Copy and Paste

You can also use the clipboard to copy objects—using the Edit | Copy command. Select the object and then select Edit | Copy, and Designer places a copy of the object in the clipboard. Move the pointer to where you want to place the copy, and select Edit | Paste. Then press and hold the mouse button. (Keyboard Shortcuts: Copy = Ctrl-Ins, Paste = Shift-Ins.)

This method is especially useful if you want to make multiple copies of an object, because the clipboard retains a copy of the object until you empty the clipboard or put another image into it. You can also use it to place copies into another Designer window.

HOW TO ROTATE OBJECTS

Rotate

The rotation commands let you spin an object around any axis. You can select the axis; it may be in the center of the object, on one of the edges of the object, or even outside the object. These are the Rotate commands:

Rotate (Shift-Ctrl-F8)	Lets you rotate the object by moving the pointer. The object rotates in increments according to the value set in the Minimum box in the Rotation dialog box.
Rotate Left/Right (F8)	Rotates the object a specified number of degrees (from the Step box in the Rotation dialog box) in the specified direction (from the Direction box). This command used to be called Step Rotation in earlier versions.
Rotate to Zero	Returns the object to the position it was in before you rotated it
Rotation	Lets you set the rotation values

We are going to rotate the helicopter, so let's set the rotation values first. Select Change | Rotation. Designer displays the Rotation dialog box, displayed in Figure 3.11.

Here's what you can set in this box:

Pivot Point	Set the pivot or axis point. You have two settings: the horizontal position (left, center, or right), and the vertical position (top, middle, bottom). Selecting both Center and Middle puts the axis in the center of the object.
Direction	Determines which direction the Rotate Left/Right command moves the object. (It doesn't affect the Rotate command.)

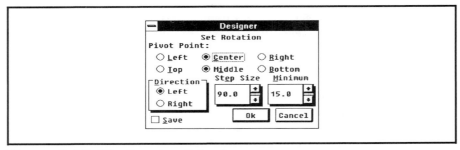

Figure 3.11: The Rotation dialog box

Step Size   Determines the number of degrees the object moves each time you use the Rotate Left/Right command. (It doesn't affect the Rotate command.)

Minimum   Determines the degree increments used by the Rotate command. If you set 10.0 here, you could use the Rotate command to move the object 10 degrees, 20 degrees, 30 degrees, and so on, but you couldn't move it only 5 degrees.

Save   Select the Save checkbox to save the displayed Rotation settings as the default.

1. Select Change | Rotation.

2. Click on the Left and Bottom option buttons.

3. Click on the down arrow in the Minimum box to change the Minimum value to 5.0.

4. Click on OK.

5. Select the helicopter.

KEYBOARD

Use the arrow keys to move between option buttons, the space bar to select an option, and Tab to move between lines. Type **5** into the Minimum box. Press ⏎ when you have finished.

---

6. Click on the Rotate tool in the Toolbox, or select Change | Rotate (Keyboard Shortcut: Shift-Ctrl-F8).

Rotate

7. The pointer now has a Rotate icon next to it. Point to an area above and to the right of the helicopter, and press the mouse button. Drag the pointer downward, and the object begins to rotate. Figure 3.12 shows what the helicopter looks like while it is rotating. Release the mouse button when the helicopter is pointing down about 40 degrees.

Figure 3.12: Rotating the helicopter

8. Look carefully for the helicopter's rotation axis—the circle with cross-hairs inside it. When you find it, drag it an inch or two to the left. Release the mouse button.

9. Try rotating the helicopter again. You will see that the helicopter now rotates around the new position.

10. Play with the rotation for a few moments, but then leave the helicopter as shown in Figure 3.13. Click on the pointer in the top of the toolbox to remove the rotation tool.

One of the things you might notice when playing with the Rotate tool is that you can use it like the standard pointer to change a selected object's size: just drag one of the object's handles in or out from the center of the object, and the object shrinks or enlarges accordingly.

HOW TO FLIP OBJECTS

Another way to change the object's orientation is by flipping it: turning it into a mirror image of itself. You can flip objects horizontally or vertically. Select the helicopter and then select Change | Flip Horizontal. The

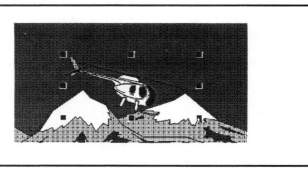

Figure 3.13: The helicopter after rotating

helicopter is now facing the other way. (Keyboard Shortcut: Flip Horizontal = F7, Flip Vertical = Shift-F7.)

SLANTING OBJECTS

You can twist an object onto its side by using the Slant tool. Select Change | Slant or click on the Slant tool. A slanted box appears next to the pointer. Click on an object, and the handles appear—except this time the handles on the corners of the object are grey. Place the pointer to one side of the object and press the mouse button.

Moving the pointer up enlarges the object, moving it down reduces it, moving to the right slants the object to the right, and moving to the left slants it to the left. You can even flip the object horizontally using this tool. Just keep moving the pointer down until the object reduces down to nothing, and continue as it increases again below its original position.

This is one of the few tools that you cannot convert to a standard pointer by clicking quickly. Clicking on an object simply selects that object for slanting.

Slant

WORKING WITH OTHER IMAGE FORMATS

You are not limited to using Designer's clip art. You can use the File | Import command to import art in a variety of other file formats. Using the File | Import command you can use art in .AI, .CGM, .DXF, .GEM, .GRF, .PCT, .PCX, .PIC, .TIF, .TXT, .WMF, and .WPG files. This is especially useful if you have a *scanner*, a device that copies pictures into your computer.

You can also use the Import command to import Designer's own .DRW files. Use it to merge two Designer files (open one file and import a copy of another file into it), or when you want to import a Designer picture that is too big to put into the clipboard.

Electronic clip art can be very expensive, but what many computer users don't realize is that your local art store or book store may have dozens of clip art books, each with hundreds or even thousands of copyright-free pictures, and that you can use a scanner to copy these pictures into your computer. You can then use the File | Import command to bring them into Designer. Scanners can be purchased very cheaply. You can find a 400 dpi (dot per inch) hand scanner for under $200, even under $100 if you find one on sale. With a scanner and a few clip art books you can build yourself a library of cheap electronic clip art.

Your scanned images may not be perfect, especially when the art is complicated. You may have to spend some time with the scanner's utility program, "cleaning" the image, before you can import the art into Designer. If you plan to use simple images, on the other hand, you will find it practical to buy a scanner and a few $10 clip art books.

Figure 3.14 is an example of an image scanned from a clip art book into my computer. I used a 400 dpi HS3000 Handy Scanner from DFI (Diamond Flowery Electric Industries). It took me about five minutes to scan it, save it in .PCX format, reopen Designer, and import the image.

Figure 3.14: Scanned clip art

Incidentally, another source of low-cost clip art is *shareware*. You can obtain shareware clip art from local electronic bulletin boards, from friends, or from companies that sell shareware (usually for between $2 and $4 a disk). Look in the computer magazines for shareware company ads and call them for a catalog.

IMPORTING

During installation, Designer automatically loaded seven *translators*, special utilities that convert file formats. Designer 3.1 also offers you the option of installing six other translators, for .AI, .DXF, .CGM, .GEM, .PCT, and .WPG. These are discussed in more detail in Appendix D. Even after Designer has loaded the translators you think you need, however, it might not be able to import your file; you may get a "memory low" message, and your system could even crash. Try reopening Windows (with the /n switch if you are using a pre-3.0 version or the runtime version), and don't open any other Windows applications or Designer windows until you have completed importing the file.

NOTE

In order to use the translators with pre-3.0 versions of Windows or with Designer using runtime Windows, you must start the program with the /n switch, or Designer won't be able to load some of them. If you didn't do this, close Designer and Windows, and re-open using /n. For example, type **win386 /n** and press ↵. See Chapter 2 for more information, or Appendix D for more information on importing and exporting art.

In this example you are going to use a .TIF file, a format used by scanners. During installation you had the option of installing sample artwork. If you chose this option (as suggested in Appendix A), Designer built a sub-directory called SAMPLES, and placed several files inside. We are going to use the file called TRACE.TIF.

1. Use the scroll bars to find a blank area in the drawing area.

2. Select File | Import, and Designer displays the Import dialog box, as shown in Figure 3.15.

3. Click on the line that says "TIF Tag Image File Format." Notice that the file extension in the text box at the top changes to .TIF.

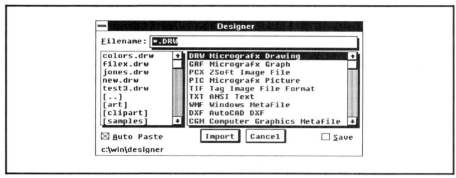

Figure 3.15: The Import dialog box

4. Now select the SAMPLES directory (the full path name is something like C:\WIN386\DESIGNER\SAMPLES, depending on the directory names you selected during installation).

NOTE

If you are still having trouble finding your way around the directory tree, try this: keep clicking on [..] until you reach the root directory, that is, until the [..] is no longer available. Now find the Windows directory, and double-click on it. Then find the DESIGNER directory, and double-click on that. Finally, find the SAMPLES directory and double-click on that.

---

5. Make sure the Auto Paste option is selected (that the box has an X in it). This keeps Designer from loading the file into the clipboard, a process that can take quite some time, especially with bitmapped images.

6. Double-click on TRACE.TIF.

7. Designer displays the TIFF Input Configuration dialog box (Figure 3.16). This configuration box tells you that the image is a color bitmap, and gives you several options.

NOTE

If you are importing one of the vector-based formats, Designer won't show you this dialog box.

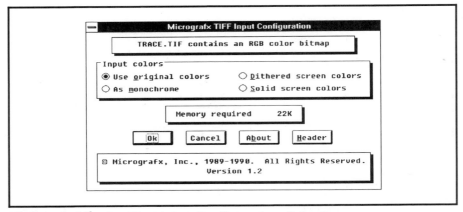

Figure 3.16: The TIFF Input Configuration dialog box

Use original colors	Imports the art with its original colors (this option is not available if you turn Auto Paste off)
Dithered screen colors	These are colors that are produced by mixing pixels of different colors; this allows a screen to display many more "colors" than it is normally capable of.
As monochrome	Imports the art without any colors, substituting black and various levels of grey shading
Solid screen colors	Substitutes solid colors for dithered colors that the bitmap may contain

8. Click on the Solid Screen Colors option button. (Note that when you select a different option in the Input Colors box, the Memory Required box updates to show how much memory will be needed to import the image.)

9. While the dialog box is displayed, click on the Header command button, to see the TIFF Header Information dialog box, as shown in Figure 3.17. Although you won't normally need to see this box, it can be useful for giving you information about the particular type of .PCX image being imported. Click on the OK command button to return to the Configuration dialog box.

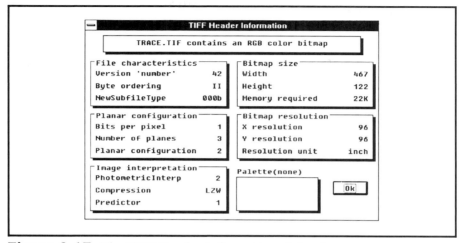

Figure 3.17: The TIFF Header Information dialog box

10. Click on the OK command button. Because you had Auto Paste on, Designer automatically draws the picture in the middle of the window.

While Designer is importing a file it displays a dialog box with a Stop command button and a Cancel command button. Click on Cancel to abort the importing, or on Stop to display what has been imported so far. This feature is supposed to allow you to see if the file you are importing is the one you want, before you have actually imported the whole thing. This may be of value in a very slow system, but if you have a fast computer it's not worth using Stop, because if the file *is* the one you want, you have to delete the partial file that resulted from pressing Stop and go through the whole procedure again.

Note that some .EPS files may contain .TIF images. You can import these images by selecting Tag Image File Format, replacing the .TIF extension with .EPS in the text box showing the path name, and clicking on the Import command button. Designer then displays .EPS files in the list box. Select the one you want and click on Import again.

USING IMPORTED IMAGES

Now that you have imported the art, what can you do with it? Because it is a bitmap file, you can't slant it, rotate it, or give it a pattern. (If you need to do any of these things, you must do so in a paint program before importing it.) You can do any of the following, though:

- Print or plot it or incorporate it into other art without modifying it

- If it is a monochrome image you can change its foreground and background colors, and change between an opaque and transparent background (see Chapter 4)

- Change its size, move it to front or back, or duplicate it

- Flip it horizontally or vertically

- Use the Array command (see Chapter 7) to duplicate the image while simultaneously rotating and changing the size of the copies—creating a repetitive pattern

- Hide sections of the picture (crop it)

- Trace it, converting it into a Micrografx format (.DRW) picture

Cropping the Bitmap

Reshape
Points

To crop the image, use the Change | Reshape Points command. Click on the picture, select Change | Reshape Points (Keyboard Shortcut: Ctrl-Click), and place the pointer on one of the handles. Press the mouse button and drag the handle inward (see Figure 3.18). Release the button and press Esc (or select Change | Reshape Points again) to get out of Reshape mode. Although at this point the bitmap appears to have been cropped, the result does not have to be permanent. If you click on the picture and select Change | Reshape Points again before going any further, and drag the handle outward, Designer restores the missing portion.

Figure 3.18: Cropping a bitmap

NOTE

Designer sometimes displays a straight black line on one or two edges of an object after cropping. If this happens, select View | Redraw, and the line should disappear.

USING AUTO TRACE

Designer's Auto Trace feature lets you turn a bitmap image into a Micrografx vector-based image, which can then be modified like any .DRW image. You can trace the entire picture, or select the parts of the picture you want to use.

Here are a few things to keep in mind when you start to consider bitmaps for tracing:

- Scan overlapping images separately, or use the scanner's bitmap editing program to separate them.

- Set your scanner to high contrast, and avoid images with lots of grey scales. Grey scales are difficult to trace, and they produce very large files that are difficult for Designer to work with. (Photographs, unless they are high-contrast, usually contain a multitude of grey scales.)

- Experiment to find the minimum resolution that will still produce acceptable results. The lower the resolution, the less memory the image requires.

- Before importing the bitmap, use a paint program to fill in spaces, making solid objects. Remove any parts you don't want to trace. (When you look closely at the image you have just imported you will see lots of holes in the fishes; you would normally use the paint program to fill in those holes before importing the picture.)

- If you are importing a color bitmap, select Solid Screen Colors in the Input Configuration dialog box; the image will then have solid colors rather than dithered colors or grey scales. Designer does a much better job of tracing solid colors, so you will get a cleaner image. (If the bitmap is black and white your only option is Monochrome).

- If you are tracing only part of a monochrome bitmap, change the bitmap to a light color before tracing, so that you can see the trace more easily. (Select Pattern | Color to see the Color Selection dialog box, click on a light color, and click on OK.) Earlier versions of Designer automatically changed the bitmap to grey when you selected the Trace tool; 3.0 and later do not do this.

- Don't import bitmaps into the clipboard. (In other words, don't set Auto Trace off). Importing bitmaps into the clipboard consumes more memory, which may be a problem for some systems.

- Don't bother tracing text—use Designer's text features instead. In the sample you have just imported you would normally want to remove the text (''Hollywood'') using the scanner's editing program or a paint program.

SETTING TRACE PREFERENCES

Before you trace your bitmap you must set the trace preferences in the Preferences dialog box (View | Preferences), shown in Figure 3.19.

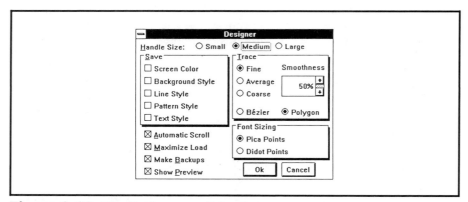

Figure 3.19: The Preferences dialog box

This box lets you customize the way Designer works. Most of its options are discussed in Appendix C; all we are concerned with here are the Trace options:

- **Fine, Average, and Coarse Accuracy**   These settings define how many *anchor points* Designer adds to the traced image. Anchor points are used to edit a curve (modifying its shape); the more anchor points you have the closer the trace follows the bit-map, and the more detailed editing you can do. The Fine setting, however, can use a lot of memory, slow down redrawing, and produce so many anchor points that editing becomes very difficult. Also, you may end up with more anchor points than your Postscript printer can handle. (These devices have problems with pictures that have more than 1500 points, but you may still be able to print them; see Chapter 14.) The coarse setting produces fewer anchor points and doesn't follow the bitmap quite as closely. Use the coarsest setting that produces acceptable results.

- **Smoothness** A high smoothness setting produces traces with a lot of rounded curves, rounding off hard corners in the image. The default setting of zero gives a trace most closely matching the bitmap.

- **Bézier** Bézier curves let you edit in more detail than "polylines," the method available through the other options in this group. Use Bézier when the object you are tracing has many curves in it.

- **Polygon** Select Polygon to trace with "polylines." Use this when the object has a lot of straight lines.

Zooming In on the Bitmap

Before you trace the picture, use the Zoom tool to get a little closer so you can see what is going on.

Zoom

1. Click on the Zoom tool in the toolbox (or select View | Zoom). The pointer turns into a pointing hand with two small boxes (Keyboard Shortcut: Ctrl-Z).

2. "Rubberband" around the bitmap, so that the dotted-line box covers all of the bitmap, as in Figure 3.20. When you release the mouse button, Designer moves in on the image, filling the drawing area with it. (Both the Zoom tool and the Block Select tools use this "rubberband-ing" technique—holding the mouse button while moving the mouse— to stretch a dotted-line box around the area you want to zoom into or around the area containing the objects you want to select.)

KEYBOARD

To "rubberband," press and hold the space bar while moving the pointer with the arrow keys.

Figure 3.20: "Rubberbanding" the bitmap

Tracing the Bitmap

There are several ways to trace an object.

- **Trace the entire bitmap**   Point to the bitmap, press Shift, and click the mouse button quickly. Release Shift.

- **Trace one object**   Click on the object quickly.

- **Trace all or a large part**   Use the pointer to "rubberband" around the area you want to trace with the pointer.

- **Trace an overlapping object**   You can tell Designer which of two overlapping objects you want to trace, or even which part of a single object you want to trace.

- **Abort Tracing**   Press Esc at any time to stop tracing. This is especially useful if Designer has traced the part of the object you want and is now tracing something you don't need. Press Esc again to leave Trace mode entirely.

The command used for selecting which of two overlapping objects to trace needs some explanation. Suppose you have two objects touching or overlapping, but you want to trace them individually. Normally Designer would trace around both objects, but you can place a line across the point at which the objects overlap and make Designer trace around just one of the objects. Actually you can also use this technique to trace just a portion of a single object.

Before you start, turn off Snap (click on Snap in the status line); this allows you to place the line across the bitmap more easily, without having the line snap to the nearest ruler increment. Then place the pointer near the overlapping section, press and hold Shift at the same time you press and hold button 1, and drag the pointer across the overlapping portion of the pictures, the point at which the objects join together. Designer draws a dotted line across the objects. Release Shift and button 1 when you have crossed the overlap.

Designer should now begin tracing the outline the shortest distance around the two objects (i.e., tracing the smallest of the two objects), from one end of the dotted line to the other. If you want to trace the longest distance (i.e., around the largest of the two objects), press and hold Shift-Ctrl while dragging the pointer. Actually this method is difficult to use, and very unpredictable. If it is at all possible, you might be saving yourself some trouble if you can break the objects apart with a paint program before importing them.

After tracing, press button 2 on your mouse. (If you have assigned a command to button 2, that command won't work while in Trace mode.) The bitmap disappears, leaving the trace visible.

Now let's try our hand at tracing our sample bitmap:

1. Select View | Preferences. In the Preferences dialog box select Polygon, Coarse, and 100%, and click on OK.

2. Click on the bitmap to select it.

Trace

3. Select Change | Trace. The handles around the bitmap turn into grey boxes.

4. Point to the map of the United States and click, quickly. (Don't hold the mouse button down for more than a split second, and make sure you don't move the mouse while you click.) Designer makes a rough trace around the image.

KEYBOARD

Use the arrows to move the pointer onto the map and click on the space bar.

CHANGING YOUR TRACE

Sometimes you make a mistake, or your work doesn't look quite right. Luckily you can go back one step, using the Edit | Undo command (Keyboard Shortcut: Alt-space). You can use this command in many editing situations—typing text, drawing objects, and so on—though it won't always work the way you think it will. For example, if you trace an entire bitmap it may not remove all the tracing; it will just remove the last section of trace. We can use it here, however, to remove the trace around the map.

1. Select Edit | Undo. Designer removes the trace from around the map.

2. Go back to the Preferences dialog box (View | Preferences) and select Bézier, Fine, and 0%. Click on OK.

3. Click quickly on the map again. This time the trace looks much closer to the original.

4. Now rubberband around the rightmost fish. When you release the mouse button Designer traces around the fish.

5. Press button 2. The bitmap disappears, leaving the trace. Press button 2 again, and the bitmap reappears.

Arrow

6. Click on the Arrow tool in the top of the toolbox, or press Esc, to leave Trace mode.

7. Drag the bitmap. As the bitmap moves, it leaves the trace in place; however, you won't be able to see the trace until you release the mouse button. Make sure the bitmap is completely away from its original position—this will allow you to work with the trace without having the bitmap obstructing your view of it.

8. Press Esc to end Trace mode.

Smoothing Curves

Designer lets you smooth out lines after you have drawn or traced them.

Reshape
Points

1. Return to the map and select it, then select the Change | Reshape Points command (Keyboard Shortcut: Ctrl-click). The map changes into an outline with more than a hundred small blocks or handles around it, as shown in Figure 3.21.

2. Select Change | Smooth (Keyboard Shortcut: F6). Designer smooths the lines in the map. Select Change | Reshape Points again to get out of the Reshape mode.

You will notice that the map now has smoother lines, with all the sharp edges taken off.

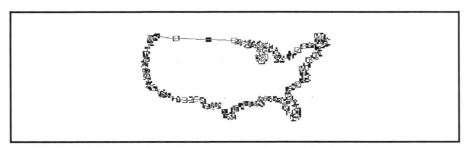

Figure 3.21: Reshaping the map using Change | Reshape Points

When you finish your work, save the file again. Select File | Save. This time Designer saves the file automatically, without prompting you for a file name.

In this chapter you learned how to bring clip art into the drawing area, make some simple modifications, and save your work. In the next chapter you will learn how to reopen a Designer file and make more advanced changes to the art.

4

Modifying the Picture

$\mathbf{I}$n the last chapter you learned how to bring clip art into the drawing area, make a few simple changes, and save the file. Now you are going to find out how to reopen that file and make more extensive changes such as adding color and patterns.

OPENING A FILE

When you imported clip art you learned how to use the Open File dialog boxes. You use the same type of dialog box to open your files.

1. Select File | Open. Designer displays the Open File dialog box.

2. Use the techniques you learned in Chapter 3 to find the file you created in Chapter 3. If you followed the exercises exactly the file will be in the subdirectory with the path name C:\WIN386-\DESIGNER\ART. (Substitute the correct Windows directory if necessary.)

3. When the box displays the ART subdirectory, double-click on FILE1.DRW to open it. Designer displays your file, with the pages positioned just as they were when you saved it.

Although you were just instructed to use File | Open, there are three different File menu commands for bringing art into the drawing area. It is important that you understand how each one is used:

- **File | Open** places a Micrografx Designer file into the drawing area. If you make changes and then use the File | Save command the original file is modified. Although there is a separate command (File | ClipArt) for loading clip art images, you *can* use Open to load a clip art file if you wish; however, *all* the illustrations in the clip art file are loaded into the drawing area. Therefore, if you do use Open to load a clip art file, make sure you immediately save the file, using File | Save As, and enter a different name. (If you use File | Save before you change the name using File | Save As, you will copy any changes you have made into the clip art file, and the only backup you will have will be on the original disks, which you would need to reload using the installation procedure described in Appendix A.)

- **File | Import** lets you bring into the drawing area art that is not in a Micrografx Designer file format. This art may be from other graphics programs, from a scanner program, or from clip art files that are not in the .DRW format. If you make changes and use the File | Save command Designer prompts you for a new file name; the original file is preserved even if you use the same name, because different file formats use different extensions. You can also use Import to merge Designer files, by selecting the .DRW format and the name of the other Designer file; Designer copies the contents of the "imported" file into the open file. This is often easier than opening both files and copying objects from one file to the other.

- **Files | ClipArt** brings selected pictures from a .DRW clip art file into the drawing area. If you make changes and use the File | Save command Designer prompts you for a new file name; the original file is not modified. If you have clip art that is not in the .DRW format you must use the Import command to use it.

HOW DESIGNER WORKS WITH COLORS AND PATTERNS

Designer's color commands are found in the Pattern and Change menus. The program has a number of color commands, which can be a little confusing when you first start out. To make matters worse, the main distinction between pattern and background can seem vague.

When you can describe a pattern in terms of lines and the space(s) between or around them, the distinction is easy to make: the *pattern* is the lines, and the *background* is the space or spaces. It is when the pattern cannot be said to be composed of lines, or when the lines are arranged such that the spaces between them could also be described as lines, that the distinction becomes ambiguous. In these cases you may have to resort to selecting a pattern color just to see which part of the image takes the color. The part that changes color would then obviously be the pattern.

- **Pattern | Color**   You use this command to select a color for an object regardless of whether or not the object has a pattern. If it does have a pattern, only the pattern itself will fill with the color you select.

- **Change | Background Color**   This command will have no effect if the object you select has no pattern, because an object that has no pattern also has no background.

- **Change | Opaque**   This makes the background color opaque. If you place the object over another, you can't see the object below. (Note that this is the default setting; that is, each time you choose a background color it is set to opaque automatically.)

- **Change | Transparent**   This makes the background color transparent. If you place the object over another, you can see through the element(s) that would normally have the background color.

- **Pattern | None**   Removes the colors as well as the pattern, leaving a transparent object.

- **Pattern | Solid**   Removes the pattern only, leaving the pattern color to fill the object.

Figure 4.1 shows the effect of transparent and opaque with different colors and patterns. In this figure the horizontal rectangles are all in front of the single vertical rectangle.

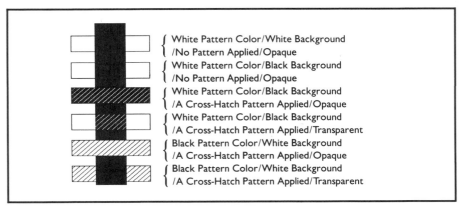

Figure 4.1: Transparent and opaque with different colors and patterns

APPLYING COLORS

To select a color, display the Color dialog box; select Change | Background Color or Pattern | Color to see the Background Color or Pattern Color dialog box (shown in Figure 4.2).

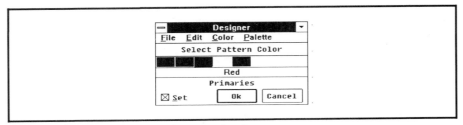

Figure 4.2: The Pattern Color dialog box

Once you double-click on a color, or click on a color and click OK, Designer uses that color as the *current* color. If an object is selected it is filled with this color, and any objects created subsequently will also be filled with this color.

Selecting a color by double-clicking or clicking on OK will usually remove the dialog box, but you can make Designer leave the box on the screen by selecting the Set checkbox; then the only way to remove the box is by clicking on Cancel. With the box permanently displayed you can quickly select a new color by double-clicking on the one you want, and you can move the box to another position on the screen by pointing to the box's title bar, pressing the mouse button, and dragging the box to its new position.

You can also reduce the dialog box's size by clicking on the arrow in the top right corner. When you do this, the checkbox and command buttons are removed from the box, so you have to select colors by double-clicking on them.

There are actually five different Color dialog boxes, displayed when you use the following commands:

- Pattern | Color

- Change | Background Color

- View | Screen Color

- Text | Color
- Line | Color

The boxes all look the same, except for the title below the menu bar. You can change the type of dialog box being displayed by selecting one of the others from the Designer menus, or by selecting one from the Color dialog box's Color menu.

Try applying color to the map of the United States that you traced in Chapter 3:

1. Find the map in file FILE1.DRW.

2. Select the traced map and then select Pattern | Color.

3. In the Color dialog box, click on the Set checkbox, and then double-click on a color. Your map fills with a color.

Using the Keyboard   Use the arrow keys to select a color. Then, to apply the color, press ←, or press Tab until the cursor is on the OK button and press ←. To return to the drawing area without selecting a color, press Tab to move the cursor to the Cancel button and press ←, or press Alt-F6.

If you have selected the Set checkbox and you are not using a mouse, press Alt-F6 to move control between the drawing area and the dialog box.

USING THE COLOR DIALOG BOX

Each Color dialog box has four menus: Files, Edit, Color, and Palette, as shown in Figures 4.3 through 4.6.

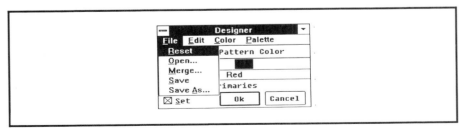

Figure 4.3: The Color dialog box's Files menu

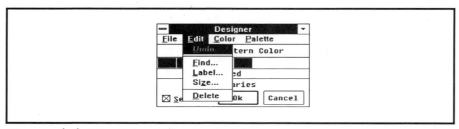

Figure 4.4: The Color dialog box's Edit menu

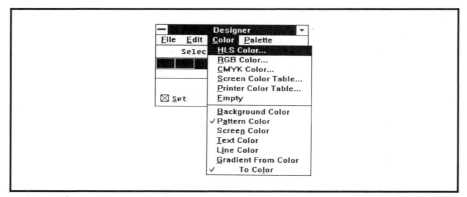

Figure 4.5: The Color dialog box's Color menu

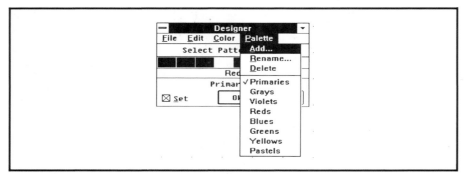

Figure 4.6: The Color dialog box's Palette menu

THE FILES MENU

Reset   Removes the current color palette set and displays the default set

Open   Opens another palette set

Merge   Lets you combine two palette sets into one

Save   Saves a palette set you have modified

Save As   Saves a palette set you have created

THE EDIT MENU

Undo   Reverses the last change you made while creating or modifying a palette

Find   Finds a named color within a palette

Label   Lets you name a particular shade or color in a palette so that you can use Edit | Find to identify it

Size   Lets you increase the number of colors or shades that can be shown in the Color dialog box

Delete   Removes the highlighted color or shade from the palette

THE COLOR MENU

HLS Color   Lets you mix new colors with the HLS model (discussed in Chapter 13)

RGB Color   Lets you mix new colors with the RGB model (discussed in Chapter 13)

CMYK Color   Lets you mix new colors with the CMYK model (discussed in Chapter 13)

Screen Color Table   Displays the colors your monitor can display, and lets you add these to a palette

Printer Color Table   Displays the colors your printer can print, and lets you add these to a palette

Empty   Inserts an empty space into the palette

THE COLOR MENU (continued)

Background Color | Changes dialog box to the Background Color dialog box

Text Color | Changes dialog box to the Text Color dialog box

Line Color | Changes dialog box to the Line Color dialog box

Gradient From Color | Changes dialog box to the Background Color dialog box (the same as the Background Color option in this menu)

Gradient To Color | Changes dialog box to the Pattern Color dialog box (the same as the Pattern Color option in this menu)

THE PALETTE MENU

Add | Adds a blank palette to the set of palettes; you can then use the commands in the Color menu to mix colors to add to the new palette

Rename | Lets you rename the palette displayed in the dialog box

Delete | Removes the palette displayed in the dialog box from the palette set

(Palette names) | Lets you select one of the other palettes in the palette set

COLOR PALETTES

Designer lets you use up to 3.6 million different colors and grey scales by using *dithering,* a process in which different-color pixels are "mixed" together to produce far more colors than your screen can actually display. (Because the pixels are so small, the colors look quite good, though they often end up looking a little grainy or spotted.)

The colors that come with Designer are arranged into three palette sets. The default set includes the primary colors palette, and seven other palettes for greys, violets, reds, blues, greens, yellows, and pastels. This is the set that is displayed each time you open Designer. If you have selected another palette you can redisplay the default set with the dialog box's Files | Reset command.

The other two palette sets, which are loaded onto your hard disk automatically, are ARTIST and CRAYON. You can display these in the Color dialog boxes by using the Files | Open command; you will see an Open Files dialog box, which you use the same as you would opening any other kind of file: just select the palette set you want and double-click on it. (These palettes are in the SAMPLES directory, and they have the .PAL extension.) ARTIST contains one set of 25 dithered colors. CRAYON has two palettes—the Primaries palette, the same one that appears in the default palette set, and one that has 64 crayon colors.

NOTE

If you have one of the early versions of Designer 3.0 you may not have the ARTIST and CRAYON palettes. These were left off some of the first copies of the software dated February 22, 1990. (Select Help | About to see the issue date for your disks.) If you can't seem to load these palettes from the Color dialog box, look through your Designer directories for files called ARTIST.PAL and CRAYON.PAL. If you can't find them you probably have one of the early issues.

You can also buy other palette sets from Designer, such as PANTONE.PAL—a file that contains the Pantone color set—and you can change the default palette set. For example, you could make Designer open with ARTIST automatically loaded. This is explained in Chapter 13.

Creating Your Own Palettes

You can also make your own palettes, by mixing new colors (using the Color menu in the Color dialog box) or by merging palettes into one new one. Working with palettes is described in detail in Chapter 13, ''More About Color.''

APPLYING PATTERNS

There are a number of pattern types available in the Pattern menu, as you can see from Figure 4.7.

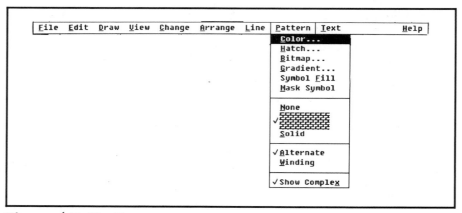

Figure 4.7: The Pattern menu

Hatch	Patterns made up of vector-based lines
Bitmap	Bitmap patterns produced by coloring individual pixels; you can edit the bitmaps and save the new patterns
Gradient	A gradual transition between two colors, so that the colors appear to merge into each other
Symbol Fill	This fills an object with a symbol you create or select
Mask Symbol	Lets you cover a pattern with a "mask" such that the only part of the pattern that is visible is that part covered by the mask
None	Removes the colors and pattern, leaving a transparent object

(sample patterns)	The last three patterns you have used, so that you can select them directly without going to their respective dialog boxes
Solid	Removes the pattern, but leaves the pattern color, so the object is filled with the pattern color
Alternate	This feature will be explained in Chapter 7
Winding	This feature will be explained in Chapter 7
Show Complex	Turns off complex fills, so that Designer can redraw quickly

USING HATCH PATTERNS

Select Pattern | Hatch to see the Hatch dialog box, as shown in Figure 4.8. To set the current pattern double-click on the pattern you want (or click on it once and then click on OK). If you have already selected an object, it will be filled with that pattern. Once you have selected a hatch, each object you draw will be filled with that pattern (the "current pattern") until you select another or select Pattern | None or Pattern | Solid.

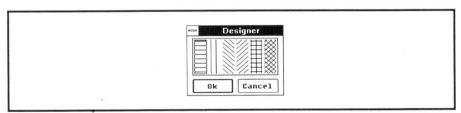

Figure 4.8: The Hatch dialog box

NOTE

When you fill an object with a hatch the white areas will take the background color, and the black lines will take the pattern color. Thus, if you selected Pattern | Color to be green, the lines will be green.

Try applying a hatch pattern to your map of the United States:

1. Select the map.

2. Select Pattern | Hatch.

3. Double-click on one of the hatch patterns. Your map fills with the pattern. Notice that the lines in the pattern are the color you selected as the pattern color.

4. In the Color dialog box, select Color | Background Color. The title in the box changes to Select Background Color.

5. Double-click on another color. Notice that the spaces inside the lines fill with the selected color.

6. Click on the Cancel button in the Color dialog box to remove the box from the screen.

KEYBOARD
You can use the Hatch dialog box the same as you use most dialog boxes: Press the arrow keys to move the cursor to the hatch you want, then press ⏎.

USING BITMAP PATTERNS

Select Pattern | Bitmap to see the Bitmap dialog box. You can use the box in the same way you use the Hatch dialog box, to add a pattern to an object or to change the current pattern. You can also create your own patterns. The box you see when you first select Pattern | Bitmap will not look quite the same as the one shown in Figure 4.9 until you add several new bitmaps. Designer will allow you to add up to 32 new bitmaps. If there is not enough space to display all the bitmaps, Designer adds a scroll bar to the bottom of the pattern box.

The Options menu in this dialog box lets you delete or edit a bitmap. To delete a bitmap, select it and then select Options | Delete. (You can delete only a bitmap that you added, not one of Designer's original set.) To edit a bitmap, select it and then select Options | Edit. Designer displays the Edit Bitmap dialog box, showing a detailed view of the bitmap. As you can see in Figure 4.10, this dialog box displays a pixel-by-pixel view of the pattern.

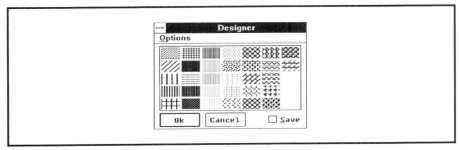

Figure 4.9: The Bitmap dialog box

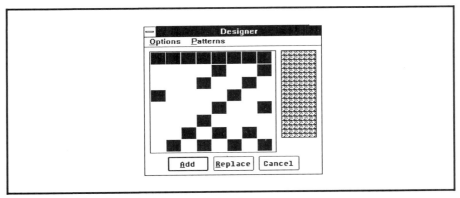

Figure 4.10: The Edit Bitmap dialog box

You can change the pattern by clicking on the squares that represent individual pixels: as you click the pixel reverses color, a black pixel becoming white and a white pixel becoming black. You can see the effect of changing individual pixels by looking at the view of the pattern in the right side of the box.

This box has a few options:

- **Options | Black** Turns the pattern entirely black. Create a new pattern by adding white pixels.

- **Options | White** Turns the pattern entirely white. Create a new pattern by adding black pixels.

- **Patterns** Displays all the patterns available for editing.

- **Add**   Click on this button to add the edited version to your bitmap selection, leaving the original unchanged.

- **Replace**   Click on this button to replace the bitmap you selected with your edited version (you can only do this if the selected bitmap was one of your creations; Designer will not let you change any of its original set).

- **Cancel**   Click on this button to close the dialog box without making any changes.

- **Save**   Select this box if you want Designer to save the bitmaps that you have created. If you don't use this option, your bitmaps are removed from the pattern set when you close Designer.

NOTE

Remember that when you fill an object with a bitmap the white pixels in a bitmap will take the background color, and the black pixels will take the pattern color.

USING GRADIENT PATTERNS

When you select Pattern | Gradient you see the Gradient dialog box. The one you see the first time won't look quite the same as the one in Figure 4.11; that is because I have added more gradients. Designer will let you add another 60 gradients.

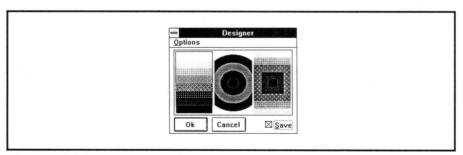

Figure 4.11: The Gradient dialog box, Designer 3.1

You can delete a gradient by selecting it and selecting Options | Delete. (Designer lets you delete all but one of the original gradients.) You can edit gradients by selecting Options | Edit, which displays the Edit Gradient dialog box (Figure 4.12). It is especially important to remember when creating a gradient that the black areas represent the pattern color, and the white areas represent the background color, because if you are using a light pattern color and a dark background color, you could easily confuse yourself by thinking the black and white relate to the dark and light colors.

The Edit Gradient dialog box has the following features:

- **Linear**   Select this button if you want to build a gradient that "fades" along a straight line (see the gradients on the left and in the middle in Figure 4.11).

- **Radial**   Select Radial if you want a gradient that fades in a circular pattern, as in the gradient on the right in Figure 4.11.

- **Square**   Select this option (found in version 3.1 only) to create a square or right-angled gradient as shown on the right in Figure 4.12.

- **Angle**   If you select Linear or Square you can determine the direction of the fade by selecting the angle of the line that runs *perpendicular* to it. (Angle has no effect on radial gradients.) Setting the Angle to 0 degrees or 180 degrees, for example, makes a line horizontal; therefore the fade would occur along a vertical line. This setting is combined with the Y setting in the Origin box to determine at what point along a linear gradient the pattern color will be its strongest.

- **Origin**   The origin of a gradient is the point from which the pattern color begins to fade to the background color. The Origin

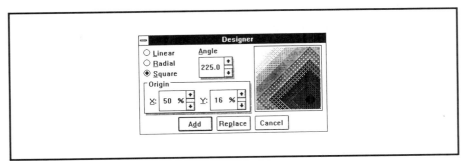

Figure 4.12: The Edit Gradient dialog box, Designer 3.1

settings, discussed in the next section, determine the location of the pattern color along the gradient.

- **Add**   Adds your new gradient to the set of gradients in the Gradient dialog box.

- **Replace**   Replaces the original gradient with your new one.

- **Cancel**   Closes the Edit Gradient box without making any changes.

You can create smooth gradients by using large objects and similar colors. The more room that Designer has to work with, the more room it has to put different shades. And the more similar the colors are, the smaller the shade ''increments'' Designer will have to use.

Note that if you want to save your changes for the next time you work with Designer, click on the Save checkbox in the Gradient dialog box.

Setting the Origin of a Gradient

The Origin settings can be rather confusing, and you really need to play around with them to get a feel for how they work. The following explanation should give you an idea of what they are intended to do.

The Origin values determine where along the gradient you will see the pattern color before it begins its fade to the background color. The spot (or band) where the pattern color is located along the gradient is thus referred to as the *origin* of the gradient, and its location is expressed in terms of its relative distance along the X and Y axes of the gradient. This relative-distance approach is actually rather intuitive, and it saves having you figure out what units of measure you are using. In this regard, the Origin settings are easy to use. The reason Origin settings can be confusing is that the orientation of the X and Y axes is not what you might expect.

Let's start with radial gradients, because they are a bit easier to explain. The X and Y axes correspond to horizontal and vertical, and the actual length of each axis is the maximum width and height of the object you have selected to fill. However, unlike the Cartesian coordinate system you are familiar with from high-school geometry, the numbers along the Y axis (the vertical component) increase as you go from *top to bottom,* not bottom to top. Thus, a setting of 0 percent along the Y axis positions the pattern color at the *top* of the object. It follows, then, that 50 percent positions it halfway down, and 100 percent positions it at the bottom.

Combining the Y setting with the X setting serves to position the origin within the object. An X setting of 0 percent positions the pattern color at the left side of the object, and 100 percent positions it at the right (as you would expect from a Cartesian coordinate system), so a setting of X = 0 and Y = 100 would locate the origin at the bottom left, and X = 100 and Y = 0 would locate it at the top right. (A setting of 50 and 50 would put the origin right in the center of the space.)

In a linear gradient, the fade occurs along only one line. Regardless of whether this line is vertical, it is defined to be the gradient's Y axis, and, for all intents, it is the gradient's only axis—any values set for the X axis will have no effect on linear gradients. What *will* have an effect is the angle of the gradient, which not only determines the direction of the gradient but also determines which end of the selected object Designer considers to be 0 percent of the way along the length of the gradient and which end is 100 percent of the way. This is unfortunately very confusing, and you will probably have to take a guess as to which end is which.

3.1

If you have Designer 3.1 you can also create square gradients. You can imagine the square gradient as a combination of four linear gradients at right angles to each other. You set a square gradient's origin and angle in much the same way you would set them for a linear gradient, except that you can adjust both the Y and the X axis. In fact, with some settings three of the lines will disappear, and you are basically left with a linear gradient. Combining the origin and angle settings lets you create not only *square* gradients but also *right-angled* gradients: you can have an actual square, two lines meeting at a right angle, or one line with two lines joining it at right angles. The best way to get an idea of how the square gradient feature works is to play around with the origin and angle settings to get a feel for how they can affect the result.

Figure 4.13 shows examples of how different Origin settings affect the placement of the gradient.

Try filling your map of the United States with a gradient:

1. Select the map.

2. Select Pattern | Gradient

3. When the Gradient dialog box appears, select Options | Edit.

4. In the Edit Gradient dialog box select Radial, with an Origin of 50 percent on the X axis and 100 percent on the Y axis.

5. Click on the Add command button. The Edit Gradient dialog box disappears.

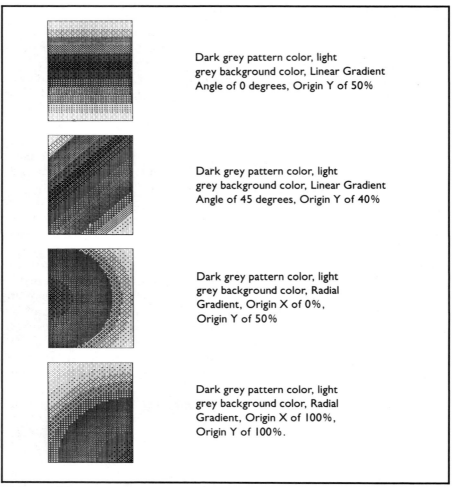

Figure 4.13: Positioning the gradients

6. Double-click on the new pattern and the Gradient dialog box disappears. The map fills with the gradient (see Figure 4.14).

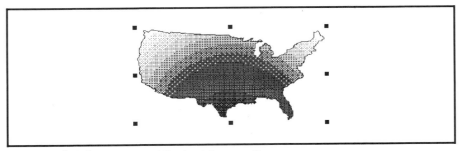

Figure 4.14: The map filled with a gradient

USING SYMBOL FILL

The Pattern | Symbol Fill feature lets you fill an object with a pattern made of multiple images of another object that you select. You can load a piece of clip art, or draw a small symbol, and then make Designer copy that symbol into the object you want to fill. (You cannot, however, use a bitmap as a fill symbol.)

The procedure is simple. First, prepare the fill symbol: either import it or draw it. Then select the object you want to fill, and select Pattern | Symbol Fill. Designer puts a dotted-line box around the object. Next select the object you want to use as the fill pattern. Drag that object into the dotted-line box and release it. Then select Pattern | Symbol Fill again. Designer fills the object with the new pattern. The combined objects will now act like one object.

If you don't like what you see, it is easy to change. Perhaps the fill object is too large, so you want to reduce it. Select the object and select Pattern | Symbol Fill again. Designer displays the objects as they were when you dragged the fill object into the dotted-line box. Drag it out of the box, reduce it, and then repeat the Fill procedure again.

Remember that the smaller the fill symbol, the more numerous it will be in a pattern. This will affect the time required for Designer to redraw. Similarly, the more complicated the fill symbol, the longer it takes to redraw.

TIP

When you fill a symbol with a fill pattern you may find your system slows down considerably; even if you switch to other applications running in Windows you may find things running sluggishly. You can speed things up a little by turning off the display of the fill. Select Pattern | Show Complex to temporarily remove the fill pattern. Operations speed up, and you can toggle Pattern | Show Complex to its previous state later on, when you need to view the pattern again.

Now fill your map with a symbol:

1. Use the File | ClipArt command to view the contents of the file called TRANS01D.DRW. (This should have been loaded during installation, if you followed the procedures suggested in this book. If you didn't load this file, use any other object; for example, you could draw a square using the Draw | Square command.)

2. Load the clip art picture called Helicopter04.

3. Reduce the helicopter in size until it is about three quarters of an inch wide. (Use one of the corner handles to reduce it proportionally.)

4. Select the map of the United States.

5. Select Pattern | None to remove the pattern and color from the map.

6. Select the map and select Pattern | Symbol Fill. Designer puts a dotted-line box around the map.

7. Select the helicopter and drag it into the dotted-line box. Release the mouse button.

8. Select Pattern | Symbol Fill. Designer slowly fills the object with the new pattern, as shown in Figure 4.15.

USING MASK SYMBOL

When you think of "masking" something you normally think of covering it up. Not so with the Pattern | Mask Symbol command, which does the opposite. When you place an object *in front of* Designer's mask symbol, the only part of the object that *shows* is the part with the mask symbol

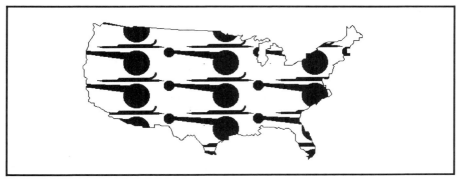

Figure 4.15: The map filled with the helicopter symbol

underneath; the parts outside the mask symbol become invisible. You might think of the Mask tool as a ''cookie cutter'' that both cuts the object and discards the portions of the object that are outside the cookie cutter. This allows you to create some unusual effects. For example, you could mask a scene with text (that is, with letters that have been converted to objects). Because a mask symbol in Designer is transparent—it has no color or pattern—the effect would be that of looking through transparent text to a picture or pattern.

Once you have masked an image, the combined objects act like one object. If you use Pattern | Show Complex to keep Designer up to speed, you can temporarily remove the pattern from the mask, effectively making the masked object disappear until you select the command again.

Use the map of the United States to mask your picture of the mountain scene:

1. Select the map and select Pattern | Symbol Fill.

2. Remove the helicopter from the map, and press Esc to get out of Symbol Fill mode.

3. Select View | Show Preview. This will turn off all the color, speeding things up.

4. Select View | View Used Pages.

5. Move the map next to the mountain scene.

6. Expand the map proportionally (using one of the corner handles), until it is a little bit smaller than the mountain scene.

7. With the map still selected, select Pattern | Mask Symbol.

8. Drag the mountain scene onto the map.

9. Select Pattern | Mask Symbol again. The mountain scene disappears.

10. Select View | Show Preview to redisplay the colors. The mountain scene is masked by the map, as in Figure 4.16.

11. Select File | Save As, type FILE2, and press ↵.

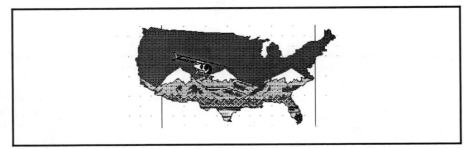

Figure 4.16: The map masking the mountain scene

5

Using the Drawing Tools

Designer wasn't intended to be used only to manipulate other people's art—you can also create your own pictures using Designer's many drawing tools.

Designer has 15 drawing tools. You can use these tools by selecting them from the Draw menu, from the toolbox, or, in some cases, by using a keyboard shortcut. The following list describes the drawing tools and includes the keyboard shortcuts when available. You will find a more detailed discussion of each of the drawing-tools, as well as a picture of each tool's icon, in the second part of this chapter.

Arc (Ctrl-A)	Draws one quarter of an elliptical arc
Bézier	Draws symbols made of Bézier curves
Circle	Draws circles
Curve (Ctrl-U)	Draws parabolic spline curves, lines made up of more than one parabola
Elliptical Arc	Draws arcs that are a portion of an elliptical arc
Ellipse (Ctrl-E)	Draws ellipses (squashed circles)
Freehand (Ctrl-F)	Lets you draw any shape you want, using the pointing device like a pen on paper
Horz/Vert Line (Ctrl-H)	Draws straight lines, horizontally, vertically, or at 45 degrees
Line (Ctrl-L)	Draws straight lines, at any angle
Parabola	Draws parabolas, lines with a single curve
Pie	Draws circles with "pie" segments, or draws individual pie segments
Polyline (Ctrl-P)	Draws straight lines, each one starting where the last one left off
Rounded Rectangle	Draws rectangles with rounded corners
Rectangle (Ctrl-R)	Draws rectangles
Square	Draws squares

There are two types of tools; those that draw simple shapes, called *primitives* (the square, rectangle, rounded rectangle, oval, and circle), and those that draw different types of lines and enable you to produce more complex shapes. If you draw a line drawing in which the two ends of the line meet, Designer automatically creates a *connected closed* object, and fills that object with the currently selected pattern and color. If the ends don't meet, the object is left as an "open" (unconnected) line or series of lines. You will learn more about *connected closed* and *connected open* objects in Chapter 7.

SELECTING AND USING A TOOL

The tools all work in a similar manner. First select the tool. Either use the Draw menu, press the keyboard shortcut, or click on the item in the toolbox. (Appendix C explains how to customize your toolbox, adding tools that are not included in the default toolbox.)

The pointer will change from an arrow to an icon that looks like a pen or pencil, with another small icon next to it; for example, the square-drawing pointer has a square next to it, and the circle-drawing pointer has a circle. Once you see the drawing pointer icon, you can draw the object by pressing the mouse button and dragging the mouse. In some cases the pointer starts at one edge or corner of the object and expands to the opposite edge or corner as you move it; in other cases the pointer starts in the center of the object and expands outward in all directions as you move it. While you are drawing, the status line shows how big the object is, so you can release the button when the object is exactly the size you want. Figure 5.1 shows the Square drawing tool at work.

When you have finished one object, you can draw another. For example, say you are using the Square drawing tool. You press and hold the mouse button, drag the mouse, and release the button, and Designer draws a square. Repeat the operation to draw another square. If you are using one of the line-drawing tools rather than one of the primitive-drawing tools, you can start a new line by clicking quickly and then continuing. For example, say you are using the Polyline drawing tool. This allows you to draw an object one line after another by pressing the mouse button, moving the mouse, releasing the button, moving the mouse, pressing the button again, moving the mouse and pressing again, and so on. However, if you click *quickly,* rather than pressing (you must click faster than the double-click speed), Designer considers the drawing finished and lets you begin a *new* object made up of polylines.

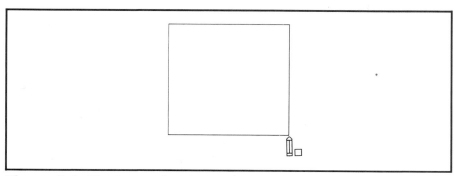

Figure 5.1: The Square drawing tool at work

When you have finished drawing, select another tool (such as the arrow pointer in the top of the toolbox), to exit the drawing mode.

Using the Keyboard   If you don't have a mouse, you can still use these tools. You can select them from the Draw menu. Or press Tab twice to move the cursor into the toolbox, press the down arrow key to move the cursor to the tool you want, press the space bar to select that tool, and press Tab several times to move the cursor out of the status line, returning control to the pointer. You can also select the tool using its keyboard shortcut. Once you have selected the tool, press and hold the space bar and use the arrow keys to move the pointer, drawing the item.

Drawing using the keyboard is a little awkward, and takes a bit of getting used to. Use it for a while, and you may decide to buy a mouse.

CHANGING PROPORTIONS

You can change the angle of a line or the proportions of an object using the Ctrl and Shift keys. When drawing a line, pressing Ctrl makes the line a straight horizontal, vertical, or 45-degree line. Pressing Ctrl while you hold the mouse button and drag, or while you use the arrow keys to move the tool, produces an object with equal proportions, a symmetrical object. Holding Ctrl while drawing an ellipse, for example, makes Designer draw a circle. (Holding it while drawing with the Circle tool has no effect on its symmetry, because a circle is already symmetrical.) The Ctrl key may, however, have another effect—in the case of the circle it will affect the circle's position. These special effects are explained later in this chapter, with the instructions for each tool.)

Holding the Shift key has an effect opposite to that of the Ctrl key, making a proportional object nonproportional. Holding Shift while using the Square tool, for example, allows you to produce a rectangle instead.

NOTE

When you use Shift or Ctrl with the mouse you must release the mouse button *before* you release Shift or Ctrl, or the symbol reverts to its normal form.

CORRECTING MISTAKES

If you make a mistake while drawing an object you can change the object back to the way it was in one of two ways. If you still have the mouse button held down, press Esc and then release the mouse button. If you have already released it, use the Edit | Undo command (Keyboard Shortcut: Alt-Backspace).

CHANGING MODES WITHOUT LOSING THE TOOL

Designer allows you to temporarily leave the drawing mode without selecting another tool. Click quickly on an object, and Designer changes the pointer into the standard arrow pointer—the tool at the top of the toolbox—and selects the object (you will see the black handles appear around the object). You can then carry out certain procedures that don't require you to select another tool—you might delete the object, copy it, or move it, for example. You can then display the drawing tool again by pointing to a blank area and clicking quickly. Designer automatically changes the pointer back to the drawing tool, and you can continue.

This feature has been known to cause confusion because people not aware of the feature don't understand why they keep losing the drawing tool, and why it seems to return for no reason. But once you understand what you are doing and try it once or twice, you will find this feature is a real timesaver. There is just one tool in the Draw menu that this feature does not work with—the Text tool. The Text tool is described in Chapter 8.

MOVING WHILE DRAWING

If you find in mid-drawing that an object you are producing is in the wrong place, you can move it even before you finish drawing it. The technique is quite easy, but only if you are using a mouse. Simply press and hold button 2 without releasing button 1, and the object "freezes." Drag the mouse to move the object, release button 2, and continue drawing.

Although you can use the keyboard to move an object you are drawing, you cannot automatically resume drawing the object after you have moved it. Simply tap the *2* on your keyboard (not on the numeric keypad) while you continue holding the space bar. The object "freezes." You can now move it using the arrow keys. Release the space bar when the object is where you want it.

THE TOOLS

Each tool works in a slightly different way, so I will describe each one individually. Experiment with each tool as you read its description.

THE ARC TOOL

Draw | Arc

The Arc tool (Keyboard Shortcut: Ctrl-A) draws curved lines that are one quarter of an ellipse. Place the pointer where you want to begin the line, press the mouse button, and drag the mouse. Release the button when you have the shape you want. You can modify the direction of the curve by pressing Shift while you drag the mouse. For example, if you drag the mouse up and to the right without holding Shift, the line will go up and then curve to the right; holding Shift will make the line curve to the right first and then go up. You can even "flip" the curve by pressing Shift after you have drawn the line (but before you have released the mouse button).

Pressing Ctrl while drawing the arc ensures that the arc has a constant curve, that it is one quarter of a circle rather than an ellipse.

The Arc tool's pointer is shown in Figure 5.2.

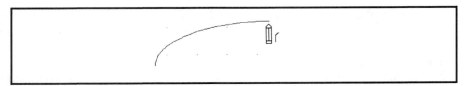

Figure 5.2: Drawing with the Arc tool

Draw |
Bézier

THE BÉZIER TOOL

Using the Bézier tool takes a bit of getting used to, because you don't actually draw a line; rather, you place the line's anchor points. You are effectively drawing and editing at the same time.

Bézier curves are lines made up of anchor points and control points. Moving these points moves the line's position and orientation.

Anchor points lie on the line itself. An anchor point may lie at the end of a line, or it may be a *common anchor point,* an anchor point that is at the beginning of one line and the end of another (thus, it appears to be in the middle of a line). Anchor points are small black boxes.

Control points are small cross symbols (made of four small black squares), that appear near the anchor point. Each anchor point has two control points, and they are connected by a straight line, with the anchor point in the middle. If you move one of the control points, the anchor point serves as a pivot, remaining where it is, while the connecting line and the opposite control point move around the anchor. As they move they drag the line with them, changing its curve; the line still goes through the anchor point, but at a different angle.

Try the following procedure to learn how to draw a Bézier curve, and see Figure 5.3 to see what the line looks like. Don't worry too much about where your line goes or what it looks like, just try to get a feel for what is happening.

1. Select the Bézier tool and place the pointer where you want the line to begin.

2. Press the mouse button, and drag the mouse to the right a few inches, to the position of the first control point. Designer draws a straight line.

3. Release the mouse button.

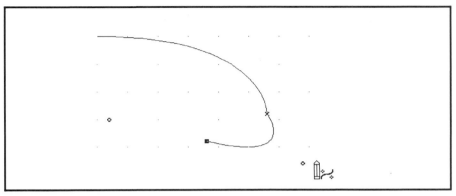

Figure 5.3: Drawing with the Bézier tool

4. Move the pointer down a few inches, to where you want to place the end of the line.

5. Press and hold the mouse button. Designer changes the line, moving the end to the pointer position, creating a curve.

6. While still holding the mouse button, drag the mouse to the next control point. As you begin moving the mouse Designer displays the line connecting the control points. (You won't be able to see the anchors or control points, though.) While you move the mouse, Designer modifies the shape of the line you are creating, so you can see exactly how it will turn out.

7. Release the mouse button. Designer displays the anchor points and control points, as shown in Figure 5.3 (in this figure you can see three control points; one control point is under the first anchor).

8. Move the pointer and press the mouse button again. Designer draws a line from the end anchor point to the pointer.

You can also use the Bézier tool in the following manner:

1. Point to where you want the line to begin and press the mouse button. Hold it down a second or so (longer than the mouse's double-click speed) and release it.

2. Move the pointer to the end of the line and press the mouse button again. (Don't just click, press the button longer than the double-click speed, and then release the button; make sure you don't move

the mouse while you do this.) Designer draws a straight line between the points.

3. Move the pointer again and press and release again. Designer draws another straight line, from the end of the first line to the pointer.

4. Continue like this, moving the pointer and pressing the mouse button. Designer draws a shape made up of straight lines (a polygon).

You can combine these two methods at any time. You could, for example, draw two or three straight lines, and then, instead of pressing and releasing the mouse button before moving the mouse, hold it while you move the mouse; Designer displays the connecting line, and lets you move it to modify the resulting curve. Then release the button, move the mouse, and press and release to draw another straight line, connected to the end of the curve you just modified.

After drawing a curve using the first of the two methods described, you can immediately modify it. While the control and anchor points are still displayed, move the pointer onto one of them. You will notice that the pointer changes from the pen icon to the arrow icon, with a small black box next to it. This is the Reshape Béziers tool; Designer automatically selects this tool for you when you move the Bézier drawing tool onto one of the control or anchor points. This tool is used for editing objects, and can also be used by selecting an object and then choosing Change | Reshape Béziers.

Press and hold the mouse button while you move the mouse, dragging the control or anchor point. The curve will be modified accordingly. You will learn more about using the Bézier tool in Chapter 9.

Draw |
Circle

THE CIRCLE TOOL

After selecting the Circle tool, place the pointer where you want to put the center of the circle, press the mouse button, and drag. Designer draws a circle, with the center where the pointer was when you started drawing. If you hold Ctrl while you drag the mouse, the starting point will not be used as the center of the circle; rather, the starting point will be the "corner" of the circle. (Imagine the circle is inside a square, with the edge of the circle touching the middle of each side of the square; the starting point will be one of the square's corners.)

If you hold Shift while dragging the mouse, Designer draws an ellipse instead of a circle.

The Circle tool's pointer is shown in Figure 5.4.

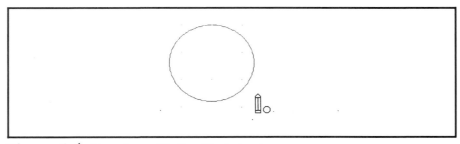

Figure 5.4: Drawing with the Circle tool

THE CURVE TOOL

Draw |
Curve

The Curve tool (Keyboard Shortcut: Ctrl-U) draws simple curved lines, or shapes made from one curved line after another. Figure 5.5 shows the Curve tool drawing a single curve.

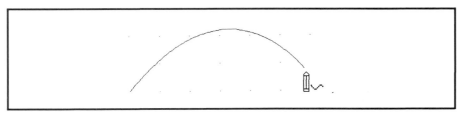

Figure 5.5: Drawing with the Curve tool

1. Select the Curve tool, then press and hold the mouse button.

2. Drag the mouse, and release the mouse button. Designer draws a straight line.

3. Move the pointer, and press and hold the mouse button again. Designer curves the line, dragging the end of the line with the pointer. After you move the mouse to alter the curve to the shape you want, release the button.

4. Move the pointer again, then press and hold the mouse button. Designer draws a curved line from the end of the first curve to the pointer. Move the mouse to alter this curve's shape before releasing the button.

5. Continue like this, moving the pointer, pressing and holding the mouse button, releasing, and moving the pointer again.

When you have finished the object, click quickly. The object is complete, but you remain in curve-drawing mode so you can begin another object.

You can use Shift or Ctrl to combine straight lines with curved lines in one object. Pressing and holding Shift while holding the mouse button and dragging makes the line remain straight, and using Ctrl instead of Shift draws a straight line that is vertical, horizontal, or at 45 degrees, whichever you are closest to.

By the way, you can use Edit | Undo to remove the segment you have just drawn if you don't like it, and then redraw it.

Draw |
Elliptical
Arc

THE ELLIPTICAL ARC TOOL

An elliptical arc is a curve that is part of an ellipse. This tool lets you draw a line that is any portion of an ellipse (unlike the Arc tool, which limits you to one quarter of an ellipse).

1. Select the Elliptical Arc tool, then press the mouse button and drag. Designer draws an ellipse. Release when the ellipse is the size and shape you want.

2. Point to the ellipse and press and hold down the mouse button again. (The ellipse may disappear.)

3. Move the pointer in a circular motion around the ellipse, or around the space where the ellipse was, and Designer draws the elliptical arc.

4. The status line indicates how much of the ellipse is being drawn (360 degrees means the complete ellipse, 180 degrees means half of the ellipse, and so on.) Release the mouse button when you have the line you want.

Holding Ctrl during Step 1 (while you draw the ''ellipse'') makes Designer draw a circle instead of an ellipse. This is useful for drawing a curve that is part of a circle's circumference.

The Elliptical Arc tool's pointer is shown in Figure 5.6.

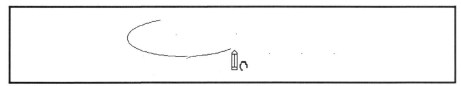

Figure 5.6: Drawing with the Elliptical Arc tool

THE ELLIPSE TOOL

Draw |
Ellipse

The Ellipse tool (Keyboard Shortcut: Ctrl-E) lets you draw ellipses. Press the mouse button and drag, and Designer draws the ellipse. Release when you have the shape and size you want. If you hold Ctrl while you draw the shape, Designer draws a circle instead of an ellipse.

The starting point is not the center of the ellipse (or circle). Rather, it represents one "corner" of the object, as described earlier for the Circle tool.

The Ellipse tool's pointer is shown in Figure 5.7.

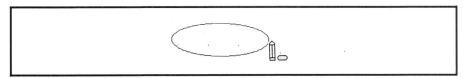

Figure 5.7: Drawing with the Ellipse tool

THE FREEHAND TOOL

Draw |
Freehand

The Freehand tool (keyboard shortcut: Ctrl-F) lets the mouse, or other pointing device, act like a pen. As you move the pointer, Designer draws a line. Where the pointer goes, the line goes. The Freehand tool in action is shown in Figure 5.8.

This tool is especially useful if you have a digitizing pad and a pen. Using the mouse is awkward for most people—it just doesn't move like a pen, so it is difficult to get the lines to go where you want them to go. But with a digitizing pad and pen you can draw objects just as you would with a real pen and paper. You can even trace pictures; you can place paper art onto the pad, select the Freehand tool, and then trace the picture with the pen.

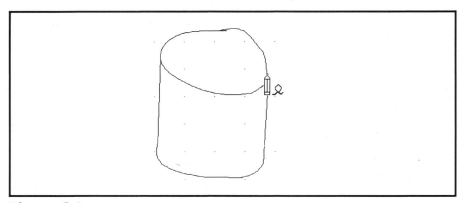

Figure 5.8: Drawing with the Freehand tool

To draw freehand, place the pointer where you want to begin, press the mouse button, and move the mouse. Designer draws a line, following the pointer until you release the button. There are several other ways to use the Freehand tool. Press Shift, hold the mouse button, move the mouse, and release the mouse button. Designer draws a straight line. You can draw more straight lines, each connected to the previous, by keeping the Shift key down while you repeat the drawing procedure for each line.

If you press Ctrl instead of Shift, the straight line will be vertical, horizontal, or at 45 degrees—whichever you are closest to. (You will not be able to draw any other kind of line while Ctrl is held down.) Make sure you release the mouse button before you release Ctrl.

You can also draw straight lines by pressing the mouse button for a second or so (longer than the double-click time), moving the mouse *without* the button held down, and pressing again for a second or so when you reach the point at which you want the line to end. Designer draws a straight line between the two points at which you pressed. (Pressing and holding Ctrl while you do this ensures that the line will be horizontal, vertical, or at 45 degrees.) The difference with this straight-line method is that you have no way to modify the line's position once you press the second time. With the first method (pressing Shift or Ctrl while holding the mouse button), you can move the mouse until you get the line in the correct position, and then release the button, but with the straight-line method you can't see the line until you press a second time, and then it can't be changed without using an entirely different command (the Change | Reshape commands, discussed in Chapter 9).

Each line you produce using the Freehand tool is automatically smoothed and converted to Bézier curves when you release the mouse button.

Draw |
Horz/Vert
Line

THE HORIZONTAL/VERTICAL LINE TOOL

The Horz/Vert Line tool (Keyboard Shortcut: Ctrl-H) draws horizontal, vertical, and 45-degree lines. Place the pointer where you want the line to begin, press the mouse button, and drag more or less in one of these three directions, as shown in Figure 5.9. Release when the line is as you want it. If you find while you are using this tool that you need to draw another straight line that is *not* limited to the vertical, horizontal, or 45 degrees, just press Shift after pressing the mouse button (not before).

Figure 5.9: Drawing with the Horz/Vert Line tool

Draw | Line

THE LINE TOOL

The Line tool (Keyboard Shortcut: Ctrl-L) lets you draw straight lines that are not limited to vertical, horizontal, or 45 degrees, unless you hold Ctrl while you draw the line. The Line tool's pointer is shown in Figure 5.10.

Both the Line tool and the Horz/Vert Line tools draw only single straight lines. To draw a series of automatically connected lines, you would use the Polyline tool.

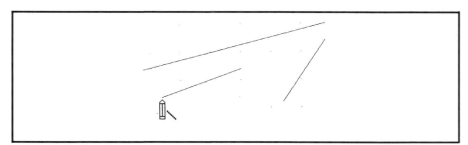

Figure 5.10: Drawing with the Line tool

Draw |
Parabola

THE PARABOLA TOOL

The Parabola tool draws a curved line; you begin by drawing a straight line, and then "pull" the center of the line out, as shown in **Figure** 5.11.

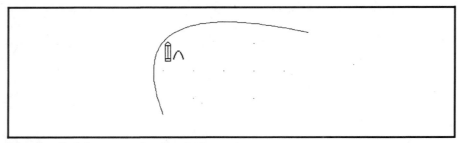

Figure 5.11: Using the Parabola tool

1. Select the Parabola tool and place the pointer where you want the line to begin.

2. Press the mouse button and drag the line to the point at which you want the line to end.

3. Release the mouse button.

4. Move the pointer to about where you want the top of the curve to be.

5. Press and hold the mouse button.

6. Move the mouse until the curve is in the position you want, and release.

If you hold Ctrl while drawing the straight line, you can limit the line to vertical, horizontal, or 45 degrees. Release the mouse button before you release Ctrl. Then press and hold the mouse button to position the apex of the curve.

Draw | Pie

THE PIE TOOL

You can use the Pie tool to draw any radial section of a circle—a straight slice from the center out to the circumference—as well as entire pie charts. The tool also enables you to create "exploded" pie sections— sections removed from the main pie, as shown in Figure 5.12.

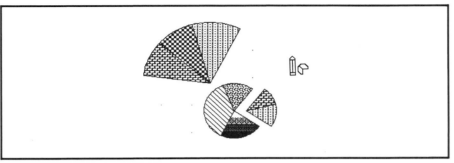

Figure 5.12: Pie segments drawn with the Pie tool

1. Select the Pie tool and point to where you want the center of the circle to be. Press and hold the mouse button.

2. Drag the mouse to draw a circle. Release when you have the size you want.

3. Point to the circumference of the circle, then press and hold the mouse button.

4. Drag the mouse in a clockwise or counter-clockwise direction. If you move clockwise, Designer draws a pie segment, which gets bigger as you move the mouse. If you move counter-clockwise, you erase the part of the circle along which you are moving the pointer, effectively creating a ''missing'' section, which gets bigger as you move the mouse. Move the mouse until the segment is the size you want.

5. Release the button and Designer adds the current color and pattern to the pie.

6. Point further along the circumference and press the mouse button again. Designer draws another pie segment.

7. Move the mouse until the next segment is the size you want, and release the mouse button.

8. Continue like this, until the circle is full of pie slices, or until you don't want to add any more.

9. Move the pointer to a blank space, and quickly click the mouse button; you are now out of the pie-slice-drawing mode, and can draw another circle.

While you are drawing a slice, notice that the status line shows you how large the slice is, in percentage of the entire pie. This lets you create perfect pie charts. For example, if you are trying to show the portion of the market held by your company's product, you can simply draw each slice to show the percentage share.

You can ''explode'' any of the slices by using button 2 on the mouse. When you have drawn a slice you want to explode, don't release button 1. Instead, press and hold button 2 as well, and move the mouse. When the slice is where you want it, release button 2, return to the pie, and continue drawing slices. The next slice will be added to the exploded slice, rather than to the main pie. (If you want to explode only a single segment, you must wait until after you have finished the pie chart.)

You may want to ''set'' the color dialog box while drawing pie charts. That way you can conveniently color each pie segment differently: select a color, click on OK in the color dialog box, and draw a slice; select the next color, click on OK, and draw the next slice, and so on. You can also select patterns from the Pattern menu while using the Pie tool, so you can apply different patterns to each slice.

Each pie slice is an independent object. You can move any slice wherever you want it. For example, you may want to ''explode'' various sections after you've created a whole pie chart, pulling one or two slices out for emphasis. If you want to move the entire circle, use the Edit | Block Select tool to grab the entire object at once.

Pressing Shift while you draw the initial circle makes the circle an ellipse—so you can slice elliptical pies—and pressing Ctrl while you draw the circle makes the beginning point one ''corner'' of the circle, as explained in the description of the Circle tool.

NOTE

You may sometimes find that Designer will not allow you to draw a slice with the number of degrees you want. It may be jumping from 5 to 10 to 15 degrees, and you want to make a wedge of 9 degrees, for example. This is due to a rounding error inside the Designer program. Try starting over from the beginning, drawing a new circle in a slightly different position, and the error might clear automatically.

Using the Keyboard   If you don't have a mouse, you will have to use the arrow keys in unison when drawing the pie slice so that you can move the pointer in a circular motion. If you want to explode any segments, press the *2* key on your keyboard (not on the numeric keypad), move the slice out, release the space bar, and press the space bar again to continue.

THE POLYLINE TOOL

Draw |
Polyline

The Polyline tool (Keyboard Shortcut: Ctrl-P) lets you draw objects with a series of connected straight lines, as shown in Figure 5.13. Each time you move the pointer and click the mouse button, Designer draws a straight line from the end of the last line. This makes it the best tool to use when producing lines that must be connected, because it is not always a simple task to go back to connect lots of individual straight lines.

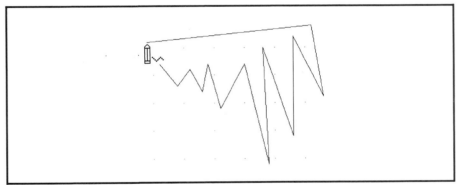

Figure 5.13: Drawing with the Polyline tool

You can change to freehand-style drawing while using the Polyline tool by holding down the Shift key while you draw. Holding down the Ctrl key limits you to vertical, horizontal, and 45-degree lines.

THE ROUNDED RECTANGLE TOOL

Draw |
Rounded
Rectangle

The Rounded Rectangle tool draws rectangles with rounded corners. As you drag the pointer with this tool selected, the rectangle expands diagonally from one of its corners.

The Rounded Rectangle tool can be deceiving at times, because until the object is at least about 0.3 by 0.2 inches it looks more like an ellipse, but as you expand it you will see that the sides flatten out and it changes into a rectangle. Holding down Ctrl while you draw the rectangle makes Designer draw a square with rounded corners.

If you don't like the angles of the corners, you can edit them later, using the Change | Reshape commands, as described in Chapter 9.

The Rounded Rectangle pointer is shown in Figure 5.14.

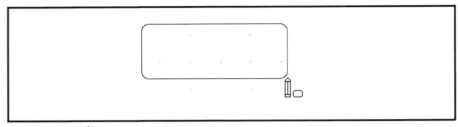

Figure 5.14: Drawing with the Rounded Rectangle tool

THE RECTANGLE TOOL

Draw |
Rectangle

The Rectangle tool (Keyboard Shortcut: Ctrl-R) works like the Rounded Rectangle tool, except of course that the end product doesn't have rounded corners. The Rectangle tool's pointer is shown in Figure 5.15. Pressing Ctrl while drawing makes Designer draw a square instead of a rectangle.

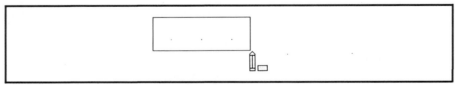

Figure 5.15: Drawing with the Rectangle tool

THE SQUARE TOOL

Draw |
Square

When you first press the mouse button with the Square tool selected, the pointer appears at the center of the square; as you drag the mouse the square expands equally in four directions. If you hold down the Ctrl key, the starting point becomes one corner of the square; as you drag the mouse you drag the opposite corner along the square's diagonal. Pressing the Shift key while drawing a square permits you to move off a 45-degree diagonal in order to draw a rectangle instead.

The Square tool's pointer is shown in Figure 5.16.

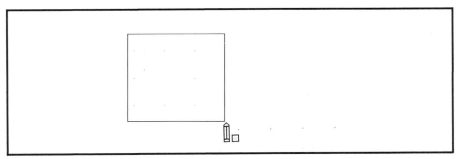

Figure 5.16: Drawing with the Square tool

6

Working with Lines

There is an aspect of drawing lines and objects that we haven't yet touched on: What does the line itself look like? For instance, what color is the line? How thick is it? What should the ends of the line look like? These are all line aspects that Designer lets you manipulate.

USING THE LINE MENU

The commands in the Line menu, shown in Figure 6.1, let you change a line's color, its width, and its style (either continuous or one of four patterns of dashes). You can even change its "pattern" color, profile, and end style.

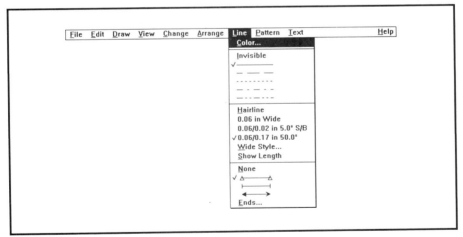

Figure 6.1: The Line menu, Designer 3.1

There are two ways to use the line commands. You can select a line and then use one of these commands to change it, or select the command to set the current line characteristic, so that subsequent lines are drawn with that characteristic.

Color   Changes the line's color. If you select a dithered color Designer actually draws the closest solid color.

Invisible	Removes all color, including black; you cannot see the line. You can use this to change an existing line, but you cannot use it to *draw* an invisible line (i.e., "invisible" cannot be the current line style).
(line styles)	Defines the line style. You can choose a continuous line style or a variety of dashed styles.
Hairline	Hairline is the thinnest line that the monitor will display or that the output device will print. This is the default line size for 3.0 as well as for 3.1. Although earlier versions don't actually show Hairline as an option, in these versions you are using the hairline width if no other line size is selected.
(line measurements)	Designer displays up to three of the most recently used widths, from the Wide Style dialog box. Information about cap style, join style, height, and pen angle will also be displayed, if you changed these.
Wide Style	Displays the Wide Style dialog box, letting you select the width, profile, cap, and so on.
Show Length	Displays the length of lines drawn using the Line or Horz/Vert Line tool.
None	Sets the end style to none, i.e., the ends of a line will not have any special symbol.
(end styles)	Displays up to three of the most recently used end styles.
Ends	Lets you select the type of symbol to show at the end of a line.

3.1 (margin marker beside Hairline row)

SELECTING A LINE'S COLOR

You have already learned how to change or select an object's color; the principle is the same for a line. Select Line | Color and the Select Line Color dialog box is displayed. (If another Color dialog box is already displayed because the Set checkbox is turned on, select Color | Line Color from the dialog box's menu bar.) Then select a color. That color becomes the *current color*, which means that subsequent lines—whether individual lines or the lines around objects—will be drawn in that color. If you have a line selected when you choose a new color, that line changes color. You can also select a background color for lines, using Change | Background color. A line has a background color only if it is one of the dashed or dotted lines; the background color is the color *between* the dashes or dots. Also, if you are displaying line lengths (explained later in this chapter), the background color appears as a background box for the line-length numbers.

SELECTING A LINE STYLE

There are five different line styles that you can select from the Line menu: the continuous line, and four types of dashed lines. You can select any of these types for any line or object border (the line around an object). Versions prior to 3.1 will not allow you to create dashed lines with anything but the default line size (the hairline). This can be distressing if you are working with a very high resolution printer, because the only lines you can dash are lines that are nearly invisibly thin. Creating a dashed line first and then applying a line width to it doesn't solve the problem; pre-3.1 Designer will simply convert the dashed line to a continuous line. (Designer 3.1, though, allows you to create dashed lines with any line width you want, up to Designer's maximum line width of one inch.)

MAKING A LINE INVISIBLE

You can make any existing line or object border invisible by selecting the line or object and then Line | Invisible. However, you cannot set Invisible as the current line style; in other words, you cannot *draw* invisible lines or objects without borders.

This feature is useful because you won't always want to see a border around objects—sometimes you need simply a colored area. But remember that if the object has no fill you are, in effect, making the object invisible.

NOTE
If you decide to connect or disconnect an object that has an invisible border, the border reappears.

SELECTING A LINE WIDTH

Designer displays up to three line widths in the Line menu. If you haven't yet selected a line width, Designer displays 0.06 inch (or 0.16 cm). Each time you select a line width from the Wide Style dialog box (Line | Wide Style), Designer adds that width to the menu, and, if necessary, removes one of the other widths, so that you can see the last three widths you have used. (If you change the line's cap or join style, or its height or pen angle, that information is also displayed with the width; you will learn more about these later in this chapter.) The maximum line width is 1 inch.

The default line width is the narrowest line your monitor can display— a *hairline*. When you zoom in on an object the hairline-width lines and borders do not change correspondingly; they don't appear to get thicker, they always remain the thinnest lines your monitor can display.

Hairlines also display on other devices at these devices' thinnest line width. When working with a very high-resolution output device, such as a Linotronic typesetter, you may have to avoid using the hairline width because it might be so thin it would be virtually invisible. (Unfortunately, in versions prior to 3.1, if you try to *increase* the width of a dashed line, Designer converts it to a continuous line.)

If you want to convert a continuous line back to the default, hairline width, select the line and then select Hairline (in 3.1) or the continuous line below Color (pre-3.1) in the Line menu.

USING THE WIDE STYLE DIALOG BOX

Figure 6.2 shows the Wide Style dialog box. You can change any of these features in this dialog box:

- Width

- Height

- Pen angle

- Cap

- Join

Notice the picture of the line in the right-hand side of the box. As you make changes, the picture changes, so you can see exactly what you are getting. Inside the picture of the line is a thin white line; this is the default line

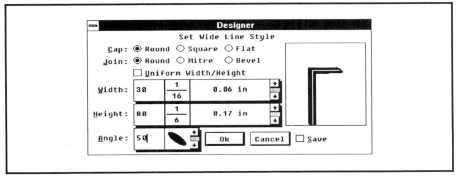

Figure 6.2: The Wide Style dialog box

(the line used if you don't select a wide line). This gives you a point of reference to see the effect of changing cap and join styles.

Width, Height, and Calligraphic Drawing

The concept of line width is obvious. The term *line height*, however, may need some explaining.

Line *width* is the width of a vertical line, and line *height* is the width of a horizontal line. Giving a line both a width and a height allows you to draw "calligraphic lines," lines that look like they were drawn with a wide-point pen. With such lines, the width of the line changes as the line curves. You can create calligraphic lines by making the height and width differ greatly, or you can use the pen angle (described later) to create a calligraphic effect when the width and height are close.

Normally the width and the height are the same thing. You can see both measurements in the Wide Style dialog box, but as long as the Uniform Width/Height checkbox has an X in it, the width and height are exactly the same. However, deselect the Uniform Width/Height checkbox, and you can change width and height independently of each other.

As you can see from the illustration of the Wide Style dialog box in Figure 6.2, both Width and Height are measured in three ways; on the left of the list box is what is called the coordinate (explained below), in the middle is the fraction of an inch (or centimeter), and on the right is the decimal measurement, from .002 to 1 inch (or centimeter).

Coordinates are, basically, a measure of the resolution of the art you are drawing. The default is 480, that is, 480 dots per inch (or centimeter); so if the line is half an inch the coordinate box will display half of 480, or 240.

(You will learn more about coordinates in a later chapter.) The fraction is the fraction of an inch or centimeter; a 0.5-inch line will show 1 over 2 in the fraction box.

You can use the Width or Height boxes by clicking on the arrows in the scroll bar, or by typing a new coordinate. If you have been adjusting width and height independently, and then select the Uniform Width/Height checkbox again, Designer automatically adjusts the current line's height to make it the same as its width. As long as the box has an X in it, changing the width changes the height, and vice versa.

KEYBOARD

Press Tab, Alt-W, or Alt-H to move to the coordinate box and type a new value. Or press Tab until the cursor is in the scroll bar, and then press the up or down arrow keys to increase or decrease the value.

Pen Angle

The pen angle is used in combination with the line width and height to create calligraphic lines. The pen angle has no obvious effect when the width and height are the same, but once they begin to differ, you can see how the pen angle modifies the line. The pen angle simulates the effect of holding a calligraphic pen at different angles. It is something you need to experiment with to get a good idea of how it works, and it is a feature that will require a lot of practice before you can use it predictably. In effect it adjusts *where* on a curve the line thins, as you can see from Figure 6.3. The

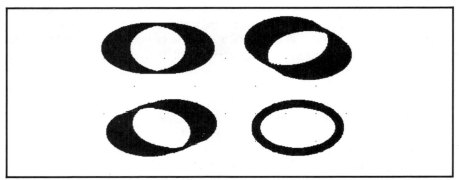

Figure 6.3: The effect of different pen angles

ellipse in the top left has a pen angle of 0 degrees, the one in the top right has an angle of 145 degrees, and the one in the bottom left has an angle of 200 degrees. All three of these ellipses have very thick line widths and thin line heights. The ellipse in the upper left has the same pen angle as the one in the lower right (200 degrees), but it has equal line width and height.

Caps and Joins

Designer also lets you adjust what the ends of a line will look like (the *cap* style), and how lines are joined together (the *join* style).

The cap style only comes into play if the line doesn't have any of the special line endings in the End Styles dialog box (which you will learn about in a few moments). You can select Round (the default), Square, or Flat. The round cap places a circle with its center at the end of the line, the square cap places a square with its center at the end of the line, and the flat cap flattens off the end of the line. Figure 6.4 shows an example of each style. (Each line is displayed as if it were selected, so you can see where the lines' handles are.)

Notice that the square and flat styles look much the same, except that the square style effectively lengthens the line, protruding past the end of the line.

The join style can be Round (the default), Mitre (squared-off corner), or Bevel (the corner "knocked off"). Round join uses a circle with its center at the point at which the two lines meet, Mitre joins the lines exactly, and Bevel averages the angles of the intersecting lines, blunting the join. Figure 6.5 shows an example of each of these styles.

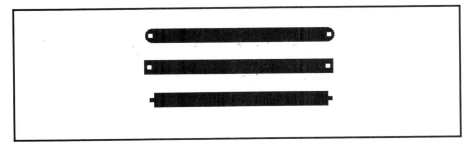

Figure 6.4: Line cap styles

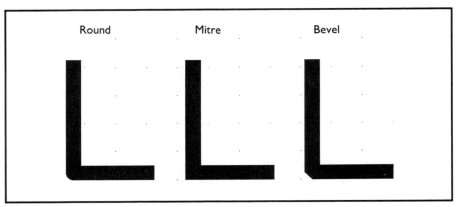

Figure 6.5: Line join styles

SHOWING LINE LENGTH

If you select Line | Show Length, Designer will display the line length in the center of each straight line. The digits in the line will be the same color as the line color; if you have selected a background color, a background box of that color will be displayed underneath the line length.

This feature only works on single straight lines drawn using the Line, Horz/Vert Line, Polyline, or Freehand tools. (With the Freehand tool you have to hold down Shift while you draw in order to create a straight line.)

The dimensions used for line length are determined in the View | Dimensions dialog box. (You will learn more about this dialog box in Chapter 11.) It is important to realize that when you change the dimensions, you are changing only the name you use for the dimension; you are not actually changing the scale (that is done in the Rulers/Grid dialog box). Figure 6.6 shows the Dimensions dialog box; your options range from feet to meters, points to picas, minutes to years. The time dimensions make it easy to create time-management charts (like Gantt charts) and schedules.

TIP

There's another way to make a line display its length besides using Line | Show Length. Select the line, select View | Dimensions, choose the dimension you want to use, and click on OK. Designer automatically displays the line length on the selected line, in the new units. Note that this method does not cause subsequent lines to have their line lengths displayed.

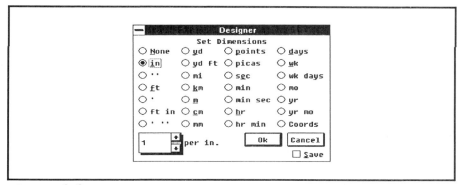

Figure 6.6: The Dimensions dialog box

Changing a line's length normally changes the dimension shown, but if you combine the line with other objects (using Arrange | Combine, Arrange | Connect Closed, or Arrange | Connect Open, explained in Chapter 7), changing the combined object does not change the line's displayed dimension. However, using Arrange | Break Apart automatically readjusts the dimension.

Using the Special Line Ends

Designer lets you choose from 14 special line-end symbols. You can select a line and then select its end style, or select an end style as the current style before drawing your lines. All lines, straight or crooked, can have end styles; even objects converted using Arrange | Connect Open (see Chapter 7) can have end styles added to their outlines—though if you select a style for both ends the symbols are joined together, because both "ends" are in the same place. Objects that are "connected closed" cannot use the special line ends.

Selecting Line | Ends displays the End Styles dialog box, as shown in Figure 6.7. The default line-end style (a line with no special symbol) is shown in the first line in the box. You will notice that the option button at each end of this line has a black dot, indicating that the style for each end of the line is selected.

You can select a line by clicking on the line itself—in which case the end styles will be the same at both ends of the line—or you can click on the individual option buttons, so that you can have one style at one end and a different style on the other. (The end styles on the right side of these sample lines determine the style for the right end of horizontal lines, or the bottom of vertical lines; the end styles on the left determine the style for the left or top ends.) When you have selected the styles you want, click on OK.

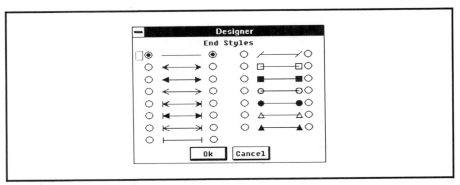

Figure 6.7: The Line Ends dialog box

You can remove line ends by selecting the Line | None option; it changes the current end style to "no symbol," or removes end symbols from a selected line.

KEYBOARD

When you first open the Line Ends dialog box, the cursor is on the current left-hand end style. Use the arrow keys to move the black dot up or down to another left-hand style, or Tab to move to the right-hand end style (and use the arrow keys again to select a right-hand style), or Tab again to move the cursor to the first *line* in the list. If you want to select a line (both end styles the same), press Tab or the down arrow key to move down the rows of lines, or Shift-Tab or the up arrow key to move up the rows, then press the space bar to select the line—the same style end will be used on both ends of your line. Press ↵ when you have finished selecting the styles.

Now that you have learned how to draw various component objects, move on to Chapter 7 to learn how to combine these objects into pictures.

7

Combining Objects into Pictures

Using Designer to make line drawings is merely the first step in the process. A finished picture is made up of many individual drawings, which may be combined in various ways. Once you have drawn an object or two, you can either combine them into a group or connect them into a single, new object using the following commands from the Arrange menu:

Combine (F5)	Groups two or more objects together. The group can then be moved, rotated, or flipped, or have its color and pattern changed, etc., as if it were one object.
Connect Closed (F11)	Closes any gaps in a line drawing (drawn with the Arc, Bézier, Freehand, Line, or Parabola tools) and fills the object with the current color and pattern. If you are connecting more than one object, the group is also combined (as with Arrange | Combine).
Connect Open (Shift-F11)	Works like Connect Closed, except that one gap is left, so the object is not filled with color or pattern. If the object has no gaps in the first place, it will act like an open object; you cannot fill it with color or pattern, for example.
Break Apart (Shift-F5)	Breaks a combined group or a connected object into its original components. If you use this command on a group of objects that were connected using the Connect Closed command, the individual objects change back to the colors and patterns they had before being connected.

COMBINING OBJECTS

When you combine objects, they remain individual objects—Designer doesn't join them together with lines or close any gaps in the drawings—but they are *grouped* together. Clicking on one of the objects selects the entire combined group, and any command you use on the group affects all the objects in the group. If you select the group and then select Change | Flip Horizontal, for example, the entire group is flipped, and if you select the group and select a new color or pattern, all the objects in the group are changed.

If you want to work on an individual object—you want to change the color of just one object, for example—you can break the group apart, using Arrange | Break Apart (Keyboard Shortcut: F5), and the group is dismantled. Then if you click on one object, only that object is selected.

Try this experiment to see Combine at work:

1. Draw several objects with the draw tools: some squares and circles, for example. As you do so, make sure they have different colors and patterns. For example, see Figure 7.1.

2. Use the Block Select tool to select all the objects, and then select Arrange | Combine. You can now move the objects as if they were one, and selecting one of the objects selects all of them. In fact, you can no longer select the objects individually.

3. Select the combined objects and select a new pattern color. Notice that the colors of *all* the objects change.

4. Try selecting different colors and line styles. Notice that all the objects change.

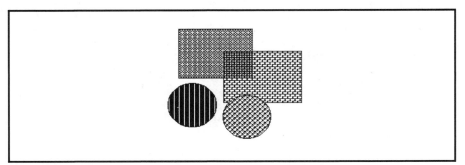

Figure 7.1: Independent objects before connecting

CONNECTING OBJECTS

The differences between combining and connecting are important to understand.

When you *combine* objects you are grouping them together for easy editing. On the one hand, you can change every object within the group with just one command. On the other hand, you can protect the group from changes you are making to the rest of the picture. In fact, one of the major reasons for combining objects is to make sure a finished picture or section of a picture isn't accidentally distorted when you are carrying out an operation on some other part. Unless you change them on purpose, the combined objects retain their original colors, patterns, and line settings, and look exactly as they did before they were combined. If, for example, one object overlaps the other, when the objects are combined the overlapping object continues overlapping.

When you *connect* objects you are actually creating a new object. Designer changes the line to the current line setting, and, if you "connect closed," even fills the newly created object with the current pattern and color. Designer will also adjust any overlaps in the drawing according to the Pattern | Alternate and Pattern | Winding settings (which you will learn about later in this chapter).

You may connect an object "open" or connect it "closed." A closed object has fill—color or pattern—and is regarded as an object, whereas an open object has no fill, and is treated as a line. Although an object has a line around it (you can make the line invisible if you wish), you might think of that as its border rather than as a line. Open objects are nothing *but* the line: without the line there would be nothing there.

USING CONNECT CLOSED

The connecting commands let you finish off an object drawn with any of the various line-drawing tools, turning a line or group of lines into a complete object. Imagine you have an object drawn with the Freehand tool, and the drawing comprises only one line. If you had drawn the object so that the beginning and end of the line met, the object would automatically be a connected object, and would have filled with the current color and pattern when you ended the freehand-drawing mode. But if you left a gap between the beginning and end of the line, you can still convert the object to a connected symbol. Click on it to select it, and then select Arrange | Connect Closed; Designer closes the gap between the beginning and the end, and fills the object with the current color and pattern. From this point on, Designer will treat the object as a connected one.

If you used several lines to draw a single object, use the Block Select tool (from the toolbox, or choose Edit | Block Select) to select all the lines, and then select Arrange | Connect Closed; Designer closes all the gaps, and fills the finished object with the current color and pattern. Designer also automatically combines them, just as if you had used the Arrange | Combine command; the lines will now be treated as a single object.

If the original objects' lines are invisible, by the way, Designer will automatically redraw the lines when you connect the objects—because connecting objects automatically draws lines in the current line setting. You can always make them invisible again after connecting the object; simply select the new object and select Lines | Invisible (Keyboard Shortcut: F11).

Although it may seem a contradiction in terms, there *is* a way to ''fill'' an open object, or at least make it look like you have done so. Try this procedure to create a picture similar to the one in Figure 7.2:

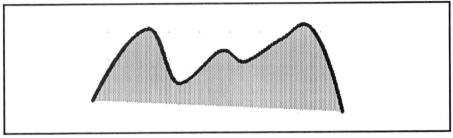

Figure 7.2: An apparently open object, with a fill

1. Draw an open object, such as the curve shown in Figure 7.3, drawn with the Curve tool.

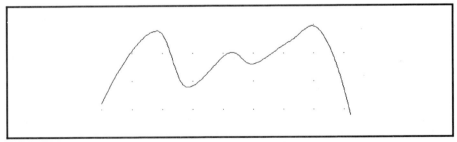

Figure 7.3: A line drawn with the Curve tool

2. Make a copy of the object.

3. Connect Close the copy, then use the Line | Invisible command to make the border line disappear.

4. Select a pattern and color for the copy.

5. Select the original (the curved line) and use the Arrange | Move to Front command (Shift-F9). (If you don't use the Move to Front command, you may find the copy slightly overlaps the original, blocking part of the line, especially if it is the default—thin—line.)

6. Change the curve to a wider line.

7. Select both objects with the Block Select tool, and press Ctrl-F5 followed by Ctrl-F6 to align them. (You will find out more about the Align commands in Chapter 12.)

Reversing the Connection

If you want to break apart a connected object, use one of these methods:

- If you connected a one-line drawing, select Arrange | Connect Open. This reopens the gap between the ends of the line.

- If you connected several lines, select Arrange | Break Apart. This returns the lines to their original states. Or, select Arrange | Connect Open to reopen the largest gap, leaving the other gaps closed, and removing all color and pattern.

- If you connected closed objects, select Arrange | Break Apart (Keyboard Shortcut: Shift-F5) to return the objects to their individual colors and patterns.

USING CONNECT OPEN

If you selected Arrange | Connect Open, all the gaps in your drawing would close, except one. This ensures that the object cannot be filled with color or pattern. You might want to do this if you are creating an object that you don't want to fill, or if you intend to combine the object with others— leaving the object open will allow you to change the rest of the group's color and pattern, while leaving the open object unchanged.

You can also use this command to ensure that the primitives (which are naturally closed objects) will not accept fills or colors. For example, a square or circle is automatically drawn closed; thus, it takes the current color and pattern. If you want to use Arrange | Connect Open on a primitive, you can't simply select the object and then select the command. You must either select *several* objects (using the Block Select tool) and then select Arrange | Connect Open; or select one object, select one of the Change | Reshape commands (to get into Reshape mode), select the Change | Reshape command again (yes, to get *out* of Reshape mode), and finally select Arrange | Connect Open. (In the case of the rounded rectangle, you must select Change | Reshape Béziers before you select Arrange | Connect Open; selecting Change | Reshape Points will not work.)

This may seem a complicated way to do things, but, like other graphics programs, Designer requires that some types of objects be converted into a different, editable form before modifying. Although most of Designer's shapes can be immediately modified, the primitives cannot. They are, as the name implies, very simple objects; they require another step before they can be turned into open objects. Going into Reshape mode converts them into an editable form.

If you use the Arrange | Connect Open command on a primitive, all color and pattern is removed, and none can be added until you change it back to a "closed" object. Note that this command doesn't actually open the object—that is, Designer doesn't open a gap in the object's outline—rather, it tells Designer to treat the object as if it is open, at least as far as fill is concerned.

CONNECTING OVERLAPPING OBJECTS

Suppose you connect two objects, one of which either overlaps or sits completely in front of the other. Remember that when you connect objects (as opposed to combining them), you create a new object. Therefore, the object in front or "on top" is no longer *overlapping* the other one, it is actually *part of* a new object.

Designer has two ways to connect such objects: Pattern | Alternate cuts out a space in the connected object, and Pattern | Winding fills in the space.

Each of these commands works in two ways. You can select one as the current setting—so that subsequent objects are connected using that method—or you can select a connected object and then select the method to convert the object from one form to the other (no need to break the object apart and then reconnect using the other setting).

USING PATTERN | ALTERNATE

The default method is the *alternating* method. The area where two connected objects overlap each other, or the area of an object that is totally inside another object, is "cut out." The effect is that you can see through it to the background drawing area. This is useful when you want to create a see-through effect (the windows in a car, for example), or when you are using two symbols to create an object that has a hole or gap in it—using two circles to create a key ring, for example.

When you are dealing with only two objects, it doesn't matter *which* object is on top once they are connected. A circle inside a square will produce a circular hole regardless of whether the circle was behind or in front of the square. Figure 7.4 shows an example of an object before and after connecting, using the Alternate method.

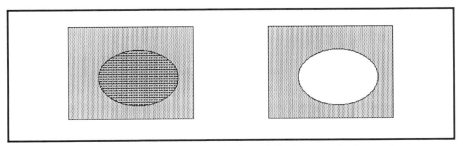

Figure 7.4: Two objects connected closed, before and after using Pattern | Alternate

What about multiple overlaps? Areas where three or more objects are on top of each other, for example? The Alternate command cuts out only those areas with an *even number* of objects overlapping; in other words, it *alternates* from one layer to the next, cutting out the area occupied by even-numbered layers and leaving the areas covered by odd-numbered layers. The area covered by Object #2 is cut out, but if Object #2 has another object, Object #3, on top, the area where it overlaps Object #2 is *not* cut out. The area where Object #4 covers Object #3 *is* cut out, though. Look at Figure 7.5 to see what five stacked rectangles look like.

On occasion you may find that an object is connected with Alternate even if Winding is selected in the menu, and that you are not able to convert the

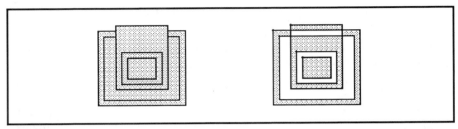

Figure 7.5: Stacked objects connected closed, before and after using
Pattern | Alternate

object to Winding. This happens particularly with some of the outline fonts—
such as Geometric—that have been converted to curves and then connected
with overlapping objects. (Converting to curves is explained in Chapter 8.)
There's nothing you can do in the case of the fonts, but if it happens to any
other objects, try breaking them apart, moving them, and reconnecting.

USING PATTERN | WINDING

If you choose not to use the default connection method, select
Pattern | Winding. Designer will fill the entire object with the current pat-
tern and color, without regard to overlaps. No part of the object will be cut
out. Instead of seeing a hole in the object, you will see the outline of the
overlapping object.

Invisible lines are automatically redrawn when you connect, of
course, but if you change the lines back to invisible after connecting the
object, remember that if one object is inside the other, it will disappear completely. Figure 7.6 shows the same overlapping squares from Figure 7.5, but
connected closed using Winding.

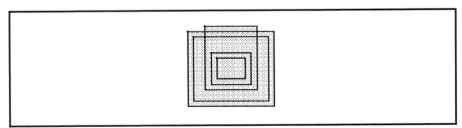

Figure 7.6: Stacked objects connected closed using Pattern | Winding

8

Working with Text

Designer has some very versatile text features. Like many other illustration packages, Designer lets you use text to add titles to your work; unlike some other illustration packages, Designer is flexible enough to let you work with large blocks of text, allowing you to use it as a page layout program. You can design flyers or brochures, for example, importing the text from a word processing file, or typing it directly into Designer.

Fonts cause some confusion, because they seem to change on screen now and again. You may notice that if you change your page view, zooming in or moving out, the font seems to change to a different one. This is because when you change a view your computer doesn't simply increase or decrease the size of the text, as it does with objects; rather, it has to find a font that is the size you want and display *that*. There are occasions when Designer doesn't have the correct size for that particular font. (This problem doesn't occur with outline fonts.) In such cases Designer will substitute another font, but only for that *view:* if you print the work, or change to the previous view, Designer uses the correct font.

It is actually Designer's flexibility that causes these problems. Unlike most graphics programs, Designer lets you use the Zoom tool to view your work at any size. For example, PageMaker allows you to view your work only at 200 percent, actual size, 75 percent, 25 percent, and "Fit in Window" size, and the last two display only very large fonts—anything small is replaced with "fuzz." In PageMaker, then, there are only five different font views at most, or five different display sizes for each font, so when you change view in PageMaker the program knows exactly how to display the fonts in the new view. Designer, on the other hand, has so many possible views that it will never have enough display fonts to always be able to display the font correctly, so on occasion your fonts will look a little different. If you use View | Actual Size or View | Page, though, the font will return to the correct one.

UNDERSTANDING DESIGNER'S FONT TYPES

Designer comes with four different font types: *outline, vector, device,* and *screen.*

- **Outline**   These are the highest quality fonts, consisting of Bézier curves. They are independent of the device on which you will print

---

NOTE

Designer 3.0 had some serious problems with text. There were a number of bugs that could make using text very difficult. The selected font would change without reason, the text display mode would often be different from the one selected, and text could suddenly jump into the wrong position within a paragraph, to name a few. Most problems were fixed by Designer 3.01, though.

---

your work: they look the same regardless of the device you use, and they print with the highest quality possible on each device. They may be resized, rotated, or even converted to curves so that you can reshape them in the same way you would a drawn object. Unfortunately, outline fonts take up a lot of memory and can considerably slow redrawing. Designer comes with 35 fonts designed by Bitstream, and 6 URW Nimbus-Q fonts from The Font Company. (You can see what these fonts look like on the inside back cover of this book.) You can buy additional fonts from Bitstream or The Font Company, or add outline fonts that you already own, as long as they are compatible with Designer.

- **Vector** Vector fonts are outline fonts of a lower quality. They cannot be converted to curves—if you try to do so Designer selects the closest outline font and converts that instead—but they can be resized and rotated. A vector font's outline will take the selected text color, but vector fonts cannot be filled. Vector fonts redraw more quickly than true outline fonts, and they are suitable for use on plotters because they plot quickly. The vector fonts are provided by Windows, and they include Modern, Roman, and Script.

- **Device** Device fonts are fonts used by specific output devices, particularly laser printers and matrix film recorders, and they generally print at the device's highest resolution. They also print quickly. Some, but not all, device fonts can be rotated and sized. If you try to print device fonts on a device that doesn't support them, Designer will substitute outline fonts. Some device fonts can be sized and rotated, though they may change to an outline font. On the screen, device fonts will display sometimes as outline fonts and sometimes as screen fonts; when they print, though, the correct font is used. The device fonts are loaded when you load the device drivers, either through Windows, or, if you have one of the devices for which Designer provides drivers, when you install Designer. Some devices also allow you to add "soft" fonts later, through the Printer Options dialog box; these will be discussed later in Chapter 10. Actually, any font that is not an outline, vector, or screen font will be identified as a device font. This includes Adobe Type Manager fonts, which are loaded using Adobe's special ATM Control Panel. (If you have Designer 3.1 you can use Adobe Type Manager fonts in the same way that you use outline fonts: you can rotate or resize them, convert them to curves, or use Text | Text Along a Curve, and the font will retain its correct proportions.)

- **Screen** Screen fonts are bitmap images that redraw quickly on the screen. They are intended for use in onscreen presentations, not for printing, and they usually have a limited range of point sizes. If you size or rotate a screen font it may change to an outline font. The screen fonts you have will depend on the computer you are using; they are loaded when you load Windows, according to your computer's configuration. You may have, for example, Courier, Helvetica, Symbol, and Times Roman.

Figure 8.1 shows examples of these different fonts.

Figure 8.1: Font types

You Should Always Use Outline Fonts (or Adobe Type Manager Fonts) When You Can The following points illustrate why they are the most versatile:

- It doesn't matter if you change printers—outline fonts are not device dependent.

- If you have a printer that doesn't print large fonts or rotated text, you can convert the outline fonts to objects. (If you convert printer fonts to objects they will be replaced with a different font.)

- You can print any size outline font. (Printer fonts generally have a limited range of sizes.)

- If you come back to a drawing later, and want to change some of the text to a special effect, you can convert it to curves and make your changes; the text will still match the font used elsewhere in the drawing. (If you try this with printer fonts Designer will replace the converted text with a different font.)

- If you are using a Matrix slide recorder you can use outline fonts converted to curves to avoid the five-fonts-per-drawing limitation imposed by that device.

ENTERING TEXT

Before entering text, you should make sure that you have selected the correct output device, the device on which you intend to produce your work; though if you will be using only outline fonts it doesn't matter. Use the File | Change Printer command to select your output device (and see Chapter 10 for more information).

T

Draw | Text

To enter text, select the Text icon from the toolbox, or select Draw | Text (Keyboard Shortcut: Ctrl-T). A black T appears next to the pointer.

NOTE

The Text tool is not in the Text menu; it is in the Draw menu (Draw | Text). This is because it is regarded as another type of drawing tool. You can also select it from the toolbox—it's the small black T, *not* the larger, outlined T (that's the Convert to Curves tool, which you will learn more about later in this chapter).

Place the pointer where you want to begin typing, and press the mouse button once. (Press and hold it for a second or two. Sometimes the text tool seems to "stick," especially if it is redrawing something at the moment that you click, or if there is a lot of text already in the drawing area.) The pointer changes into a text bar—a small vertical line with short offshoots at the top and bottom—and a vertical black line is displayed on the drawing area. The size of this line depends on the size of the font you are using. When you begin typing, Designer displays the text.

If the rulers are displayed, the top ruler shows the text margins. (You can turn the rulers on and off in the Rulers/Grid dialog box, which is displayed when you select View | Rulers/Grid). When you reach the right margin the text wraps around onto the second line, just like in a word processing program. You can adjust these margins, as you will learn later.

You may remember that when you use the other drawing tools you can jump in and out of drawing mode by clicking the mouse button quickly. The procedure was pretty simple: Point at an object, click quickly, and the drawing tool disappears, allowing you to work on the selected object. Then click quickly in an empty area and the drawing tool reappears.

This procedure no longer works with the Text tool. Previous versions of Designer *did* allow you to select objects while using the Text tool, but many people found the Text tool awkward, so Micrografx modified it. As of Version 3.0, clicking quickly on an object has no effect. There *are* three ways to exit the Text mode, but once you exit, you must select the Text tool again in order to use it again.

- Double-click the mouse button anywhere in the drawing.

- Select another tool from the toolbox.

- Select a tool or command from the menus.

EDITING TEXT

To edit what you have typed, first use the pointer or the cursor-movement keys to move the text cursor within the text.

arrow keys	Move the text bar one space or line at a time
Home	Moves the text bar to the beginning of a line
End	Moves the text bar to the end of a line
Ctrl-Home	Moves the text bar to the beginning of the text
Ctrl-End	Moves the text bar to the end of the text

Once you have placed the text bar where you want to change text, use the Delete and Backspace keys to erase characters, or begin typing, and Designer automatically inserts new characters, pushing existing text to the right. If you want to *overstrike* (replace) text, press the Ins key to toggle from Insert to Overstrike mode, and begin typing; Designer replaces the old characters with the new. (Whenever you select the Text tool, Insert mode is active, even if the last time you used the tool you were in Overstrike mode.)

NOTE

If you want to place the text bar into an existing block of text, make sure it is not combined with other text or objects. Use Arrange | Break Apart to separate combined objects.

SELECTING TEXT

You may also select a block of text and modify it. If you hold the mouse button while you drag the mouse, or hold Shift while you use one of the cursor-movement keys, Designer will select the text by highlighting it as the text bar moves over it.

Once the text is highlighted, you can perform operations on the whole block:

- Select another font

- Select another font style

- Select another text color

- Select another text leading (line spacing)

You can also delete the block by simply typing. As soon as you type a character, the highlighted text is removed, and replaced with whatever you type (even if you have not toggled into Insert mode).

NOTE

Designer has a bit of a delay after you select another font, style, or leading before it gets back to typing—you will notice a short lag between when you begin typing again and when Designer begins inserting text. And if you select another color while Set is on in the Color dialog box, you must actually reposition the text bar in the text; the act of selecting a color removes the text bar from the text.

USING THE TEXT EDITOR

Sometimes Designer will use a *text editor* to work on the text. This is a small window into which the text is typed. Figure 8.2 shows an example of the text editor box at the top of the main window. The text editor appears for the following reasons:

- When you select the text tool, press and hold Shift, and click the mouse button.

- When the selected page view and the selected text size are such that the text will be too small to be legible, Designer automatically displays the text editor when you select the text tool and press the mouse button.

- When you select the text tool, point to rotated text, and click the mouse button. Designer automatically displays the text editor so you can edit the rotated text.

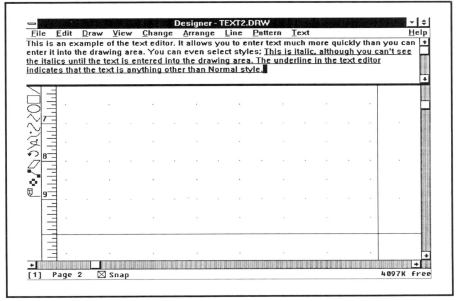

Figure 8.2: The text editor

You may want to use the text editor whenever you type or edit blocks of text, because it works much faster than entering or editing text on the drawing area itself. The tradeoff to using the text editor is that, while you are entering or editing the text, you will not be able to see the text exactly as it will appear on screen. The color and any underlines will display, but not in the selected font, size, or attribute (bold, strikeout, or italic). These characteristics *will* display, though, once the text is placed in the drawing area.

You can adjust the size of the text editor using the mouse to drag the lower border. (The next time you open the text editor the window will be the new size.) You can also use the text editor's scroll bar to scroll through the window, or use the PgUp and PgDn keys to move up and down one window's worth of text at a time.

3.1

KEYBOARD

If you have Designer 3.1 you can also adjust the size of the text editor using the keyboard. Press Ctrl-F8 (a two-headed arrow appears on the bottom of the text editor's window), then use the arrow keys to move the border up or down. Press Enter to return to the text, or Esc to cancel the sizing operation. This feature will not work with versions prior to 3.1.

Once you have entered or edited the text, press Esc or select another tool or command. Designer closes the text editor and places the text into the drawing area, using the specified font, size, and attributes.

NOTE

Designer 3.0 has a few problems with the text editor. It doesn't always display all the text lines. Lower lines just seem to "disappear," though they may reappear when you insert a character. (However, inserting a character may also make lower lines that *are* visible disappear.) Also, some characters disappear off the right side of the window, even if the window is maximized. These problems were fixed in Designer 3.01.

SPEEDING UP TEXT
REDRAWING WITH TEXT DISPLAY

Using text can slow down redrawing dramatically, so Designer has a command that lets you speed up redrawing by displaying low-quality text. When you are working on other parts of the drawing, or when you are simply entering text and are not yet concerned with how it actually *looks*, you should use the *draft* or *greyed* text—which will be explained shortly—to speed things up. This doesn't affect the output, and you can change back to high-quality text at any time.

Select Text | Display, and you see the Display dialog box (Figure 8.3), which allows you to adjust how text should be displayed during viewing and during editing. (By viewing, it means any time you are not entering or editing text.)

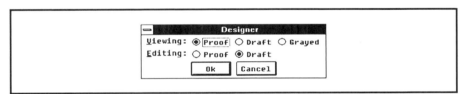

Figure 8.3: The Display dialog box

Viewing has three options:

Proof   The highest-quality display, as close to the printed text as possible. This is the slowest font display to work with.

Draft   The text is of a lower quality, and doesn't look exactly as it will when it prints. Outline fonts are not filled with color. However, it may redraw quicker than proof.

Greyed   The text is replaced by a grey box, which makes it unreadable. This is the fastest display.

The setting you select here affects *all* text in the drawing, not just selected text.

Editing has just two options, Proof and Draft. (You can't edit in Greyed mode because you can't see the text.) Unless you are in the text editor, which does not display the font or size, the option you select affects the text as you enter it or when you return to edit it.

IMPORTING TEXT

There are two basic ways to import text from other documents:

- Copy text from another Windows application into the clipboard, then paste from the clipboard into the text editor or drawing area.

- Use the File | Import command to import ASCII text files either straight into the drawing area or into the clipboard.

In either case, bringing the text into the clipboard enables you to paste it into the text editor to let you change it before pasting it into the drawing area. Importing or copying text into the text editor is also a quick way to handle it. For one thing, redrawing the text is much faster in the text editor than it is in the drawing area, because the text editor uses screen fonts. You can import into the text editor, delete the pieces of text you don't want to use, make any changes, and then place the text into the drawing area. This is especially useful if you want to import text from a document and put different parts of it in different parts of the drawing area. Just paste it into the editor, remove the parts you don't want, and press Esc to exit Text mode and place the text into the drawing area. Then return to the editor again and repeat the procedure; the text in the clipboard remains there until you delete it or replace it.

NOTE

There is one restriction on this procedure: in pre-3.0 versions of Windows you are limited to 64K of text. If the text takes up more memory than 64K you will not be able to import it, even if you try to import directly using Auto Paste to bypass the clipboard. In this case you will have to break the file to be imported into manageable pieces.

IMPORTING THROUGH THE CLIPBOARD

All Microsoft Windows programs can use the clipboard, so you can import text from any of your other Windows programs. For example, if you have Microsoft Word 5.0 that you run in Windows, you can copy blocks of text into the Windows clipboard from your word processing documents.

You can then open or return to Designer and select Edit | Paste to copy the text directly into the drawing area; it will have the font and characteristics currently selected in the Text menu, but of course you can use the Text tool to edit it. Alternatively, you can open the text editor and then select Edit | Paste; the text is pasted into the text editor so you can edit it immediately. The text may appear in the text editor in "inverse" video—that is, the background may be black, until it is highlighted, at which point it turns white—but don't worry, it still works the same.

IMPORTING THROUGH FILE | IMPORT

If you don't have a full version of Windows, or if you want to import text from programs that won't run in Windows, you can still do so, as long as the program will save the text in ASCII format. You can paste ASCII files directly into the drawing area, or you can import them into the clipboard and then paste the text into the drawing area or text editor.

Select File | Import and Designer displays the Import dialog box, shown in Figure 8.4. In the list of file formats select the line that says "TXT ANSI Text." In the list box on the left Designer displays all files with the .TXT extension. Find the file you want to import and select it. (If your file does not have the extension .TXT, either rename it with this extension before you try to import it, or change the extension in the Filename box to the one your text file has.)

You now have two options. You may turn Auto Paste *on* (in the checkbox in the lower left corner of the Import dialog box) and click on OK to place the text directly in the center of the Designer window. Or you can

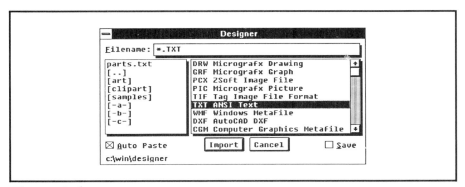

Figure 8.4: The Import dialog box

turn Auto Paste *off* and click on OK to copy the text into the clipboard. In either case, if you are in the text editor when you click on OK Designer closes it and ends Text mode before placing the text. When you import text into the clipboard, Designer displays the Paste tool, the large cross. You can place the cross where you want to place the text, and press the mouse button to paste it in. Of course once the text is in the clipboard you don't have to paste it immediately; you can click on the arrow in the top of toolbox—or select any other tool or command—to exit Paste mode, and return to paste the text later (as long as you don't use Edit | Cut or Edit | Copy to put something else in the clipboard). At this point you could, for example, open the text editor and then paste the text into the editor.

MODIFYING TEXT

There are a number of ways you can modify your text. You can select the font, the size, the margins, the leading (rhymes with *bedding*, and means the space between the lines of text), the color, the alignment, and the style—normal, bold, italic, underline, and strikeout. If you have Designer 3.1, you can also change character and word spacing.

The Text menu contains most, but not all, of the text tools you will use in Designer.

Text | Normal	Text that is not bold, italic, underline, or strikeout
Text | Bold	Bold text
Text | Italic	Italic text
Text | Underline	Underlined text
Text | Strike Out	Text marked by means of a horizontal line through it
Text | (font names)	The names of the last three fonts used
Text | Font...	Lets you select another font
Text | Color...	Lets you select the text color
Text | Alignment...	Lets you align the text around a point

Text | Leading...	Lets you set the line spacing (pre-3.1 versions only)
3.1 Text | Spacing...	Lets you select leading, inter-character spacing, and inter-word spacing (Designer 3.1 only; replaces Text | Leading)
Text | Paragraph...	Lets you set the text margins
Text | Display...	Lets you set the display mode, adjusting the redraw speed
3.1 Text | Text Along a Curve	Lets you place text on an object so that the text conforms to the shape of the object
Text | Convert to Curves	Changes text into Bézier curves
Text | Split Text	Breaks up blocks of text
Text | Join Text	Joins blocks of text

The other text commands you will use are listed below:

Draw | Text	Selects the Text tool
Change | Background Color	Fills the rectangular area immediately around and behind the text with the background color, or changes the background color
Change | Opaque	Fills the text background with background color
Change | Transparent	Removes background color from the text

SELECTING FONTS

Choosing a font has two effects; it determines the font in which text will appear when you type it, and it *changes* the font of the text block that is selected at the time you choose the font.

There are two ways to select a font. The simplest way is to open the Text menu and select one of the fonts listed at the top of the second group of options. The menu lists up to three fonts, the last three that you have used during that session.

The second way to select a font is using the Font dialog box, displayed when you choose Text | Fonts. On the left side of this box (shown in Figure 8.5) is the Typeface list box, listing the available fonts. In the bottom center of the dialog box is a sample character (the default is an uppercase A). This gives you an idea of what the font highlighted in the Typeface list box will look like; if you need a better idea you can click on the box and type in another character (a lowercase letter, perhaps, or a number or percent sign). Remember, however, that when you select a device or screen font Designer has to display the closest screen font, so the printed text may not look the same as the sample.

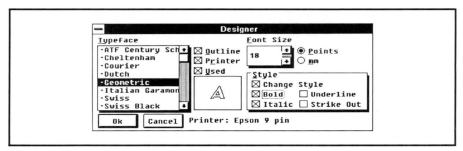

Figure 8.5: The Font dialog box

The checkboxes on the right side of the Typeface list box determine which fonts will be listed therein. If Outline is checked, all the outline and vector fonts are listed; if Printer is checked, all the appropriate device fonts are listed (or if no device is selected, the screen fonts are listed); and if Used is checked, all the fonts used in the current file are displayed, regardless of what type they are. You can, of course, select all three of these. Also, Designer always includes the current font in the Typeface box. For example, if you select a printer font, go to the Fonts dialog box and deselect Used and Printer; Designer will display only Outline and Vector fonts, *and* the current font, which is a printer font.

By appropriate device fonts, I mean those that are supported by the printer or output device displayed at the bottom of the dialog box. In Figure 8.5 the dialog box says "Printer: Epson 9 pin," so the only device fonts displayed in the list box are those that are supported by an Epson 9-pin printer. If you don't have a printer or other device selected, it says "None" in the Printer line. If this is the case, and you select the Printer checkbox, Designer actually displays the *screen* fonts in the list box, because there are no printer fonts.

- **To list outline fonts**   Click on the Outline checkbox. The outline fonts will be listed with a small dot in front of their names.

- **To list printer or device fonts**   Select a printer or other device in the Change Printer dialog box (File | Change Printer). Then go to the Fonts dialog box, select one of the outline fonts, click on OK, and redisplay the Fonts dialog box (this is to ensure that the current font is not a screen or printer font). Click on Printer in the Fonts dialog box and deselect Outline and Used. The only fonts now displayed *without* a dot in front of their names are printer fonts. Remember that Designer will also regard as a device font any font that is not an outline, screen, or vector font. If, for example, you have Adobe Type Manager fonts, they will be displayed in the list box when the Printer checkbox is selected.

- **To list screen fonts**   Select None in the Change Printer dialog box (File | Change Printer). Then go to the Fonts dialog box, select one of the outline fonts, click on OK, and redisplay the Fonts dialog box (this is to ensure that the current font is not a screen or printer font). Click on Printer in the Fonts dialog box and deselect Outline and Used. The only fonts now listed *without* a dot in front of their names are screen fonts.

- **To list vector fonts**   Select Outline in the Font dialog box, and deselect Printer. Then select one of the outline fonts, click on OK, and redisplay the Fonts dialog box (this is to ensure that the current font is not a screen or printer font). The only fonts now listed *without* a dot in front of their names are vector fonts.

Selecting Font Styles

Immediately to the right of the sample character is the Style box. You can click on Change Style, and then select the style you want; or you can choose bold, italic, or underlined text, or text with a "strikeout" line through it, or any combination of the four. (Until you select Change Style the other four options are ghosted, so you cannot use them.) Selecting an option in this box is the same as selecting it from the Text menu, except that in this case you can look at the sample character to see what the result will look like.

Some of the outline fonts, by the way, don't let you turn them into bold, italic, or bold-italic. The following fonts are limited:

Italian Garamond, Aldine 525	No bold-italic
Swiss 721 Light	No bold
Swiss 721 Black	No bold
Vivaldi	No bold, italic, or bold-italic

You can, however, use the strikeout or underline on any font.

Although each normal, bold, italic, or bold-italic font is a single font, the styles for a single typeface all carry the same name. Therefore, you will usually see fewer fonts listed in the Fonts dialog box than you thought you had loaded. If you are not sure if you installed a font variation, there's a quick way to check. Go to the Font dialog box, select the font you want to use, and try to apply bold, italic and bold-italic to it. If the sample letter in the box doesn't change, you didn't install that font.

The text style you will see whenever you open Designer depends on what you selected the last time you clicked on the Text Style checkbox in the Preferences dialog box. Set up the style that you would like to see whenever you open Designer. Then select View | Preferences. Click on the Text Style checkbox on the left side of the Preferences dialog box. Click on OK and Designer enters that style into the Windows WIN.INI file, the file that tells Windows how to open Windows applications. You can now return to your work, and change the style if you wish. The style that will be displayed the next time will be the one selected at the time that you closed the Preferences dialog box.

Selecting a Font Size

Above the style options is the Font Size box. Font sizes are normally measured in points, but you can change the dimensions to millimeters, using the option buttons to the right of the box. The scroll bar lets you change the size in increments of 1 point, from 1 to 144 points. The points used in the United States and the United Kingdom are based on the pica (one pica equals 12 points). Six picas almost equal one inch (0.996 inches), so a point is 0.0138 inches. Ten-point type is approximately a seventh of an inch high, and one inch is about 72.5 points. If you have Designer 3.1 you can choose to use *didot* points, a system used in some European countries. This is a

3.1

slightly larger point size; one didot point is 0.0148 inches. You can select didot points in the Preferences dialog box. The default is pica points. If you select millimeters you can use the scroll bar to change the size in 0.5 millimeter increments, from 1 to 50 millimeters.

You can also type a size into the Font Size box, in 0.1 point or 0.1 millimeter increments. However, unless the screen resolution (set in the Rulers/Grid dialog box) is high enough, Designer will not allow the 0.1 increments, and will change the font size to the nearest acceptable size. The default screen resolution of 480, for example, does not allow 0.1 increments.

At the other end of the scale, large font sizes can also run into problems. Your printer might not be able to print fonts larger than a certain size. Check your printer's manual to see if it limits the font size.

If your printer doesn't support the type size you want to use, there is a way around the problem: convert the fonts into graphics. Although the printer may not be able to handle large type, if it thinks the type is actually a picture, it will print it like any other object. You can convert text into pictures using the Text | Convert to Curves command, explained later in this chapter.

A Quick Way to Adjust Font Size There's a quick way to get the font just the size you want it, relative to your drawings. Select the text block, point to one of the handles, and drag the handle in or out, until the block is approximately the size you want. Release the handle, and Designer redraws the font at the new size. If you look in the Text menu you will see that Designer has entered the new font size. If you use the corner handles to adjust the size, the font will be adjusted equally in all directions and maintain its proportions. However, if you use the handles on the sides, you can change those proportions to create tall thin fonts or short fat ones, or whatever else you want. Figure 8.6 shows Century Schoolbook that has been stretched out of shape.

If you try to change a screen or device font to a size that it does not support, Designer will substitute a vector or outline font.

WORKING WITH MARGINS AND ALIGNMENT

Designer lays out text between text margins. Designer inserts text into an invisible box, the width of which is defined in the Paragraph dialog box.

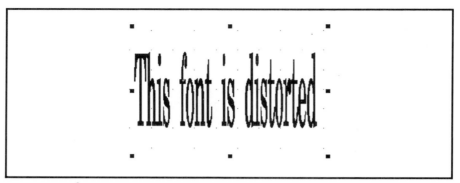

Figure 8.6: You can distort fonts by dragging the side handles.

When you are typing text into this box and you reach the right margin, Designer wraps the text down onto the next line, just as a word processor does. You can set an indent, the position at which a new paragraph begins, and you can also align the text in different ways.

SETTING MARGINS

When you select Text | Paragraph, Designer displays the Paragraph dialog box (Figure 8.7), which allows you to set the left margin, the right margin, and an indent. The left margin does not refer to the left margin of the page; it refers to the point at which you place the text bar. The dimensions are the same as those for the ruler units selected in the Rulers/Grid dialog box (View | Rulers/Grid). The values determine the number of units the

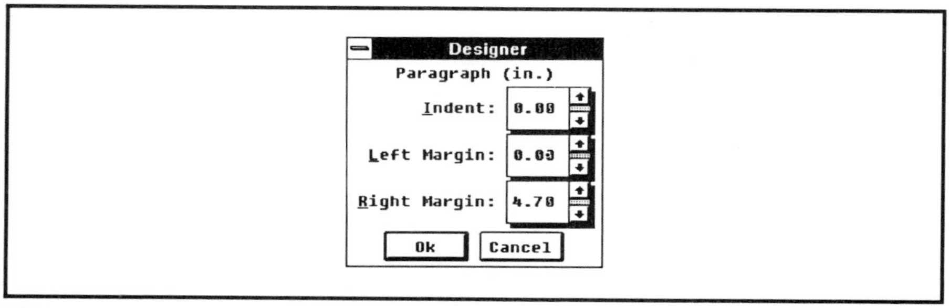

Figure 8.7: The Paragraph dialog box

indent and the right margin are from the left margin. For example, if the left margin is 0.00, and the indent is 1.00, then the indent is one inch to the right of the left margin. If the indent is – 1.00, the indent is one inch to the *left* of the left margin.

Actually, if you want to enter a "negative indent" you should use a left-margin value that is higher than 0.00. For example, rather than entering – 1.00 as the indent, enter 0.00, and enter 1.00 for the left margin. (Don't forget to add an extra inch to the right margin too.) You could enter the negative indent value if you really want to, but Designer will convert it to this second method anyway—and it may miscalculate when it does so!

Designer 3.1 has an extra option in the Text menu: Word Wrap. If Word Wrap is selected, the text will wrap when it gets to the right margin set in the Paragraph dialog box. If Word Wrap is *not* selected the text will *not* wrap. Also, when Word Wrap is turned off, the Indent you entered in the Paragraph dialog box is ignored, even if you press Enter to begin typing text on the next line; the first line will be at the same margin as the subsequent lines. In effect the Word Wrap option turns the paragraph settings on and off.

3.1 ADJUSTING THE MARGINS

As you've just seen, you can set your margins before you begin typing, but you can also set margins during text mode. In fact, you can even select single paragraphs within the block of text and change the margins to affect only those paragraphs. (Recall, however, that it can be difficult to determine where paragraphs begin and end since there are no visible paragraph markers once the text is entered.)

You can do this in one of two ways: by opening the Paragraph dialog box, or by moving the margins in the ruler. You may find it easier to set margins using the ruler. (The ruler display must be turned on, of course, in the Rulers/Grid dialog box.) The margins are displayed in the ruler below the menu bar. The left margin is a small triangle pointing to the right; the right margin is a triangle pointing to the left, and the indent mark comprises two triangles, back to back. See Figure 8.8.

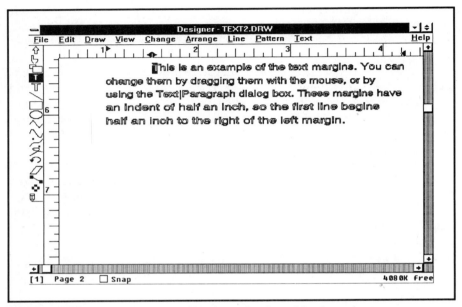

Figure 8.8: The text margin markers displayed in the rulers

You can drag these marks to the positions you want. Point to a mark, press the mouse button, drag the mouse, and release the button when it is in the position you want. Your text will automatically readjust.

KEYBOARD

There is no way to directly move the margin markers if you don't have a mouse. Instead, press Alt, press *T* and *P* (Text | Paragraph), and enter the values you want, using Tab to move around in the Paragraph dialog box.

ALIGNING TEXT

The text can be aligned within the text margins and in relation to the point at which you click the Text tool. Select Text | Alignment to see the Alignment dialog box, as shown in Figure 8.9.

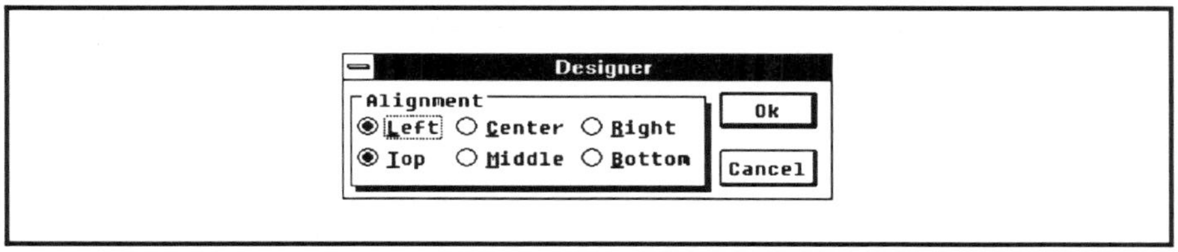

Figure 8.9: The Alignment dialog box

The top row of selection buttons sets the horizontal alignment, and the bottom row sets the vertical alignment, so you can select one from the top row and one from the bottom row.

For example, suppose you select Right and Bottom. You click on OK, select the Text tool, and click in the drawing area. When you begin typing, the text is inserted at the text bar and pushed to the left and—when it wraps onto the next line—upwards. In this way the bottom right of the text box will always be at the point at which you clicked the Text tool, regardless of how much text you enter. The default setting for the Alignment dialog box is Left and Top, of course, because normally when you enter text the top left of the text box remains at the point at which you clicked the Text tool.

This text alignment tool is very useful when you are entering labels into a drawing. Say, for example, that you want to label a component such that the label is situated to the right and just above the component. Just set the alignment to Left and Bottom and click the Text tool where you want the bottom left of the label text to appear. This lets you situate text exactly, without having to enter it and then move it into position.

You can also use the Alignment dialog box to align text *after* you have entered it. Select the text and then set the horizontal alignment (the vertical alignment will have no effect once you have entered the text). You might, for example, decide to move a block of text against an object, and you might want to change the text justification—you can center the text, right-justify it (have a straight line against the right side), or left-justify it. (If you use the Alignment dialog box on selected text the block of text may leap across the page at the same time its alignment is adjusted! If it does this, just move it back into position.)

Aligning Text in Objects

Designer has another way to align text: you can line it up inside an object you have already drawn. You might want to use this for labeling drawings or building flow charts, for example. The text is automatically aligned around the center of the object.

Of course this is also a quick way to set margins: you can use this method to align your text within a specific blank area. Just draw a rectangle in the area you want to place your text, enter the text, delete the rectangle, and—if necessary—realign the text.

1. Select the object.

2. Press Shift and select the text tool by clicking on the tool or select Draw | Text. (Keyboard Shortcut: Shift-Ctrl-T).

3. Release Shift. The text bar appears in the middle of the object.

4. Type the text. The text is automatically centered, as shown in Figure 8.10, and Designer automatically changes the Alignment dialog box settings to Center and Middle.

When you have finished typing you can change the text alignment if you want. Click away from the object (remember, the object is selected, not the text), and then click on the text. Then set your new alignment.

WORKING WITH LINE SPACING (LEADING)

The distance from the bottom of one line of text to the bottom of the next is called *leading*. It is normally measured in points. You may have seen word processing programs expressing font and leading as 9/11 or 10/12, for example, which means a font of 9 points and a leading of 11 points or a font of 10 points and a leading of 12 points, in both cases leaving 2 points between the bottom of one line and the top of the next.

Select Text | Spacing, or, in pre-3.1 Designer, Text | Leading, and Designer displays the Text Leading dialog box (Figure 8.11). The box tells you the name of the current font (or the font used in the selected text), and, below that, displays a box with two figures separated by a slash—the font size followed by the leading. You can change the value for the leading by using the scroll arrows or typing in a value. (If you want to change the value for the font size you must go to the Font dialog box.)

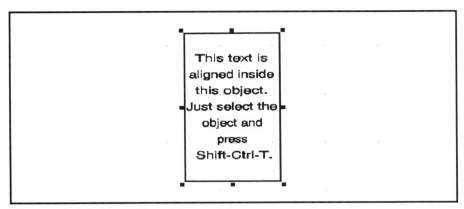

Figure 8.10: Text aligned in an object

Figure 8.11: The Text Leading dialog box (pre-3.1 Designer only)

Each of Designer's fonts has a default leading, the leading that will be used if you don't make any adjustments. Click in the Default Leading box to set the leading back to the default.

If you enter a value less than that of the default leading, Designer 3.1 accepts it, but pre-3.1 versions ignore it. Designer *3.01* and *3.02* ignore it, that is; Designer *3.0* lets you use a leading less than the default to change existing text (though it won't allow you to *enter* text with such a leading). Designer 3.0 even allows you to apply a leading that is less than the font size, causing the text lines to overlap. If you want to do that in Designer 3.01 and 3.02 you must use the Text | Split Text command and then move the lines on top of each other.

You can use the selection buttons to select the dimensions: points or millimeters. However, these are, to some degree, overridden by the settings in the Font dialog box, so if you have "Points" selected in the Fonts box and then select "mm" in the Text Leading box, Designer will display the size in millimeters, but it will change back when you close the dialog box—that is, the next time you open the box the dimensions will be points again.

You can also use this dialog box to find out what leading a block of text is using. Select the text and then select Text | Leading, and the dialog box displays the font and leading that is used.

There's a shortcut to changing leading. Select the text, point to one of the handles, press and hold Shift while you press and hold the mouse button, and drag the mouse. When you release Shift and the mouse button, Designer redraws using the new leading, leaving the text the same size; it still won't allow you to reduce the leading below the default, though. This shortcut doesn't seem to work on rotated text, at least not consistently, but you can still use the Leading dialog box to change leading in rotated text.

CHARACTER AND WORD SPACING

There will be times that you want to adjust character spacing (kerning) and word spacing. For example, some combinations of letters seem to have too much space between them. There appears to be more space between an uppercase *T* and a lowercase *o,* or between an uppercase *W* and a lowercase *a,* than between most other pairs. These differences are not too noticeable in large blocks of text, but they become much more apparent in headlines, especially with white type against a black background. You also may want to adjust letter spacing to create special effects, spreading a headline across the page, for example, in effect creating a graphic element from text. And you may wish to change the space between words, to reduce or increase the *density* of type in a block of text, for example.

In Designer 3.0 it was not too easy to adjust character and word spacing. In effect you had to make each word or character an individual block of text, and then move each word or character into the correct position. An alternative method was to type the text as one block, convert it to curves (Text | Convert to Curves) and then adjust spacing. Designer 3.1, however, lets you adjust the spacing between characters and words as you type the text, or will automatically adjust spacing in an existing block for you. Figure 8.12 shows the Designer 3.1 version of the dialog box that was shown in 8.11. This dialog box is displayed when you select Text | Spacing. You can enter both character and word spacing in the range – 25 percent to 200 percent. (The negative numbers reduce the normal spacing between characters and words.) You can see that inter-character spacing is measured in *ems,*

3.1

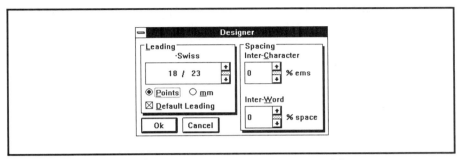

Figure 8.12: The Text Spacing box (Designer 3.1 only)

while inter-word spacing is measured in spaces. An em is the size of the lowercase *m* in the particular font you are working with; therefore it will vary from one font to another. The size of the em, by the way, also includes the space normally left after the letter—if you adjust inter-character spacing to 100 percent, the space between letters will be the size of an *m* plus the space normally placed before and after the *m*. (Imagine an old block of type—the block extended a little beyond each side of the actual letter.) You can adjust kerning for individual characters by typing the first character, adjusting the kerning, typing the next character, adjusting the kerning again, and so on. Or you can select a block of text and adjust the spacing for all the characters at once.

If you adjust the word spacing, the amount specified is added to the amount of space normally left when you press the space bar. So if you select 100 percent, Designer will actually leave two spaces when you press the space bar (one plus the space from the space bar); if you enter 150 percent, Designer will leave two and a half spaces (one and a half plus the one from the space bar), and so on.

SPLITTING AND JOINING BLOCKS OF TEXT

You will often find that you need to break apart blocks or lines of text. The need for this arises from the fact that it is difficult to get the leading to look the way you want it when you work with a variety of font sizes within a single block.

To break apart a block of text, select it and then select Text | Split Text. The text is broken into individual lines, each line becoming a block of text.

You can also join text together. Use the Block Select tool to select all the text you want, and then select Text | Join. All the text is moved to the left, to the position of the leftmost text, and placed in a column. If two or more blocks of text are on *exactly* the same horizontal line, the block originally on the right is placed below the block originally on the left.

Before you join text, make sure there are no objects in the way. If you select objects at the same time that you select the text, Designer will not allow you to join the text.

APPLYING COLORS TO TEXT

There are two ways to apply color to text. You can change the color of the font itself, or you can change the color of the text's background, a rectangular area behind the text. You can apply the colors to existing text, or you can select the colors before entering the text. You learned about colors in Chapter 4, and the principles are exactly the same. Use Text | Color to adjust the text's color, and Change | Background Color to apply or change the background color. Change | Transparent removes the background color, and Change | Opaque reapplies it. The defaults are black for the font itself and *no* background color (that is, a transparent background).

You can change text colors without leaving Text mode. Type some text, select a new color, replace the text bar in the text, and continue typing. Or, select several of the characters using the techniques described earlier in this chapter and select a color, and Designer applies that color to the selected text.

You can even apply dithered colors to your text. (Dithered colors are created by combining pixels of differing colors.) While you are entering or editing text, however, the dithered color is displayed as a solid color.

Incidentally, unlike objects, fonts don't have outlines, so if you make the text the same color as the screen background, the text disappears. If you want to use white text on the screen background, for example, you should convert your screen to another color using the View | Screen Color command. If you are going to print your work on a screen background other than white, it's a good idea to change the screen color to that color anyway. Matrix slide printers, for example, let you select a background color. (If you *want* an outline around the text, you must convert it to an object, a process discussed later in this chapter.)

TEXT SPECIAL EFFECTS

Once you have the text on the screen you can play with it to get special effects. You can use any of the following commands:

Change | Rotate	Spins the text around a pivot point
Change | Rotate Left/Right	Rotates the text a set number of degrees
Change | Rotate	Returns the rotated text to its starting point
Change | Opaque	Fills the text's background with the Background color
Change | Transparent	Removes the background color from the text's background
Change | Background Color	Fills the text's background with the Background color or change the color
Arrange | Align	Lines the block of text up with other blocks of text or objects
Arrange | Array	Creates multiple images while rotating, resizing, and moving the text
Text | Color	Changes the color of the text

Of course you can also move, copy, or duplicate the text, as well as combine it with other objects and move it in front of and behind objects. You *cannot* slant it or flip it, or use any of the reshape commands on it (unless you convert it into an object, which we'll discuss in a moment).

Not all text can be rotated. You can rotate outline fonts, and some device fonts, but if you try to rotate screen fonts or device fonts that cannot be rotated, Designer substitutes an outline font before rotating the text, and the replacement may not look like the original.

CONVERTING TEXT INTO OBJECTS

Designer allows you to convert text into objects. You can convert outline fonts exactly, and the object will look just like the typed characters. You can also convert printer, screen, and vector fonts, but not directly. Designer has to select an outline font first, and then convert *that* font, and the end result often doesn't look much like the original.

3.1   Designer 3.1 can also convert Adobe Type Manager fonts directly into objects.

Why would you want to convert text into objects? As I mentioned earlier in this chapter, it is one way to get your printer to print fonts that are too big for it. Some printers cannot print fonts above a certain size, but if you convert the font to an object first, the printer will print the text without knowing the difference. The same goes for rotated text. Though some printers can't print rotated text, if you convert an outline font to an object, the printer won't know it is text and will print it anyway.

Another reason is that converted text can be used just like any other graphic. You can now apply patterns to it, for example. You can break the text apart, and not just line by line (as you can do with Text | Split Text), but character by character, allowing you to move each character into exactly the position you want. You can also flip or slant the text, something you can't do with real text—and you can even flip or slant individual characters within the text. You can modify the size of individual characters disproportionately, increasing the height but not the width, for example, and you can also use the Change | Reshape commands, so you can edit the very *shape* of each character. The special effects you can create are limitless once you convert your text into graphics.

To convert text to graphics, just select the text and then select Text | Convert to Curves (or click on the Convert to Curves tool—the outline T—in the toolbox). Designer converts the text into Bézier-curve objects. Each character is an individual object, and the entire text is *not* combined, though of course you can combine it if you wish. If you want to use the Change | Reshape commands on your converted text, use a large font, make your changes, and then reduce the finished objects. Larger fonts—say, over 72 points—have more Bézier anchors, so they are easier to manipulate.

Designer has a tendency to slightly increase the size of the text when it converts it to curves, so in some cases you may need to reduce it slightly. Also, remember that once the text is a graphic, *there's no going back!* (Except, of course, by immediately using Edit | Undo). You cannot convert back to text, and none of the text commands will have any effect. These are pictures now, and work just like any other object.

Also, remember that once converted to an object, text has pattern, background, and *line* color, the line color being the color of the font's outline. Real text does not have an outline color.

3.1 PLACING TEXT ALONG A CURVE

Text Along a Curve, a new feature found in Designer 3.1, is really a "text along an object" feature: not only can you place the text on a curve, circle, or ellipse, you can actually place it on *any* object drawn with one of Designer's drawing tools—even a complex object created with the Free-hand tool. You can't place text on objects that have been combined, though, or on bitmaps or on blocks of text. Furthermore, as with converting text to curves, placing text on an object doesn't work well with any but outline fonts. If you use another type of font it will be converted to something different (though perhaps similar). Adobe Type Manager (ATM) fonts may be alright—Micrografx has made them work almost as well as outline fonts—but they are not totally reliable when being placed on an object. The result may look okay on the screen, but some characters may be misplaced or even disappear when you print the art.

Also, Text Along a Curve does not convert to all the export file formats very well. In some vector formats the text will be displayed as normal (straight) text. However, once you have placed the text on an object you can convert the text to curves (Text | Convert to Curves) and *then* export the file.

Text Along a Curve is very easy to use. First, select both the text and the object (by using the block select tool or by clicking on one, pressing and holding Shift, and then clicking on the other). Then select Text | Text Along a Curve. The text is placed on the object, conforming to the object's shape. If the object is a primitive (a square, circle, ellipse, rectangle, or rounded rectangle) the text begins at the top left "corner" of the object and runs clockwise. If the object is a line of some kind (freehand, polyline, horizontal/vertical line, and so on), the first character is placed at the object's starting point. (The case of an open object that has been connected closed is more complicated, with the position depending on the location of the original starting point on the closed object.) You can reverse the positioning of the first character by holding the Shift key when you select Text | Text Along a Curve: with primitives, the text is placed inside the object, going counterclockwise; with lines, the text is positioned with the first character at the end of the line.

If there is too much text for the object, the text that "overshoots" will continue on the same course that it left the object. For example, if you place text on a square but you have more text than can fit on that square, the extra text at the end will continue off the last side—the left vertical side—in a straight line going up the page. The text in Figure 8.13 shows text placed on a rounded rectangle. (I inserted spaces for the first few characters of this text, by the way, once I realized that the overflow at the end of the text string would run right through the beginning of the string.)

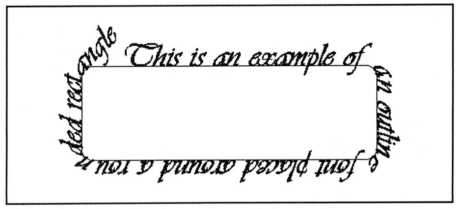

Figure 8.13: Text placed around a rounded rectangle

To remedy the problem of overflow, you could use the Text | Spacing feature to try to compress the text a little in order to fit it all onto the square.

Once on an object, the text remains text. You can edit the text in the normal way (although regardless of the text's size the text editor is automatically displayed when you try to do so). You can change character and word spacing, and move and rotate the text. For example, you might want to rotate text you have placed on or in a circle, in order to have the starting and ending points in the correct position. You can also remove the object you placed the text on and leave the text floating in space in the shape of the object—the text and object are independent of each other, so you can use an object as a "form" and then delete the object when you are finished with it. The text "remembers" the shape it was placed on, so even if you have removed the object you can change the character or word spacing and the text will be reformatted and placed back into the remembered shape. You can always remove the shape from text—straighten out the text—by selecting the text alone and then selecting Text | Text Along a Curve. (You can tell when you have selected the text rather than the object, incidentally, because the middle handles will be grey instead of black.)

Placing Text on a Curve with Pre-3.1 Designer

With pre-3.1 versions of Designer, positioning text on a curve, or around a circle, takes quite a few steps:

1. Draw a circle. The larger the circle, the shallower the curve will be, of course. If you want to place your text on a gentle curve, draw a very large circle—you can delete it when you have finished.

2. Enter your text in a single line and convert it to curves (Text | Convert to Curves).

3. Exit Text mode, select the text, and select Arrange | Align to display the Align dialog box (you will learn more about this in Chapter 11). Figure 8.14 shows the Align dialog box.

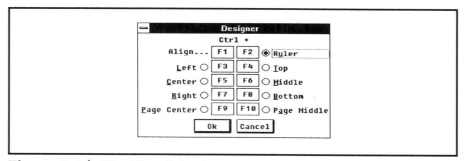

Figure 8.14: The Align dialog box

4. Click on Center, and click on OK. Designer places all the letters in your text on top of each other, with the first character on the bottom.

5. Move the text onto the curve.

6. Select the circle, and then select Edit | Snap Mode to display the Snap dialog box. Click on Center, and click on OK. (You will learn

more about Snap Mode in Chapter 11). Designer places blocks around the circle and in its center.

7. Click on the text again. Designer will select the top character, which was the last one on the line of text.

8. Select Change | Rotate or press Shift-Ctrl-F8. Designer displays a pivot point in the center of the block of text. Drag the pivot point onto the circle's center point.

9. Now place the pointer outside the selected character, press the mouse button, and drag the character away from the others. The character will rotate around the center point of the circle. Release the mouse button when the character is in the position you want.

10. Repeat this procedure for all the characters. The result should look something like Figure 8.15.

11. Click on the arrow in the top of the toolbox to exit Rotate mode.

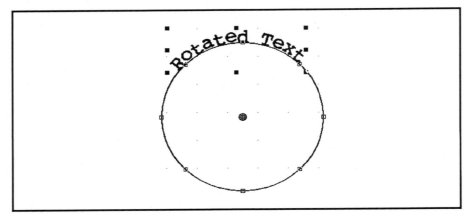

Figure 8.15: The text spread along the circle, with the pivot point in the middle

You can use the Rotation dialog box (Change | Rotation) to set the character spacing—as you drag the characters around the circle they "jump" the number of degrees set in the Minimum Step Size checkbox in the Rotation dialog box. Experiment with different settings until you get the right one. Once you have positioned the characters around the circle you can turn off

Object Snap (select Edit | Object Snap), select all the characters, and combine them into one object (using Arrange | Combine). Then use the same procedure to rotate the completed block around the circle until it is in the correct position.

SHADOWING TEXT

Another text effect you might want to try is "shadowing" text:

1. Type your text. Then make a copy of the text block. (You can use the Drag-Shift method, the Duplicate tool, or, best of all, the Arrange | Array command, which is described in Chapter 11.)

2. Use the Text | Convert to Curves command to change the copy into an object.

3. Change the new text object's color or pattern using the Pattern menu commands. It's a good idea to select a lighter color or shade. Select Line | Invisible to make the text object's outline disappear.

4. Use Arrange | Combine to combine the individual text object characters into one object.

5. Turn off Snap to Rulers by clicking on Snap in the status line or by selecting Snap to Rulers in the Rulers/Grid dialog box (View | Preferences). Then drag the text object onto the original text, trying to block out the original. (If you used the Arrange | Array command using 0.00 for the movement and size settings, the object is already exactly on top of the original.) If the text object is larger than the original text, reduce it until it almost exactly covers the original.

6. Select Change | Slant. The pointer turns into the Slant tool. Drag one of the top corners up and to one side of the text, distorting the text object. Release when the block is in the position you want, and click on the pointer in the tool box.

7. If the shadow is still *on top* of the original text, use Arrange | Move to Back to put it behind the original.

In this example, if you had converted the text to curves and *then* made a copy, you would not have to reduce the text object in size to fit the original text. Figure 8.16 shows an example of shadowed text.

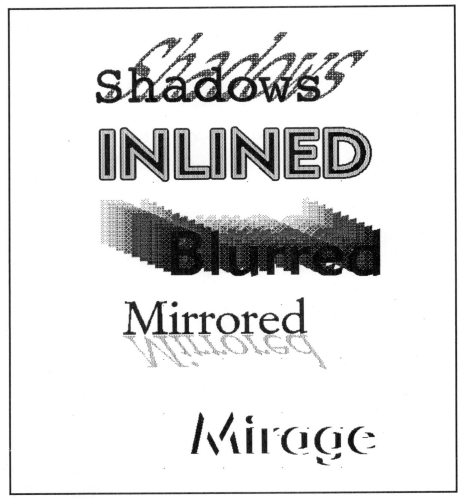

Figure 8.16: Shadowed text and other text effects

OTHER SPECIAL EFFECTS

You can create great special effects with Designer's text tools—you are limited by only your imagination. (Some of these effects depend on the Array dialog box, which is explained in Chapter 11.) Here are a few ideas for effects that can be created once you have converted the text to curves:

- **mirrored text**   Make a copy and flip it to create a mirrored effect. Make the mirror image a lighter shade, and reduce it in size a little to make it look like a reflection. Or use the Slant tool to flip and slant the image at the same time. This also gives a ''backlit'' shadow effect.

- **mirage text**   Place a white copy of the original text on top and slightly offset, and remove the copy's border (Line | Invisible).

- **gradient text**   Fill the text with a gradient pattern and color.

- **inlined text**   Give the text a thick line using Line | Wide Style—0.04 inch for example. Then use Arrange | Array to place an exact copy on top. Then give the copy a thinner line width, and use Line | Color to give it a different color.

- **blurred text**   Remove the border from the text (Line | Invisible) and then set its pattern color to white. Then use Arrange | Array to produce 10 or 15 slightly offset copies, and to grade the copies from white to black.

SPEEDING UP TEXT OPERATIONS

Text slows down your computer tremendously. Even working with text on a fast 386 can be frustrating, so anything you can do to speed things up is worth trying. Here are a few tips:

- Don't add the text to your drawings until you really have to, as close to completion as possible.

- Use the text editor to enter text. The editor is as quick as a word processor.

- Create all your diagram labels in the text editor at one time, then use Text | Split Text to break them up into blocks. With the display set to Greyed you can then move the blocks to the correct positions.

- Use Text | Display to change the way your screen displays text. Display text you are not using as grey boxes, or in Draft mode—limit your use of Proof mode to when you have to know exactly what the finished work will look like. Don't edit text in Proof mode.

- If you are entering large blocks of text, enter them in one of the screen fonts, which redraw relatively fast. Then, when you are near completion, convert to the outline or drives font you want to use. (You won't be able to do this if you are using a font size that the screen fonts don't have.)

- Convert outline text to curves if you are sure you won't need to edit it later as text. It will redraw more quickly.

- Keep text "off screen" whenever possible, so your system doesn't have to keep redrawing it.

9

Reshaping
Curves

Designer has some powerful editing tools that let you treat any line or object—including text—as a curve. This gives you remarkable control over any point you choose on an object, allowing you to fine-tune all your drawings, adjusting a line's position and angle to get perfect results.

Of course, you have already learned some simple editing methods; you learned how to change an object's size, both linearly and proportionally, and how to flip or rotate the object. But the tools described in this chapter go much further, using complex mathematical formulas to "micro-edit" your work. The tools you will learn about in this chapter all come from the second group of options in the Change menu:

Reshape Points (Ctrl-click)	Lets you alter the shape of an object
Reshape Béziers	Converts the image into Bézier curves, and lets you use anchors and control points to edit it
Reshape Connected	Lets you modify a component of a connected object, without disconnecting the object first
Smooth (F6)	Smooths a symbol or a selected portion of a symbol
Unsmooth (Shift-F6)	Unsmooths a symbol or a selected portion of a symbol

STEP ONE:
TURN OFF SNAP TO RULERS?

Snap to Rulers is a special mode that helps you to line up and position objects, by forcing the pointer to "jump" from ruler increment to ruler increment. (You will learn more about this in Chapter 12.) When you are editing curves, though, you may find this to be a limitation. You have more control over curves if you turn off Snap to Rulers. That way, the pointer—and thus the line it is dragging—can move anywhere on the drawing area, not just on the ruler increments.

Snap to Rulers can be awkward if the object you are editing was created with Snap to Rulers off. The handles, anchors, and control points seldom line up on ruler increments, and the pointer jumps right past them if you are trying to edit with Snap to Rulers turned *on*. For this reason, it is a good idea to turn Snap to Rulers off before using the Reshape tools.

USING THE
RESHAPE POINTS COMMAND

The Reshape Points command displays handles that you drag to modify the shape. You can use this method on any symbol, even text if you change it into an object first (using Text | Convert to Curves—see Chapter 8).

NOTE

Using Reshape Points on an imported bitmap *crops* the image. See Chapter 3 for more information.

Change |
Reshape
Points

There are three ways to enter Reshape Points mode:

- Select the object and then click on the Reshape Points tool

- Select the object and then select Change | Reshape Points

- Point at an object, press and hold Ctrl, and click the mouse button

To leave Reshape Points mode once you have finished editing, use one of these methods: use Ctrl-click again; select the Reshape Points tool again; select Change | Reshape Points again; select one of the drawing tools; or press Esc. (Pressing Esc doesn't always work, so you may sometimes have to use one of the other methods.)

When an object is in Reshape Points mode it loses its color and pattern, its border line changes to the default (fine) line, and a black handle appears at each corner or curve. You can drag one or several of these handles at a time, distorting the image. You can also delete, duplicate, or add handles. Figure 9.1 shows an image in Reshape Points mode.

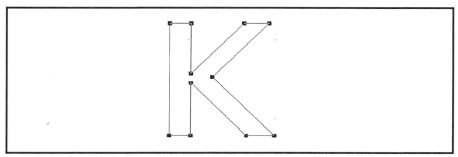

Figure 9.1: An image in Reshape Points mode

Generally, if a handle is displayed it is selected, and dragging the mouse will drag the handle. You may, however, decide to select only certain handles from those displayed. To select the handles you want to move, use one of these methods:

To Select	Do This
one handle	Point to the displayed handle. A black box appears next to the pointer, indicating that it is in Reshape mode. Press and hold the mouse button.
	or
	Click near a corner. The handle at that corner appears (or remains displayed), and all other handles disappear.
more than one handle	Use the Block Select tool (Edit | Block Select, Ctrl-B, or the Block Select icon) to rubberband around the ones you want.
	or
	Point to a corner and click, then press and hold Shift while you click next to the other corners you want.
	or
	Rubberband with the Block Select tool, then press and hold Shift while you click next to the other corners you want.

To Select	Do This
all handles	Select Edit | Select All (F2)
all handles not presently displayed	Press and hold Shift while you select Edit | Select All (F2)

To deselect a handle, leaving the others selected, point to the handle, press and hold Shift, and click the mouse button.

NOTE

You may notice that a handle sometimes doesn't appear when it should. Point to where it should be; if a black square appears next to the pointer, the handle *is* there, it is just invisible. As long as it's there it should act normally: you can still drag it even though you can't see it.

Editing the Objects

Now that you know how to select handles, you can use one of the following techniques to edit the object:

- **to move handles** Press button 1 and drag the mouse. The selected handles move, dragging the lines with them. If all the handles are selected, the entire object moves, without distorting the lines.

- **to move the entire object** There are two methods. You can press button 1 (making sure you don't move the mouse), then press button 2, and, with both buttons held, drag the mouse. The entire object moves. When you release the buttons, the same handles are selected that were selected before you moved the object. Alternatively, you can select all the handles, press and hold button 1, and drag the mouse.

- **to delete handles** Point to a handle and click, then press Del. The handle disappears and the object's line changes correspondingly, straightening out to make a direct line between the two handles on either side of the deleted handle. Deleting a handle at the end of a line "cuts" the line back to the next handle.

- **to add handles**   Point to the line, hold Shift, and press button 1 (hold it down longer than a click). Adding a handle enables you to distort the image in an area that doesn't have a handle.

- **to duplicate points**   Point at a handle, press and hold Shift, press and hold button 1, and drag the mouse. The original handle remains where it was, and a new one is dragged out, pulling the line with it. It's easy to accidentally draw loops in the line with this method, so move the mouse around until you get the shape you want.

- **to break handles**   Select the handle (make sure no other handles are displayed) and then select Arrange | Break Apart (Shift-F5). If you look closely you will see the line in the handle is broken. You can point to either side of the handle to pull that side of the break away. Once the lines are apart, Designer adds a handle to each new end. When you leave Reshape mode, select Arrange | Break Apart to complete the operation. (Breaking an object like this makes the object an "open" object, removing the color and fill.)

Remember to use the space bar in place of button 1 if you are using the keyboard.

NOTE

Sometimes, after you drag the entire object while in Reshape Points mode, Designer leaves a line or two where the object used to be. Select View | Redraw (F3) to remove these "phantom" lines.

Copying and Cutting Part of the Object

While in Reshape Points mode you can copy a selected part of an object into the clipboard, or actually remove it and place it in the clipboard, by selecting the handles in the area you want and then selecting either Edit | Copy (Ctrl-Ins) or Edit | Cut (Shift-Del). You can then continue editing (and paste the image later), or you can immediately select Edit | Paste (Shift-Ins), place the pointer where you want the object, and press and hold the mouse button. (Pasting the object takes you out of Reshape Points mode.)

Figure 9.2 shows an example of a copy produced from just part of an object in this manner. On the left is the K image with certain of the handles selected. On the right is what the copy will look like once you have used Edit | Copy and Edit | Paste.

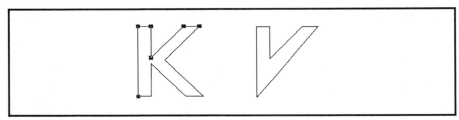

Figure 9.2: The effect of copying with Reshape Points

NOTE

Except for the fact that a copy of the removed piece is placed in the clipboard, cutting is the same as deleting the handles: if you cut part of an object from the middle, the object adjusts itself just as if you had deleted those handles.

When you cut or copy an image like this, you must make sure you get all the handles you need. If you miss a handle or two the image placed in the clipboard will look as if those handles had been deleted, and the line will be straightened out between the two handles on either side of the missing handle. Also, if you include an extra handle from somewhere else in the drawing, the picture in the clipboard will contain an image that has been distorted to connect the extra handle.

To avoid these problems, either use the Block Select tool to select the handles, or select all the handles by pressing F2, and then deselect the ones you don't want by pressing and holding Shift, pointing to the handles, and quickly clicking (make sure it's a quick click, or you will add a new handle instead).

Also, before you cut or copy part of an object you may need to add one or two new handles to be the "cut" points; Designer cuts at the last selected handle, so if you don't have a handle in a suitable position you will need to add one.

Splitting Images

You can remove or break apart a section of the object using Edit | Cut, as just described, but you may also use the following method:

1. Decide on the two places that you want to break the object. If those spots don't have handles, add them (pointing to the line, holding Shift, and pressing and holding the mouse button).

2. Press F2 and then Shift-F2 to make all the handles disappear.

3. Select the first handle you want to break and press Shift-F5 (Arrange | Break Apart).

4. Repeat for the second break point.

5. Leave Reshape Points mode (press Esc or select Reshape Points again).

6. With the object still selected, press Shift-F5 (Arrange | Break Apart) again. The object is now broken in two, and you can drag the two pieces apart. Figure 9.3 shows the K broken in two using this method.

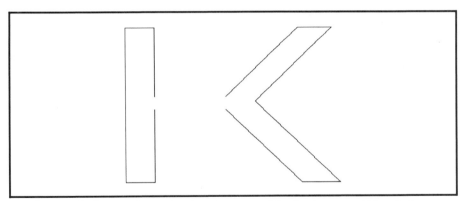

Figure 9.3: An object broken in two with the Arrange | Break Apart method

Once you have broken the object apart, you could use Arrange | Connect Closed to create two new objects, and fill them with color and pattern.

Editing Rounded Rectangles

Rounded rectangles are a special case, as far as editing goes. Reshape Points mode affects this type of object in two ways, according to whether or not it has been converted to Bézier curves. Selecting an object and then turning on Reshape Béziers converts the object to Bézier curves. If the rounded rectangle has been converted to Béziers, it can be edited in the same way you would edit any other object. (Change | Slant also converts it to Béziers.)

However, if the rectangle hasn't yet been converted to Béziers, the only part of it that you can edit in Reshape Points mode is the roundness of the corners. If you want to edit other parts of the rectangle you must use Reshape Béziers, which is explained in the next section.

When you select a non-Bézier rounded rectangle and then select Change | Reshape Points, a handle appears just inside the rectangle, near the top left corner. (If you did something else to the rectangle first, such as rotate or flip it, the handle may be *outside* the object, but it works much the same.) This is the only handle you will see, so you don't need to select it or point at it. Just place the pointer in the rectangle near the handle, hold the mouse button, and drag the mouse toward the top left to reduce the curves and to the bottom right to increase them. You can reduce the curves until they are almost completely gone, or increase them until the object looks more like an ellipse than a rectangle.

Snap mode effects the way the curves change. With Snap turned on, the curves move in increments, jumping from one setting to the next. With Snap off, the curves move more smoothly, and you can get a finer setting. You will learn more about Snap in Chapter 12.

If you need to adjust the curves on your rounded rectangles, remember to do it *before* you use Reshape Béziers on them—it will be too late afterwards.

USING THE RESHAPE BÉZIERS COMMAND

Bézier curves (or, more correctly, Bézier splines) were invented by Pierre Bézier in the 1960s. Bézier was a Renault engineer looking for ways to help computers design the curves of an automobile's body panels, and he came up with a mathematical system for duplicating a *spline*. A spline, at that time, was a thin, flexible piece of wood or metal that could be anchored to form a curve. Bézier managed to build a mathematical formula that could do the same thing, and Designer uses this formula (or at least a similar one) to build Bézier curves.

The great advantage of Bézier curves is that it gives tremendous control over the form of the curve, allowing you to perform detailed editing and allowing you to add sharp angles at any point in a curved object. Anything you can draw using Bézier curves can probably be drawn using one of the other tools, but it can be a slow, complicated process, and it may also use a lot of memory.

If you draw an object with the Bézier tool (Draw | Béziers) the lines are Bézier curves, and if you use the Freehand tool the lines are converted to Bézier curves when you finish. Other objects can be converted to Bézier curves simply by selecting them and then selecting Change | Reshape Béziers. Text can even be converted to Béziers and then edited. To do this you would select the text, use the Text | Convert to Curves command, select an individual letter, and then select Change | Reshape Béziers.

Designer's simple curves consist of three anchor points or handles, with the line curved smoothly through them. Designer's Bézier curves, however, consist of groups of anchor points and control points. There are two control points for every anchor, except at the ends of a line, where there is one control point per anchor. (Note that you can't see a control point when it is on top of an anchor.) The control points define the angle of the line curving through the anchor—or, at the end of a line, a control point defines the angle of the line ending at the anchor. Figure 9.4 shows an object in Reshape Béziers mode, with the anchors and control points shown. Notice that the anchors without control points on top look just like handles—black boxes—and control points by themselves look just like the Reshape Béziers icon—four small boxes.

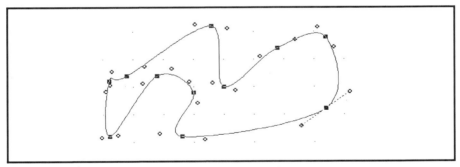

Figure 9.4: A curve in Reshape Béziers mode

The simplest Bézier curve consists of two anchor points—one at each end of a line. Each anchor point is associated with one control point. Although you can't always see the control points, because they may be directly on top of the anchors, anchors that have control points on top look different from regular anchors. As you can see in Figure 9.5, they look somewhat like stars.

Figure 9.6 shows a simple curved line. Once again, each anchor has one control point, and the control point on which the pointer is resting has a line running from it to the anchor; this is the *direction line*. The distance from the anchor to the control point defines how far toward the control point the curve must move before bending around to the anchor point. Notice that the angle of the line as it enters the anchor point on the left is not as steep as the angle of the line entering the anchor point on the right. This is because the control point on the left is closer to its anchor point.

Of course most drawings comprise more than two anchor points. In such drawings the anchors between the end anchors have *two* control points, each defining the angle of the line entering one side of the anchor. Each control point has its own direction line, and when the two direction lines make one straight direction line running through the anchor, as in Figure 9.7, the lines entering and leaving the anchor have the same angle, so the curve is smooth. When the direction lines form an angle, a *cusp* is formed; depending on the angle, a distinct, "sharp" point may be drawn, as in Figure 9.8.

Using Béziers is an art, something that requires a little practice. However, it is simpler than all this talk of control points and mathematical formulas might imply, and you can quickly learn how to edit objects in Reshape Béziers mode.

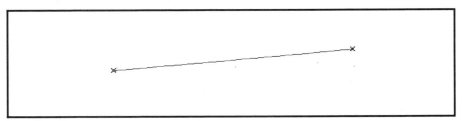

Figure 9.5: A straight line in Reshape Béziers mode

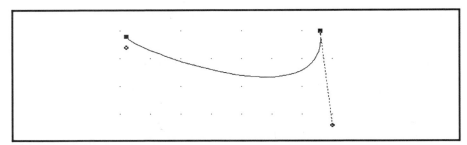

Figure 9.6: A curved line in Reshape Béziers mode

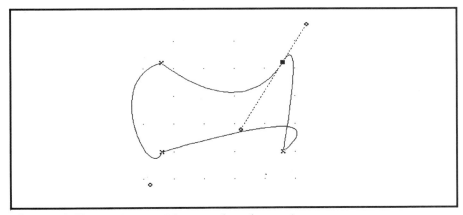

Figure 9.7: An object with several anchor points

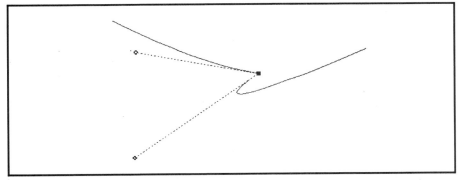

Figure 9.8: A cusp is formed where the direction lines join the anchor at different angles

EDITING BÉZIER CURVES

You can edit Bézier curves while you are using the Bézier drawing tool, or by selecting an object and then selecting Change | Reshape Béziers. Designer converts the object to Bézier curves, removes color and pattern, changes the lines to the default (fine) line, and displays the anchor points and control points.

Once in Reshape Béziers mode you can use all of the techniques available in Reshape Points mode. (If you want to duplicate an anchor point, though, make sure that the black box is displayed; if you try to duplicate an anchor that has a control point on top of it you will just move the control point.) In fact you can jump from Reshape Béziers mode to Reshape Points mode and back, just by selecting the icons or commands (however, Ctrl-click will not select Reshape Points while you are in Reshape Béziers).

Of course, in addition, Reshape Béziers lets you move the control points. There are three ways to do this.

- Point to the control point, press the mouse button, and drag the mouse—the point moves. If the point is associated with an anchor that is not at the end of a line, the other control point associated with the anchor also moves, such that the direction lines remain at the same angle. For example, if the direction lines make one straight line, that line remains straight. If the lines form a 90-degree angle, the lines remain at 90 degrees.

- If you press and hold Ctrl while you drag one of the control points, Designer will not only keep the angle of the line the same, it will also keep the proportional distances the same: double the distance from the anchor to the control point you are dragging, and Designer automatically doubles the distance from the anchor to the *other* control point.

- You can also move one control point independently of the other. Point to the control point, press and hold Shift, and then press and hold the mouse button while you drag the mouse. The control point and its direction line move, while the other point and its line remain still. This is how you build a cusp, making the object's line enter the anchor point at a different angle on each side.

TIP

Sometimes, when you are trying to place a control point on top of an anchor, you will find that it doesn't seem to move quite where you drag it. A simpler way to do this operation is to select the anchor (make sure none of the others are displayed), and then select Change | Unsmooth (Shift-F6). The control points are automatically moved onto the anchor.

USING THE
RESHAPE CONNECTED COMMAND

Change | Reshape Connected lets you reshape a connected object one component at a time. Select the object and then select Change | Reshape Connected. The object's color and pattern disappear, the lines change to the default (fine) line, and handles appear around the entire object (see Figure 9.9).

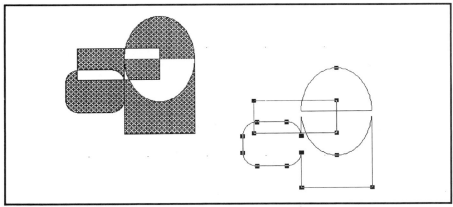

Figure 9.9: An object in Reshape Connected mode

Now, click on the object you want to edit. The handles are removed, and new ones appear around the object you clicked on. (If the object you click on is a large one, its handles may be in exactly the same place as the handles for the combined object, fooling you into thinking that Designer hasn't selected the object you pointed at.)

You can now carry out most of the simple editing methods you learned earlier in the book: you can move the object, change its size, rotate or slant it, or delete it (using Delete or Cut). You can also smooth or unsmooth it, even if it is a primitive that hasn't been in Reshape Béziers or Reshape Points mode. However, you cannot flip it or duplicate it—using the Duplicate tool simply moves it—nor may you do any Reshape Points or Reshape Béziers editing without actually selecting the appropriate command.

If you want to use Reshape Points or Reshape Béziers, select the command, and the selected component is put into the appropriate Reshape mode. You will not be able to modify the other objects. When you have finished editing, select one of the other Reshape commands (you can swap between Reshape Points, Reshape Béziers, and Reshape Connected modes at will), or select the same one to exit Reshape mode entirely.

SMOOTHING AND UNSMOOTHING SYMBOLS

Designer's Change | Smooth command smooths out sharp edges on selected objects. Objects drawn with the Freehand tool are automatically smoothed when you finish them, but other objects and lines must be smoothed by command. When you select the object and then select Change | Smooth, Designer rounds off the corners. (Keyboard Shortcut: F6)

Designer smooths an object by moving its control points. An angled corner, for example, has its control points on top of its anchor; Designer takes these and puts them on a straight line, equidistant from the anchor, ensuring a smooth curve through the anchor.

If you want to smooth a square or rectangle, you must convert it to Bézier curves first. (Primitives must be converted to a form that allows editing first.) To do this, you could select the object, then select Reshape Points (Ctrl-click) or Reshape Béziers, and select Change | Smooth.

SMOOTHING ONE PART OF AN OBJECT

You can also smooth a selected portion of the object while in Reshape Points or Reshape Béziers mode. Simply select the handles or anchors on the corners or curves you want to smooth and select Change | Smooth.

"UNSMOOTHING" THE OBJECT

You can also "unsmooth" an object. Whereas smoothing an object entails moving the control points onto a straight line, equidistant from the anchor, unsmoothing takes the control points and places them *on top of* the anchor. Don't think of unsmooth as being the exact opposite of smooth.

If you smooth an object and then unsmooth it, it may not return to exactly the same object.

Suppose you have an object with sharp curves. The control-point pairs are neither on top of the anchors nor on straight directional lines that pass through the anchors. When you *smooth* the object the curves are smoothed out, the control points being placed on a straight directional line that passes through the related anchor, and equidistant from the anchor. When you *unsmooth* the object, Designer takes the control points and puts them on top of the anchors, turning curves into sharp joints, or vertices. The unsmoothed image is clearly not the same as the original or pre-smoothed image, as you can see in Figure 9.10.

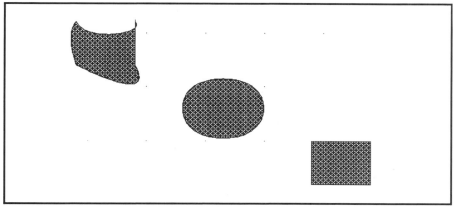

Figure 9.10: Original, smoothed, and unsmoothed versions of an object

Unsmoothing is as easy as smoothing. Just select the object and then select Change | Unsmooth (Keyboard Shortcut: Shift-F6). If you want to unsmooth one of the primitives, you must do so in one of the Reshape modes: to unsmooth a circle (making it a rotated square) or an ellipse (making it a diamond), you must be in Reshape Points or Reshape Béziers mode, and to unsmooth a rounded rectangle ("flattening" the corners), you must be in Reshape Béziers mode.

Of course you can also unsmooth a selected section of the object, in the same way that you can smooth selected sections, by selecting the handles or anchors in Reshape Points or Reshape Béziers mode.

USING UNDO IN RESHAPE MODE

The Edit | Undo command affects Reshape mode in two ways. Using Undo while still in Reshape mode undoes the last change made to the object (Keyboard Shortcut: Alt-Backspace), and using Undo immediately after you have exited Reshape mode undoes *all* the changes made during Reshape mode, returning the object to the shape it had before you entered that mode.

There is also a way to duplicate one effect of Undo. If you have modified part of a curve and still have the mouse button pressed, press Esc. The curve jumps back to its previous position. Unfortunately this also takes you out of Reshape mode, so you probably won't use this alternative very often.

10

Printing

You already have the knowledge necessary to produce usable art, so you may be ready to print your work. By printing I mean producing a final product; you can use a printer or a plotter to put your art onto paper, or use a film recorder to put your work onto slides, transparencies, or photographic prints, or even save your work in a *print file* so that it can be printed later. To make things simple, I (and Micrografx) talk about *printers* and *printing* when talking in general terms. In fact, whether you are printing, plotting, or producing slides, you will use the same commands. You will use a different device driver and connect a different type of device to your computer, of course, but all outputs are grouped together by Designer under the *printing* label.

This chapter describes how to prepare for printing and produce basic printed art. It doesn't explain everything about printing. The more advanced printing techniques that most users do not require—such as producing color separations—are explained in Chapter 14. And Chapter 15 explains more about producing slides from your work.

PREPARING THE DRAWING AREA

Before you think about printing you need to consider whether your drawing area is properly prepared. First, do you have the correct page size, orientation, and borders? For 90 percent of devices the setup *is* correct; it is configured for pages 8.5 inches wide and 11 inches tall, with 0.25 inch borders at the sides and 0.5 inch borders at the bottom, and it is unlikely that you will have to change it. If you do need to change this (for example if you have installed a Matrix Film recorder—which has Landscape orientation and different margins), you will have to use the View | Pages command. See Chapter 11 for more information.

Second, do you have the correct resolution? Most laser printers have a 300 or 400 dots-per-inch (dpi) resolution, and Designer's default resolution is 480. But if you are using a typesetter, or a Matrix Film recorder, you may want to use a much higher resolution. Some Matrix Film recorders have resolutions much higher than this, up to 8192 by 5464, so you may want to use a higher resolution in the drawing area; Designer lets you go as high as 2900 dpi. Resolution is set in the Rulers/Grid dialog box, and is explained in Chapter 11.

Make sure that when you create your art, you do so with the printer on which you intend to print selected. If you *don't* do this you might use fonts that are not supported by that printer, or you may draw your art assuming that you have more room on the page—or less—than your printer actually has.

PREPARING YOUR PRINTER

There are several procedures that must be carried out before you can use a printer:

- Load the printer drivers

- Connect the printer to a communications port

- Select the default printer

- Set up the communications port (if you are using a serial device)

The following printer setup procedure affects not only Designer, but, if you are using full Windows, all the programs you run under Windows.

LOADING THE PRINTER DRIVERS

There are many different types of printers or output devices, each working in a slightly different way. Different printers expect to receive data in different formats, so your computer needs a *printer driver*, a program that tells the computer what sort of data your printer expects to see. Microsoft Windows comes with a number of printer drivers that you can use, and these are loaded during the Windows or runtime Windows installation, but Micrografx also provides drivers for the following devices:

- PostScript printers

- Toshiba printers

- HP PaintJets

- HP-compatible plotters

- Matrix film recorders

- VideoShow film recorders (if you request it from their technical support)

If you have one of these devices you must load the driver from the Designer installation disks. Use the Designer installation procedure (see Appendix A); you will not be able to use the Windows Control Panel to install these drivers, because they are in compressed files that Windows cannot read. (However, if you want to load a printer driver that came with Windows, use the Windows Control Panel—see your Windows manual or the instructions that came with your runtime windows.) You can load as many printer drivers as you want, as long as you have enough disk space to spare, and then swap between drivers as the need arises.

PostScript Printer Drivers   Designer has a special PostScript printer driver that supports most PostScript devices; see Designer's Help screens— or the Driver installation screen in Designer's installation program—for a list of those devices.

This driver has a variety of features that allow Designer to print faster and to support rotated text, text kerning, custom page sizes, and so on. If you are using a PostScript printer you would be well advised to use Designer's driver. If you use the Windows PostScript driver instead you will not be able to use downloadable fonts, which the Micrografx driver does support.

CONNECTING THE
PRINTER TO A COMPUTER PORT

Not only must you physically connect the computer to one of your computer's *ports*, but you must also tell Designer where the printer is, which printer is the default printer, and, in the case of serial devices, what *protocol* to use when sending a document. You do this from the Control Panel.

If you have full Windows, select the Control Panel using the Windows commands—in Windows 3.0 you will double-click on the Control Panel icon in the Program Manager Main window, but if you have an earlier version of Windows you will double-click on CONTROL.EXE in the MS-DOS EXECUTIVE window. If you only have a runtime version of windows, you will have to use Designer's commands to get to the Control Panel. Unfortunately it is hidden away, several levels down; Select File | Print | Utilities | Controls. (That is, select the File menu on Designer's menu bar; select Print from the File menu, select the Utilities menu from the Print dialog box; and select Controls from the Utilities menu.) Figure 10.1 shows the Windows 3.0 Control Panel, and Figure 10.2 shows the Control Panel used by earlier versions, with the Setup menu open.

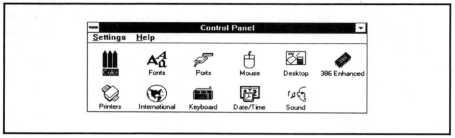

Figure 10.1: The Windows 3.0 Control Panel

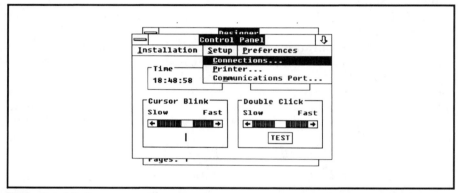

Figure 10.2: The pre-3.0 Windows Control Panel, with the Setup menu selected

As you can see, the two Control Panels are entirely different. I shall explain how to use the Windows 3.0 Control Panel, and then explain the earlier version.

Selecting a Computer Port

Double-click on the Printers icon to see the Printers dialog box (Figure 10.3). This box displays a list of the printer drivers you have installed.

You will soon learn about the different options in this box, but the first thing you will do is select the printer you want to set up and click on the Configure command button. The Printers-Configure dialog box appears (Figure 10.4).

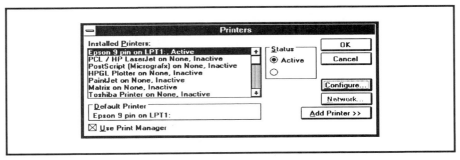

Figure 10.3: The Printers dialog box

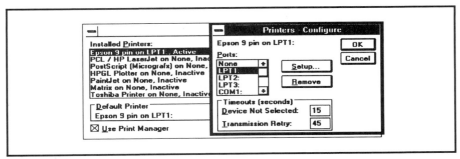

Figure 10.4: The Printers-Configure dialog box

Select the port to which you want to connect the printer—the scroll box contains the following options:

LPT　　Parallel ports

COM　　Serial ports

EPT　　Used by some special printers such as IBM Personal Pageprinter; if you don't have the required computer board, this operates like a FILE port.

FILE　　Print-to-File port. If you print to this "port" Designer will build a print file called FILE. See Chapter 14.

None　　　　No port selected

LPTx.OS2　　If your printer doesn't seem to work well through Windows, you can use this to get to a printer port through DOS, bypassing the Windows print-management software. You can also use this to connect two printers to the same physical port. For example, if you have an ''A/B'' switch on LPT1 with two printers connected to it, you could ''connect'' one printer to LPT1 and one to LPT1.OS2. Then, when you want to swap printers, you don't need to come back to the Control Panel; just switch your A/B switch and select the other printer in the Select Printer dialog box. (You will learn about this dialog box later in this chapter.)

MGXPrint.prn   A print-to-file port installed by Designer 3.1. See Chapter 14.

Refer to your computer and printer manuals to find out whether your printer is connected to a parallel or serial port, and which of these you have used.

You may also have other options, print-file names added to the Windows WIN.INI file—names you can assign yourself—such as PRINTFIL. These work like FILE ports; if you connect your printer to this option, a print file named PRINTFIL is placed in the Designer directory each time you print.

Instead of actually printing your art Designer produces a file that contains all the information needed to print the art; that file can then be taken to another computer and printed, or be given to a print shop or service bureau to handle. You may not have the actual output device connected to your computer, but you still need the device driver so you can create the correct print file.

In such a case you would load the driver, but leave it assigned to None, FILE, EPT, or to one of the special ports you add to your WIN.INI file. See Chapter 14 for more information.

You can, if you wish, change the printer timeouts. Device Not Selected is the number of seconds Designer should wait before sending you a message telling you the printer is offline (it may be turned offline, unconnected, or switched off), and Transmission Retry is the time it should wait for the printer to respond before telling you that it cannot print to the device. You won't normally change these numbers, unless you have a printer that seems to take a long time to respond to Windows.

Selecting Printer Options

When you have selected the printer port, click on Setup. You will see the Printer Options dialog box. The box varies depending on the features of the selected printer. Figure 10.5 shows the box you see if you have an HP LaserJet, and Figure 10.6 shows the box for a 9-pin Epson printer. In some boxes you will see a list of printers; having selected, for example, a LaserJet, you must now select the exact model of LaserJet that you have. (If your exact printer model is not listed, pick the closest model number, or check your printer manual to see which alternative setting is recommended by the manufacturer.)

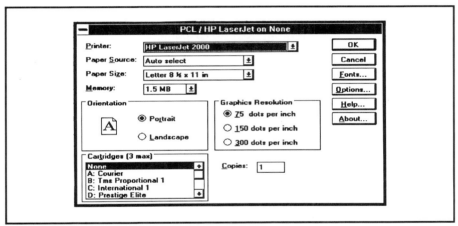

Figure 10.5: The HP LaserJet Options dialog box

You should also make sure the other options are set correctly: the paper size, print orientation (Portrait is the normal page orientation for most printers, and Landscape is on the "side," with the bottom of the picture along the longest side of the paper), the amount of memory on the printer, the types of font cartridges, and so on.

IMPORTANT

If you change the orientation setting here, make sure you change it in the Pages dialog box (View | Pages). See Chapter 11 for more information.

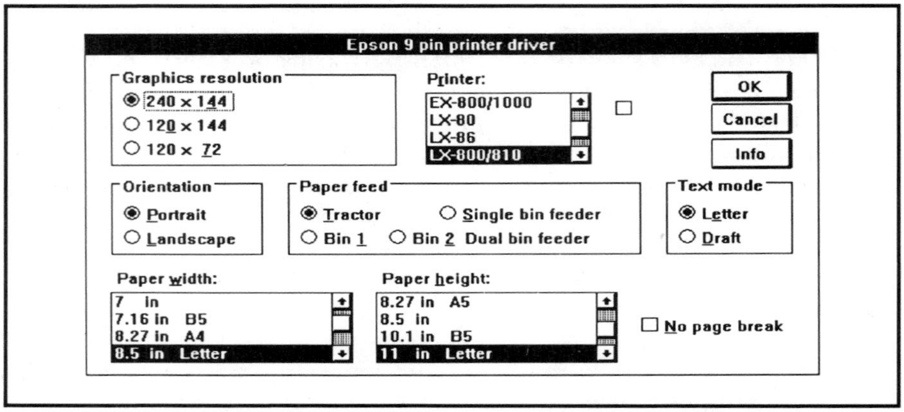

Figure 10.6: The Epson 9-pin Options dialog box

The Printer Options dialog box may also have a command button labelled Info (click on it for specific information about setting up your printer for use with Windows), or a button labelled Fonts. The Fonts button lets you load *soft fonts*, fonts that you load from computer disks. It may also have a command button labelled Reset—click on this to change the printer settings back to the standard settings. And in some cases you will see an Options button; for example, if you select the HP LaserJet 2000 in the HP LaserJet Options dialog box the Options button can be used to view a small dialog box that lets you select duplex printing.

The settings available depend on the type of device you are using. Each option refers to a feature of that device, so refer to the device's manual to find more information about the Printer Options dialog box options.

NOTE

Some of the Printer Options dialog boxes have a Help menu option. You should read all the Help messages, as they contain important information about using your particular device. See Appendix B for information on using Help screens.

Selecting the Active and Default Printers

When you have finished setting up the printer, click on OK, and the box is removed from the screen. Make sure the correct printer port is selected in the Printers-Configure dialog box, and click on OK.

Now you must select the "active" printers. Unlike earlier versions of Windows, Windows 3.0 allows you to assign as many printers as you want to a printer port. However, only one of those printers may be *active*. Select the appropriate printer in the scroll box and click on the Active option button. You will not be able to select a printer as active if it does not have a port selected (if it says "*Printername* on None" in the list box).

Now decide which printer will be the default. Each time you start Designer it will assume the default printer is the one you are going to use for printing, unless you give it other instructions. Double-click on that printer, and the name is displayed in the Default Printer box at the bottom of the dialog box. (If only one printer is Active, it is automatically the default printer.)

There are a couple of other options in this box that you might want to know about. You can turn off the Print Manager if you want. Print Manager is a *print spooler* used by Windows to manage your print jobs; Designer sends print jobs to the Print Manager, which then sends them on to the printer while you continue working. If you turn off Print Manager the job will print faster, but you won't be able to work while it is printing, nor will you be able to view print status information.

Use the Add Printer command button if you want to add a Windows printer driver (not a Designer printer driver—you must use the Designer installation procedure for that), and use the Network command button to select a network printer.

Configuring Serial Devices

If you are using a serial device, you have another job to do before leaving the Control Panel. Double-click on the Ports icon, and Windows displays the Ports dialog box, a box showing you four serial ports. Double-click on the port you are using, and Windows displays the Ports-Settings dialog box (both these dialog boxes are displayed in Figure 10.7). Select the correct baud rate, word length, parity, stop bits, and handshake—this information can be found in the device's documentation—and click on OK. Then click on OK in the Ports dialog box.

USING EARLIER VERSIONS OF WINDOWS

The Control Panel and associated dialog boxes are very different in earlier versions of Windows. If you are not using Windows 3.0, read the Windows 3.0 description above to get an idea of what you are trying to do,

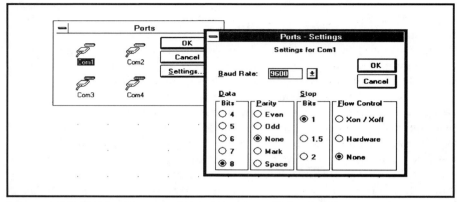

Figure 10.7: The Ports and Ports-Settings dialog boxes

IMPORTANT

Once you have finished in the Control Panel close it by double-clicking in the Control-menu box in the top left corner of the Control Panel, pressing Alt-space bar to select the Control menu and press C, or selecting Settings | Exit. The Control Panel is an *application*, just like Designer or any other program you run in windows. If you don't close it you can continue working in Designer, but Control Panel will remain open, use memory, and cause confusion; if you continue using Designer without closing the Control Panel the Control Panel disappears behind Designer's window. Then, later, when you try to swap windows, you may end up in the Control Panel again. Or if you try to open Control Panel again you will see a message saying it's already open (it's hidden behind a window).

---

and then read the following summary of the way the Control Panel works in earlier versions. (Remember that Designer 3.1 cannot be used with earlier versions of Windows.)

Begin by selecting Setup | Connections in the Control Panel; Designer displays the Printer Connections dialog box, shown in Figure 10.8. You can see the printer drivers you installed on the left of the box, and your computer's ports on the right. Click on the printer you are using, and then click on the port to which you connected it.

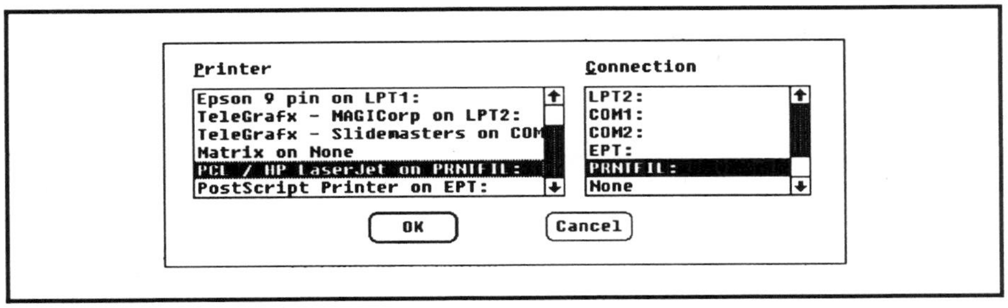

Figure 10.8: The Printer Connections dialog box

Set up the ports for all the printers, and then click on OK once you have made your selection. If you selected a port more than twice (even one of the "fake" ports such as FILE or one you added to WIN.INI), you will see an error message and will have to go back and straighten out the problem.

When the Printer Connections dialog box disappears, select Setup | Printer, to see the Default Printer dialog box (Figure 10.9). The list box shows all the printer drivers installed on your system, with the port to which each is connected. Simply click on the default printer and then, if you wish, change the printer timeouts. Then click on OK.

Designer now displays the Printer Options dialog box, with various printer options. They look similar to the ones in Windows 3.0, though they may not have as many options or command buttons; while the earlier HP LaserJet dialog box has only OK, Cancel, and Fonts command buttons, for example, the Windows 3.0 version also has Options, Help, and About.

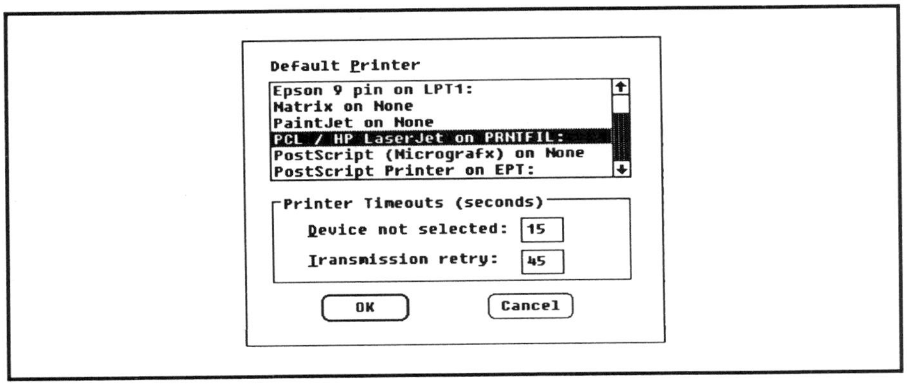

Figure 10.9: The Default Printer dialog box

When you have finished setting up the printer, click on OK, and the Printer Options and Select Printer dialog boxes disappear.

If you are using a serial device, select Setup | Communications Port. Designer displays the Communications Settings dialog box (Figure 10.10). First, look at the last line in the box, Port. Click on the port to which you connected the serial device (COM1 or COM2). Then, select the correct baud rate, word length, parity, stop bits, and handshake. Then click on OK to close the dialog box, and then close the Control Panel by double-clicking in the Control-menu box in the top left corner of the Control Panel or by pressing Alt-space and pressing *C*.

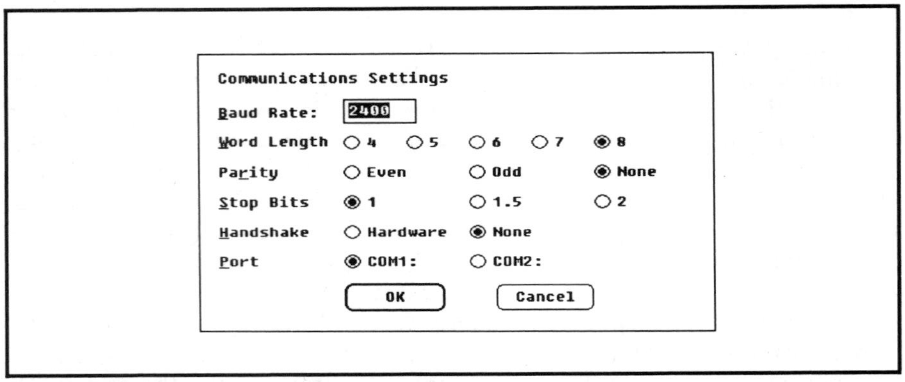

```
Communications Settings
Baud Rate:    2400
Word Length   ○ 4    ○ 5    ○ 6    ○ 7    ◉ 8
Parity        ○ Even      ○ Odd       ◉ None
Stop Bits     ◉ 1         ○ 1.5       ○ 2
Handshake     ○ Hardware  ◉ None
Port          ◉ COM1:     ○ COM2:
              [   OK   ]    [ Cancel ]
```

Figure 10.10: The Communications Settings dialog box

SELECTING ANOTHER PRINTER

When you installed your printer drivers and selected the connection (in the Printer Connections dialog box), you may have set up several options—perhaps a couple of different printers and a slide recorder. You have already set the default printer, in the Printers dialog box (in pre-3.0 Windows it's called the Default Printer dialog box); this is the printer that Designer automatically uses when you print. If you want to use one of the other printers, select File | Change Printer to see the Select Printer dialog box (Figure 10.11).

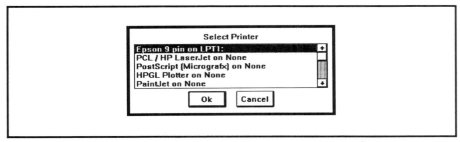

Figure 10.11: The Select Printer dialog box

Select the printer you want to use and click on OK. Designer displays that printer's Options dialog box, so you can make sure that the settings are all correct. Click on OK, and both dialog boxes disappear. The next time you print, Designer will use the printer you just selected. (However, the next time you start Designer the printer chosen in the Printers dialog box will automatically be selected again.)

The Select Printer dialog box has an extra option: None. If you select None, you won't be able to print at all, even to a file. However, you can use this setting to turn off the display of printer fonts, which you might want to do if you are producing screen presentations.

INSTALLING MORE FONTS

You are not limited to the fonts Designer provides you. You can buy more outline fonts from Bitstream or The Font Company (the company that sells URW Nimbus-Q fonts and ATF American Type Foundry), or you can install printer fonts. If you already have Bitstream fonts, they may be compatible with Designer—look for the Bitstream diamond logo on the disk label; if the logo is there, the fonts can be used with Designer. If it isn't, call Bitstream to send you an upgrade of the fonts.

These are the different ways to add fonts:

- Add Bitstream and URW fonts through Designer's installation program

- Add printer fonts through the Printer Options dialog box

- Install a font cartridge on your printer, and select the cartridge in the Printer Options dialog box

- Add screen fonts through the Control Panel
- Add Windows fonts using special applications such as Adobe Type Manager or Bitstream Facelift.

In Designer 3.1 the outline fonts are installed in a subdirectory named MGXFONTS. In pre-3.1 Designer, the outline fonts are installed in subdirectories of the Windows directory, not in the Designer directory. A subdirectory called MGXLIBS contains the font program files, plus the subdirectories called BITFONTS (Bitstream fonts), SPDFONTS (Bitstream Speedo fonts), and URW-FONTS (URW fonts).

Installing Bitstream and URW Outline Fonts

If you want to install more Bitstream or URW outline fonts, you must use Designer's installation procedure (see Appendix A). One of the options in the installation menu is called Add Retail Outline Fonts. Select this option and follow the instructions.

Installing Cartridge Fonts

If you use an HP LaserJet or compatible, you can use "cartridge fonts," fonts contained in a cartridge that you install in the printer. When you have installed the cartridge, display the PCL/HP LaserJet Options dialog box and select the appropriate cartridge from the list at the bottom of the dialog box.

Installing Printer Soft Fonts

Printer "soft fonts" are similar to outline fonts in that they are software fonts: that is, they are fonts produced by a program as opposed to fonts dependent on a piece of hardware installed in your printer. Unlike outline fonts, though, printer soft fonts are designed for use by a specific printer.

There are a number of different ways to install printer "soft fonts," depending on the device you are using. Select File | Change Printer to see the Select Printer dialog box. Select the device for which you want to add fonts, and click on OK. Designer displays the Printer Options dialog box. In some cases you cannot add soft fonts—if you are using the Windows PostScript Printer driver, for example, there is no way to add soft fonts. If you are using Micrografx's PostScript driver, though, you can.

NOTE

Designer has a lot of Help screens that explain the various Designer printer drivers. The drivers presented in this chapter may not be exactly the same as the ones you have, so once you have displayed the Printer Options dialog box, select the Help menu or press F1. Read all the messages, because they contain important information about your printer.

PostScript Fonts   Figure 10.12 shows the dialog box that is displayed when you select "PostScript (Micrografx)" from the Select Printer dialog box, and then select Fonts | Install. (The driver shipped with Designer 3.1 is different. You select Fonts | Select to see the Fonts dialog box, and the box looks slightly different.) You select the fonts you want from the list box, and then click on OK. Designer converts the font metrics files on the disk to .WFM fonts files, and places them in the directory you specified with the Fonts | Path command. In the driver shipped with 3.1 you will click on the Path button to select a directory, then highlight a font from the Available Fonts list box.

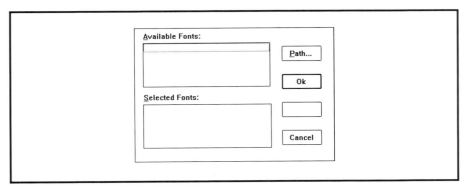

Figure 10.12: The PostScript Fonts dialog box

You can install the following fonts with this technique:

- .PFA Image Club

- .PSO Bitstream

- .PFB Adobe

- .PSF Publisher's Type Foundry

Once you have installed the fonts, you must restart Windows and download the fonts to the printer, using the Fonts | Download command. Downloading copies the fonts onto the printer's hard disk or memory. See the Help screen for detailed instructions.

The Matrix Fonts　　The Matrix printer driver shipped with Designer 3.1 automatically installs all its fonts. If you have an earlier version, though, you must specify the fonts you want. Figure 10.13 shows the Fonts dialog box that is displayed when you select Style | Fonts from the Matrix Printer Options dialog box (which is displayed if you select the Telegrafx-Slidemasters or Matrix drivers).

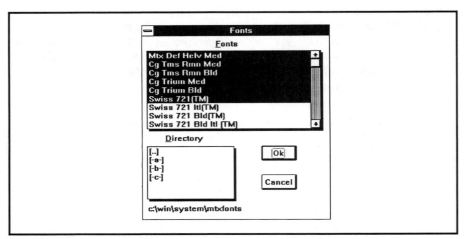

Figure 10.13: The Matrix Options Fonts dialog box

This box displays the selected fonts, and the directory in which the fonts are stored. Designer assumes the fonts are in a subdirectory called MTXFONTS, because that is where Designer puts them when you install the Matrix driver, but you can select another directory if you wish. See your Matrix manual for information about loading fonts onto the hard drive.

To make fonts available to Designer, you must select them. Click on the font you want, and hold Shift while you click on additional fonts. Then click on OK, and click on OK in the Matrix Options dialog box. Now, if you go to the Fonts dialog box and click on the Printer checkbox, you will see the fonts you just selected.

HP LaserJet Fonts　　Figure 10.14 shows the Soft Font Installer, displayed when you click on PCL/HP LaserJet in the Select Printer dialog box and then click on the Fonts command button in the PCL/HP LaserJet Options dialog box. To add new fonts, click on the Add Fonts command button. Designer displays another dialog box, telling you to put the disk with the soft fonts in drive A:. You can select another drive if you want. When you click on OK Designer displays a list of fonts in the list box on the right. Click on the ones you want and then click on Copy. The fonts are copied onto your hard drive, and displayed in the list box on the left.

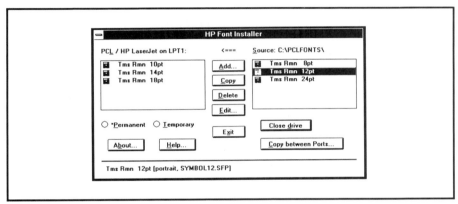

Figure 10.14: The HP LaserJet's Soft Font Installer dialog box

You can also use this dialog box's options to load the fonts into your printer's memory, to change a font's name, to delete fonts, or to copy fonts to a printer on another computer port. This dialog box has a Help command button—use it to find detailed instructions.

Other Devices

Some devices don't have soft fonts available. For example, the Epson 9-pin printer has a couple of built-in fonts, but you cannot add soft fonts; if you go to its Options dialog box you will not find any menu options or command buttons that let you do so. If your device *does* have soft fonts, go to the device's Options dialog box and look for commands similar to the ones just described. Remember to read the Help messages.

Adding Screen Fonts to the Control Panel

You may occasionally need to install screen fonts if you have installed printer fonts that don't display their equivalents on screen. If the manufacturer provides screen fonts for those printer fonts, you can load them using the Control Panel.

In Windows 3.0 you will select the Fonts icon or the Settings | Fonts menu option; if you are using an earlier version you will select Installation | Add Fonts. Windows will prompt you to insert the appropriate Windows installation disks.

Using Add-on Windows Fonts

A number of companies make special programs to add fonts to Windows. Working within Windows, these programs make the fonts available to all Windows applications, including, of course, Designer. Perhaps the best known of these programs are Adobe's *Type Manager,* Bitstream's *Facelift,* and Atech Software's *Publisher's Powerpak.* These fonts can be printed on most printers, and include screen fonts that make the font displayed on screen very close to the font that is printed.

While these are not actually device fonts, Designer treats them as such to some degree. They are only displayed in Designer's Font dialog box if you select the Printer checkbox, and if you try to convert them to curves, rotate them, or place text on a curve, Designer selects another font. The one exception is Adobe Type Manager (ATM) fonts; if you have Designer 3.1 you can generally use ATM fonts in the same way you use outline fonts (though you must still select the Printer checkbox to see them). ATM fonts may not work too well with Text | Text Along A Curve, though.

PRINTING YOUR WORK

Now that you have set up your printers, you are ready to print. Designer gives you several options. You can print a single page or object, print an area you specify using a "rubber band" tool, or give Designer detailed instructions on what to print and how. You can also select a printer other than the default printer and change the printer settings without going to the Control Panel. The File menu gives you various options:

Print Page	Prints the page currently displayed
Print View	Prints an area you define
Print	Lets you define print criteria
Change Printer	Lets you select another printer

NOTE

Print Page and Print View are ghosted if the default printer is None. See the discussion of the Select Printer dialog box earlier in this chapter.

USING FILE | PRINT PAGE

When you select File | Print Page (Keyboard Shortcut: Shift-F4), Designer automatically prints a page. This page is either the page with images selected, or, if no images are selected, the page that is displayed in the top left of your window. Even if, for example, the bottom right square inch of page 5 is displayed in the top left of the window and most of the window is taken up by other pages, only page 5 will print.

Designer automatically uses the default printer (or the printer you selected in the Select Printer dialog box), with the settings you selected in the Printer Options dialog box. It also uses the options selected in the Print dialog box (except, of course, the settings that select which pages will print), explained later in this chapter.

Spooling to Printer

Figure 10.15 shows the Spooler dialog box. This tells you that the drawing is being sent to the Windows Print Manager, a special application that transmits the file to your printer (in versions of Windows prior to 3.0, Print Manager was called Spooler). While the Spooler dialog box is displayed you cannot use your computer except to cancel the printing, which you can do by clicking on Cancel, using the dialog box's Control menu to close it, or pressing Esc.

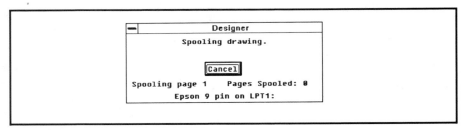

Figure 10.15: The Spooler dialog box

When the file has been transmitted to the Print Manager you can continue working with the file printing "in the background." Actually the practicality of doing this depends on the type of computer, the amount of memory, the version of Windows, and the number of applications you have open—you may find you cannot work until the printing is almost over, or that your computer is just too slow to use while it is spooling.

File | Print
View

USING FILE | PRINT VIEW

The File | Print View command (Keyboard Shortcut: F4) gives you a bit more flexibility; it lets you use a rubber band, similar to the Block Select tool, to show Designer exactly what you want to print. Rubberband around the object and then release the mouse button; Designer prints the object on the default printer, using the settings you selected in the Printer Options dialog box. You can rubberband around objects as often as you want—each time you release the mouse button the object is sent to the printer. When you have finished, select another tool or select View | Print View to end the Print View mode.

Print View doesn't print the objects at their actual sizes. If the object is bigger than a page Designer shrinks it to fit. The size also depends on how much blank space you left around the object when you rubberbanded it: the more blank space, the smaller the object will print; the less space, the larger it will print.

This command is very useful for reviewing an object or part of an object, but because it resizes the art you may want to use one of the other print commands to produce the final copy. On the other hand, with a little practice you can use this tool to intentionally expand or reduce the size of the printout, to fit the available space in a document into which it will be pasted, for example.

USING FILE | PRINT

The File | Print command gives you more print options. You can select the number of copies or the range of pages, have Designer collate multiple sets, and select tools that help you prepare your work for professional printing. Select File | Print to display the Print dialog box, as shown in Figure 10.16.

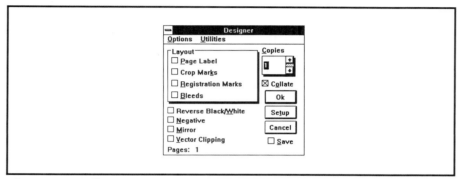

Figure 10.16: The Print dialog box

Copies	The Copies box lets you tell Designer how many copies you want Designer to print, from 1 to 100.
Collate	Select this box if you are drawing multiple copies of more than one page; Designer will print one copy of the set, then go back and print the next copy of the set, and so on. Using collate may slow down laser printers, though.
Reverse Black/White	This will reverse the black and white when the picture is printed, but leave other colors as they are (so this is not the same as a negative image). See Chapter 14 for more information.
Negative	Produces a negative image: black is printed as white, white as black, cyan as red, magenta as green, and yellow as blue. See Chapter 14 for more information.

Mirror	Produces a mirror image of the art; all the work is flipped horizontally (and text will read backwards). This lets you use the art for T-shirt transfers, or for professional printing. Not all devices support this feature, so the option appears ''ghosted'' if you don't have a suitable device driver selected.
Vector Clipping	Improves the output on plotters by stopping the plotter from drawing the parts of objects that are overlapped by other objects in front. This only works for plotters (so it is ''ghosted'' if you don't have a plotter driver selected), and slows down the output. Without vector clipping the plotter will draw objects over each other, producing transparent-looking objects, but possibly affecting the performance of the pens (if the pens have to draw over different colors).
Save	Select this checkbox if you want Designer to save the settings as the defaults. Designer writes the changes into the Windows WIN.INI file as soon as you click on OK.

Layout Options

The Print dialog box also has Layout options. You can select these options to make Designer print lines and text in the page margins. (The layout options are generally used in color separation and multi-page printing.)

NOTE

These layout options only print if you have wide margins. See Chapter 14 for more information.

Page Label	Prints a label on each page, showing the document name, page number, and ink color used.

Crop Marks	Produces crop marks that show the actual page size. See Chapter 14.
Registration Marks	Registration marks help a print shop line up process-color and spot-color separations. See Chapter 14.
Bleeds	Makes pictures "bleed" over into the margins. See Chapter 14.

The Print Dialog Box Menus

There are two menus in the Print dialog box: the Options menu and the Utilities menu. The Options menu includes the following choices:

No Separation	Tells Designer not to produce a print separation, that is, to print all the colors on one page. See Chapter 14.
Separate	Tells Designer you want to produce a spot-color or process-color separation. See Chapter 14.
To Printer	Tells Designer to send the printout to the selected printer. This option is "ghosted" if the selected device is connected to None in the Printers dialog box (i.e., the device has not been assigned to a computer port or a print file named in WIN.INI), or if no device is selected (i.e., None is selected in the Select Printer dialog box).
To File	Tells Designer to send the printout to a special file, that you can use to print the art later. See Chapter 14.
Print All Pages	Tells Designer to print all the pages that have something drawn on them.
Print Current Page	Tells Designer to print only the current page; this is the same as the File | Print Page command.
Print Page Range	Lets you specify the pages you want to print; this may be a range or several ranges. This is explained in more detail later in this chapter.

CHAPTER TEN

The Utilities menu includes the following options:

Batch Print	This takes you to the Batch Print utility, which allows you to print .DRW, .GRF, .PCX, and .TIF files as a set, without having to open each file first. This utility is described in Chapter 14.
Controls	Displays the Control Panel, as explained earlier in this chapter. (The Control Panel is further described in Appendix C).
TeleGrafx	This takes you to the special TeleGrafx utility that allows you to transmit files from your computer to a print shop or slide shop. See Chapter 15.

The Print dialog box also has three command buttons:

OK	Prints the art, using the settings you made in this dialog box. This is ghosted if None is selected in the Select Printer dialog box.
Setup	Displays the Printer Options dialog box (Figures 10.5 and 10.6), letting you change printer settings. This is ghosted if None is selected in the Select Printer dialog box.
Cancel	Closes the Print dialog box without printing and without saving changes to the dialog box; however, if you changed settings in the Printer Options dialog box (using the Setup command button to get there), or if you used the Utilities menu to go to another dialog box and change something, those other changes *are* saved.

When you click on OK, your art is printed, and the *next* time you print using one of the other commands (File | Print Page or File | Print View), the printout will use options you selected in the Print dialog box.

Selecting Specific Pages

You can tell Designer exactly which pages you want to print. Select Options | Print Page Range to see the Page Range dialog box (Figure 10.17).

This box shows a layout of the entire drawing area, with each page numbered. Pages colored black are the ones Designer will print. If, before entering the Page Range dialog box, Options | Print All Pages were selected, all the pages would be black. If Options | Print Current Page were selected, only the current page would be black.

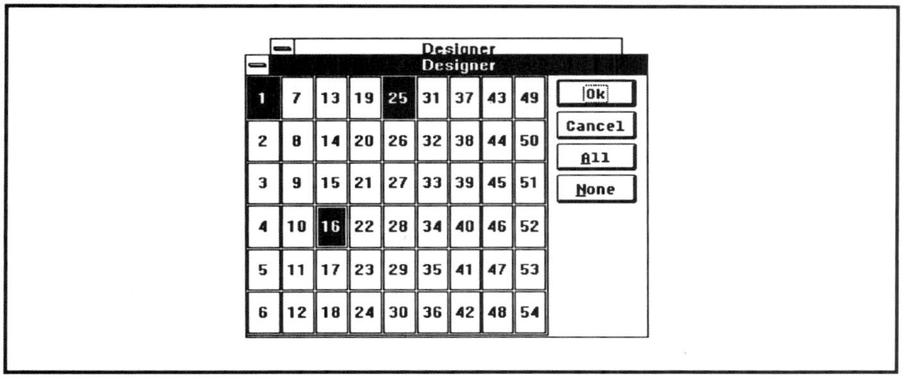

Figure 10.17: The Page Range dialog box

Click on a page to select it or deselect it. Alternatively, click on the All command button to select all the pages, or the None command button to deselect all the pages. You can select multiple ranges: you could select pages 1 and 2, 15 to 27, and 32 to 40, for example. If you click on OK, Designer will display the selected pages in the "Pages" row at the bottom of the Print dialog box. (If there's not enough room to display all the selected pages, you will see an ellipsis at the end of the list.)

KEYBOARD

Use the arrow keys to move from one page to another in the Page Range dialog box. Unfortunately you will toggle each page as the cursor lands on it—if it wasn't selected, just moving the cursor to it selects it, and if it was selected, moving the cursor deselects it. If you want to move across several pages to get to the one you want, press arrow-space-arrow-space and so on: the space bar also toggles the page.

Printing your work is a simple matter, but there is more to learn if you want to produce slides or color separations. These processes are explained in further detail in Chapters 14 and 15.

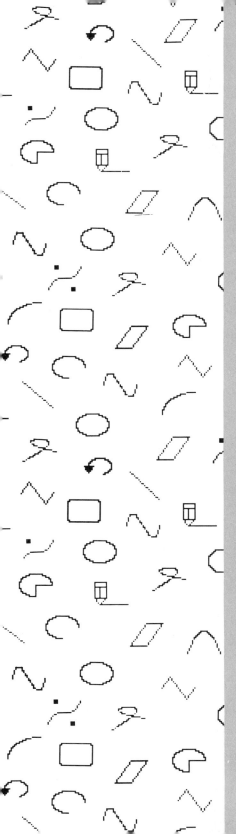

PART II

More Advanced Techniques

11

Using
Drawing Aids

$\mathbf{T}$his section describes Designer's special drawing aids. You can use aids such as the rulers and grids, cross-hairs, dimensions, the status line, and so on to make drawing quicker and easier.

CROSS-HAIRS, RULERS, AND GRIDS

Designer has four indicators to assist you in lining up objects as you draw and move them:

rulers	Bars at the top and the left of the drawing area indicating dimensions
ruler guides	Small dotted lines that move along the rulers, indicating the pointer position
cross-hairs	Two solid lines—one horizontal and one vertical—that cross the drawing area, meeting at the pointer position. (The pointer is not visible when cross-hairs are turned on.)
grids	Dotted lines dividing the drawing area into squares or rectangles

Figure 11.1 shows all four of these indicators.

USING RULERS

Select View | Rulers/Grid to display the Rulers/Grid dialog box (Figure 11.2). On the left side is a box with the Rulers settings. Two boxes let you set the horizontal and vertical ruler divisions independently of each other. You can set them from 1 division per unit to 100 divisions per unit (inch or centimeter).

These divisions will not always display, however. If you are zoomed in close, are using inches, and have a resolution of 480, you can see 100 divisions along the ruler. But if you change to centimeters, or if you move out again—using View | Page, for example—some of those divisions are removed, because there simply isn't any room for them. Or, if you change

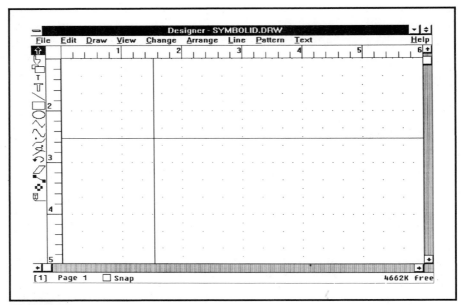

Figure 11.1: Rulers, guides, cross-hairs, and grids

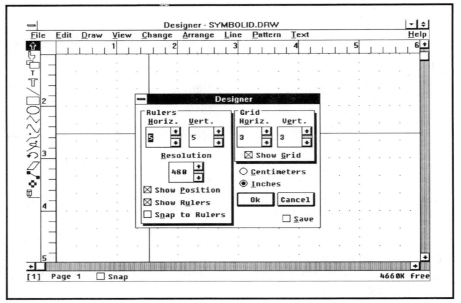

Figure 11.2: The Rulers/Grid dialog box

the resolution to 250, only 50 divisions will be seen in each inch. In fact, if you set 100 divisions per inch and then display a full page, you will see only *1* division per inch! You would do better setting only 10 per inch, because all ten would be displayed. The lesson here is that you should use the large settings only when you need to work zoomed in on your objects.

Ruler divisions can be used in several ways. You can use them in conjunction with the ruler guides or the cross-hairs (as I will explain in a moment), or with Snap to Rulers, a way to make Designer "jump" from one division to another so you can place objects precisely. Snap to Rulers is described in Chapter 12.

The Rulers section of the Rulers/Grid dialog box has four other components. The Show Position checkbox lets you turn the ruler guides on and off (explained next), and the Show Rulers checkbox lets you actually remove the rulers from the drawing area. The Snap to Rulers checkbox turns Snap to Rulers mode on and off, and the Resolution box lets you set the drawing-area resolution (explained later in this chapter).

You can also set the units—inches or centimeters—in this dialog box (this is also explained later in this chapter), and you can use the Save checkbox to save the current settings for future sessions. If you select the checkbox and click on OK, Designer writes the settings to the WIN.INI file, so the next time you open Designer it will use these settings. However, Designer saves these settings for *that particular file* even if you don't click on Save.

Ruler Guides

The dotted lines in the ruler that point to the pointer position are *ruler guides* (see Figure 11.1). As you move the pointer, the guides move along the rulers. You can use these to position the pointer rather precisely. Use them in conjunction with Snap to Rulers for even more control. The guides also indicate the position of an object you are moving or duplicating. When you move or duplicate an object you will see *four* ruler guides, two in each ruler, that point to each side of the object.

The ruler guides are turned on and off by clicking on the Show Position checkbox in the Rulers/Grid dialog box. There's a quicker method, though: click on the corner of the two rulers, the box at which the rulers intersect.

Using the Keyboard   Keyboard users can turn the guides on and off in the Rulers/Grid dialog box, of course, but they can also use the shortcut. Press Tab once to move control from the pointer to a cursor in the box at the ruler intersection. Press the space bar to turn the guides on or off, and then press Tab several times, until control moves back to the pointer.

USING CROSS-HAIRS

Select View | Cross-hairs (Keyboard Shortcut: Ctrl-C) to turn the cross-hairs on and off. The cross-hairs actually replace the pointer. In fact, you will not even see selected tools—the tools will work the same as normal, but the cross-hairs remain displayed. The cross-hairs can be used in conjunction with the ruler—as a sort of extended ruler guide, though the ruler guides still work when the cross-hairs are displayed—or to line up objects with others. Figure 11.3, for example, shows how you can use the cross-hairs while you are drawing a square to make sure that the edge of the new square is lined up with the edge of an existing one. When the objects are lined up exactly, the cross-hair is on top of the edge of the existing object—and that edge will change color when the cross-hair is on top of it.

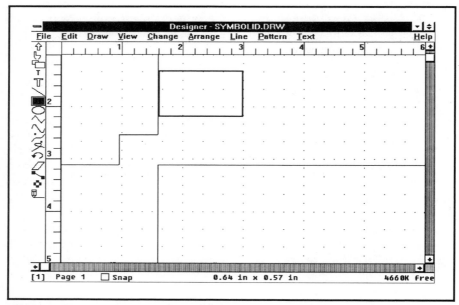

Figure 11.3: Using cross-hairs to line up objects

USING THE GRIDS

The top right-hand box in the Rulers/Grid dialog box has the Grid settings. Use the Show Grid checkbox to add the grid to the drawing area or remove it, and use the Horiz. and Vert. boxes to adjust the horizontal and vertical divisions. The Horiz. box determines the number of horizontal divisions, or, put another way, it determines how many vertical lines will be displayed in each unit. The Vert. box, similarly, determines how many horizontal lines are displayed in each unit. You can select from 1 to 100, but if you select more than Designer is able to display at a particular view, Designer will not display a grid at that view. Even if only the horizontal setting is too high, Designer will remove *all* grid lines. Zooming in on the drawing may redisplay the grid, though. When you are using inches, with the default resolution of 480, entering 7 or more into either the Horiz. or Vert. box will not display a grid at the Page View; if you change to Actual Size, though, you *will* see the grid.

IMPORTANT

The grid helps you line up objects, but don't confuse the grid with Snap to Rulers. When Snap to Rulers is turned on, the pointer snaps from one *ruler* point to another, not from grid line to grid line as some programs do. (See Chapter 12 for more information on Snap to Rulers.)

RESOLUTION, UNITS, AND DIMENSIONS

Designer lets you work in inches or centimeters. You can also set the *resolution,* the degree of accuracy with which you can work and display your objects. In addition, Designer has a Dimensions dialog box that changes the *displayed* units (which have no effect on the real size or resolution).

UNDERSTANDING RESOLUTION

Think of resolution this way. Designer has only a limited number of *coordinates,* or divisions, in its drawing area. You can't see these coordinates, but Designer knows they are there and uses them to place objects in the drawing area. For example, if you have 480 coordinates per inch—the default setting—Designer has an invisible grid in each inch, 480 lines across and 480 lines high. Designer can use the intersections of these lines, but not the spaces in between. For example, if you try to draw a line at point 132.6X and 256Y, Designer actually begins the line at 133X and 256Y. Of course you can't see all this going on—the divisions are too small for you to notice the pointer move to the next intersection.

Designer's default drawing area has a resolution of 480 coordinates per inch and displays pages 7 inches wide and 10 inches high. It has a total of 54 of these pages—6 pages high by 9 pages wide. So, the default area is 30,240 coordinates wide and 28,800 coordinates high. What happens if you change the resolution setting?

You saw the Resolution and Unit settings in the Rulers/Grid dialog box in Figure 11.2. You can use the Resolution box to adjust the resolution, from 250 to 2900 coordinates per inch, or 100 to 1100 per centimeter. Remember, though, Designer only has a limited number of coordinates. If you change resolution to 1000 coordinates, you can't expect to see 54 pages. In fact, if you change to 1000 per inch you might expect to get a drawing area about 3 pages high and 4 pages wide, and that is exactly what you do get. (Although the default setting is 30,240 times 28,800, there's actually more than this available, because Designer has some "slack" to work with at the edges.)

Change to 2900 coordinates per inch, and we get just 1 page in the drawing area. Designer can't give you 2 pages, because that would take a width of 40,600 coordinates, far more than what is available. What happens if you go the other way, if you change the resolution to 250? You get 18 pages wide by 13 pages high, a total of 32,500 coordinates wide by 22,750 high, a bit larger than the default setting (because of the "slack" that's left over), but still in the same general range.

What Does Resolution Do?

So what does all this actually mean to you, apart from the fact that you have fewer—or more—pages available?

It affects the degree of accuracy with which you can draw, because it limits how close you can zoom in on an object. Designer does not let you zoom in close enough to see the coordinates or "feel" their effect—in fact, the fewer coordinates on a page, the further away Designer keeps you. For example, set resolution to 250 and zoom in as far as you can (use the zoom tool and move it just a fraction before releasing the mouse button). Depending on your screen, you will see about 2.5 inches on the horizontal ruler.

Now change the resolution to 2900, and try the experiment again. You can now get so close that a mere 0.2 inches is enough to fill the screen! That's a difference of approximately 12 times, about the difference between the minimum and the maximum resolutions.

This allows you to produce either lots of simple drawings on more than 230 pages, or to produce extremely accurate work on just 1 page. Micrografx selected the default setting of 480 coordinates per inch as a compromise, the setting that they felt suited most people, giving reasonable accuracy and lots of room. And 480 dots per inch is more than most printers can print anyway. The typical laser printer outputs about 300 or 400 dots per inch.

If you need more room, but don't need great accuracy, you can reduce the resolution; or if accuracy is most important to you, you can increase resolution. Consider the resolution of your printer too, though. There's little point to drawing with an accuracy of 2900 points per inch, when your printer can output only 300 per inch. But if you are using a printer with 1200 dots per inch, you might want to set your resolution to 1200.

Converting Drawings

Set your resolution *before* you begin a drawing. (Use the Save checkbox in the Rulers/Grid dialog box to save the settings you usually work with.) If you *do* try to convert the resolution after you have begun a drawing, you have to tell Designer whether to leave objects the same *unit size* (the same number of inches), or leave them the same *coordinate size* (the same number of coordinates). If you have an object one inch wide, for example, and change resolution from 480 to 960, keeping the coordinate size will make the new object only half an inch wide—because 480 coordinates now equals half an inch.

When you change the resolution of a drawing area that contains objects, Designer displays the dialog box shown in Figure 11.4.

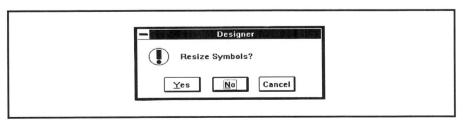

Figure 11.4: The Resize Symbols dialog box

If you click on No (or press ←) Designer keeps the unit size. The object remains one inch wide (for example), so Designer has to readjust the number of coordinates in the object. You will see a warning that "Some precision may be lost in conversion." Click on OK to continue. If, on the other hand, you click on Yes, the symbol is converted to the new size corresponding to the new resolution. The new object then has the same coordinate size, but a different actual size.

Viewing the Coordinates

You can display the coordinates in the status line. Select View | Status and Designer displays the Status/Coordinates dialog box (Figure 11.5).

Click on the Coordinates checkbox in the left half of this dialog box to make Designer display the coordinates in the status line (Figure 11.6). The display shows the X coordinates in the left side of the parentheses, and the Y coordinates in the right. (The X coordinates are left to right, the Y coordinates are up and down.)

You can also set the "origin," by typing new values into the brackets in the right side of the Status/Coordinates dialog box. For example, if you enter 100 on each side of the comma and click on OK, moving the pointer to the top left of the drawing area will display "(– 100, – 100)" in the status-line coordinates display. The new origin will be 100 coordinates in from the left and 100 down from the top, and when the pointer is in that position the status-line display will show "(0,0)." You might want to use this feature to make the numbers easier to work with. Say, for example, you are drawing a line beginning at coordinate 1342,2614 and want the line to go 112 coordinates to the right and 55 down. If you type those figures into the Status/Coordinates dialog box and click on OK, that position will now be 0,0. Now

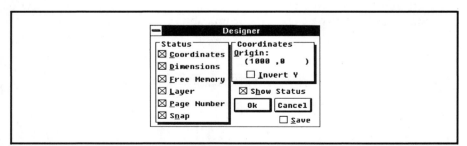

Figure 11.5: The Status/Coordinates dialog box

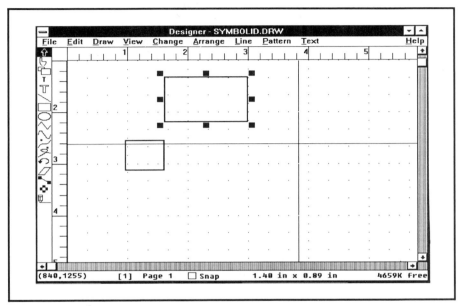

Figure 11.6: The coordinates display in the status line

draw the line—when the coordinates say 112,55, the line is in the correct position. That's easier to work with than 1454,2669.

You can also invert the Y coordinates so that the Y origin is at the bottom of the page. This helps you draw graphs, because in graphs and charts you probably want the X and Y origins in the bottom left corner. Combine "Inverting" the Y with resetting the coordinates to zero, and the bottom left corner of your graph begins at 0,0.

Viewing the coordinates helps you place items in the correct position, especially when your drawings require great accuracy, and when the highest Snap to Ruler setting (100 per inch) isn't enough. If the 100 setting *is* sufficient, however, you will probably find it easier to use Snap to Ruler.

CHANGING UNITS

The Rulers/Grid dialog box has two selection buttons: Centimeters and Inches. The default is inches, but you can work in centimeters if you want. When you convert to centimeters Designer keeps the page size the same, converting the dimensions into centimeters. If you have a page that is the default size of 7 inches by 10 inches (Designer displays the print area, not the total page, as described later in this chapter), changing to centimeters changes the page size to 17.79 by 25.4.

If you are converting a drawing area that already includes objects, you can either *convert the dimensions* of the objects—converting 1 inch to 2.54 centimeters, so the object is the same size—or *resize* the object, so that 1 inch is now 1 centimeter. This works just like modifying the resolution. You will see the same Resize Symbol dialog box you saw in Figure 11.4. Click on Yes to change the size of the object (a 1-inch object becomes 1 centimeter), or No to keep the same size, and just convert the units (a 1-inch object becomes 2.54 centimeters).

Having changed units to centimeters, you may notice that although the numbers in the ruler have changed, dimensions displayed elsewhere still say inches. For example, if you select or draw an object the dimensions in the status line still show inches. That's because Designer lets you set the displayed dimensions independently of the units you are using.

DIMENSIONS—NOT THE SAME AS UNITS!

It is important to understand the differences between selecting dimensions and changing units from inches to centimeters. The dimensions of an object are simply displayed numbers; this allows you to draw objects "to scale."

Select View | Dimensions to see the Dimensions dialog box (Figure 11.7). This box lets you set the dimensions that will be displayed in various locations in Designer's screen, including

- the Dimensions display in the status line
- the line width in the Wide Style dialog box
- the line widths in the Line menu
- the number of divisions in the ruler
- lines that were drawn with Line | Show Length turned on, or were selected and had the Line | Show Length command applied
- the dimensions displayed in the Array dialog box

The Dimensions setting has *no effect* on the page size, borders, resolution, grid position, or the ruler increments. *The dimensions are the scale.*

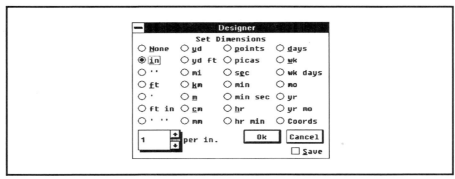

Figure 11.7: The Dimensions dialog box

For example, you can be using inches, but select centimeters for the dimensions. You might want to draw a diagram where one inch on paper equaled five centimeters on the screen. In the Dimensions dialog box you would select "cm." In the box at the bottom of the dialog box you would enter 5. When you click on OK you will notice that the number of divisions in the ruler changes. Where the ruler used to say 1, 2, 3, etc., it now says 5, 10, 15, (etc.), because you now have five centimeters per inch. If you select an object you will notice that the Dimensions display in the status line displays the units (cm), and dimensions that used to say 1 inch now say 5 cm. The line width and height in the Wide Style dialog box are now in centimeters, and if you use the Line | Show Length command the line will display a dimension in centimeters. However, lines already added to the Line menu remain in the previous dimensions, as do lines already displayed with Show Length.

NOTE

If you select a line and then select a new dimension with View | Dimensions, Designer automatically applies Line | Show Length to the selected line, using the new dimension.

These dimensions are purely for display, to help you when you are drawing. A 1-inch object will still *print* as 1 inch (not 5 centimeters!). And if you select a ruler setting of 10 in the Rulers/Grid dialog box, Designer displays 10 units per inch, even though the numbers are set according to the number in the Dimensions dialog box.

Let's take a look at the Dimensions dialog box options.

The None option removes the unit name (ft, in, hr, etc.) from the status line, the Wide Style dialog box, and lines drawn with the Line | Show Length command on. It does not remove the unit name from wide lines already in the Line menu or previously drawn lines. Also, this does not affect the number in the box at the bottom of the Dimensions dialog box. If it says 5, a 1-inch line will show as 5 (not 1) in the status-line Dimensions display, and the rulers will show five units for every one actual unit.

The other dimensions should be self-explanatory. Those that might look a little peculiar at first glance are actually familiar once you put them in context. For instance, ft in, yd ft, min sec, wk days, and yr mo are all combination settings that show both the larger and the smaller unit on the same measure, thus feet and inches, yards and feet, minutes and seconds, week and day, and year and month. The double and single "primes" or "hash marks" under in, ft, and ft in, respectively, of course stand for inches, feet, and feet and inches. Points and picas are units of measure for type size.

The box at the bottom left of the Dimensions dialog box permits you to select the number of units displayed per inch or centimeter. The Save checkbox saves the current settings for future sessions. If you select the checkbox and click on OK, Designer writes the settings to the WIN.INI file. (Designer automatically saves Dimension settings for *that particular file* even if you don't click on Save.)

Why would you want dimensions in hours? Or days or years? An obvious choice is for charts and schedules, but Designer has provided enough variety here to satisfy most needs. You might, for example, use points or picas if you are diagramming fonts, or miles or kilometers when drawing maps.

ADJUSTING THE PAGES

Although your drawing area is split up into "pages," it is not entirely accurate to refer to them as such. You may have noticed that the default page size is only 7 by 10 inches, which means that these pages are actually *printing areas,* the area of the paper after subtracting the borders. Adjustments to this size are made in the Pages dialog box. Before you learn about this box, however, there are a few points you need to keep in mind:

- The higher the drawing resolution, the fewer the pages that Designer can display; some page-size options are not available at high resolutions.

- The inches or centimeter setting also determines how many pages can be displayed, as well as, of course, the dimensions.

- When you open the Pages dialog box Designer checks to see what printer is installed, and the size of the print area provided by that printer. You can change the selected printer (and thus, possibly the print area), using File | Change Printer.

THE PAGES DIALOG BOX

Select View | Pages to see the Pages dialog box (Figure 11.8). This dialog box lets you define the page size, change the borders, change the page orientation, and turn off the page-border display.

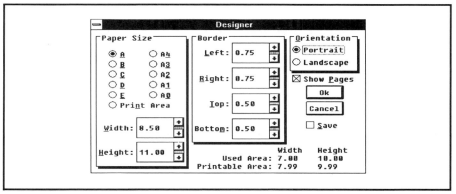

Figure 11.8: The Pages dialog box

Page Sizes

In the left of the dialog box is a group of options for selecting paper size. The different options display different values in the Width and Height boxes at the bottom. I am listing them here for reference purposes in case you are unable to select all the buttons to see the sizes available.

A	8.5 × 11 in	21.6 × 27.9 cm
B	11 × 17 in	27.9 × 43.2 cm
C	17 × 22 in	43.2 × 55.9 cm

D	22 × 34 in	55.9 × 86.4 cm
E	24 × 44 in	86.4 × 111.8 cm
A4	8.27 × 11.69 in	21 × 29.7 cm
A3	11.69 × 16.54 in	29.7 × 42 cm
A2	16.54 × 23.39 in	42 × 59.4 cm
A1	23.39 × 33.11 in	59.4 × 84.1 cm
A0	33.11 × 46.81 in	84.1 × 118.9 cm

You may not be able to select from all of these options, depending on the resolution of the drawing area and whether you are using inches or centimeters. Any options that are therefore unavailable are "ghosted." For example, if you are using the default resolution and inches, you can see all options. But if you increase resolution, some of the options disappear. Also, if you keep the default resolution but change to centimeters, options D, E, A1, and A0 are not available.

You can use the Width and Height boxes to enter a different page size; when you do so the black dot disappears from the previously selected option button.

Page Borders

To the right of the selection buttons are four boxes used to enter borders. The larger the border, the smaller the print area on the page, of course, but also the greater the number of "pages" that Designer can display. (Remember, they are not really pages, they are print areas, so if you are using only half of a page, Designer can display twice as many.) You can mark the borders on the page with crop marks, lines in the corners of the printed page that show where the borders begin. (For more information on borders, see Chapter 14.)

Page Orientation

In the top right of the box are the Orientation options; you can set up your pages to be in Portrait (8.5 inches wide and 11 inches high, for example) or Landscape (8.5 inches high and 11 inches wide). The default setting depends on the device you have installed. If you have a printer installed, the Portrait button will probably be selected, but if you have a Matrix film recorder installed, Landscape will be the default.

If you are changing the orientation of your pages you must also change the orientation of the printer, in the Printer Options dialog box (see Chapter 10 for more information). Otherwise the objects will still be printed the same way, and you will get a message saying "Page size too large—reduce to fit?"

The Print Area

Designer knows what device you have selected in the Select Printer dialog box (File | Change Printer), so it knows how large the page can be. In the bottom of the dialog box are two text lines: Used Area and Printable Area. Used Area is the area that you can draw in, the available area minus the borders; as you change the borders the Used Area changes. Printable Area is the area that is available to you if you want it, the total area on which the printer can print.

Below the Paper Size box on the left is another option: Print Area. If you click on this button Designer automatically adjusts the borders and sets the Used Area to the same as the Printable Area. In other words, Designer sets the drawing area to use the maximum space possible on the page. You can reduce the borders even more, increasing the print area *beyond* the available area, but when you try to print you will get the "Page size too large—reduce to fit?" message, and the page will be reduced—and distorted—if you continue.

The Show Pages Command

On the right of the box under the Orientation options is a Show Pages checkbox. When there is an X in the box Designer shows the page *boundaries,* lines across the drawing area that indicate the boundaries between the "pages"—or print areas, that is. If you are using paper that is 8.5 inches wide, and you set the left and right borders to 3 inches each, the boundaries between pages will be displayed every 2.5 inches across the display area. The reason it is important to understand that Designer does not display *pages*—that, instead, it displays the *area available* on the page—is because some programs do display the entire page, with borders marked on the page. The way Designer handles page boundaries is in some ways superior— it gives you more usable area, and it makes sure you don't place objects into unprintable areas—but you must remember that you are not seeing the entire sheet of paper.

Saving the Settings

When you click on OK you accept the settings for the current session, but the chances are that you need those settings for the next time you use Designer. Click on the Save checkbox before clicking on OK, and Designer immediately saves those settings in the WIN.INI file for subsequent sessions. (Designer saves these settings for that particular file even if you don't click on Save.)

THE STATUS LINE

The status line is used to display six different types of information that may be of use to you. Figure 11.9 shows an example of the status line, with all six items displayed.

coordinates	The coordinate position of the pointer. You can click on the coordinates and enter a new setting to move the pointer to an exact location.
layer	The layer number currently in use (or the layer's name, if you have named it). If you are also displaying the coordinates you may not see all of the layer name. You can jump between layers, and even open new layers, by typing a number or name in here and pressing ←┘. Or place the cursor here and press the up or down arrow keys to move through the layers.
page number	The page number of the page currently displayed in the top left corner of the window even if most of the window is taken up by a different page
snap	Click on this checkbox to turn Snap to Rulers mode on and off.
dimensions	The size, rotation, and movement of the selected object.
free memory	The amount of RAM available to Designer

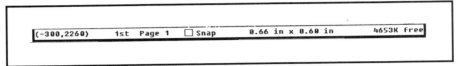

Figure 11.9: The status line

Select View | Status to see the Status/Coordinates dialog box that you saw in Figure 11.5. Click on Show Status to turn the status line on and off— you may want to remove it if you need the extra room on the screen.

Clicking on the status options turns them on and off. You can also adjust the Coordinates display using the options in the top right of the box, as described earlier in this chapter.

Using the Keyboard   Designer lets you move the pointer using the Coordinates box. Press Tab three times to move control from the pointer to a cursor in the status-line coordinates display. Enter the coordinates of the position to which you want to move the pointer, and press ←┘. (Press Backspace to delete characters, or the arrow keys to move the cursor into the numbers.) The pointer jumps to that position. If you selected a drawing tool, the tool is automatically enabled, the equivalent of pressing button 1 or the space bar. Press Tab to move the pointer out of the status line, and then press the arrow keys to move the pointer. It begins drawing an object, even though you are not holding the space bar.

If you specify coordinates off your screen—the other side of the drawing area, even—the pointer moves to that area, but your screen doesn't, so you can't see the pointer. Pressing the arrow keys a couple of times will bring the pointer back into view, however far away it is, drawing its object as it moves.

This is a difficult technique to use; try it, but if you have no specific need for it you probably won't use it again. (The real answer is to get a mouse!)

SPEEDING UP REDRAW

Like all graphics-intensive programs, Designer can be slow, especially on slow machines. The faster your computer, hard disk drive, and graphics board, the faster Designer will work, but there are also several software tools to speed up your system. You have seen some of these before, but here they are in one place for easy reference.

View | Show Preview	Turns on and off the display of patterns, colors, wide lines, and end styles. It also makes text display in Draft mode if Proof is the selected Text Display mode. Turning off Show Preview blanks out imported bitmaps, leaving a box around them, and, in effect, carries out a Pattern | Show Complex command.
Pattern | Show Complex	Turns on and off the display of symbol fills (Pattern | Symbol Fill), masking (Pattern | Mask Symbol), and gradient fills. Gradient fills display the solid pattern color when Show Complex is turned off, and Masked Symbols show only the masking symbol.
Text | Display	Changes the mode of text display, while viewing or editing text. Text may be displayed in Proof mode (filled with the selected color), Draft mode (empty, outline only), or Greyed (the text is obscured by a grey box). See Chapter 8 for more information on Text.
to interrupt redraw	You can select a command at any time, even when Designer is redrawing. Designer will carry out the command before continuing redraw.

Use these commands to make your work easier. If you don't need to view the text at present, put it in Greyed or Draft mode. If you are adding objects and are not yet ready to fill or color them, turn off Show Preview. If you have a number of imported bitmaps—which can redraw very slowly— turn off Show Preview. Show Preview also lets you select objects that are behind other objects. Turn off Show Preview to remove the patterns and colors, and then click on a line in the desired object.

These commands don't have any effect on what your work looks like when it is printed; it always prints with all colors and fills, regardless of how it is displayed.

Designer lets you interrupt redraw by selecting another command. The interruption feature is especially useful. Many programs make you wait while they finish what they are doing, which is often of no use to you anyway after you have realized that you want to carry out a different command. Now and again, however, if you are too "fast on the draw," Designer will lock up. Pressing Esc usually frees things up again.

There are also a few other ways to speed things up. Don't open other Windows applications, including the clock or calendar. When you have finished viewing the clipboard, close it. Save your file frequently. And keep large, complicated objects off screen until you need them.

By the way, you can change the default setting for Show Preview. Click on the Show Preview checkbox in the Preferences dialog box (View | Preferences) to *remove* the X if you want Designer to open with Show Preview turned *off.* This also automatically changes the Text Display mode so that it displays text in Draft mode when viewing text.

USING ZOOM

View |
Zoom

You have already used the Zoom tool, but there is a way it can be used that I haven't yet explained. Select the Zoom tool from the toolbox, or select View | Zoom (Keyboard Shortcut: Ctrl-Z). The pointer changes into the Zoom tool, a pointing hand with two overlapping boxes next to it.

You normally use this tool by rubberbanding around an object—pointing to one side of the object, pressing button 1, dragging the "rubber band" to the side of the object diagonally opposite, and releasing button 1.

But try this. Don't release button 1; hold it while you press button 2. The rubber-band box "freezes." Move the mouse, and the box moves, allowing you to position it over another object. Release button 2 and you can continue expanding or reducing the box. Release button 1 when you are satisfied with the zoom area.

There is, of course, a limit to how far you can zoom in, and that is determined by the resolution of the drawing area, as discussed earlier in this chapter.

Using the Keyboard   There is a keyboard equivalent for at least part of this frozen-zoom method. You zoom by selecting the Zoom tool, pressing and holding the space bar, and moving the pointer with the arrow keys. While holding Shift, press and release the *2* on the alphanumeric part of the keyboard (*not* the the numeric keypad). The rubber-band box is now "frozen" so you can move the box into position. You can no longer change the size of the box, though—when you release Shift the view zooms in on the box.

USING SYMBOL IDs AND PARTS LISTS

Designer lets you assign names to images (symbols). These names are called symbol identifiers, or symbol IDs. The fact that you can refer to symbols by name makes it easy to

- build a library of symbols, either as you draw them or from existing drawings;

- load symbols from the library, using the ClipArt command;

- find particular symbols in your drawing;

- select all occurrences of a particular symbol in your drawing;

- print a *parts list,* a list of all the symbols in your drawing; and

- replace all occurrences of a particular symbol with the contents of the clipboard.

Although you can assign 80-character names or IDs, only 30 characters will display in the parts list, so you might as well limit names to less than 30 characters. This should still be enough to clearly describe the symbol. You have already used symbol IDs—the names you saw in the ClipArt dialog box are symbol IDs.

NAMING SYMBOLS

To name a symbol, select the symbol and then select Edit | Symbol ID. (Keyboard Shortcut: F12.) The Edit Symbol ID dialog box appears, shown in Figure 11.10.

Type the name you want to assign to the symbol—including spaces in the name if you want. If the symbol already has an ID, the ID is displayed in the dialog box—you can replace or edit the name if necessary. Click on OK to close the dialog box. The symbol will keep that name even if you

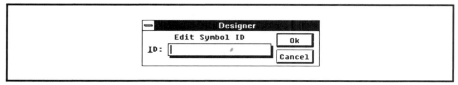

Figure 11.10: The Edit Symbol ID dialog box

reshape it, flip it, change its color or pattern, and so on. If you copy the symbol to another Designer window, the symbol ID is copied with it.

If you duplicate the symbol, using the Shift-draw method or using the Arrange | Array command, the copies will have the same symbol ID.

If you combine several objects that already have names, the combined object has no name. (You can assign a name, of course.) If you later break the object apart, the original components' names reappear.

Building a Symbol Library

Building a symbol library is easy.

1. Select a named object and then select Edit | Copy to put it in the clipboard.

2. Display the Control Menu (Alt-space, or click on the bar in the top left of the window).

3. Select the Add a Window command. Designer displays a new window, on top of the original.

4. Move the pointer onto the new window's drawing area by using the mouse or by pressing Alt-Tab. The pointer automatically changes to a Paste tool, the cross. Position the pointer where you want to put the symbol, and press and hold the mouse button. Designer pastes the symbol from the clipboard into the drawing area.

5. Click on the first Designer window. The second one disappears.

6. Select the next symbol. Select Edit | Copy to put it in the clipboard.

7. Press Alt-Tab to redisplay the second Designer window. Again, paste the symbol into the drawing area.

8. Continue like this until you have copied all the symbols you need. When you have finished, save the new file.

If you want to put most or all of a drawing's symbols into the library, or if you have a symbol that is too big to fit into the clipboard, use the File | Import command while in the library file. This will load the entire file into the library. You can then delete the symbols you don't want and reposition the others. (Actually, you may *have* to use this method if you have a slow computer, because on some computers opening a second Designer window slows the system down to a crawl.)

To further identify your symbols, you might want to type the symbol ID under each symbol in the library. This will help you find the one you want later. Use a screen font so it doesn't slow down redrawing too much, or a simple outline font with Text | Display set to Draft.

If you have a lot of symbols you want to save, consider building several files. You could create a subdirectory called LIBRARY, and then have several files—one called BOLTS, one called VEHICLES, and so on, in the same way the clip art files are organized.

Using the Symbol Library   You can use the symbol library files just like the clip art files (see Chapter 3). In fact your library files *are* clip art files, built in the same way that Micrografx builds their clip art files. You can use the clip art commands to preview the clip art files before loading symbols. You could also use the File | Import command to load an entire clip art file into the drawing area if you will need most of the symbols in your current work.

USING THE PARTS LIST

Designer automates the process of producing a parts list. You can even have Designer build a word processing file for you, listing all the parts in your drawing.

Click somewhere in a blank space, so no object is selected, and then select File | List Parts. (If you display the parts list while a single object is selected, the list displays only the ID of that object, not of the entire file. Or block-select several objects to see their names.)

Figure 11.11 shows an example of the Parts List dialog box. The names or IDs of the symbols appear in the left side of the list box, while on the right you can see the number of times that each symbol appears. At the bottom, "Other" indicates the number of symbols in the file that do not have IDs.

You can leave this dialog box displayed on the screen while you work, if you want, or use the mouse to push it most of the way off the screen so it's not in the way. You can't use the File | Clipboard command while the parts list is displayed, though. Close the dialog box using the Control menu, or click on the top left corner.

Figure 11.11: The Parts List dialog box

This dialog box also has two menus (in addition to the Control menu, that is). The File menu gives you the following commands:

New   You can work in the drawing area while the parts list is displayed, but if you add or remove symbols or IDs the parts list does not automatically update. Use File | New to update the list.

Save As   Saves the parts list as a text file. Designer displays a dialog box in which you can name the file and specify whether you want to save the file in .TXT (ASCII), .DIF, or .SLK formats. Use the .TXT file in a word processor, the .DIF or .SLK in databases or spreadsheets that use those formats.

Print   Prints the parts list. First Designer asks if you want to place dots or spaces between the ID and the quantity.

Titles   Displays a dialog box that lets you change the titles (Part List, Part, Qty) that are displayed on the Parts List dialog box, the copy of the parts list pasted into Designer, the printout, and the saved file. You can also save the titles as the defaults.

The Edit menu within the Parts List dialog box gives you, the Copy command, to copy the parts list into the clipboard. You can then paste the parts list into your drawing area or word processor.

Figure 11.12 shows an example of the Parts List dialog box with its titles changed. Next to it you can see the parts list pasted into the drawing area, and under that is the Titles dialog box.

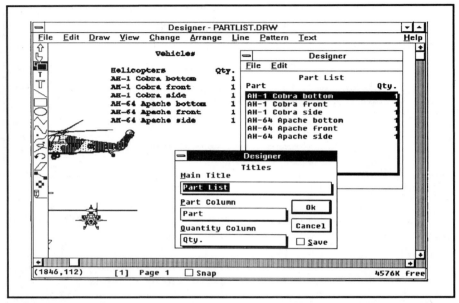

Figure 11.12: The Parts List dialog box, the Titles dialog box, and the parts list pasted into the drawing area

You can also use the parts list to confirm which object in a library or clip art file is which. Select the object and display the Parts List (or select File | New in the Parts List dialog box if it is already open) and the list displays only the name of the selected object.

USING LAYERS

Designer lets you build up to 64 different layers. Think of a layer as a piece of transparent paper on which you can draw. When you place layers on top of each other you can see through the layers to the objects below, but you can (usually) draw on only one layer at a time.

Why would you want to work like this? Well, you might be a technical drafter, doing a series of circuit boards. Each board has the same basic layout, and some have a secondary board mounted on top. You could draw the basic layout and save that as a template. When you want to draw another board, you could copy the template file and open it (or use the File | Import command to bring it into the drawing area). Then you can go to another layer to add the components. If this board has one of the secondary boards on top, you can import that into another layer. This way each layer remains distinct and cannot be accidentally changed or get in the way of the other layers. You can even tell Designer not to display certain layers when you are drawing below them, and to print specific layers.

Another use for layers is tracing bitmaps. Put a bitmap on layer 1 and then go to layer 2 and trace around it using the mouse or a digitizing pad.

You can use the View | Status command to display the layer name or number in the status line, and then use that display to move up and down the layers. Click on the layer name or number in the status line, type the name or number of the layer you want to go to, and press ←┘. Or use the up or down arrow keys to move to each layer in sequence.

THE LAYERS DIALOG BOX

Select Arrange | Layers to view the Layers dialog box (Figure 11.13).

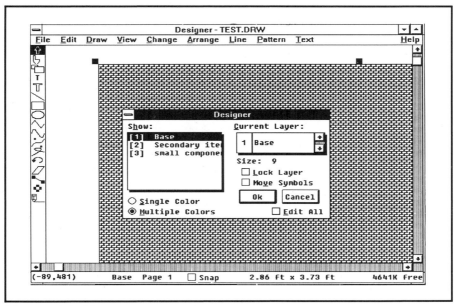

Figure 11.13: The Layers dialog box

These are features of the Layers dialog box:

Show	Lists all the existing layers. The layers that are selected will be displayed, those that are not selected will not. Usually all are selected, but you can click on one to select it, deselecting the others. Press Shift and click on another to select that also, and so on. You cannot deselect the current layer. If you print the file, only the selected layers are printed.
Current Layer	Use this to select the current layer, the one on which you are going to work. You can also type a layer name in the box between the layer number and the scroll bars. The name will appear next to the layer number in the Show Layer list.
Size	The number of objects in the current layer. This may give you an idea of whether you have selected the correct layer. (Combined objects count as one object.)
Lock Layer	Locks the layer indicated by the Current Layer box. You will not be able to move or change objects, or even add new ones.
Move Symbols	Lets you transfer objects from one layer to another. Select the objects you want to move, open the Layers dialog box, and click on Move Symbols. Then change the current layer in the Current Layer box and click on OK. The objects are moved.
Edit All	Click on this checkbox if you want to edit *all* the layers at the same time, not just the current layer. The objects will act as if they are all on one layer.
Single Color	This makes Designer revert to the last color used in a layer when you move to that layer.
Multiple Colors	Turns off the Single Color feature.

Unless you name a layer or place objects on it, Designer will not save it, even if that means having a layer 5 and a layer 7, but no layer 6, for example. You can use the layer name to ''sign'' art, by the way, in the same way Micrografx artists signed their work in the samples that came with pre-3.1

versions of Designer (look at, for example, CAMERA.DRW). However, if you have the coordinates displayed in the status line much of the layer name is obscured.

You can use the Show command to print layers separately. Simply select the ones you want to print, click on OK, and then print the file using one of the Print commands.

NOTE

Arrange | Move to Back and Arrange | Move to Front have no effect on layers. They only move the position of objects in a single layer.

MAKING OBJECTS TRANSPARENT

Making objects on higher levels transparent can be confusing. Simply selecting Change | Transparent won't always do it. If you have Pattern | Solid set on, the object will still be opaque. It is easy enough if you want the object to have no color or pattern—just select Pattern | None (it doesn't matter what you select for the background, Change | Opaque or Change | Transparent).

If you want to use a transparent pattern, though, select the pattern and then select Change | Opaque to make the background color opaque. You cannot make a Pattern | Solid object transparent.

USING SINGLE COLOR

The Single Color feature is a timesaver when you are jumping frequently from one layer to another. If Single Color is set on, Designer automatically changes back to the last color used in a layer when you move to that layer. For example, if you have selected green in layer 4, but move to layer 1, where you used blue the last time you drew an object or applied a color, Designer automatically reverts to blue—you don't need to use the Color dialog box to select blue.

The color selected in the Color dialog box *does not* change—when you jump to layer 1 green will still be selected in the box (it remains the current color), but blue will be used if you create *a new object*. However, if you click on the OK button before creating an object, green becomes the current color for that layer, and the new object will be green. Or if you select an object and click on the OK button in the Color dialog box, the object will be filled with green, and the next object you create will also be green.

When you go to a *new* layer and create an object, that object will be *black,* unless of course you select another color first. Select Multiple Colors to turn this feature off.

12

More
Editing Methods

$\mathbf{T}$his section is a sort of potpourri of techniques to make working with Designer easier. From aligning objects and building arrays, to using snap modes and selecting objects, these tools will make Designer quicker and easier to work with.

USING THE CLIPBOARD

Designer uses the Windows clipboard to store, move, and copy objects. The clipboard has a few advantages over a real clipboard, not least of which is the ability to make copies of the object it is holding. Once an object is saved in the clipboard it remains there until you copy something else into it, tell Designer to empty it, or close Windows. You can copy the same image over and over again, so the clipboard is an easy way to duplicate a symbol.

The clipboard is a Microsoft Windows application, so other programs designed to run under Windows can use it. This allows you to copy objects from one Windows application to another. Although this chapter describes how to use Designer's clipboard commands and Designer's Clipboard dialog box, you can also view the contents of the clipboard by double-clicking on the clipboard icon in the main window of the Program Manager in Windows 3.0, or by double-clicking on CLIPBRD.EXE in the MS-DOS Executive window in pre-3.0 versions of Windows.

Windows 3.0 has an improved clipboard. It now has four menus that allow you to save the contents of the clipboard in a .CLP file, open a .CLP file, empty the clipboard, or view the contents in several different formats (the clipboard stores the image in different formats so you can transfer objects between different applications). The new clipboard also has a Help menu, and can contain much larger files.

PLACING OBJECTS IN THE CLIPBOARD

You have already learned a few of the ways you can put objects into the clipboard. Edit | Cut *removes* the selected picture from the drawing area and puts it into the clipboard, and Edit | Copy places a *copy* of the selected object into the clipboard.

You may also place an object into the clipboard when you use the File | Import and File | ClipArt commands, if you don't have Auto Paste selected. If Designer loads art using Auto Paste the art is loaded straight into the drawing area, but with Auto Paste turned off the art is loaded into the clipboard. You can then copy it into your drawing area. Although you won't be able to use the clipboard for very large objects, this is a good method for when you want several copies of a piece of clip art or an imported file. Instead of loading it into the drawing area and then copying it, load it directly into the clipboard and then paste it as many times as you need it.

NOTE

Designer 3.0 had some problems importing bitmaps through the clipboard. In some cases it will not display the imported bitmap, leaving a blank space instead. This can happen while using the File | Import command, and while using the Edit | Cut or Edit | Copy commands to import from other Windows applications. Try using the File | Import command with Auto Paste turned on (to bypass the clipboard).

You can also load objects into the clipboard from other Windows applications, and then copy these objects from the clipboard into Designer. And, of course, you can go the other way, loading a Designer drawing into the clipboard and then copying it into another Windows application. You could, for example, copy a spreadsheet graph into the clipboard and then into Designer, or use Designer art to spruce up a spreadsheet.

OPENING THE CLIPBOARD

Designer lets you select the type of formats used by the clipboard. Select Edit | Clipboard to view the Clipboard dialog box, shown in Figure 12.1. This box lets you select the formats you want to use, view the contents of the clipboard, and empty the clipboard. (You may want to empty the clipboard if you are trying to carry out an operation that requires a lot of memory, and your system can't quite manage it.)

The default setting has all the formats selected. The Input Formats are those that can be used when copying objects from other Windows applications into Designer, and the Output Formats are those that may be used when copying objects from Designer into other applications. These are the

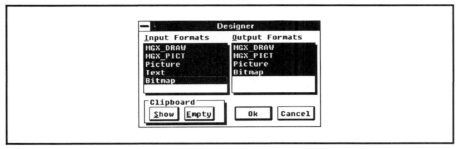

Figure 12.1: The Clipboard dialog box

formats with which the clipboard can work:

MGX_DRW	The Micrografx Designer format
MGX_PICT	The Micrografx .PIC format, used by earlier Micrografx products such as In*a*Vision
Picture	.WMF, Windows metafile format, read by Windows Write and Pagemaker
Text	ASCII text
Bitmap	.MSP, Microsoft Paint format, the format used by Windows Paint, and .BMP, Microsoft Paintbrush format

You may deselect some of these formats—for example, if an application supports more than one of these formats, and you want to ensure that you import only a specific format.

Use the Clipboard dialog box in the following manner:

Show	Displays the clipboard window, displaying the clipboard's contents (Figure 12.2). In pre-3.0 Windows the bar below the clipboard title bar displays a message telling you if the clipboard is empty or, if it has an object in it, in which formats the data can be pasted.
Empty	Empties the contents of the clipboard, freeing memory for other uses. The same as the Edit | Delete command in the Windows 3.0 clipboard.

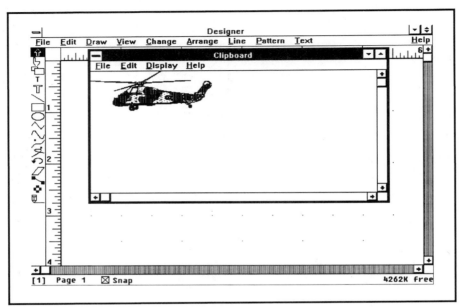

Figure 12.2: The Windows 3.0 clipboard

Input and Output Formats	Click on a format to select or deselect it.
OK	Clicking on OK closes the dialog box; until you return and change the formats again, only the selected formats will be used.
Cancel	Closes the dialog box without changing the format selection.

The clipboard runs independently of Designer. When you click on the Show command button in the clipboard dialog box (or when you open the clipboard from Windows), you start the application; closing the Clipboard dialog box will not close the clipboard window. If you move between windows the clipboard may end up out of view; if you want to see it again you must use the Alt-Tab or Alt-Esc commands to jump to the window again. (You will not be able to use the Edit | Clipboard command or open the clipboard from Windows, because it is already running. If you open the Clipboard dialog box you will see that the Show command button is "ghosted.") Close the clipboard by double-clicking on the Control menu, selecting Close from the Control menu, or (in Windows 3.0) by selecting File | Exit.

ALIGN

No graphics program is complete without an align command. Arrange | Align (Keyboard Shortcut: Ctrl-F1), which displays the Align dialog box in Figure 12.3, offers several alignment combinations. Although it contains ten options, each with a Ctrl-key/function-key shortcut, this dialog box allows three main types of alignment:

- You can snap an object onto the nearest ruler increment.

- You can align a group of objects relative to each other.

- You can move an object or group of objects to the middle or center of the page.

To use the individual align commands, select the objects, select Arrange | Align, then either click on the command you want, and click on OK, or simply press Ctrl and the appropriate function key.

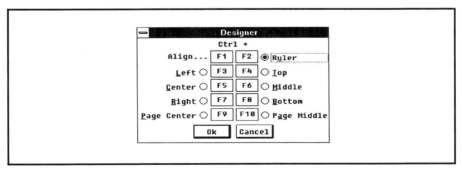

Figure 12.3: The Align dialog box

ALIGNING TO RULERS

If you select an object or a group of objects, select Arrange | Align, click on Ruler, and then click on OK, the top and the left sides of the object will snap to the nearest ruler divisions, even if there are divisions closer to the bottom and right sides. (Keyboard Shortcut: select the objects and press Ctrl-F2.) Of course if the object was created using Snap to Rulers it is already against the nearest ruler, so usually this won't do anything. Align to rulers works under any of the following conditions:

- The object was created when Snap to Rulers was turned off.

- The object was moved or reshaped when Snap to Rulers was turned off.

- You have changed the number of ruler divisions in the Rulers/Grid dialog box, and the division that the object was next to is gone.

- You used the Array command to duplicate an object and enlarge the copies, and the copies ended up off the ruler increments.

ALIGNING OBJECTS RELATIVE TO EACH OTHER

The Align commands let you align objects "together," or relative to each other. For example, say you have a number of labels on your drawing, but they aren't on the same line. If you want to level them out, you would select all the blocks of text and apply Align Bottom to them. Designer puts them all on the same level as the lowest in the group.

There are six ways to align objects together:

Align Left	Designer places the objects on the same vertical level as the object furthest to the left.
Align Center	Designer places the objects along a vertical line down the center of the group.
Align Right	Designer places the objects on the same vertical level as the object furthest to the right.
Align Top	Designer places the objects on the same horizontal level as the highest object in the group.
Align Middle	Designer places the objects along a horizontal line across the center of the group.
Align Bottom	Designer places the objects on the same horizontal level as the lowest object in the group.

Figure 12.4 shows several examples of these alignments. The group in the top left is the original group; the others show how Designer aligns them.

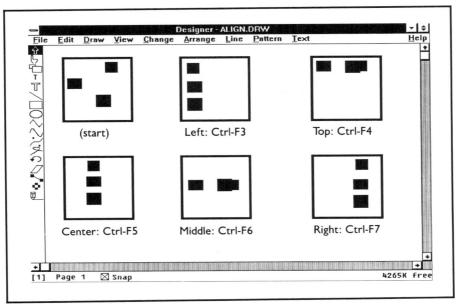

Figure 12.4: Aligning objects relative to each other

ALIGNING OBJECTS
IN THE MIDDLE OF THE PAGE

You can also use Align Page Center and Align Page Middle to align objects in the center or middle of the page. By "center" Designer means the *horizontal* center. The object is moved to the left or right to put it in the horizontal center. If you use Align Page Middle the object is moved up or down to put it in the "middle," which is the *vertical* center. If you use both commands on the same object it is moved into the actual center of the page, both horizontally and vertically.

SNAP MODES

Designer has two Snap modes: Snap to Rulers and Object Snap. These commands help you line up objects in exactly the right position. These are the various Snap commands:

Edit | Object Snap (Ctrl-O)	Turns on and off the Object Snap mode, using the settings in the Object Snap Mode dialog box
Edit | Snap Mode (Ctrl-N)	Displays the Object Snap Mode dialog box, letting you set up Object Snap mode
View | Rulers/Grid	Displays the Rulers/Grid dialog box. Click on the Snap to Rulers checkbox to enter or exit the Snap to Rulers mode. This is the same as clicking on Snap in the status line.
View | Status	Displays the Status/Coordinates dialog box. Click on the Snap checkbox to turn on the status-line display of Snap to Rulers.
Arrange | Align (Ctrl-F1)	Displays the Align dialog box. Use the Align to Rulers command to line up an object drawn or positioned when Snap to Rulers was turned off.

SNAP TO RULERS

The status line has a checkbox next to the word Snap. This controls the Snap to Rulers mode. When the Snap checkbox has an X in it, Snap to Rulers is turned on, and moving or drawing an object is controlled by the ruler divisions. As you move an object the object "jumps" from one division to another, and when you draw an object you will find that Designer draws the lines only to ruler divisions, even if you move the drawing tool to a position between divisions.

You can demonstrate this quickly. Make sure the Snap box in the status line has an X in it—if it doesn't, click on it—and that the ruler guides are turned on. (These are the dotted lines—explained in Chapter 11—that appear in the ruler to indicate the pointer position.) Now select the Rectangle drawing tool and draw a rectangle. Watch the ruler guides as they jump from one ruler increment to the next. Now click on Snap again, to turn off Snap to Rulers, and draw another rectangle. This time the lines are drawn smoothly, without any jumping.

The Snap to Rulers feature helps you line up objects and draw objects of just the right size. You can adjust the jumping by adjusting the ruler increments, as explained in Chapter 11; and when you need to place an object *between* ruler increments, turn off Snap to Rulers by clicking on Snap in the status line.

You can also turn Snap to Rulers on and off by selecting View | Rulers/ Grid and, when the Rulers/Grid dialog box is displayed (Figure 12.5), clicking in the Snap to Rulers checkbox. Also, you can remove (or redisplay) the Snap checkbox from the status line by selecting View | Status and clicking on Snap in the Status/Coordinates dialog box. Snap to Rulers works even when the rulers are not displayed.

If you drew or positioned an object when Snap to Rulers was turned off, and then turn Snap to Rulers back on, you may find that the object does

---

NOTE

Don't confuse Snap to Rulers with the Snap to Grid or Snap to Guide feature that some programs have. In Designer, the objects snap to the ruler increments, regardless of the grid increments. If you are used to working with systems that snap to the grid—and like it that way—simply make the ruler and grid settings the same.

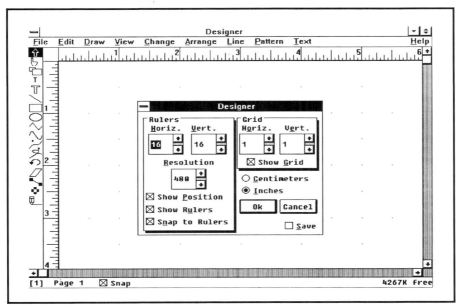

Figure 12.5: The Rulers/Grid dialog box

not move to the ruler increments. For example, if the ruler increments are one tenth of an inch apart, the object will normally move from 0.1 to 0.2 to 0.3, and so on. But if you drew the object with one edge at 0.05, turned on Snap to Rulers, and then tried to move the object, it would move from 0.05 to 0.15, to 0.25, and so on. It will move the correct increment, but remain offset from the correct position. Select the object and use the Align to Ruler command in the Align dialog box (Arrange | Align), as described earlier in this chapter, to move the object back to the correct ruler position.

You have already learned that Designer cannot always display all the ruler divisions. If you set 100 per inch, for example, and then use View | Actual Size, and you will see 25 rather uneven divisions. Snap to Rulers, however, will still use 100 snap points per inch, not the 25 displayed.

SNAPPING OBJECTS TO OTHER OBJECTS

You can use Edit | Snap Mode to snap objects together when you are drawing them. It is often difficult to get lines positioned exactly in their correct place; they look alright on your screen, but once you print them you notice small—but distracting—gaps between lines and the objects they are supposed to join. Object Snap mode makes sure that when you connect a line to another line or an object it mates exactly, leaving no gap. The snap position could be the center of an object, the middle of a line, the middle of an object's edge, the joint between two lines, or an object's corner . . . or even a point in the middle of nowhere. This tool is very useful when drawing flow diagrams, Gantt charts, circuit diagrams, and so on, because you can make sure that not only do connecting lines connect without leaving gaps, but that they do so exactly in the middle of the edges or on the corners.

Select Edit | Snap Mode (Keyboard Shortcut: Ctrl-N) to see the Object Snap Mode dialog box shown in Figure 12.6. This box lets you decide where

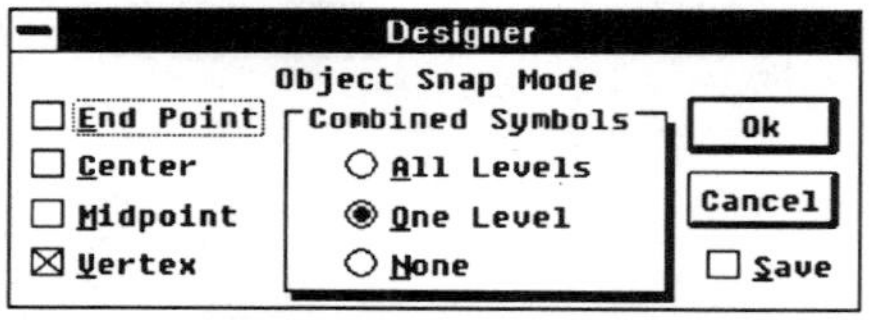

Figure 12.6: The Object Snap Mode dialog box

on the object Designer should display snap points:

Center	The middle of a line, or the center of a primitive object. This has no effect on multiple-section lines and non-primitive closed objects.
Midpoint	The middle of a line or the middle of the straight lines in a closed object or multiple-section line
Vertex	The end points of a line, the corners of a closed object, and the joints in a multiple-section line
End Point	The end points of a line or a multiple-section line. This has no effect on closed objects.

NOTE

Remember that primitives are those drawn with the square, rectangle, rounded rectangle, ellipse, or circle drawing tools.

Even the circle has midpoints and vertices, by the way. Though it doesn't really have corners or straight lines on which to place midpoints, Designer improvises and places snap points spread evenly around the circle.

This dialog box also allows you to tell Designer how to work with combined objects, that is, what to do if you apply Object Snap Mode to an object comprising individual objects that have been combined with Arrange | Combine.

All Levels	Gives all the components snap points
One Level	Gives only the most recently combined objects snap points. If you combined all the objects at the same time, all will have snap points.
None	Does not apply any snap points to combined objects

Notice also the Save checkbox in the dialog box. Check on this if you want to save the current settings for future sessions. Designer will save the settings—writing them to the Windows WIN.INI file—as soon as you click on OK.

By the way, if you have one or more objects selected when you open this dialog box, those objects will be placed in Snap mode as soon as you click on OK—you don't need to use the Edit | Object Snap command. But you can use Edit | Object Snap (Keyboard Shortcut: Ctrl-O) to apply the *current settings* to the selected objects.

Figure 12.7 shows a square with Center, Midpoint, and Vertex snap points.

You will notice that with the snap points displayed, your drawing tool will snap lines to those points. Select a drawing tool, and then move the pointer onto one of the snap points. You can begin drawing while the pointer is anywhere in the snap point, and the line (or object) will begin in the very center of the snap point, mating exactly with the existing object. Snap to Rulers is overridden. Even though the corner of the object may not be on a ruler, your line begins at the corner.

TIP

To put snap points in "thin air," draw an object, apply Snap Mode, and then delete the object. The snap points remain, even after the object has gone, and will operate as normal. This will let you snap objects into position even when you have no object onto which you can snap them.

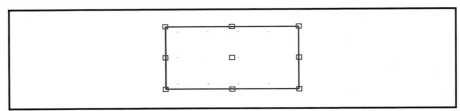

Figure 12.7: Center, Midpoint, and Vertex snap points

ARRAY

The Arrange | Array command is a great way to produce special effects, and to duplicate objects. Select an object and then select Arrange | Array, and the Array dialog box is displayed (Figure 12.8).

If you used all of the Array options you could take a square and duplicate it 50 times; move each copy slightly to the left and down, each copy being slightly further from the original than the last one; rotate each copy, each one more than the last; make the copies diminish in size, so #1 is 5 inches wide and #50 is only 1 inch; and change the colors, with the pattern

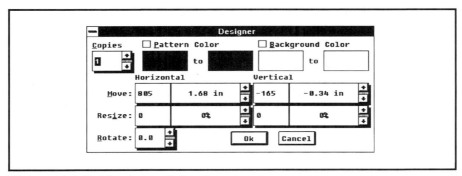

Figure 12.8: The Array dialog box

color changing from black to white in increments and the background color changing from red to green in increments.

The Array command can be used to simply duplicate an object and place it exactly where you want it, or to create many unusual effects. For example, if you are drawing part of a machine that has bolts every 1 inch along one side, a total of 15 bolts, you could draw one bolt, and then use the Array command to duplicate—and position—the other fourteen. Or, if you are producing something a little more artistic, use Array to build blurred or "fuzzy" images. You can also use Array to make very precise enlargements of objects.

The array in Figure 12.9 was created by copying an object 24 times, rotating it 5 degrees each time, moving it both down and to the right, enlarging it about 11 percent each time, changing the pattern color from black to white, and changing the background color from white to dark grey.

You enter movement and resizing settings in coordinates, so it helps if you understand what these are. (Coordinates are explained in Chapter 11.) Here are the adjustments you can make in the Array dialog box:

Copies	You can make from 1 to 100 copies.
Move	Tells Designer how far to move the object; you can set the horizontal and vertical movements individually. A negative horizontal movement is to the left and a negative vertical movement is up, not down. Each box displays both coordinates on the left, and dimensions—feet, centimeters, hours, etc.—on the right. You can type the coordinates value in the small box, or use the scroll arrows; however, you cannot enter anything in the dimensions side of the box.

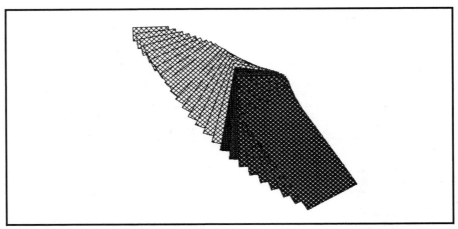

Figure 12.9: An object copied and modified by means of the Array dialog box

Resize	Tells Designer how much to increase (positive numbers) or decrease (negative numbers) the size of the object. The values are displayed as the number of coordinates on the left of each box and the percentage change on the right (as explained for the Move settings).
Rotate	Use the scroll bars to scroll 5 degrees at a time, or type a value directly into the box. The rotation is counterclockwise, so 5 degrees means move the top of the object 5 degrees around to the left.
Pattern Color	To adjust the pattern color, click on the Pattern Color checkbox then click in the second color sample (the one after the word "to"). Designer displays the Pattern Color dialog box. Double-click on the color you want the *final* copy in the series to have. (You cannot change the "from" colors while using this dialog— you must do that before you open the Array dialog box.) Figure 12.10 shows the effect of changing the pattern color from light to dark grey in an array of 23 copies.
Background Color	Change the background color in the same way as the pattern color.

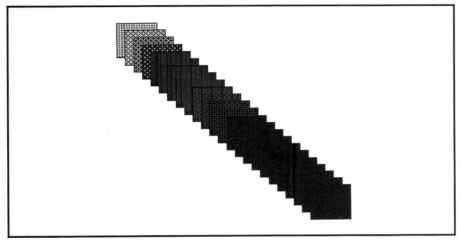

Figure 12.10: Changing pattern color in an array

As I just explained, you can enter the Resize setting in coordinates or by percent. To enter it by percent simply use the scroll arrows until you have the percentage increase you want—50% means half again as large, 100% means twice as large, and so on. If you enter it in coordinates, you are giving Designer the exact number of coordinates by which the object should be enlarged. If an object is 100 coordinates wide, for example, and you enter 10, the first copy will be 110 coordinates wide, the next will be 120, and so on.

If you are applying the Array command to a horizontal or vertical straight line, only the appropriate adjustments will be available. And if you are rotating an object, you will not be able to set the horizontal and vertical values independently of each other.

You can quickly learn to produce ''fun'' stuff with the Array command, and with a bit of practice you can also use it to control your art very precisely.

By the way, you may frequently find that Designer ''ghosts'' the OK button in the Array dialog box. When it's ghosted, it means Designer can't carry out the command according to the settings displayed. Look at all the settings and figure out why. It may be that it can't carry out the command without pushing the array out of the drawing area, for example, or perhaps you typed a bad number into one of the boxes (0 – .5, for instance). If you catch the OK button just as it ghosts, it means the setting you just entered was wrong. Fix the setting and Designer will ''unghost'' the button.

NOTE

You cannot enter the pattern or background colors into the Array dialog box unless you have a mouse.

3.1

BLENDING OBJECTS

If you have Designer 3.1 you have a new feature that allows you to "blend" one object into another. Designer draws several objects between two selected objects, each one modified slightly. The effect is a series of metamorphosing objects, each with a slightly different size and shape, that seem to merge from the first selected object to the second.

Designer will blend the object's pattern and background colors, but it cannot blend patterns—all the objects in the series will have the *starting* object's pattern, the object that Designer begins with. Which is the starting object? The one at the front. If it is important which is the starting object, select it and use Arrange | Move To Front before blending.

Note that you cannot blend bitmaps, combined objects, or text (though of course you could convert a character to curves and then blend it).

To use Blend, select your two objects and then select Arrange | Blend. The Blend dialog box (Figure 12.11) appears.

Use the Blend Steps scroll box to enter the number of new images you want Designer to draw (from 1 to 99). The Reverse Points checkbox reverses the way the images are blended. Each object created by Designer has a "direction." The direction depends on the object's type and how it was drawn. For example, primitives have a counterclockwise direction; they were drawn by Designer counterclockwise. Objects drawn with line-drawing tools may be

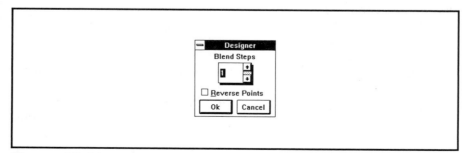

Figure 12.11: The Blend dialog box

clockwise or counterclockwise, depending on exactly how you drew them. The direction in which the objects were drawn affects the form of the series of blended objects, as seen in Figure 12.12. The two series of blended objects at the bottom of the figure began with the same objects, but in one case the direction has been reversed. If you blend two objects and don't like the result, press

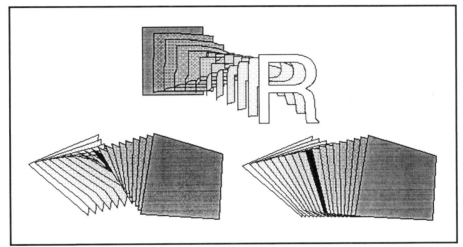

Figure 12.12: Blended objects

Alt-Backspace to Undo the blending, reselect the objects, and try blending with the Reverse Points checkbox selected.

Of course you can also use this feature to create a series of objects with the same shape but different sizes: create an object, duplicate it, reduce or enlarge the copy, and then blend the two to create up to 99 duplicates, each one slightly larger than the other.

SELECTING OBJECTS

You have already learned a couple of ways to select objects, but there are others. Here are the different ways to make selections:

to select one object | Point and click the mouse button.

to select several objects	Press Shift and click on the objects you want to select, then release Shift.
to "rubber-band" the objects	Edit | Block Select selects the objects enclosed by the Block Select tool's "rubber band."
to select all the objects	Edit | Select All selects all the objects in the file.
to select a symbol ID	Edit | Select lets you select all the objects with a particular ID.
to select symbol styles	Edit | Select lets you select all objects of a specified type (color, line size, or pattern).
to select line styles	Edit | Select lets you select all lines of a specified type (color, width, style, or end style).
to select text styles	Edit | Select lets you select all text of a specified type (color, font, or size).
to deselect an object	To remove an object from a group of selected objects, press and hold Shift, click on the object to be removed, and release Shift.

Edit | Block
Select

THE BLOCK SELECT TOOL

Use Edit | Block Select (Keyboard Shortcut: Ctrl-B) or click on the Block Select tool in the toolbox. Because the Block Select tool draws only rectangles (you can't trace around the objects you want as you can in some programs), you will sometimes block-select more objects than you want, and sometimes fewer than you want. For example, if you block-select a group you want to move, but you want an object in the middle of the group to stay where it is, you can press Shift, point at that object, click, and release Shift. When you move the group, the object in the middle stays where it is. You can also use this method to add unselected objects to the selected group.

You can "freeze" the Block Select tool in the same way you can freeze the Zoom tool. Before you release button 1, press button 2. The rubber band freezes, and moving the mouse moves the entire square rather than enlarging it. Position this rubber-band square where you want it and then release button 2. You can now continue rubberbanding.

Using the Keyboard   There is a keyboard equivalent for at least part of this frozen Block Select method. You normally use the Block Select tool by pressing and holding the space bar and moving the pointer with the arrow keys. While you are holding Shift, press and release the 2 on the alphanumeric part of the keyboard (not the 2 on the numeric keypad). The rubberband box is now "frozen," permitting you to move the box into position. Releasing Shift selects the objects inside the box, however; it does not return you to the rubberbanding mode.

SELECT ALL THE OBJECTS

Use Edit | Select All (Keyboard Shortcut: F2) to select every single object in the file. You can then use the Shift-click method just described to deselect some objects if you want. You might want to select all the objects in a file so you can shift them all over a page or two, or apply a line style or pattern to them all, for example.

USING THE SELECT DIALOG BOX

The Select dialog box is Designer's equivalent to a word processor's "Search for Style" command. In the same way some word processors will search your document for, say, all the bold text, or all text with a particular font, Designer will search the drawing area for all objects, lines, or text with specified styles, or all objects with a specified ID.

You can then use the Shift-click method described above to remove objects from, or add objects to, the selected group.

Before you start, select View | Used Pages, so you will be able to see all the objects. Then select Edit | Select (Keyboard Shortcut: Shift-F3) to display the Select dialog box, as shown in Figure 12.13.

Specifying IDs

At the top of the Select dialog box is the Symbol ID text box, in which you enter the name of the ID you want to select. (Symbol IDs are described in Chapter 11). You can use *wildcards* if you want: a question mark (?) stands for any one letter, and an asterisk (*) stands for several. Say you want to select all the bolts in your drawing (for example, in order to change the pattern on all of them), and you know that the only symbol ID beginning with a

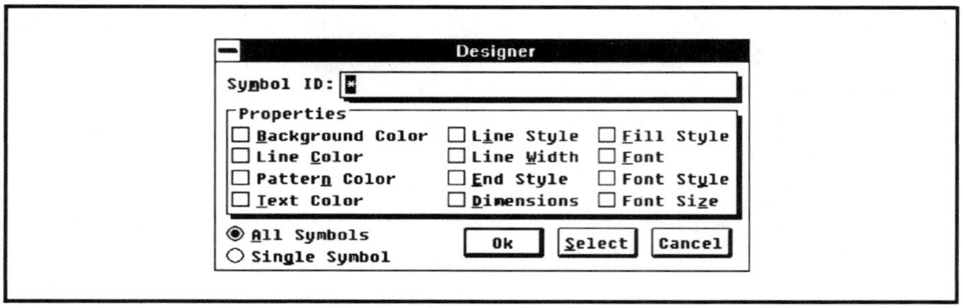

Figure 12.13: The Select dialog box

b in that drawing is "bolt." When the Select dialog box opens, press the left arrow key to move the cursor to the left of the asterisk that is initially displayed and type the letter *b*. Press ← or click on OK, and Designer selects all the objects with IDs beginning with b—in this case, all the bolts.

Perhaps you want to select the coccyx in the clip art file called SKELAV.DRW. There are other IDs beginning with c—so entering simply c* won't suffice—but none of them end in x. Therefore, you can enter c*x to select *coccyx*.

The question mark is used when you are not sure of the character in that position or when you know that several IDs contain it. For example, you may have several different bolts—bolt1, bolt2, bolt3, and so on. Enter bolt? to select all of these. If you have a bolt10, however, it won't be selected, because the question mark stands for only one character, and bolt10 has two at the end of *bolt*.)

Specifying Properties

Selecting an object, line, or text property begins before you open the Select dialog box. First select the characteristics you want to search for as the current settings. If you want to select all the green lines, select green as the current line color. If you want to search for all text in Swiss Light, select that as the current font.

Then display the Select dialog box. Click on the properties for which you want to search. For example, if you want to search for all lines and objects using the current line width, click on the Line Width checkbox. If you want to select only the objects that have both the current line width and the current pattern color, click on both Line Width and Pattern Color. This works the same way if you enter a symbol ID and check some of the Properties checkboxes: Designer will select only those objects that have both the ID and the specified properties.

NOTE

If you only want to search for object, line, or text properties, just leave the asterisk by itself in the ID box.

Most of the Properties checkboxes in the Select dialog box are self-explanatory, but two require more explanation. Fill Style makes Designer search for the same pattern and pattern color; objects with the same pattern but different pattern color are not selected, and the background color has no effect. Dimensions makes Designer select lines that have a Show Length dimension in the current dimensions; if the current dimensions are centimeters Designer will select all lines with a Show Length dimension in centimeters, but not those in other units.

EXECUTING THE
SEARCH AND USING SELECT

Once you have specified the symbol ID or the properties you are looking for, select either the All Symbols or Single Symbol button. All Symbols selects all the objects that fit the specifications you have entered; Single Symbol selects only one of them.

Now you can click on OK to close the dialog box and select the objects. You will usually use this command button if you selected the All Symbols option. If you selected Single Symbol, though, you will probably want to click on the Select command button. Designer will select one of the objects, and leave the dialog box displayed. Click on Select again, and Designer selects the next object that fits the specifications. Continue clicking on Select to select each appropriate object, one by one.

If the object happens to be off the screen you won't be able to see it—Designer doesn't shift the drawing area for you—so select View | Actual Size to move to that object, or View | Used Pages to see where it is. (Or remember to select View | Used Pages before using the Select dialog box.)

13

More
about Color

$\mathbf{I}$n Chapter 4 you were introduced to the basics about color—applying colors, selecting other palettes, learning how colors interact, and so on. In this chapter you will learn commands that give you even more control over color, letting you combine palette sets, create new palettes, mix new colors, and label colors so that you might find those colors quickly.

ADDING AND MIXING NEW COLORS

There are three ways to mix new colors—using the HLS (Hue, Lightness, Saturation), RGB (Red, Green, Blue), and CMYK (Cyan, Magenta, Yellow, and Black) dialog boxes. The dialog box names refer to the process by which the colors are produced:

HLS	Select from as many as 360 hues, set a percent lightness to add white or black to the hue, and set a percent saturation to adjust the amount of color in the hue.
RGB	Mix three primary colors together (red, green, and blue, the equivalent of mixing cyan, magenta, and yellow).
CMYK	Mix cyan, magenta, yellow, and black, the four colors required for four-color printing.

Begin the color-mixing process by selecting the color closest to the one you want to mix. Then open the appropriate dialog box from the Color menu (Figure 13.1).

HLS Color	Lets you mix new colors with the HLS model
RGB Color	Lets you mix new colors with the RGB model
CMYK Color	Lets you mix new colors with the CMYK model
Screen Color Table	Displays the colors your monitor can display, and lets you add these to a palette
Printer Color Table	Displays the colors your printer can print, and lets you add these to a palette

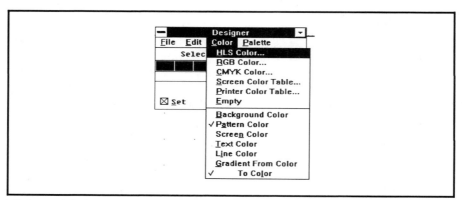

Figure 13.1: The Color dialog box's Color menu

Empty	Inserts an empty space—a "placeholder"—after the color highlighted in the palette
Background Color	Changes dialog box to the Select Background Color dialog box
Pattern Color	Changes dialog box to the Select Pattern Color dialog box
Screen Color	Changes dialog box to the Select Screen Color dialog box
Text Color	Changes dialog box to the Select Text Color dialog box
Line Color	Changes dialog box to the Select Line Color dialog box
Gradient From Color	Changes dialog box to the Select Background Color dialog box (the same as the Background Color option in this menu)
Gradient To Color	Changes dialog box to the Select Pattern Color dialog box (the same as the Pattern Color option in this menu)

Incidentally, to make it easier to mix and work with colors, Designer lets you keep one of these color-mix dialog boxes open while you are working in Designer. You can draw new objects or use the Color dialog box menus to open other dialog boxes, without closing the color-mix dialog box. However, if you select another color-mixing method, the displayed box is replaced by the selected one.

USING THE HLS DIALOG BOX

Display the HLS dialog box by selecting Color | HLS Color from the Color dialog box's menu bar. When it appears, the color you selected in the Color dialog box is shown in the sample box on the right side (Figure 13.2), and the Hue, Lightness, and Saturation bars all show the appropriate settings for the selected color.

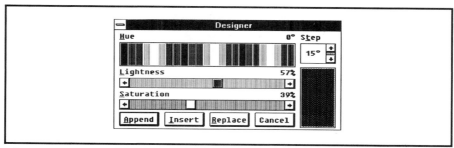

Figure 13.2: The HLS dialog box

The Hue bar at the top of the box displays up to 360 hues (0-359). If you select a primary color before displaying the HLS dialog box, only 24 hues are shown. As you select a hue the degree number above the right side of the bar changes. The Hues range from red at one end to magenta at the other. These are the degree numbers for the primary colors:

Red	0
Yellow	60
Green	120
Cyan	180
Blue	240
Magenta	300

The number of hues shown is also determined by the Step box in the top right. You can use this to set the hue "step" to 1, 5, 10, or 15 degrees. When the step is set to 1 degree, 360 colors are displayed in the hue bar—a scroll bar appears underneath the bar so you can scroll through the color bar. When the step is set to 15 degrees only 24 hues are shown, and the scroll bar is removed.

The Lightness bar determines how much white to mix into the color, and the Saturation bar determines how much color to mix. For example, if you leave Saturation at 0 percent, you have no color—anything you mix will be black, grey, or white.

Primary colors have a Lightness setting of 50 percent and a Saturation of 100 percent. For example, if you select hue 240 in the Hue bar, and set Lightness to 50 percent and Saturation to 100 percent, the sample box displays the primary color blue. And black can be created from *any* hue in the bar by setting Lightness to 0 percent.

0% Lightness	Always produces black, regardless of the saturation
100% Lightness	Always produces white, regardless of the saturation
0% Saturation	The color will be black, grey, or white, depending on the saturation
50% Lightness and 100% Saturation	Produces the exact hue selected in the Hue bar

Once you are in the HLS dialog box you can select another color from the Color dialog box, and use that color as a starting point for the new color you are mixing. Click on the Set checkbox in the bottom of the Color dialog box to turn Set on (Set makes the Color dialog box remain on the screen even after you have selected a color), select the color you want and click on OK, and then select Color | HLS Color. The HLS dialog box changes to show the settings for the new color. Or select a hue from the Hue bar and mix a new color from that.

When you have finished mixing the color, click on one of the command buttons at the bottom of the box.

Append	Adds the new color *after* the color selected in the Color dialog box; if the color already exists, the highlight moves to that color instead of adding a color
Insert	Adds the new color *before* the color selected in the Color dialog box; if the color already exists, the highlight moves to that color instead of adding a color

Replace   Replaces the color selected in the Color dialog box with the new one; if the color already exists, the highlight moves to that color instead of adding a color

USING THE RGB DIALOG BOX

Display the RGB dialog box by selecting Color | RGB Color from the Color dialog box's menu bar. When it appears, the color you selected in the Color dialog box is shown in the sample box on the right side (Figure 13.3). The RGB box uses both the *additive* and *subtractive* models to mix your colors. The additive model works by mixing red, green, and blue; it is known as additive because combining these three colors (100 percent of each one) produces pure white. The subtractive model, on the other hand, produces white by *removing* colors (cyan, magenta, and yellow).

White   100% red, 100% green, 100% blue
         0% cyan, 0% magenta, 0% yellow

Black   0% red, 0% green, 0% blue
         100% cyan, 100% magenta, 100% yellow

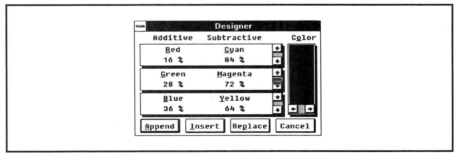

Figure 13.3: The RGB dialog box

Mix your colors by adjusting the amounts of red/cyan, green/magenta, and blue/yellow—as the percentage of one set goes up, the percentage of the other goes down. You can also adjust the amount of black in the mix, using the scroll bar at the bottom of the sample Color box: click the right arrow to increase the black, the left arrow to decrease it. All the numbers in the scroll boxes to the left adjust accordingly. If you want to create a grey, use this scroll bar to remove all the color from the mix, and then adjust the amount of black until you get the grey you want.

As in the HLS box, you can select another color from the Color dialog box and use that color as a starting point for the new color you are mixing. Once you have finished mixing your new color, use the command buttons to add the color to the palette.

USING THE CMYK DIALOG BOX

Display the CMYK dialog box by selecting Color | CMYK Color from the Color dialog box's menu bar. When the dialog box appears the color you selected in the Color dialog box is shown in the sample box on the right side (Figure 13.4).

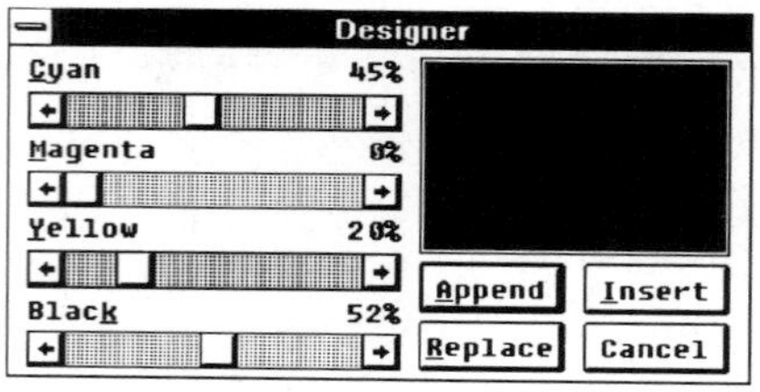

Figure 13.4: The CMYK dialog box

This dialog box lets you mix cyan, magenta, yellow, and black. When all are set to 0 percent, the sample box displays white. The Black allows you to produce a true black, required for four-color printing (the RGB dialog box does not create a true black). A 100 percent black setting is always black, regardless of the other settings, but a 0 percent black only creates white if the other settings are 0 percent also.

When you are adding a color to the mix, note the Black setting. If, for example, you have 60 percent black, you can add only 40 percent of another color. Adjusting the percent setting of any other color *above* 40 percent will not change the color. (The total percentage of the other colors is not limited to 40 percent, though). You will also notice that if you add a new color to the Color dialog box, close the CMYK dialog box, and then reopen it, the settings seem to have changed. Because there are a number of ways to produce that one color by mixing these four, Designer has simply adjusted the settings to normalize them for the maximum possible black.

As with the other dialog boxes, if you want to select another starting point, you can click on the color in the Color dialog box and click on OK to display that color's settings in the CMYK dialog box. Once you have finished, click on one of the command buttons to add the color to the Color dialog box.

ADDING SCREEN AND PRINTER COLORS

You can also add your screen or printer colors to a palette. Select Color | Screen Color Table to display the Screen Display dialog box (Figure 13.5) or Color | Printer Color Table to display the Printer Colors dialog box. Click on the color you want to add, and then click on Append, Insert, or Replace to add it to the palette.

If you are using a printer driver or video card that does not allow programs to "inquire" about colors, the Color menu option is ghosted and you will be unable to add the color to the palette.

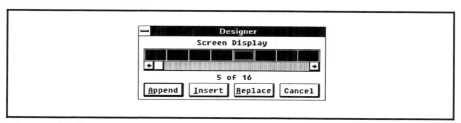

Figure 13.5: The Screen Display dialog box

ADDING AN EMPTY SPACE TO A PALETTE

The Color | Empty command adds a blank space in the palette, immediately after the selected color; this space acts as a "placeholder." Use this to place a color in the palette in a specific position. Click on the color in front of where you want the space and select Color | Empty; Designer adds a blank space, and places the highlight on it. Select or mix the color you want to add, using the other Color menu commands, and then click on the Replace command button to put that color into the placeholder. Of course you don't have to use a place-holder to add a color to a palette—just use the Append or Insert command buttons instead—but you might want to put placeholders into a palette while you plan the changes you are going to make.

DELETING COLORS FROM A PALETTE

You can remove a color from a palette by highlighting the color and selecting Edit | Delete. The color is removed and the other colors move up to take its space, so no blank place is left.

WORKING WITH PALETTES

You have learned how to add colors to a palette, and how to remove them, creating new palette and palette sets. But having created these new palettes, what do you do with them? Designer has commands that allow you to save the new palette sets, select a palette set from a list, merge two sets together, and delete palettes. These are the commands available:

THE FILES MENU

Reset	Removes the current palette set and displays the standard set
Open	Displays a File Open dialog box so you can open another palette set
Merge	Lets you combine two palette sets into one
Save	Saves a palette set you have modified
Save As	Saves a palette set with a new name

THE PALETTE MENU

Add	Adds a blank palette to the set of palettes; you can then use the commands in the Color menu to mix colors to add to the new palette

THE PALETTE MENU (continued)

Rename	Lets you rename the palette displayed in the dialog box
Delete	Removes the palette displayed in the dialog box from the palette set
(palette names)	The names of the other palettes in the palette set; lets you select one of these other palettes

OPENING ANOTHER PALETTE SET

When you first open Designer the color palette set displayed in the Color dialog box is the standard set. This set contains eight individual palettes: Primaries, Greys, Violets, Reds, Blues, Greens, Yellows, and Pastels. But Designer has two other palette sets that were loaded into the SAMPLES directory when you installed Designer. These are ARTIST.PAL—a "set" containing only one palette, Artist, which has 25 dithered colors—and CRAYON.PAL—a set of two palettes, Crayon with 64 colors, and the same Primaries palette that is included in the standard palette set. The dialog box title bar shows the name of the palette set (unless the set displayed is the standard set).

NOTE

Some early copies of Designer 3.0 did not include ARTIST.PAL and CRAYON.PAL.

Use File | Open to open one of these other palette sets. Designer displays a File Open dialog box; use it to look in the SAMPLES subdirectory—in the DESIGNER directory—for files with the .PAL extension. The File | Reset command removes the selected palette set and restores the standard palette set. (The standard palette set is *not* stored in a .PAL file, so you won't be able to find this file in your directory.)

Unfortunately, selecting File | Reset modifies your WIN.INI file, so if you had selected a palette set other than the standard as your default, that change is removed.

CUSTOMIZING THE COLOR PALETTE

If you will normally need to use a color palette set other than the standard set, open the Color dialog box and select File | Open from the dialog box's menu bar. When the File Open dialog box appears, click on the Save checkbox, select the palette set you want to use, and click on OK. The selected palette set is displayed in the Color dialog box, and the Windows WIN.INI file is changed so that the palette set becomes the default, appearing the next time you begin a Designer session.

There is one minor problem with this, however. If you want to see the standard palette set again, you normally have to select File | Reset to have Designer load the standard set and remove the previous palette name from the WIN.INI file, which makes the standard set the default again. Unless you remember to reselect the palette (and click on the Save checkbox), the palette setting in WIN.INI is removed. There is a way around this. Display the standard palette set, select File | Save As, and name the file STANDARD. Click on OK, and Designer saves a copy of the Default palette in a file called STANDARD.PAL. The next time you want to see the standard set, don't use File | Reset; rather, use File | Open and select STANDARD.PAL.

MERGING PALETTE SETS

Designer lets you join palettes together. For instance, you might build a palette, and later decide you would like to add the palette to the ARTIST.PAL palette set. In such a situation, you would load ARTIST.PAL using File | Open, and then select File | Merge. The File Open dialog box is displayed. Select the palette set you want to add to ARTIST.PAL, and click on OK; the palette sets are merged together. The individual palettes from the set you added are displayed in the Palettes menu. If you want to merge colors to or from the standard set, first save the standard set as STANDARD.PAL, using the File | Save As command, and then load this new palette file using File | Open.

SAVING PALETTE SETS

The File | Save and File | Save As commands work just like Save and Save As commands elsewhere in Designer. Select Save to save the changes you have made to a palette, or Save As to save a palette with a new name (you might make changes to a palette, but want to keep the original palette unchanged). You cannot make changes to the standard palette, incidentally—if you select File | Save, Designer displays a box asking for a new filename—but if you save the standard set with a new name (STANDARD.PAL for example) you can then use that new palette just like any other palette.

If you forget to save a new or modified palette set before you close Designer, or before you select another palette, you will see a dialog box asking you if you want to do so.

Take care when you name a palette file; if you check the Backup checkbox Designer will create a file with the same name as the palette file but with a .BAK extension. If that name is the same as another type of backup file—a backup of a .DRW file, for example—the other backup file will be written over.

Because you can create and save your own palette sets you could create sets for each type of art; for example, you might create a set that has only greys and use it for technical drawings printed in black and white.

ADDING A NEW PALETTE TO A SET

If you want to create a whole new palette of colors—rather than just modify an existing palette—use the Palette | Add command to create a blank palette. Designer displays a box prompting you for the palette name (Figure 13.6); type the name and click on OK. All colors are removed from the Color dialog box, and the name you typed is displayed above the OK command button. Now use the Colors menu options to mix or add colors to the palette. When you have finished, use the File | Save command to save your changes. (You cannot save new palettes in the standard palette set—Designer will ask you to save the file with a new name.)

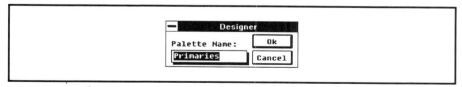

Figure 13.6: The Palette Name dialog box

RENAMING PALETTES

Every palette has a name—Primaries, Crayon, Greys, and so on. You can change a palette name using the Palette | Rename command. You will see the same dialog box that was displayed when you selected Palette | Add; simply type the new name and click on OK. The name displayed above the OK command button changes. When you have finished, use the File | Save command to save your changes. (You cannot save renamed palettes in the standard palette set—Designer will ask you to save the file with a new name.)

REMOVING A PALETTE FROM A SET

You can completely remove a palette from a set. Simply display the palette using Palette | (palette name), and then select Palette | Delete. The palette is removed from the set. Use the File | Save command to save your changes. (You cannot save the standard palette set with deleted palettes—Designer will ask you to save the file with a new name.)

LABELLING COLORS

The Edit menu contains commands that allow you to label each color in a palette, and to find a color by name:

Undo   Reverses the last change you made while creating or modifying a palette

Find   Finds a named color within a palette

Label   Lets you name a particular shade or color in a palette so that you can use Edit | Find to identify it

Size   Lets you increase the number of colors or shades that can be shown in the Color dialog box

Delete   Removes the highlighted color or shade from the palette

If you would like to name a color you have created, or would like to change the name of one of Designer's colors (except, of course, in the standard palette set), select the color and then select Edit | Label. The Color Label dialog box appears (Figure 13.7). Type the name and click on OK. That name appears in the Color dialog box below the strip of colors.

Why bother giving a color a name? If you have a range of similar hues, one of which you are using in your art, it is sometimes difficult to tell if you

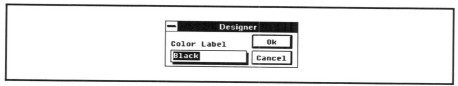

Figure 13.7: The Color Label dialog box

have selected the right one. If you label the color, though, you can make sure you are using the exact shade you want.

The label can be any size, can consist of numbers, letters, spaces, and characters, and will be centered in the dialog box when the color is selected. The dialog box can display only 34 of the characters, so there's not much point making them any longer than that. (Furthermore, long names are harder to use in the Find dialog box.)

The colors in the standard set's palettes—other than the Primaries and Greys—are not named. Unfortunately, Designer does not let you make changes to the standard palette. However, if you save the standard palette as STANDARD.PAL with the File | Save As command, you can then label the colors.

You can also use this dialog box to rename a color, or to remove a name, and Designer allows you to use the same name more than once in a palette—you could, for example, name colors according to the type of picture you are using them in, so all the colors used in a drawing would have the same name. This makes finding them with the File | Find command easy (assuming, of course, you are not using shades that are very close to each other). You can easily duplicate palette sets with the File | Save As command, and, because sets don't take up much disk space (CRAYON.PAL is only 1288 bytes), you could create a palette set for each type of art you create, and name all the colors you currently use according to the picture type.

FINDING COLORS

Once you have labelled a color, or if you are using a Designer palette with labelled colors, you can use the Edit | Find command to find the color. Type the name of the color you want to find and click on OK. Designer searches the displayed palette, from the selected color toward the right end of the palette. If Designer doesn't find the color by the time it gets to the right end, it starts searching from the left end. When Designer finds the color it places the highlight on it. The dialog box remains displayed, though—if you click on OK again Designer resumes searching for the next color with that name.

You can type the color's name in uppercase or lowercase—if you are looking for *Red* it doesn't matter if you type *Red, red,* or *RED.* You can also use wildcards. Type * to represent several missing characters, or *?* to represent one missing character. For example, if you type * and click on OK, Designer will search for *any* named color—keep clicking on OK to view every named color in the palette. If you type *b* * Designer searches for all the colors beginning with *b,* or if you type **d* Designer searches for all the colors ending with *d.* If you type *?d,* though, Designer would find only colors with two-letter names ending with *d.*

When you have finished searching for a color, click on Cancel to remove the Find dialog box.

RESIZING THE COLOR DIALOG BOX

The Edit | Size command lets you modify the size of the Color dialog box—use this command to display all the colors in the box at the same time, so you don't have to use a scroll bar to find the one you want. In the Size dialog box (Figure 13.8) click on a selection button to select whether you want colors displayed in columns or rows. The value in the text box at the top is neither the number of rows (if you selected By Row) nor the number of columns (if you selected By Column); it is the number of colors in each row

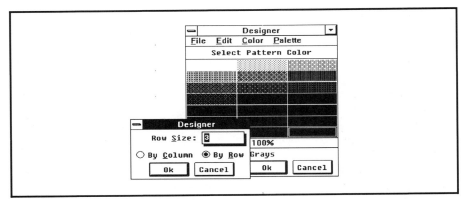

Figure 13.8: The Size dialog box

or column. For example, Figure 13.8 shows the Color dialog box after selecting By Row and entering *3* in the text box: the greys are displayed in rows, with 3 in each row.

DETERMINING A SYMBOL'S COLOR

If you need to know a symbol's color, use this procedure. Select the symbol and then open the Color dialog box. If the object's color is not in the first palette, the OK command button is ghosted. Select another palette from the Palette menu. When you find the correct palette, the object's color is highlighted, and the OK button is no longer ghosted.

EDITING THE WIN.INI FILE

3.1

If you have Designer 3.1 you can edit the Windows WIN.INI file to adjust color separations. You can adjust separations to get better color reproductions, and to fix gaps that appear at the boundaries between colors. By adding lines to the [Designer 3.1] section of the WIN.INI file, you can also tell Designer how to adjust colors when printing color separations.

At the time of this writing Micrografx acknowledged that there were still problems with the color correction procedure, and they are working on an improvement. These settings may be difficult to work with, and require some experimentation. The procedure is based on an algorithm published in the June 1987 edition of *PostScript Language*.

Colors are created by mixing four colors: cyan, magenta, yellow, and black (CMYK). But due to Windows' graphics limitations Designer only stores RGB colors (colors created with red, green, and blue). So when you print a color separation Designer has to make a conversion from the RGB model to the CMYK model. The RGB model can easily be converted to the CMY model (cyan, magenta, and yellow), but in order to complete the conversion—that is, in order to add black, the K component of CMYK—a certain amount of "fudging" is necessary. The conversion is completed by reducing each of the CMY numbers, adding the reduced amount as black, and then "boosting" the black a little more.

You reduce the amount of the CMY colors by using *Black under-color removal* (BlackUCR). Lets say, for instance, that you have added BlackUCR = 30 to WIN.INI. Designer checks to see if each of the CMY colors in a mix are above

30 percent. If they are, Designer then finds the color with the lowest value, subtracts the BlackUCR value from it, and reduces all three colors by the result. Lets say the CMY values are 100C, 100M, and 40Y. Designer subtracts the BlackUCR (30 percent) from 40 percent, and then subtracts the result (40 minus 30 = 10) from each of the CMY colors. The colors are now 90C, 90M, and 30Y. The result is then added as K (black), so the final mix is now 90C, 90M, 30Y, and 10K. All three of the CMY colors must be above the BlackUCR value, by the way. For example, if the Yellow value is 25 percent and you are using Black-UCR = 30, no changes will be made.

Having adjusted the colors, you now have a problem called *additive failure.* To fix the problem you must now boost the black to compensate for the reduction in the other three colors. With BlackUCR = 30, you may now want to enter Blackboost = 125. This increases the amount of black in the mix to 125 percent of its original value. As the original value was 10, the new value is 12.5 (125 percent of 10). Thus the final setting would be 90C, 90M, 30Y, 12.5K. The smaller the UCR value, the smaller the boost that will be required.

When you install Designer the following defaults are used. (These will not actually appear in the WIN.INI file.)

> BlackUCR = 50
> Blackboost = 125
> YellowUCR = 0
> MagentaUCR = 0

These default settings should fix most gap problems where space is left at the boundary between colors. Micrografx's art department, however, favors the following settings:

> BlackUCR = 25
> Blackboost = 150
> YellowUCR = 0
> MagentaUCR = 0

(Actually it may not be necessary to use a Blackboost setting as high as 150; you may find that 125 or 130 is sufficient.)

Generally the WIN.INI settings are used to adjust the amount of black in a color, but you can also adjust for Yellow, Cyan, and Magenta to allow for impurities in the printer's inks, and to make subtle variations in the colors. Few Designer users need this sort of fine tuning, though. If you do want to experiment, these are all the possible WIN.INI settings, in the order in which Designer will carry them out (they can appear in WIN.INI in any order you want):

CyanUCR =
MagentaUCR =
YellowUCR =
BlackUCR =
Blackboost =

14

More about Printing

In Chapter 10 you learned how to print your art using Designer's basic printing commands. Now you are going to find out about Designer's more advanced printing commands, commands that let you produce color separations, mirror images of your art, and layout information.

See Chapter 10 for information on loading printer drivers and using the Control Panel to configure printers, and using Print | Page, Print | View, Print | Change Printer, and the basic Print dialog box commands.

PRODUCING COLOR SEPARATIONS

The professional, high-resolution reproduction of color art requires *color separations*. Several sheets or separations are printed, one each for cyan, magenta, yellow, and black, or one for each color (if producing spot-color separations). The print shop then prints the layers on top of each other to create the final copy.

Producing color separations using Designer is a simple procedure, but actually understanding color separations and knowing which settings will bring the best result is not. Before you attempt printing with color separations, educate yourself: read a book on professional printing techniques, and ask your print shop for advice. I describe how to use Designer's separation features in this chapter, but to use these techniques successfully you will have to learn more about color and printing.

Some of Designer's color separation features are designed for use with the Micrografx PostScript printer driver, though you can produce simple color separations with any printer that has a Windows or Designer driver. You *cannot* use the following features, unless you use the Micrografx PostScript driver:

- process-separation color angle
- line screen setting
- spot-color spread setting

Also, you should purchase the PANTONE.PAL palette set from Micrografx if you want to use spot-color separations (see Chapter 13 for information about color palettes)—professional print shops use PANTONE colors, so you can accurately match colors if you use this palette.

You can use Designer's Separations dialog box to print process-color separations or spot-color separations, or to print both at the same time. Select File | Print to see the Print dialog box, and then select Options | Separate to see the Separations dialog box (Figure 14.1).

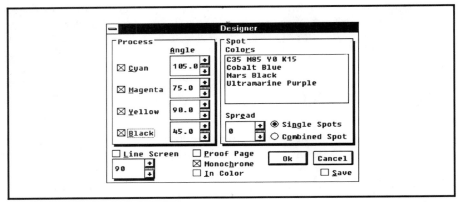

Figure 14.1: The Separations dialog box

PRODUCING
PROCESS-COLOR SEPARATIONS

Process-color printing uses four color separations: cyan, magenta, yellow, and black. By printing these four layers together, your print shop can produce "four-color" pictures. The layers are printed on top of each other, precisely aligned. In the same way that Designer uses "dithering" to produce colors on your screen—mixing dots of different colors together—four-color printing mixes dots of these four colors to produce any other color.

To print process-color separations, click on the checkboxes in the left side of the dialog box. If you are using the Micrografx PostScript driver you can also set the "angle" of the dots of ink that are printed, to avoid cloudy patterns caused by the misalignment of the dots. You can set the angle from 0 to 360 degrees. The angle required varies from machine to machine, even machines of the same models. The only way to discover the correct angle for a particular machine is by trial and error, but your print shop should be able to tell you the correct settings for their machines.

PRODUCING SPOT-COLOR SEPARATIONS

Spot-color separations print a separate sheet for each color in the drawing. Use this method with the PANTONE palette to get the most accurate rendition of your art.

Notice the list of colors in the Separations dialog box—these are the colors in your drawing. If the palette from which those colors come is loaded, the names of the colors are listed in the box. If the palette is not loaded, or if the colors don't have names (see Chapter 13 for information on naming colors), the CMYK mixture is listed instead. For example, a shade from the Violets palette in the default palettes set might have the mixture C35 M85 Y0 K15, meaning 30 percent cyan, 80 percent magenta, and 20 percent black. (This is another reason why it is a good idea to name colors—it is very hard to identify a color by its CMYK mix.)

Click on the colors for which you want to print separations, or click on a highlighted color to deselect it—if you don't want to print a spot-color separation, simply ensure that none of the colors in the Spot Colors list are selected.

You can also select Single Spots or Combined Spot. Single Spots means that Designer will print a separate sheet for each color, and Combined Spot means that it prints all the selected colors on one page.

If you are using the Micrografx PostScript printer you can adjust the colors' spread, the amount that the colors overlap. This ensures that no white space is left between colors if the colors are not exactly aligned, but adding too much spread can also make the final product look fuzzy. Talk to your print shop about the amount of spread that would be ideal for their equipment. The spread is measured in dots, and can be set from 0 to 29.

OTHER COLOR SEPARATION FEATURES

Designer has several other commands that make working with separations easier. At the bottom of the Separations dialog box you will see the following options:

Line Screen   Selects the number of dots per inch used to print the colors or grey scales, from 0 to 300. The default is 90. Low settings produce coarse images (80 might be suitable for newsprint), while higher settings produce smoother color transitions (160 could be used for magazine illustrations). This option is available only if you are using the Micrografx PostScript printer driver.

Proof Page   In addition to the separations, you will get a proof copy that shows the "final version," all the components together on one page.

Monochrome   Each separation is printed in black. At the top of the page, Designer will print the name of the color represented by the printout.

In Color   Each separation is printed in its actual color, or, on a black-and-white printer, in shades of grey. If you select both In Color and Monochrome you will receive two separation sets.

OTHER PRINT DIALOG BOX OPTIONS

There are several other options in the Print dialog box (Figure 14.2) that make print jobs easier to work with. The Layout options at the top of the dialog box help you crop and line up your art, let you label the art with the file name and page number, and cause objects that overlap pages to "bleed" into the margin.

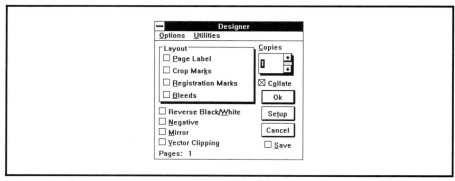

Figure 14.2: The Print dialog box

NOTE

The crop marks and registration marks print only if you have wide margins (about an inch at the top and 0.9 inches at the sides). Experiment with the margins until you have enough space for these marks. See Chapter 11 for instructions on adjusting margins.

Page Label	Prints a label on the top left of each page, showing the document name and page number
Crop Marks	Produces black lines in the corners of the page, showing the actual page size; this shows the print shop where to cut (or "crop") the page to get the correct size.
Registration Marks	Registration marks, printed outside the drawing area, help a print shop line up process-color and spot-color separations. Each registration mark is a circle with four radiating lines.
Bleeds	Selecting this option causes pictures to "bleed" over into the margins. That is, when printing a page that has an image overlapping onto the next page, the overlapping portion is printed in the margin. That allows you to join the adjoining pages together with no gap between the two parts of the image.

Figure 14.3 shows the Layout options in the margins of a page to be printed.

There are several more options at the bottom of the Print dialog box:

Reverse Black/White	This swaps black and white when the picture is printed. Why would you want to do this? Some people, used to working with programs such as AutoCAD, like to set up their screens with a black background and white lines. Unlike AutoCAD, though, Designer won't automatically convert the picture when it is printed. Use this option to print the art with a white background and black lines. Colors in the picture are unchanged by this option.

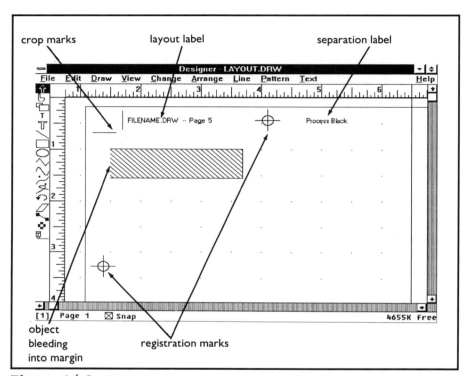

crop marks   layout label   separation label

object bleeding into margin   registration marks

Figure 14.3: The Layout options

Negative	Produces a negative image: black is printed as white, white as black, cyan as red, magenta as green, yellow as blue, 40% grey as 60% grey, and so on. Few users need this option, but some may need to produce a negative image (just like a negative of a photograph) for certain photographic processes.
Mirror	Produces a mirror image of the art: all the work is flipped left for right (and text reads backwards). This lets you use the art to make T-shirt transfers, for example, or just to create interesting effects. Not all devices support this feature, so the option

appears "ghosted" if you don't have a suitable device driver selected.

Vector Clipping   Improves the output on plotters by stopping the plotter from printing the part of an object below an overlapping object. This only works for plotters (so it is "ghosted" if you don't have a plotter driver selected), and slows down the output. Without vector clipping the plotter will draw objects one on top of another, producing transparent-looking objects, and possibly damaging the pens (if the pens have to draw over different colors).

Save   Select the Save checkbox if you want Designer to save the current settings as the defaults.

PRODUCING A PRINT FILE

You can make Designer create a print file instead of actually printing your work, and use the file to produce a printout later. For example, you may want to produce art on a device that you don't actually have. You may be sending color separations to a print shop and want to send the files rather than paper. You can load the correct device driver and set it up as if you actually have the device connected to your computer; the only difference is that instead of printing the art on paper or on film, you will "print to file."

You can then take the file to the print shop to have the final art produced, or print the art from another computer.

There are several ways to print to file:

- Using the Options | To File command in the Print dialog box

- Using the Windows EPT port

- Using the Windows FILE port

- Using the Designer MGXPrint.prn port

- Using a Windows port you create yourself

USING THE
OPTIONS | TO FILE COMMAND

Select Options | To File from the Print dialog box, and the dialog box shown in Figure 14.4 appears. Simply type the name and path name of the file you want to produce, and click on OK. Designer displays the Printer Options dialog box, the same box you saw when you selected a default printer in the Default Printer dialog box. If this is the printer with which you will be creating the print file, and if everything is set up as you want it, click on OK and Designer builds the file. Of course if this *isn't* the printer you want, you need to cancel, close the Print dialog box, and use File | Change Printer to select the appropriate one.

If you didn't include an extension in the file name the print file will be given a .PRN extension.

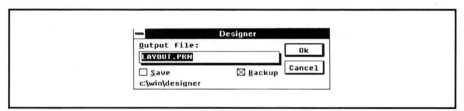

Figure 14.4: The Output File dialog box

NOTE

The Save checkbox does not work in Designer 3.01, 3.02, or the first release of 3.1.

Notice that this box also has Save and Backup checkboxes. Use these if you want to use the same path for print files the next time you open Designer, and if you want to create a backup file.

Once you have set up the Print dialog box to print to file, the Output File dialog box appears each time you select File | Print Page or File | Print View. The next time you want to actually print something, use File | Print—and when the Print dialog box appears, select Options | To Printer.

USING THE WINDOWS EPT PORT

When you start Windows it looks in the WIN.INI file—which is in the Windows directory—to see how it is supposed to act. One of the blocks of information in the WIN.INI file contains the communications ports, and one of those ports is called EPT. This is used by certain printers such as the IBM Personal Page Printer. If you don't have this type of printer, you can connect your printer to the EPT port so that when you print, a print file (called EPT), is created in the Designer directory. The advantage of this is that when you select one of the print commands Designer prints it to the file without asking you anything; you don't have to go to the Print dialog box or enter a filename or confirm the printer setup. The disadvantage is that it will always print to a file called EPT, so to avoid having the previous EPT file overwritten you must rename or move it.

When you set up your printer you can select the EPT port in the Printers-Configure dialog box (Windows 3.0) or the Printer Connections dialog box (pre-3.0 Windows).

USING THE WINDOWS FILE PORT

Windows 3.0 has another printer port called FILE. If your printer is connected to this port, Windows displays the Print To File dialog box whenever you try to print. You can enter a file name and path name in this dialog box (Figure 14.5). This method is basically the same as using the Options | To File command in the Print dialog box.

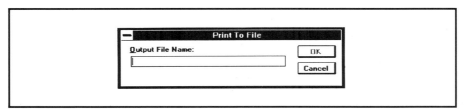

Figure 14.5: The Print To File dialog box

If you have a device driver from which you *always* want to print to file, you could connect it to the FILE port to save time. Connect the driver to the port in the Printers-Configure dialog box (Windows 3.0) or the Printer Connections dialog box (pre-3.0 Windows).

USING THE
DESIGNER MGXPRINT.PRN PORT

When you installed Designer 3.1 it added a special port called MGX-Print.prn. This works just like the EPT port. You can connect a printer to this port, and when you print, a print file (named MGXPRINT.PRN) is created and placed in the root directory.

ADDING PRINT FILES TO WIN.INI

The WIN.INI file is a file that tells Windows and Windows applications how to act when they are first opened. Most of the WIN.INI settings are made when you install Windows and Designer, or when you use additional commands described in Appendix C. The WIN.INI file is stored in the Windows directory, and can be opened using any text processor such as Windows Notepad.

You can if you wish add a port to the [ports] section in WIN.INI. Call it whatever you want—PRINTFIL or PRINTFIL.PRN, for example. Start by searching WIN.INI until you find the heading [ports]. You will see something like the following:

```
[ports]
; A line with [filename].PRN followed by an equal sign causes
; [filename] to appear in the Control Panel's Printer
  Configuration dialog
; box. A printer connected to [filename] directs its output into
this file.
LPT1: =
LPT2: =
LPT3: =
COM1: = 9600,n,8,1
COM2: = 9600,n,8,1
EPT: =
FILE: =
LPT1.OS2 =
LPT2.OS2 =
```

You can have as many as eight ports in pre-3.0 Windows, or ten ports in Windows 3.0. Few computers have that many physical ports, so you could even set up two or three print files. Type the name of the print file you want to add. Type the equals sign after the name, but don't include a colon before the equals sign like in the other port names. For example, you could add the following line:

PRNTFIL1.PRN =

You can even delete lines that are unused and replace them with print file names. When you have finished making the changes, save the file, close Windows, and reopen. See your Windows documentation for more information on modifying WIN.INI.

PRINTING YOUR PRINT FILES

Now that you have the print files, what do you do with them? Some imaging centers or print shops can use these files to produce your art, but you can also use print files to print on a device connected to a colleague's computer. For example, say you have a dot-matrix printer and want to use your colleague's HP LaserJet. Use the HP LaserJet driver to print to file, and take the file to the other printer. You can then print using the DOS COPY command.

For example, typing

copy c:\win\designer\printfil.prn lpt1 /b

at the DOS prompt prints the file called PRINTFIL.PRN from the DESIGNER directory to the lpt1 parallel computer port. The /b switch may be required; it prints the file as a "binary" file. See your DOS manual for more information. You may also be able to use the Windows File | Copy command in pre-3.0 versions of Windows (or the File Manager File | Print command in Windows 3.0) to send print files to a printer. This is not a reliable method though—it's really designed for printing text files—so you may have to go to DOS to do it.

You could use this method to create files during the day, and use a DOS batch file to print them at night, to reduce the time lost waiting for the printer.

PRINTING ON POSTSCRIPT PRINTERS

If you are trying to print very complex art, or if you have traced bitmaps with a Fine setting, you may have more points on a page than your printer can handle. PostScript printers can generally only print 1500 points on a page, and if they find more than that they may print a blank page.

You can add a line to your WIN.INI file to tell the printer to reduce the resolution of the art: in the section containing the printer settings, add the line

```
CurvePrintQuality = 5
```

Then close Windows, open again, and try printing your work. If it still doesn't work, try a lower value. When you have finished, remember to remove this line from WIN.INI.

The Micrografx PostScript printer allows you to adjust certain other settings by entering commands in the WIN.INI file. You can change the number of lines per inch, change the angle of the printed dots, send printer commands before or after the art, and turn off the printer's ability to print rotated or Béziers art, for example. See the PostScript Options dialog box's Help screens for more information, and the WIN.INI Options in the table of contents in Designer's Help screen.

3.1 BATCH PRINT

Designer 3.1's Batch Print utility lets you select a group of files, set the number of copies for each and define which pages you want, and then print all the files at once. You could set up a large print job to run at night or lunch time, for example, rather than having to open and print each file individually. You could even print files to different places—a couple of different printers, for example, or several print files. And you're not just limited to .DRW files; you can also print .TIF, .PCX, and .GRF files. (With earlier versions of Designer you have to open a Designer file before you can print it, so you can only print one at a time.)

NOTE

Batch Print is often unable to use .PCX files created by Windows 3.0 Paintbrush; Micrografx reports that Paintbrush saves its files in a nonstandard way. You can get around the problem, though, by saving the image once, then reopening the file and saving it again. Now Batch Print will be able to print the image.

Batch print is actually an independent application, just like SlideShow or TeleGrafx, so there are several ways to start it. You can use the Batch Print icon that the Designer installation program created, you can double-click on the MGXPRINT.EXE file name in File Manager, or you can open it directly from Designer; select File | Print | Utilities | Batch Print. Figure 14.6 shows the Batch Print dialog box, with several files already entered into the list.

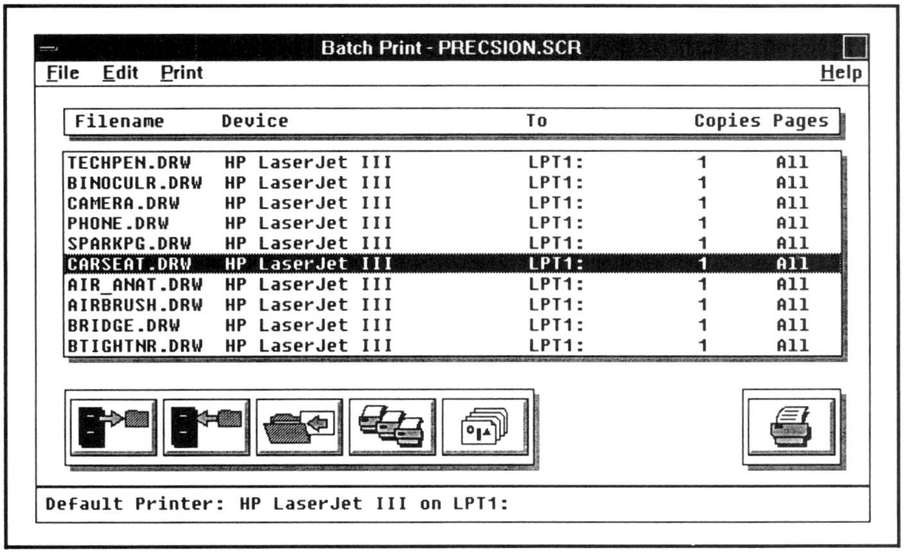

Figure 14.6: The Batch Print dialog box

Batch Print creates *print scripts,* instructions that tell Batch Print exactly what you want to print: the file names, how many copies of each, which pages in each file, which printer, and so on. The script can be saved in a .SCR file; if you have several files that you want to print often a print script can speed things up for you. You can also open and print .SHW files (Slide-Show scripts—see Chapter 16 for information on SlideShow).

The large buttons at the bottom of the dialog box duplicate several of the menu options:

First Button	File | Open
Second Button	File | Save
Third Button	File | Add File
Fourth Button	Print | Change Printer
Fifth Button	Print | Copies
Sixth Button	Print | Start

You can remove the buttons by turning off the Display Button Icons option in the Preferences dialog box (File \| Preferences).

USING THE FILE MENU

The File menu lets you select the files you want to print, or select an existing script, using the following menu options:

New	Clears the Batch Print dialog box so you can create a script
Open	Lets you select an existing .SCR or .SHW script so you can edit the script and print the files. This menu option is the same as the first icon button at the bottom of the dialog box.
Save	Saves the script. This menu option is the same as the second icon button at the bottom of the dialog box.
Save As	Lets you save a script with a new name
Add File (Ctrl-F)	Lets you add another file name to the script. This menu option is the same as the third icon button at the bottom of the dialog box.
Preferences	Displays the Batch Print Preferences dialog box, which lets you select various operating preferences
Exit	Closes Batch Print

If you have an existing script, select File | Open to see the Open File dialog box (Figure 14.7). You can click on the .SCR option button to see the print scripts, or .SHW to see the SlideShow scripts. (In fact you might want to experiment with the sample .SHW scripts loaded by Designer's installation program.)

When you open the script file the file names are displayed in the Batch Print dialog box's list box; if there are more than will fit in the list box a scroll bar is displayed. You can now add more files. Select File | Add File to see the Add File dialog box (Figure 14.8).

Select the type of file you want to add (.DRW, .GRF, .PCX, or .TIF) and then select the file name and click on OK. The selected file name is added to the end of the list. Notice the Set checkbox, by the way. This works like the Set checkbox in the Color dialog boxes; select it and the dialog box remains open so you can select one file after another without having to select File | Add File each time.

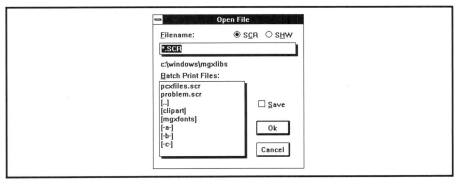

Figure 14.7: The Open File dialog box

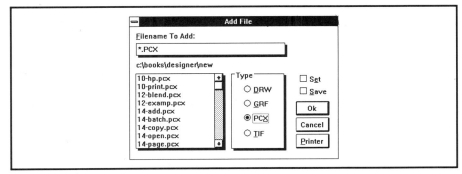

Figure 14.8: The Add File dialog box

If you want to print a file on a printer other than the default printer, click on the Printer button and select another printer from the Change Printer dialog box (Figure 14.9). Select the printer from the list box and then click on the Change button. (If you want to display the printer's Options dialog box, click on the Setup button first.) There are two option buttons: Change Default and Change Select File(s). When you display this dialog box from the Open File dialog box only the Change Default option is available. (Both options are available if you open the dialog box using the Print | Change Printer command). Change Default simply means that you are changing the default printer for all files you add. All files added subsequently will use this printer, until you select the Change Printer dialog box and change again.

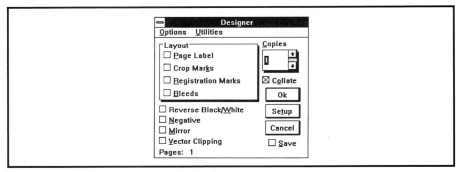

Figure 14.9: The Change Printer dialog box

Changing Preferences

You can use the File | Preferences command to change the program's preferences. The Preferences dialog box is shown in Figure 14.10.

The Preferences dialog box lets you select several checkboxes:

Record error log	Keeps track of error messages that are generated while printing by placing them in an ASCII file with the same name as the script and a .ERR extension. If the script doesn't have a name—if it hasn't been saved—the error log will be named BATCH.ERR. The file is placed in the directory specified when you click on the Directories button (which is the subject of the next list).

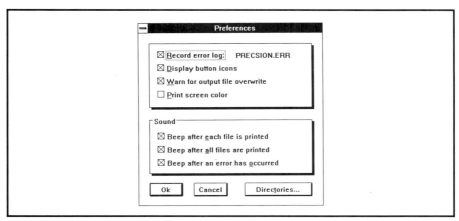

Figure 14.10: The Preferences dialog box

Display button icons	Turns the icon buttons—the buttons at the bottom of the Batch Print dialog box—on and off.
Warn for output file overwrite	Displays a warning if the batch-print operation will create a print file when an existing print file has the same name. The warning will appear when you begin the batch print job, and you will have the chance to continue (thus overwriting the file) or abort the entire print job.
Print screen color	If you print a file from Designer, the drawing-area color (set using View | Screen Color) is printed. The Print Screen Color option lets you print files without the screen color being printed.
Beep after each file is printed	Makes a beep sound when a file is printed.
Beep after all files are printed	Makes a beep sound when the batch-print operation is finished.
Beep after an error has occurred	Makes a beep each time an error occurs.

If you click on the Directories button the Set Directories dialog box appears (Figure 14.11). This is where you define which directories Batch Print will use. Click on the appropriate option button and then select the directory you want to use. Click on the Set button to set that directory, and then click on the next option button or click on Close to close the dialog box.

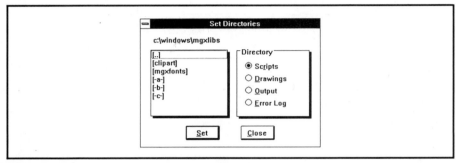

Figure 14.11: The Set Directories dialog box

You can specify four directories:

Scripts   Sets the default Scripts directory, the directory that will be displayed when you select Files | Open. (This directory is also set when you select a file in the Open File dialog box while the Save checkbox is selected.)

Drawings   Sets the default Drawings directory, the directory that will be displayed when you select Files | Add File. (This directory is also set when you select a file in the Add File dialog box while the Save checkbox is selected.)

Output   Sets the directory in which print files will be placed

Error Log   Sets the directory in which the error log will be placed

USING THE EDIT MENU AND SELECTING FILES

The Edit menu lets you cut and copy file names from the list of files to be printed, paste file names back into the list, and select or deselect all the file names in the list. This can be extremely useful when you want to print certain files on two different printers or if you want to shuffle the order of the files in the batch so that the printouts you need right away are done first. The Edit menu options are presented below:

Cut (Shift-Del)	Removes the highlighted file name from the list, placing the name in the clipboard
Copy (Ctrl-Ins)	Copies the highlighted file name from the list, placing the name in the clipboard
Paste (Shift-Ins)	Copies the file names from the clipboard back into the list, immediately after the highlighted file name. (Paste won't work if you haven't selected a file name.)
Delete (Del)	Removes the highlighted file name from the list
Select All (F2)	Highlights all the file names in the list
Deselect All (Ctrl-F2)	Removes the highlight from all file names in the list

There are several ways to select files. You can use the Edit | Select All (*Keyboard Shortcut: F2*) and Edit | Deselect All (*Keyboard Shortcut: Ctrl-F2*) commands; you can click on an individual file name; you can press Shift and click on two file names to select those files and all the files in between; or you can press Ctrl and click on file names to select and deselect them (without selecting the files between). You can also select a block of file names using the keyboard—by pressing Shift and then the up or down arrow key. (You can't use the keyboard to select noncontiguous file names, though).

USING THE PRINT MENU

The Print menu lets you specify exactly what you want to print and how you want to print it:

Pages (Ctrl-P)	Lets you select the pages you want printed in the highlighted files
Copies (Ctrl-C)	Lets you select the number of copies needed for the highlighted files. This menu option is the same

as the fifth icon button at the bottom of the dialog box.

Copy To (Ctrl-T)	Lets you redirect a highlighted file. (The file must be one that is being sent to a "print-file" port.)
Remove Hidden Lines	This option is only available when you are printing to a plotter. It does the same as the Vector Clipping checkbox in Designer's Print dialog box, improving output by stopping the plotter from drawing the parts of objects that are overlapped by other objects.
Change Printer (Ctrl-H)	Lets you select another printer for the highlighted files. This menu option is the same as the fourth icon button at the bottom of the dialog box.
Setup Printer (Ctrl-E)	Displays the Printer Options dialog box for the current printer (which is not necessarily the same printer selected for the highlighted file)
Start (Ctrl-S)	Begins printing the files in the script. This menu option is the same as the sixth icon button at the bottom of the dialog box.

Specifying the Pages

You can specify exactly which pages should be printed in each file. (If you don't specify which pages should be printed Batch Print will print all of them—all the ones that contain drawings, that is.) Select the file (or select several files) and then select Print | Pages. You will see the Pages dialog box (Figure 14.12).

When the dialog box first appears all the pages are selected, but you can click on the None button to deselect all the pages and then select just one or two (click on All to reselect all the pages). If you don't have a mouse you can press the arrow keys to move around, but each time the cursor lands on a page it will select it. The space bar toggles the page also, so you may have to press arrow-space-arrow-space and so on to cross pages to get to the page you want to select. Only .DRW files have pages, by the way; if you open one of the other types you will find that there is only one "page."

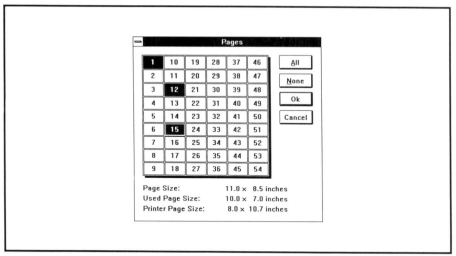

Figure 14.12: The Pages dialog box

Selecting the Number of Copies

Batch Print will normally print one copy of each file, unless you tell it otherwise. Select the file or files you want to print more copies of, and then select Print | Copies. The Copies dialog box appears (Figure 14.13). You can enter however many copies you need, from 1 to 999, and click on OK.

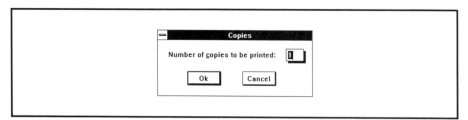

Figure 14.13: The Copies dialog box

Redirecting the Print Output

If one of your files is being sent to a print-file port, you can redirect the output. For example, say you have told Batch Print to print a file on the Micrografx PostScript driver to a printer port called PRNTFIL1.PRN (you learned about print files earlier in this chapter). You can use the Print | Copy To command to redirect the output to a file with a different name, or to a printer port. Figure 14.14 shows the Copy To dialog box.

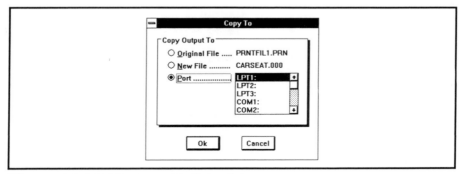

Figure 14.14: The Copy To dialog box

There are three Copy To option buttons:

Original File	The file is directed to the original print-file port.
New File	The file is directed to a print-file port with a different name. The name will be the same as the file's name, with a .000 extension. However, if you copy the file name and paste it into the list (perhaps you want one copy of some pages but two or three of others), the extension on subsequent print files in that script will be incremented; the first copy will be .001, the second .002, and so on.
Port	The file will be directed to the print-file port, which is then copied to the port you select from the list box (you can only redirect the file to an actual hardware port, not to another print-file port). You could use this option if you wanted to create a print file and print the file at the same time. But make sure that the printer connected to the port is compatible with the print file. For example, you couldn't send the file to the driver named "PostScript (Micrografx) on PRINTFIL1.PRN" and then use the Port option to copy the file to a port with a non-PostScript printer.

You can tell which files have been redirected with the Print | Copy To command: they have an asterisk next to the port name in the Batch Print box's *To* column.

Specifying a Different Printer

You don't have to send all the files to the same printer. You could send some files to your LaserJet on LPT1 and others to your Epson dot matrix on LPT2, for example. You could also send some to print files. To select a different printer or print file for a particular file (or group of files), select it and then select Print | Change Printer. You will see the Change Printer dialog box (Figure 14.9), the box you saw when you clicked on the Printer button in the Add File dialog box. But the dialog box is slightly different now; the Select File(s) option is now selected (remember that if you open the box from the Add File dialog box the Select File(s) option is ghosted). The printer you now select is the one the highlighted files will be sent to. If you click on the Default option button and then select a printer, the highlighted files are not changed, but all files added subsequently will be directed to the selected printer. (Of course if you select Print | Change Printer while no files are highlighted the Default option button is already selected).

PRINTING YOUR FILES

When everything is ready, select Print | Start and the batch job will begin. You will see a status box that shows the elapsed time, the current operation (Loading, Printing, Copying, or Skipping), and file information (Figure 14.15).

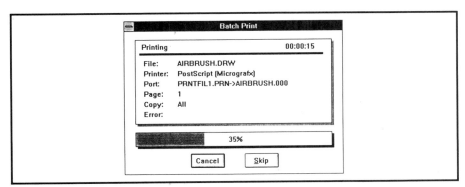

Figure 14.15: The Batch Print status box

Notice that in Figure 14.15 the Port line shows that the file is being sent to a print-file port (PRNTFIL1.PRN), which is being redirected to another print-file name (AIRBRUSH.000). There are two buttons in this status box: Cancel, which aborts the print operation, and Skip, which skips the file being printed at that moment.

Each time you run a batch print job an error file is created—even if there are no errors. The file is an ASCII file that you can open in a word processor; it's stored in the directory you specified in the Set Directories dialog box. This would be especially helpful if you run a batch print job while you are at lunch, for example, because you will be able to read the error file to find out if the operation went smoothly, and, if not, you will also be able to determine what went wrong.

15

Producing Slides and Using TeleGrafx

You have learned how to produce Designer's art on paper in your office or home, and you have learned about producing color separations using a print shop. But what if you want to use a photographic process to produce your work? One of the most popular products for business graphics is the 35mm slide, but you can use Designer's art to produce other products as well: color or black-and-white prints, flip charts, offset printing, overhead transparencies, etc.

Designer has three ways to produce these items:

- **Matrix film recorder driver**   prints your work directly to a Matrix film recorder, or to a .SCD (SCODL) print file that can be put on floppy disk, taken to an imaging center, and printed on a Matrix film recorder.

- **TeleGrafx-Slidemasters driver**   produces .SCD Matrix files for transmission to Slidemasters. These files can be used to produce slides, prints, overheads, etc. Also allows you to transmit .DRW files to Slidemasters.

- **TeleGrafx-MAGICorp driver**   produces .SLI-format files and transmits them to MAGICorp or puts them on floppy disk. These are used on Celco film recorders to produce slides, or can be used to produce Canon color laser prints, Cibachrome photographic prints, transparencies, etc.

At the time of this writing, TeleGrafx—the telecommunications program—can only be used when transmitting files to Slidemasters (Richardson, Texas) or MAGICorp (Elmsford, New York). (The European version is being shipped with a driver for EGG's COMPUTERGRAPHICS in Germany.) Micrografx hopes other companies will soon join this service, but in any case, if you have a favorite imaging center that *can't* use the TeleGrafx program, they can probably still receive your work over telephone lines

---

NOTE

The TeleGrafx drivers were still in development at the time of writing; when you contact Slidemasters or MAGICorp, ask them for the latest program. The instructions in this chapter will vary slightly depending on the changes made.

---

using a generic telecommunications program, or you can send the file on a disk—call them for details.

This chapter describes two procedures: using Designer to produce art that can be used to produce slides, and using TeleGrafx to transmit your slide files to Slidemasters or MAGICorp.

PREPARING THE DRIVER

Before you produce your art you should load the driver you are going to use to generate the slides. These are loaded during the Designer installation procedure (see Appendix A). During this procedure Designer gives you the option of loading the printer drivers. Select the Matrix driver from this list if you are not going to use TeleGrafx. Select TeleGrafx if you want to use the services of either MAGICorp or Slidemasters (see the end of the chapter for their addresses).

Once the drivers are installed you must enter Designer and configure the drivers in the Control Panel, using the same procedure explained in Chapter 10 for installing printers. If you are using TeleGrafx, of course, the driver is connected to one of your computer's serial communications ports.

MODEM SETTINGS

When you set up your communications port in the Windows Ports-Settings dialog box (Windows 3.0) or the Communications Settings dialog box (pre-3.0 Windows), use these modem settings:

SETTING	MAGICORP	SLIDEMASTERS
baud rate	1200 or 2400	up to 9600
bits	8	8
parity	no	no
stop bit	1	1
flow control	none	none

USING THE MATRIX DRIVER

If you have your own Matrix film recorder, or don't plan to use Tele-Grafx (for instance, if you plan to send the files on disks, or use another tele-communications program), load the Matrix driver, following the procedure described in Chapter 10. If you have your own Matrix recorder you will assign the driver to the port to which the recorder is connected. If you don't have your own Matrix recorder, assign the driver to None.

Figure 15.1 shows the Matrix Options dialog box, displayed when you click on Setup in the Printers-Configure dialog box (Windows 3.0) or when you select the Matrix driver in the Default Printer dialog box and click on OK (pre-3.0 Windows).

NOTE

If you own a Matrix film recorder you should have received special software for outputting files to the recorder, and documentation explaining how to use it. The rest of this chapter assumes you are using an imaging center, not your own machine.

The Matrix Options dialog box has a number of settings, so you should talk to your imaging center—or read thoroughly your film recorder's documentation—before you try to produce slides. These are the options:

File | Change Output Directory	Lets you tell the driver where to place the .SCD files

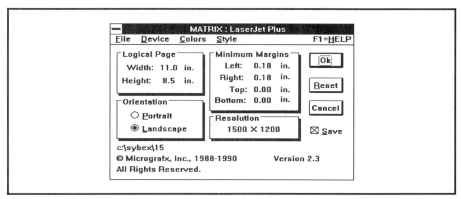

Figure 15.1: The Matrix Options dialog box

File | Confirm Picture Filename	If this option has a checkmark, the driver will display a filename box each time you print a file, so you can change the file name. Otherwise, it just adds a number to each file name.
File | Append Log File	If this option has a checkmark next to it a log file is produced for each file, and placed in the output directory. The file contains a list of colors, fonts, the date and time, etc.
Device	Select the specific output device from a list of film recorders and printers. You can use the Colors | Reverse Black and White command to output to the printers.
Colors | Background Solid	Uses the screen color in your drawing area as the background color on your slide. Use View | Screen Color to change the color.
Colors | Background Gradient	Lets you add a color gradient background to your slide
Colors | Picture Intensity	Lets you adjust the contrast and lightness of the picture (it doesn't affect the background you selected). The Contrast setting adjusts the level of color shading in the image—the higher the contrast, the fewer the shades, so the closer to black-and-white; the lower the contrast, the more shading and subtlety. The Lightness setting adjusts the amount of white. The higher the lightness, the more white in the colors.
Colors | Picture Saturation	The Picture Saturation dialog box lets you select the level of color saturation in your picture (again, not the background). The higher the saturation level, the purer the color; the lower the level, the more grey the image has. Threshold determines *which* colors are affected by the saturation command. A 40 percent saturation threshold, for example, means that colors that are 40 percent or more pure will be saturated; colors below 40 percent are not adjusted.

Colors | Picture Filter	Lets you filter out certain colors. The Additive option allows you to remove reds, greens, and blues, and the Subtractive options let you remove cyan, magenta, and yellow.
Colors | Device Colors	Lets you select Pure Colors (up to 16 million colors) or Color Palette (256 colors). The first option produces very big files, and takes more time to produce the image. If you use the latter option a message will tell you if your image has too many colors for the palette—this could happen if you are using gradients. If you choose OK the colors are converted to the nearest equivalent in the palette.
Colors | Reverse Black and White	Reverses the image so you can print on one of the black-and-white printers in the Devices list, such as the HP LaserJet. You can use this option to print a preview.

The following menu options do not appear in the Matrix driver installed by Designer 3.1, as they are obsolete. There is no longer any need to adjust line width, and all the Matrix fonts are installed automatically; you can see them all in Designer's Font dialog box when the Printer checkbox is selected. They are listed here for those who have earlier version of the program.

Style | Line Width	Lets you adjust the width of the lines in objects, vector text, and crop marks. Normal is the standard "hairline." Designer's dotted and dashed lines are converted to solid lines when you create a slide using the Matrix driver. You will usually leave this setting on normal; the other settings are rarely used, though they may be necessary if you have many polygons in your drawings.
Style | Fonts	Lets you select the fonts you wish to use, from a choice of about 30. To save memory, select only the fonts you will actually use, and don't use more than five per slide.

As you can see, there is a lot you can do to adjust your slides. It is beyond the scope of this book to explain color saturation and filtering and so on, so talk to your imaging center about these options; they will be able to tell you the best settings to work with.

USING THE TELEGRAFX-SLIDEMASTERS DRIVER

The TeleGrafx-Slidemasters driver is a Matrix driver, built into the Tele-Grafx program that allows the files to be transmitted to Slidemasters. The only real difference between setting up the Matrix driver and the TeleGrafx-Slidemasters driver is that you must connect the latter to the communications port to which your modem is connected, and then configure the port in the Ports Settings dialog box (Windows 3.0) or the Communications Settings dialog box (pre-3.0 Windows or runtime Windows).

USING THE TELEGRAFX-MAGICORP DRIVER

Some of the early versions of the MAGICorp driver did not work with Windows 3.0 in 386 enhanced mode—if you want to use one of these MAGI-Corp drivers you must open Windows 3.0 in *real* mode by typing win /r at the DOS prompt.

In addition, if you create MAGICorp files and then close the TeleGrafx window (the window opens automatically when you create a file), you will not be able to open TeleGrafx again through the Print dialog box—at least not until you have closed Designer and Windows and reopened them. (Opening TeleGrafx through the Print dialog box is explained later in this chapter.) If you have Designer 3.1, though, you will not have these problems with your MAGICorp driver.

If you want to use the MAGICorp services you must call to establish an account; before calling check the version of the MAGICorp driver you have and ask them if they can send you the latest driver. (You can see the version number when you open the MAGICorp Options dialog box from the Select Printer dialog box.)

Install the MAGICorp driver as explained in Chapter 10, connecting the driver to the communications port. When the MAGICorp Options dialog box is displayed, select the directory in which you want the .SLI files saved. The box displayed in Figure 15.2 is from the driver shipped with Designer 3.0; more recent versions allow you to select fonts and to turn off "Verify slide file name," the dialog box that asks for a file name when you print. The MAGICorp driver has up to 84 Bitstream font families, a total of over 200 fonts. (A *family* comprises several variations of the same font: italic, bold, etc.)

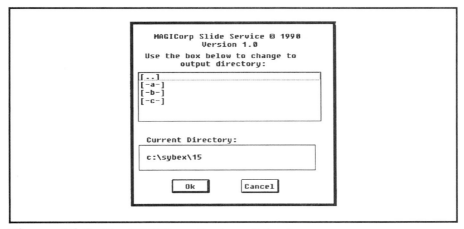

Figure 15.2: The MAGICorp Options dialog box

MAGICorp uses a proprietary file format, .SLI, which is used by its Celco film recorders. The Celcos can produce slides with an 8000-line resolution, depending on the film used—MAGICorp usually uses Ekta-chrome, which provides a 4250 dot by 2060 dot resolution.

PREPARING THE SLIDES

Having set up your driver, you should now set the page size. Go to the Pages dialog box (View | Pages) and click on the Page Area selection button. This will give you the correct page size, borders, and orientation. Here are a few points to remember when you produce your art:

- Dotted and dashed lines are converted to solid lines by the Matrix driver.

- Don't use screen fonts, or device fonts other than those provided by the driver with which you will create the slide.

- Slidemasters recommends that you use outline fonts converted to curves rather than the Matrix fonts.

- You can't add underlines or strikethrough to Matrix fonts. Use outline fonts instead.

- If you use Matrix fonts, don't resize or rotate them.

- MAGICorp recommends that you use only their fonts, to ensure perfect kerning (spacing between characters). You can still use outline fonts, though—but you should convert them to curves. You can use underline and strikethrough.

- To make the slide file smaller, and to make it generate quickly, use only the device fonts, those provided by the Matrix or MAGICorp drivers.

- You can use gradients and bitmaps in your slides, but they may slow the imaging process.

ADDING
BACKGROUNDS TO YOUR SLIDES

There are several ways you can add backgrounds to a slide:

- Change the screen color (View | Screen Color)
- Add a colored rectangle in the background
- Use the Matrix driver to add backgrounds
- Use the Backgrounds dialog box in the TeleGrafx-MAGICorp window to add backgrounds

The simplest way to add a background is to change the screen color, the color of Designer's drawing area, using the View | Screen Color command. If you want to use the screen color make sure that you select Colors | Background Solid in the Matrix Options dialog box, or Original in the MAGICorp Backgrounds dialog box (explained later in this chapter).

You can also draw a large rectangle in the drawing area and fill it with a gradient or solid color using Designer's Pattern | Gradient or Pattern | Color commands. Then place the rest of the art on top of this background.

It is faster, and the file produced is smaller, if you have the driver or imaging center add the background for you. You can use the Colors | Background Gradient command in the Matrix Options dialog box to add a gradient background—a dialog box appears that allows you to select the colors.

If you select Colors | Background Solid in the Matrix Options dialog box, a dialog box appears. Don't make any changes in this box; simply click on OK to close it. In Designer 3.01 the settings in this dialog box are ignored, and the color you have as your screen color—the drawing area color—is used as the background color.

NOTE

The Matrix driver is also used with programs other than Designer. In these other programs the Matrix driver's Background Solid settings might not be ignored.

If you use one of the commands in the Matrix Options dialog box, you must add the gradient *before* you produce the .SCD file.

If you are using the MAGICorp driver you can use the Info | Backgrounds command in the TeleGrafx-MAGICorp window, which will be described later in this chapter. MAGICorp has over 50 special backgrounds available, such as the marble or the dollar-bill background. The MAGICorp backgrounds are added *after* you have produced the .SLI file, because the background you want to use is described in the information files that are transmitted to MAGICorp when you send the slide files. Remember that your art sits on top of the MAGICorp background, so if you added a gradient box or any other type of background in the original file, the MAGICorp background will be obscured.

Most imaging centers use the Matrix SCODL files, so you can add backgrounds from the Matrix driver. Some centers may also be able to add backgrounds for you. Ask your center for details.

GENERATING THE SLIDES

Once the image is ready, print your art using the File | Print Page command. You will see a filename dialog box that allows you to modify the name (unless you are using the Matrix or TeleGrafx-Slidemasters driver and turned off the File | Confirm Picture Filename option or turned off the "Verify slide file name" option in some versions of the MAGICorp driver). Enter the file name and click on OK and the file is generated. A dialog box will probably appear displaying the message "Page size too large—reduce to fit?" This may be due to some kind of software rounding error. Click on No if this question appears. You will then see another dialog box telling you "Image received by TeleGrafx." This means the TeleGrafx window has opened. (It will be stored as an icon at the bottom of your screen, under the Designer window if Designer is maximized). Click on the OK button, and continue with the next slide.

When you have finished all your slides you are ready to go to the Tele-Grafx window and transmit them. Before you do so, however, you might like to "preview" your slides using Designer's SlideShow application. This will let you see, on your screen, what your slides are going to look like. See Chapter 16 for more information.

USING TELEGRAFX

TeleGrafx lets you transmit your art across telephone lines—using a modem, of course—to MAGICorp and Slidemasters. You can use this utility to transmit files directly to the imaging center, saving the time and cost of delivering or mailing the disks.

OPENING TELEGRAFX

There are three ways to open TeleGrafx. (Note that you must have already connected the driver to one of the communications ports.)

- The window is automatically opened when you print a file using one of the TeleGrafx drivers.
- You can open it from Designer.
- You can open it from Windows.

As described in the preceding section, the TeleGrafx program was automatically opened as an icon at the bottom of the screen when you "printed" your slides. (You won't be able to see it if the Designer window covers the entire screen, though.)

Press Alt-Tab until the TeleGrafx window title bar appears. Release Alt-Tab, and the TeleGrafx window appears. Alternatively, close Designer (to make best use of available memory), and then double-click on the TeleGrafx icon. (If you don't have a mouse, use the Alt-Tab method to open the window.)

Even if you *haven't* just produced slides, you may still want to open TeleGrafx—to enter the login information, for example, or "just to look around." You can open it from Designer by selecting File | Print to display the Print dialog box, and then selecting Utilities | TeleGrafx. The Imaging Center dialog box appears (Figure 15.3). If nothing happens when you select Utilities | TeleGrafx, the TeleGrafx window is already open somewhere—use Alt-Tab repeatedly to find it. Select the imaging center you want to use, and click on OK.

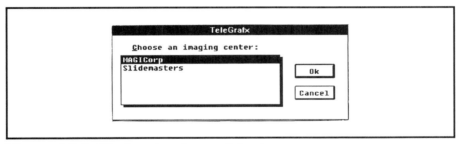

Figure 15.3: The Imaging Center dialog box

You can also open TeleGrafx directly from Windows. If you have Windows 3.0, go to the Program Manager [Windows Applications] window and click on the TeleGrafx Application icon.

If you have a pre-3.0 version of Windows, go to the MS-DOS EXECUTIVE window, display the DESIGNER directory, and double-click on the file named TELEGRFX.EXE. The Imaging Center dialog box appears. Select the imaging center you want to use and click on OK.

NOTE
If you have Designer 3.1 you can bypass the Imaging Center dialog box by clicking on the MAGICorp or Slidemasters icons in the Micrografx Program Group window.

Whichever method you use, the result is the same: the TeleGrafx window is displayed (Figure 15.4). The window lists all the files in the appropriate directory (the directory selected in the Matrix or MAGICorp Options dialog box). The procedures for using the two drivers are very similar, so I will describe how to use the MAGICorp driver first, and then explain the differences in the Slidemaster driver.

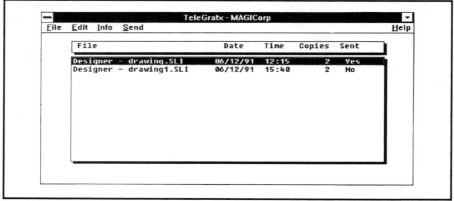

Figure 15.4: The TeleGrafx-MAGICorp window

TRANSMITTING WITH TELEGRAFX-MAGICORP

The TeleGrafx window has four menus, with the following options:

FILE MENU

Record Session (Ctrl-R) Creates a .TXT file of the telecommunications session, recording logons, prompts, responses, etc. You can use a word processing program to read .TXT files.

Exit Closes the TeleGrafx window

EDIT MENU

Cut (Shift-Del)   Removes the selected file names from the list, and places them into the clipboard. If you close Tele-Grafx without pasting the names back into the list (or if you cut or paste other files before pasting the first set), *the files are deleted from the directory, with no warning!*

Copy (Ctrl-Ins)   Copies the selected file names into the clipboard.

Paste (Shift-Ins)   Copies the file names in the clipboard back in-to the TeleGrafx window. If no file name is se-lected, the names are pasted to the end of the list, but if a name *is* selected the names are pasted *after* the selected name, allowing you to insert files between others. (If more than one is selected the names are pasted after the highest selected file name in the list.)

Delete (Del)   Deletes the selected file from the directory. A warning dialog box appears, asking you to con-firm the deletion.

Select All (F2)   Selects (highlights) all the names in the list

Modem (Ctrl-D)   Opens the modem dialog box, where you enter modem settings

INFO MENU

Login   Opens the Login dialog box where you enter your MAGICorp account number

Deliver To   Opens the Deliver To dialog box, where you enter your name and address

Media   Lets you select the type of product you need

Copies   Lets you select the number of copies of each type of medium

Backgrounds   Lets you select from MAGICorp's special backgrounds

SEND MENU

Automatic   Automatically transmits the selected files to MAGICorp

To Disk   Copies the selected files onto floppy disk

Selecting Files

To use the Edit menu commands and the Info | Copies command you must select the slide on which you want to work. Click on a slide either to select it or deselect it.

If you are using the keyboard, press the right or down arrow keys or Home to move down the list, and the left or up arrow keys or End to move up the list. You can select a block of slides by pressing the arrow keys while holding down the Shift key. You can also use Edit | Select All (Keyboard Shortcut: F2) to select all the files in the list at once.

Make sure you have the right ones selected or you may carry out operations on the wrong files.

Shuffling the Files

As long as the files remain in the directory, they will appear in the list, and all the files in the list are transmitted. This means that on occasion you will have more files in the list than you really want to send.

NOTE

This may be changed in later MAGICorp drivers to work more like the Slidemasters driver, which transmits only the slides indicated in the Copies column.

You can use the Cut and Paste commands to remove the files, transmit the remaining files, and then paste the files back into the list. If you *Cut* a file and forget to Paste it back before you close TeleGrafx, that file will be *deleted from the directory, without any warning to you*. The *Delete* command, on the other hand, lets you remove files from the directory intentionally. When you select the files you want to remove and press Delete, TeleGrafx displays a dialog box asking you to confirm that you want to delete the files. Click on OK, and they are removed from the directory.

You can also use the Copy command to print a list of the slides. Press F2 to select all the slides, then select Edit | Copy; all the information in the list is copied into the clipboard. You can then copy this information into another Windows application and print the list.

Preparing For Transmission

Before you are ready to transmit your files you must enter information concerning your modem and account. First, select Edit | Modem to see the Modem Settings dialog box (Figure 15.5).

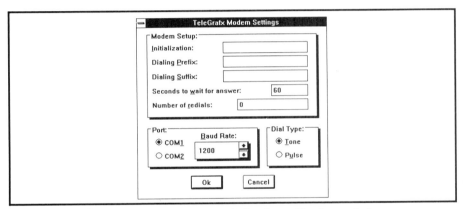

Figure 15.5: The Modem Settings dialog box, Designer 3.1

Initialization	The number required to access the modem, if you are using an office phone system. Enter ! or { to duplicate a carriage return.
Dialing Prefix	The number required to get an outside line
Dialing Suffix	Any numbers required before dialing the MAGI-Corp number, such as the number of a long-distance network
Seconds to wait	The number of seconds to wait for MAGICorp to respond, from 0 to 9999
Number of redials	The number of times to retry if MAGICorp doesn't answer

Port	The communications port to which the modem is connected (should be the same as the port to which you connected the driver)
Dial Type	If your phone "beeps" when you dial, select Tone; if it "click-click-clicks," select Pulse.
Baud Rate	If you have Designer 3.1 you can select a baud rate of 1200, 2400, or Automatic, which lets MAGICorp select according to your modem. Earlier versions use the baud rate set in Windows' Ports dialog box.

3.1

Next, select Info | Login to display the Login dialog box (Figure 15.6). Enter the account code (Site Code) that MAGICorp gave you. The telephone number your modem will dial is probably the "US Residents" number near the bottom of the box. This number is good from any place in the United States, including local (New York) calls. Only enter a number in the Other box if MAGICorp instructed you to do so.

Select Info | Deliver to see the Deliver To dialog box (Figure 15.7). This box is self-explanatory—just enter the required information.

Select Info | Media to see the Media dialog box (Figure 15.8).

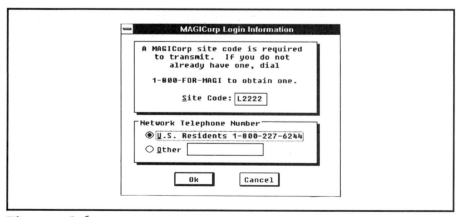

Figure 15.6: The Login dialog box

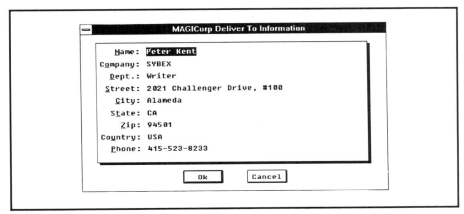

Figure 15.7: The Deliver To dialog box

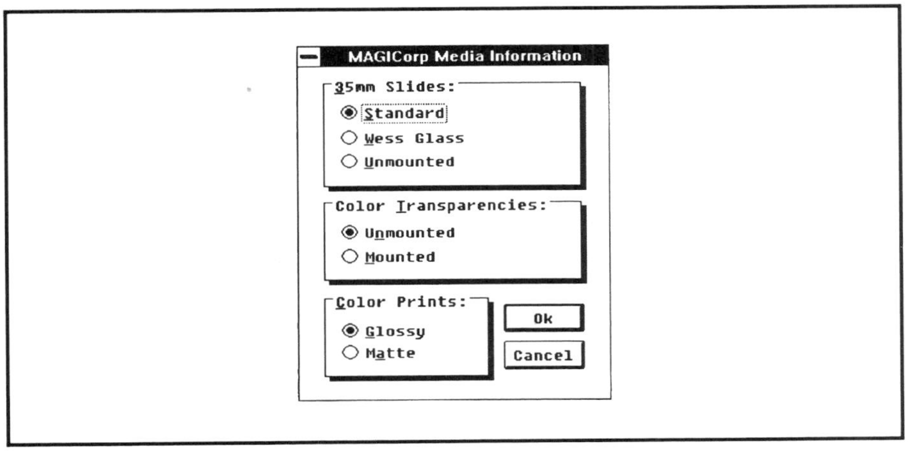

Figure 15.8: The Media dialog box

This dialog box doesn't *define* the medium to be delivered; rather, it's a "what if" box. *If* you order 35mm slides, do you want standard, Wess glass, or unmounted? *If* you order color transparencies, do you want unmounted or mounted? *If* you order color prints, do you want glossy or matte? You actually order using the Info | Copies command, which displays the Copies dialog box (Figure 15.9).

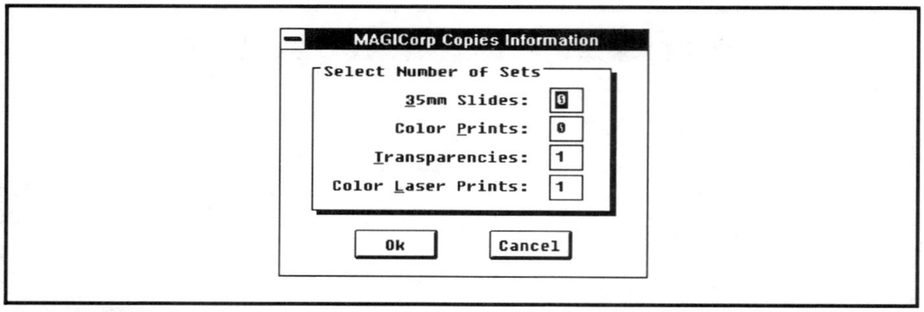

Figure 15.9: The Copies dialog box

Select Info | Copies, select the number of copies of each type of media, and click on OK—the Copies column in the TeleGrafx window is modified to reflect the changes you made.

NOTE

At the time of this writing the MAGICorp driver shipped with Designer modifies *all* the slides in the window according to the number of copies you select, not just the highlighted copies. Later versions of the driver may work differently. The Slidemasters driver lets you select the number of copies for each file individually.

MAGICorp has a number of special backgrounds you can add to your slides. Select the files to which you want to apply a background and select Info | Backgrounds to see the Backgrounds dialog box (Figure 15.10).

There are five types of background: Original (the art is printed with the screen color you applied to the drawing area), Solid (a solid color), Graded (graduated colors), Showstopper (special backgrounds such as dollar bills or marble), and Shadows, which allows you to add shadows to the objects in your art.

Click on the type of background you want, and the appropriate area of the dialog box is "unghosted," allowing you to make the changes. If you select a solid background you can then adjust the color of Color 1, the small sample box in the left side of the Colors area; you adjust the color by mixing the red, green, and blue in the scroll-bar boxes. If you select Graded you can adjust both Color 1 and Color 2, as well as select the type of gradation—from top to bottom, from the middle out to the top and bottom, or one of

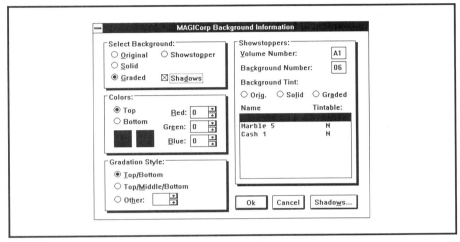

Figure 15.10: The Backgrounds dialog box

MAGICorp's special gradations, selected from the scroll-bar box. At the time of this writing MAGICorp had six special gradations, including radial and top left to bottom right.

If you select Showstopper you can enter the volume and background numbers of the design you want (see the MAGICorp brochure), and, where available, the background tint. The list box displays several backgrounds—click on the one you want and the volume and background numbers change. More than fifty are available. Talk to MAGICorp for details.

If you select Shadows the Shadows command button in the lower right corner "unghosts." Click on that button and the Shadows dialog box appears (Figure 15.11).

The Shadow Direction box within this dialog box lets you select the way the shadow will fall—notice that when you select one of the buttons the icon to the right changes to show you the direction you selected. You can then use the scroll bars to select the Shadow Properties: the darkness, the distance, and the sharpness of the shadow.

Transmitting the Files

Now that you have made your selections, you are ready to transmit. First, make sure your modem is on and ready to receive the files. Select Send | Automatic, and the Copies dialog box is displayed again, so you can

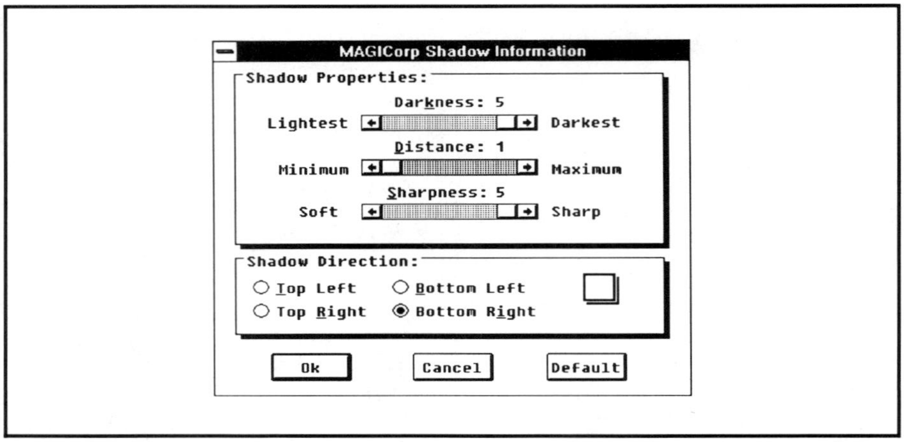

Figure 15.11: The Shadows dialog box

confirm the settings. When you click on OK you will see the Order Information dialog box, shown in Figure 15.12 (unless you didn't fill in the login, delivery, payment, and media information, in which case these dialog boxes are displayed first).

You *must* enter a Presentation Name (any name, as a reference to that set of files); if you want, you can also enter a priority setting and comments. When you click on OK the transmission begins.

The driver compresses the files, initializes the modem, and begins transmission. Figure 15.13 shows the Transmission window. The Cancel

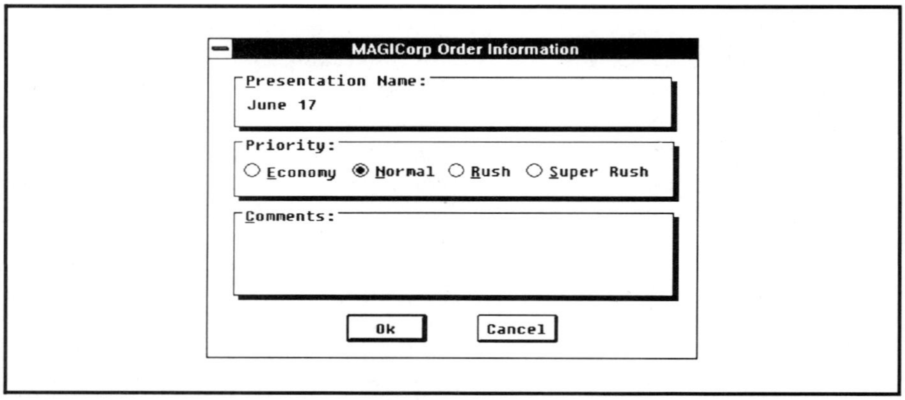

Figure 15.12: The Order Information dialog box

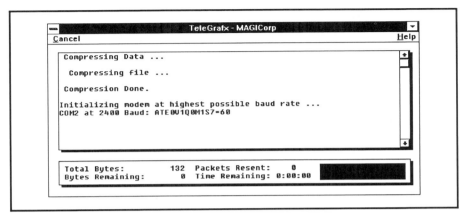

Figure 15.13: The TeleGrafx-MAGICorp Transmission window

menu option lets you abort the operation, and the Redial option becomes available if there is no answer—use this option to tell TeleGrafx to try again. When the operation is completed the menu bar shows the Done option; click on this to end the session.

Putting the Files on Disk   The MAGICorp driver lets you load the slide files onto a disk using the Send | To Disk command. You might want to do this if the files are very large, for example, or if you don't have a modem. You still have to enter the same information, but the driver prompts you for a disk drive on which to copy the files. You can then mail the disk to MAGICorp.

USING THE SLIDEMASTERS DRIVER

The TeleGrafx-Slidemasters driver differs from the TeleGrafx-MAGICorp driver in several ways. It doesn't have the Info | Backgrounds or Send | To Disk options (you can add the backgrounds using the Matrix driver, and if you want to send a disk just use the Matrix driver to produce the slide, and copy that onto a disk); it requires that you add a logon password (for which you are prompted when you transmit your files); and it has three menu options the MAGICorp window doesn't have:

File | Add (Ctrl-A)   Displays a dialog box that lets you select other files, such as .DRW format files, to add to the transmission. The .DRW files allow Slidemasters to fix or recreate your slides if there were problems with the SCODL files they received.

Info | Payment   Lets you enter a credit card, Slidemasters account, or purchase-order number, and a password. When you try to use the Info | Payment command again you are prompted for the password—if you can't remember it click on the Delete button to delete the payment information and reenter it. Figure 15.14 shows the Payment dialog box.

Send | Interactive   Lets you transmit your files in interactive mode, answering prompts from Slidemasters manually instead of allowing TeleGrafx to do so automatically. You can use this option if you want to fill out a separate order form or include additional information. Follow the prompts at the bottom of the window; you have an extra menu option, Upload, that you use when you are ready to transmit the files.

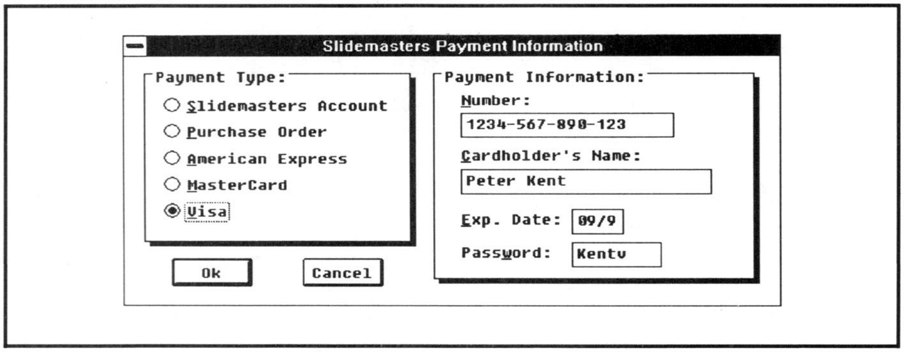

Figure 15.14: The TeleGrafx-Slidemasters Payment dialog box

The other TeleGrafx-Slidemasters dialog boxes may look slightly different from their MAGICorp equivalents, but they work much the same. One important difference is the way the Copies dialog boxes work—in the present MAGICorp driver the number selected in Copies affects *all* files in the list, whereas in the Slidemasters driver only *selected* files are affected.

Another difference is the way files are transmitted—the MAGICorp driver transmits *all* files in the list, and the Slidemasters driver transmits only those with a value in the Copies column.

TELEGRAFX FILES

There are a number of files associated with TeleGrafx slides. These files are all saved in the same directory as TELEGRFX.EXE, unless otherwise noted.

*.NFO	An information file related to a .SCD file of the same name. This is saved in the directory designated in the Matrix Options dialog box.
*.SDL	SCODL files, produced by the Matrix and TeleGrafx-Slidemasters driver when you generate your slides. Saved in the directory designated in the Matrix Options dialog box.
*.SLI	MAGICorp slide files, produced by the TeleGrafx-MAGICorp driver when you generate your slide. Saved in the directory designated in the MAGICorp Options dialog box.
COMPRESS.TMP	A temporary file of compressed images, generated during the transmission process
MAGICOR.CFG and SLIDEMA.CFG	Contain the information entered in the Info menu dialog boxes
MAGICOR.LOG and SLIDEMA.LOG	The list(s) of slide files
MAGICOR.SRV and SLIDEMA.SRV	These are ''server'' files that contain part of the program that tells TeleGrafx how to transmit to MAGICorp or Slidemasters.
TELEGRFX.EXE	The TeleGrafx executable program file
WORKORDR.TMP	A temporary file with information required for the transmission

MICROGRAFX-COMPATIBLE SERVICE BUREAUS

The following companies have TeleGrafx drivers:

MAGICorp
770 Old Saw Mill Road
Tarrytown, NY 10591
1-800-367-6244

Slidemasters, Inc.
401 Business Parkway
Richardson, TX 75081
214-437-0542

If you have a later version of Designer other services may be available—check the list in Designer's online Help (Help | Presentations | Slide Services).

Other imaging centers can work with your Designer files. The following companies can use Designer files, but cannot use TeleGrafx. Call them for information about their services and how you can transmit files to them.

UNITED STATES

Beekman Group, Inc.	New York, NY	212-406-0766
Better Image Production	San Jose, CA	408-441-0955
Brilliant Image	New York, NY	212-736-9661
Cimarron Productions, Inc.	Aurora, CO	303-368-0988
Graphic Presentation Services	Los Angeles, CA	213-930-1315
Strade Corporation	Lakewood, CO	303-232-8282
Telegraphics, Inc.	Philadelphia, PA	215-561-4500

UNITED STATES

FILMGRAPHICS, Inc.	Dallas, TX	214-690-4606
ImageAccess, Inc.	Indianapolis, IN	317-576-8080
Alban/Bruce Communications, Inc.	Baltimore, MD	301-828-1220
Capital Presentations, Inc.	Silver Spring, MD	301-588-9540
Repricolor Computer Graphics	Salt Lake City, UT	801-580-2432
Meteor Photo Business	Troy, MI	313-583-3090
Stokes Imaging Services	Austin, TX	512-458-2201
The Color Place	Dallas, TX	214-631-7174
Image Center, Inc.	Roanoke, VA	703-343-8243

GERMANY

EGG's COMPUTER GRAPHICS		89-699330

GREAT BRITAIN

Syrox Presentations	Kingston, Surrey	011-549-3444

16

Using SlideShow

Designer comes with an associated program called SlideShow, which takes selected files and uses them to produce an onscreen presentation—a kind of electronic slide show. SlideShow works independently of Designer—in fact it's better if you close Designer before you run SlideShow—and uses not only Designer images, but images in .PCX, .GRF, .PIC, and .TIF formats, so you can use art created in other programs. (Note that each slide or screen you want to display must be a separate file.)

NOTE

Because SlideShow is an independent application that is updated periodically, it's difficult to say exactly which features it has for each version of Designer. So some of the features I have described as Designer 3.1 features (that is, features of the SlideShow version shipped with Designer 3.1) may also have been included with some earlier versions of Designer.

Don't confuse SlideShow with an *animation* program, though, which actually makes your images move; SlideShow is just like the traditional slide presentation, showing one slide after another, but with a bit more flair. You can use a variety of special effects to control how Designer removes one slide and displays the next.

NOTE

Designer used to have a driver for VideoShow equipment, a machine that creates onscreen slide shows. Micrografx may still have this driver available if you ask for it, but SlideShow is a superior product.

For what might you use SlideShow? For in-house sales presentations, or even sales presentations taken to your client's office on a laptop or portable computer. For trade shows—set up a large, color screen near your booth and let it run automatically. For producing videos—with the right software and hardware you can copy the slide show onto video tapes and distribute them to sales people, or use the tapes as part of a training course. For creating simple computer-based training courses—you can produce slides illustrating concepts and techniques, and your trainees can move from screen to screen at their own pace. If you own a store, or an office with street-front windows, you might want to build a slide show you can leave running at night, for strollers to view. Or scan photos from the company picnic and use SlideShow to produce a show for the break room. The possibilities are endless.

CREATING SLIDE SHOWS

Building a slide show is a remarkably simple procedure; you can learn all the techniques in a few minutes. This is the basic procedure you will follow to create a slide show:

1. Create the art in individual files, in Designer or an application that produces .PCX, .GRF, .PIC, or .TIF images.

2. Close Designer (or the other application) and open SlideShow.

3. Select the files you want to include in the show, and determine the sequence.

4. Select Manual or Automatic slide progression.

5. If using Automatic slide progression, specify how long each slide should be displayed.

6. Specify which special effect (if any) Designer should use when moving between slides—you can select from 24 laser, fade, wipe, or blend effects.

7. Specify whether the art should be "predrawn" in memory before displaying on the screen.

8. Save the SlideShow "script" you have just written.

9. Begin the slide show.

CREATING YOUR FILES

Each slide in the presentation consists of one file; SlideShow displays the art that is in the top left corner of the file; the complete page is displayed, plus any extra area required to fit the page on the screen. For example, if the pages are 7 inches wide by 10 inches tall, SlideShow has to display another few inches of art from the right of the first page—if there isn't any art to display on that page, SlideShow centers the page in the screen, leaving blank space on both sides.

Designer provides several templates you can use to build your own slides. These templates have pages 5 inches high and 6.67 inches wide, a proportion of 1 : 1.334. When you produce your own slides, set Designer's page size (using View | Pages—see Chapter 11) to about the same proportions; you might have a page size of 10 inches high and 13.3 inches wide, for example. The actual size of your pages will depend on the type of screen you are using—experiment until you get the correct size. Set the borders to 0.00 all around (you don't need borders) in the Pages dialog box, and set the orientation to Landscape.

When you build your files, make sure you use outline fonts; they will look better, and the printer fonts may not be available if you move the script (and associated files) to another computer.

If you want to use the sample templates you must tell Designer to install the sample art during the installation procedure. Designer puts them in a subdirectory called SAMPLES in the DESIGNER directory. These are the templates:

EXTITLE.DRW	A title slide
EXBULLET.DRW	A bulleted list
EXORG.DRW	A three-layer organization chart
EXGRADNT.DRW	A screen with a gradient background

Make sure you copy and rename these templates before using them so they will be available the next time you need them. These files are arranged in a sample slide show called SAMPLE.SHW—you will find out how to run this show later in this chapter.

When you save a slide-show script in a file, all you get is a set of instructions; the script, saved in a file with the extension .SHW, does not contain art. The script tells SlideShow which files to use—in which directory the files are stored and what they are called—and if those files are not there, the script won't work. So, when you create your art files, put them in a directory and leave them there; you might create a special directory for slides, to make them easy to find. If you move them after you've written a script, you will have to correct the script. (You can't just copy a .SHW file onto a disk and take it to another machine and expect it to run.)

STARTING SLIDESHOW

There are two ways to start SlideShow—by using the File | SlideShow command in Designer, or by selecting SlideShow directly from Windows (regardless of whether Designer is open). It is actually best to start Slide-Show from Windows while Designer is *not* open, particularly if you have a slow machine or one with little RAM.

When opening a pre-3.0 version of Windows, or runtime Designer, use the /n switch (win /n, for example—see Chapter 2 for more information) to maximize available memory.

In order to open SlideShow from Windows, double-click on the MGX-SLIDE icon in the Windows Applications box inside the Program Manager window (if you have Windows 3.0), or double-click on the file named MGX-SLIDE.EXE in the MS-DOS EXECUTIVE window (if using a pre-3.0 version of Windows). Figure 16.1 shows the SlideShow "dialog box" displayed over the Program Manager; notice the MGXSLIDE icon above it. (Figure 16.1 shows the dialog box *after* the Micrografx sample show has been loaded—when you first open SlideShow the box is empty.)

Even though SlideShow is an independent application, it operates in a sort of dialog box rather than a window. You can minimize the box to icon size, but you can't maximize it or adjust the size in any other way.

If you are using runtime Windows you can close Designer once SlideShow is running; click on the Designer window (or press Alt-Tab to move to it) and then close it by double-clicking in the Control menu box or by using the Control menu's Close command or by using File | Exit.

In the middle of the SlideShow dialog box is a list of the slides in the show; if you fill the box with slides, a scroll bar appears on the right of

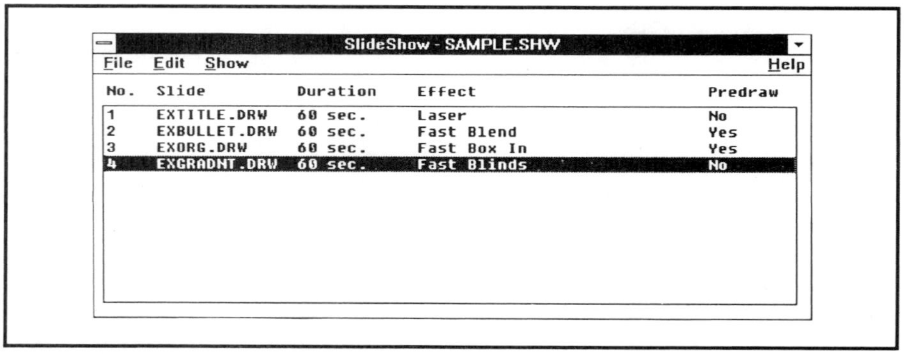

Figure 16.1: The SlideShow dialog box, displayed over the Windows 3.0 background

the box so you can move through the list. There are five columns in the slide list:

No.   The sequence number of the slide

Slide   The name of the file in which the ''slide'' is stored

Duration   The length of time the slide will be displayed on the
             screen; if the entry in this column is ''Manual'' the slide
             remains on the screen until you use a keyboard or mouse
             command to move to the next one

Effect   The special effect used to change from one slide to
             another; if the entry says Replace, no special effect
             is used

Predraw   Indicates whether or not the slide will be ''drawn'' in
             your computer's memory before being displayed on
             screen (predrawing creates a smoother transition
             between slides)

The SlideShow dialog box also has four menu options: File, Edit, Show, and Help. See Appendix B for information on using Help menus. The other menus are explained later in this chapter.

USING THE FILE MENU

After you have created a script you will save it in a script file, a file with the extension .SHW. You use the File menu to work with files in the same way you use Designer's File menu to work with art files. For example, if you want to see the sample script (SAMPLE.SHW) provided by Micrografx, select File | Open; SlideShow displays a File Open dialog box. Find the file (it's in the SAMPLES subdirectory) and click on OK.

New   Clears the SlideShow dialog box so you can create a
               new script

Open   Selects an existing script so you can edit the script or
               view the show

Save (Ctrl-S) Saves the script

Save As   Lets you save a script with a new name

Exit   Closes SlideShow

ADDING SLIDES
TO THE SLIDESHOW LIST

The next step is to add the slides you want to include in the show. Use the Edit | Add command (Keyboard Shortcut: Ctrl-A) to do this; SlideShow displays the Add dialog box shown in Figure 16.2.

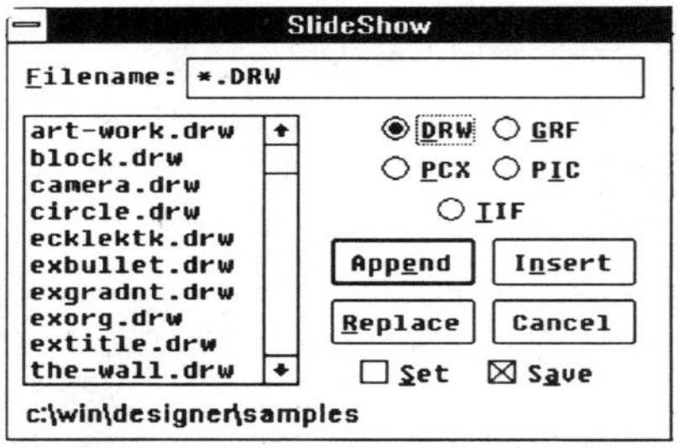

Figure 16.2: The Add dialog box

This dialog box is like a File Open dialog box—for instance, you use the list box on the left to find the file you want to use. You also have a few choices for how the file should be added to the SlideShow dialog box: you can Append, Insert, or Replace the file.

Append	Adds the file name you selected in the list box to the end of the list in the SlideShow dialog box
Insert	Inserts the file name you selected in the list box *above* the slide selected in the SlideShow dialog box. If you have more than one slide selected, the file name is inserted above the one highest in the list; if no slides are selected the file name is appended to the end of the list.
Replace	Replaces all the slides selected in the SlideShow dialog box with the file name you selected in the list box

The Set checkbox works like the Set checkbox in the Color dialog boxes—select it and the dialog box remains open, so you can select one file after another without having to select Edit | Add each time.

WARNING

If you want to use the REPLACE command button, make sure that you have selected a slide in the SlideShow dialog box. With 3.0 SlideShow may crash if you haven't selected a slide, and you will lose any changes you made since the last time you saved.

You can also select the file format. (The extension in the Filename box at the top automatically changes when you select a file type). These are the file types you can use in a slide show:

.DRW   A standard Designer art file; also used by Micrografx's Charisma

.GRF   A file from Micrografx's Graph Plus and Charisma

.PCX   A Z-Soft bitmap image, from scanners, PC Paintbrush, and many other programs

.PIC   A Micrografx picture file, from In*a*Vision or Windows Draw

.TIF   A TIFF (Tag Image File Format) bitmap file, from many scanners and paint programs

---

NOTE

SlideShow is often unable to display .PCX files from Windows 3.0 Paintbrush; Micrografx reports that Paintbrush saves its files in a nonstandard way. You can get around the problem, though, by saving the image once, then reopening the file and saving it again. Now SlideShow will be able to work with the image.

Not only does this allow you to use art from other programs, but it may also help you speed up your slide presentations. Some images may display more quickly in another format, so you could try exporting the file before adding it to the slide-show script. However, translations are not always exact—colors and shapes may change—and some formats may slow SlideShow to such an extent that it seems to have frozen. Color PCX images in particular are very slow.

Selecting Slides

If you are using a mouse, you select or deselect files by clicking on them. If you are using the keyboard, press the right arrow or down arrow key to move down the list, and the left arrow or up arrow to move up the list. Select and deselect by clicking the space bar. You can also use the Edit | Select All and Edit | Deselect All options if you have Designer 3.1.

Make sure you have the right slides selected or you may apply characteristics to the wrong slides.

NOTE

If the SlideShow dialog box contains more slides than can be displayed, a scroll bar appears on the right side of the box. In Designer 3.0 SlideShow has a habit of shifting this list when you use one of the Edit or Show commands, so that the first 12 are displayed again. However, if you had selected a slide below number 12 it remains selected, even though you can't see it.

Shuffling Slides

Once you have the slides displayed in the SlideShow dialog box, you can use the other Edit commands to "shuffle" the slides around, to get them into the correct position. The Edit menu contains the following commands:

Undo (Alt-Backspace)	Undoes the last change you made to the script
Cut (Shift-Del)	Removes the selected slide names and places them in the clipboard
Copy (Ctrl-Ins)	Copies the selected slide names into the clipboard
Paste (Shift-Ins)	Copies the slide names from the clipboard into the list of slides. Unlike the Insert command in the Add dialog box, using Paste puts the names *after* the selected slide. If no slide is selected they are put at the end of the list, and if more than one slide is selected the names are put directly after the one that is highest up the list.
Delete (Del)	Deletes the selected slides

3.1	Select All (F2)	Highlights all the slides
3.1	Deselect All (Ctrl-F2)	Removes the highlight from all the slides
	Add (Ctrl-A)	Opens the Add dialog box (explained earlier in this chapter)

You can even use these commands to create new scripts: open two Slide-Show dialog boxes, copy or cut slide names in one, and paste them into the other.

DEFINING THE SLIDE CHARACTERISTICS

Now that you have decided which slides will be shown, you must decide *how* you want to show them. You must decide

- whether to progress manually or automatically from slide to slide,

- how long you want the slide to be displayed,

- which transition method you want to use, and

- whether the slide should be predrawn in memory.

These options are set using the Show menu commands:

Duration (Ctrl-D)	Lets you set manual or automatic progression, and how long the slide is displayed
Replace (Ctrl-R)	Changes slides without using special effects
Laser (Ctrl-E)	Uses the Laser special effect
Fade (Ctrl-F)	Lets you select from 3 fade speeds
Wipe (Ctrl-W)	Lets you select from 17 wipe effects
Blend (Ctrl-L)	Lets you select from 3 blend speeds
Predraw (Ctrl-P)	Makes the image draw in memory before displaying

Preferences   Lets you set the duration increment and the fine-fade coarseness, and select audible and visible slide-ready cues

Begin (Ctrl-B)   Begins the slide show

SETTING THE SLIDE PROGRESSION AND DURATION

Select Show | Duration (Keyboard Shortcut: Ctrl-D) to see the Duration dialog box, shown in Figure 16.3.

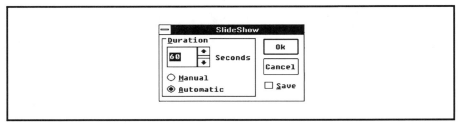

Figure 16.3: The Duration dialog box

You can use this dialog box in two ways: select the slide (or slides) you want to adjust and then make the adjustments, or make the adjustments and then add the slide using the Add dialog box (Edit | Add).

Select Manual if you want the slide to remain on the screen until you use a keyboard or mouse command to display the next one, or select Automatic to make the slide display only as long as the number of seconds set in the Duration box. You can select from 1 to 65,535 seconds (over 18 hours). You can type a value into this box, or use the scroll arrows, but if you use the arrows the number displayed in the box will increment according to the increment value set in the SlideShow Preferences dialog box.

By the way, the duration you set has nothing to do with the time it takes to change slides; it only defines the time from when the slide is fully displayed to when it begins changing to the next one.

DEFINING THE SLIDE TRANSITION METHOD

You have a number of ways to change slides:

Replace (Ctrl-R)   A blank screen is displayed before the next slide—if you are using Predraw, though, it will simply look like a very quick top-to-bottom wipe.

Laser (Ctrl-E)   Lines "shoot" from the top left corner of the screen, and blocks of the next slide fill the screen piece by piece in a seemingly random order.

Fade (Ctrl-F)   Blocks of the next slide are filled in piece by piece—similar to Laser, but without the lines shooting in from the corner.

Wipe (Ctrl-W)   17 different methods are offered for moving the slide off the screen in a "wiping" motion, exposing the next slide.

Blend (Ctrl-L)   Horizontal strips of the next slide appear throughout the screen, gradually filling in the entire picture.

Again, you can use this dialog box in two ways; select the slide (or slides) you want to adjust and then make the adjustments, or make the adjustments and then add the slide using the Add dialog box (Edit | Add).

Using Replace

The Replace method is like changing the slides without using any special effect. If the slide is not being predrawn (explained in a moment), SlideShow displays the slide file's drawing-area background and then draws the slide on it. If the slide is being predrawn, SlideShow quickly replaces the old slide with the new one, in a very quick top-to-bottom "wipe."

Using the Laser Effect

The Laser effect seems to "shoot" blocks into place on the screen, using lines that come from the top left hand corner. You can change the way

Laser works using Predraw (explained in a moment). If the slide is being pre-drawn, then Laser shoots blocks of the completed slide into place. If the slide is *not* being predrawn, Laser shoots blocks of the slide file's drawing-area background into place, and then draws the slide onto the completed background.

Selecting a Fade Effect

When you select the Show | Fade option you see the Fade dialog box (Figure 16.4).

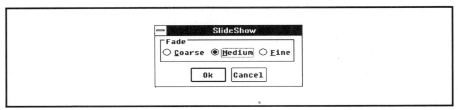

Figure 16.4: The Fade dialog box

A Fade is the gradual replacement of blocks of the previous slide with blocks of the next one. You can select Coarse for a quick fade using large blocks, Medium for a fade using medium-size blocks, or Fine for a (slow) fade using small blocks. The Fine setting can be further refined in the Preferences dialog box (Show | Preferences) by setting the Fine Fade "Coarseness Index." You can set the coarseness index from 1 to 5, with 1 being the "coarsest" fine fade, and 5 being the "finest" fine fade.

This sounds a little confusing (and it's difficult to understand why Micrografx broke Fade into two dialog boxes like this), so for further clarifi-cation: The Fine-Fade Coarseness Index in the Preferences dialog box only has an effect if you have selected Fine as the fade for one or more slides (it will affect all of those slides). Selecting a low number makes the fine fades use relatively large blocks, and a high number makes the fine fades use very small blocks (and makes it take a *very* long time to change slides).

Selecting a Wipe Effect

Select Show | Wipe to see the Wipe dialog box (Figure 16.5).

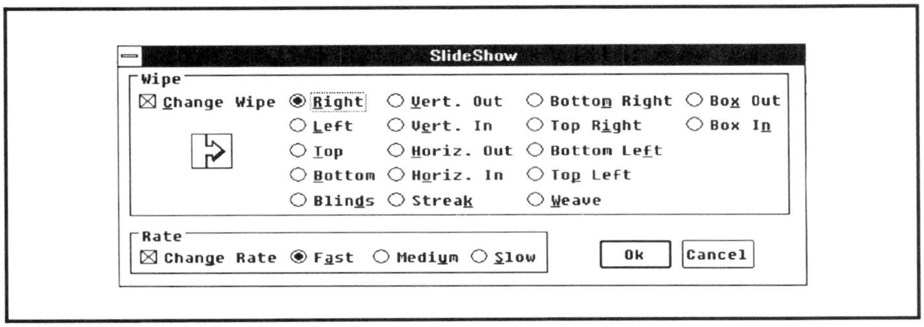

Figure 16.5: The Wipe dialog box

A wipe is an effect that moves the slide across the screen, exposing the next slide ''below.'' Right wipe is an example of a simple wipe; the left border of the slide moves toward the right, covering up the old slide as it goes, and exposing the next slide underneath. As you can see from the dialog box there are more complicated wipe effects than this. For example, Box In is when all four sides of the slide move toward the center at the same time, and Weave is when parts of the right side move to the left and parts of the left side move to the right.

If you want to change the wipe effect, make sure the Change Wipe box has a checkmark in it. Then click on the effect you want; the icon under the Change Wipe box changes to give an indication of what the effect will look like (the arrows show the direction of movement).

In order to change the speed you must check the Change Rate checkbox; you can select a fast, medium, or slow wipe.

The Streak wipe, by the way, moves from top to bottom (not left to right as the icon implies), in a sort of ''wobbly line.'' The Blinds wipe is when a series of horizontal lines, spaced out across the screen from top to bottom, wipe downward, each wiping away just a portion of the old slide.

The Change Wipe and Change Rate checkboxes allow you to select several slides and change only their wipe effects or only their wipe rates; if Change Wipe is selected, for example, and Change Rate is not, the wipe effects will be changed for all the selected slides when you click on OK, but their rates will be unchanged.

Selecting a Blend Effect

The Blend effect is when thin horizontal lines from the next slide appear on top of the old one, gradually filling the screen. Select Show | Blend to see the Blend dialog box, and simply select Fast, Medium, or Slow.

USING PREDRAW

Predraw is a way to make the slide transitions smoother. Without Predraw, each time SlideShow has to display a new slide it has to completely redraw it. In some cases this may take a long time, a minute or more, and this tends to distract from the slide show. But with Predraw turned on SlideShow begins "drawing" the slide in your computer's random access memory as soon as the last slide is fully displayed. While you are talking, SlideShow is preparing the next slide, and when you instruct it to continue, it simply sends the completed slide to the screen.

Predrawing takes a lot of memory, especially if you are using very high resolution screens, so it may not work if you don't have enough available. To see how much memory you will need, and how much is available, select Help | About—the About dialog box displays (Figure 16.6).

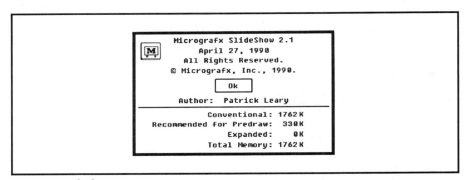

```
                Micrografx SlideShow 2.1
          M       April 27, 1990
                  All Rights Reserved.
                © Micrografx, Inc., 1990.
                      ┌──────────┐
                      │    Ok    │
                      └──────────┘
                  Author:  Patrick Leary

                      Conventional: 1762 K
          Recommended for Predraw:  330 K
                         Expanded:    0 K
                     Total Memory: 1762 K
```

Figure 16.6: The About SlideShow dialog box

If you don't have enough memory, try one of the recommendations at the end of this chapter. You can still use Predraw if you have less than the recommended memory, but displaying the slides will be slow; 5K too little may be acceptable, but the greater the deficit the slower the slides will be. Any deficit greater than 5K will probably be too slow. If you don't have enough memory you will see a warning message when you begin the show.

In versions previous to 3.1, if you try to display the next slide before it is fully predrawn, or if you have set a slide duration too fast for the next slide to predraw, SlideShow will display what it has finished so far, and then clear the screen and start again! This can be quite a problem, but there is a tool you can use to get around it: the Next-Ready Cue in the Preferences dialog box, explained next.

THE SLIDESHOW
PREFERENCES DIALOG BOX

Select Show | Preferences to display the Preferences dialog box, displayed in Figure 16.7. (Releases before 3.1 do not include all the options shown.)

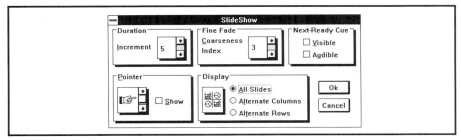

Figure 16.7: The Preferences dialog box, release 3.1

The Next-Ready Cue is a visual or audible indicator (you can select either or both) used during a SlideShow presentation to tell you that the next slide has been predrawn and is ready to display. The audible indicator is a beep, and the visual indicator is a small arrow pointing to the right in the bottom right of the screen. If you didn't select Predraw for the next slide, the indicators appear or sound almost immediately after the current slide has finished being drawn.

These indicators are very useful in two ways. First, if you are using Manual progression from slide to slide you need to know when the next slide is ready. Second, if you are using an Automatic progression you can use the indicators to help you set the display duration.

Use the following procedure to figure out the duration. Set all the slides to Manual and run through the show. Time each slide, from the moment SlideShow seems to have finished drawing the slide, to the moment the cue appears. That is the minimum time you should set for the slide's duration. You can then set the duration times, and remove the cue indicator.

As I already mentioned, you can adjust the duration increments in the Preferences dialog box—from 1 to 60 seconds. Setting the duration increment does not affect the selected slide's duration—it simply changes the way the Duration dialog box (Show | Duration) functions. For example, if you set 9 seconds as the increment, the duration increases by 9 seconds when you click on the up arrow in the Duration dialog box. (You can still type in any value you want, though).

The Coarseness Index in the Fine Fade part of the Preferences dialog box has already been described earlier in this chapter, under ''Selecting a Fade Effect.''

3.1 Designer 3.1 has two more options in the Preferences dialog box. The Pointer option lets you tell SlideShow to display a mouse pointer during the slide show, by clicking on the Show checkbox. You can then choose from eight different pointers (hands, arrows, and triangles) to direct your audience's attention to specific areas of your slides.

The other option is the Display choice. Designer 3.0 displays the first page in each slide file, but Designer 3.1 lets you place more slides in a file, and then tell SlideShow which pages to display. You can display All Slides (every page in the file that has *anything* on it, whether text or graphics); Alternate Columns (only pages in *columns* one, three, five, and so on); and Alternate Rows (only pages in *rows* one, three, five, and so on).

SAVING AND VIEWING YOUR SLIDE SHOW

You have now finished your slide-show script. If you want to use this show later, you should save it using File | Save As. You might want to print the script, so you can refer to it during a slide show. To do this, select all the slides in the list and then select Edit | Copy to copy the information into the clipboard. Then paste the information from the clipboard into Windows Write or Windows Notepad, or into a Windows-compatible word processor, and print it.

Now you are ready to see the slide show itself. Simply select Show | Begin (Keyboard Shortcut: Ctrl-B), and SlideShow starts displaying the first slide. But *which* first slide? If no slides are selected, the show begins with number 1, but if any are selected, the show begins with the highest selected slide in the list. SlideShow makes it easy to view a particular slide without seeing the whole show—just select that slide and begin the show, and when you've seen the slide press Esc to stop the show.

It may take a few seconds to begin the show if the first slide is being predrawn. When the show begins, you can use the following keyboard and mouse commands:

Display the next slide	Right arrow or button 2
Display the previous slide	Left arrow or button 1
Go to a particular slide	Type the slide number and press ◄┘
Pause the show	F2
Continue the show	Next slide, previous slide, or go-to slide commands
Stop the show	Esc

The show runs in a loop; once the last slide has been displayed for its defined duration, the first slide displays again. If you don't want that to happen, just make sure the last slide is set to Manual; then it remains displayed until you end the show by pressing Esc (or continue the show, or go to another slide, or whatever). By the way, going back to the previous slide—by pressing button 1 or the left arrow key—doesn't actually reverse the sequence. For example, say Slide #8 is displayed and you press button 1. Slide #7 will be displayed for its defined duration (if automatic), but then Slide #8 will be displayed again—the show continues in the original sequence.

SPEEDING SLIDESHOW

SlideShow moves very slowly on slow systems, and may not be able to predraw on systems with insufficient RAM. Follow these steps to improve performance:

- Run SlideShow on its own, without any other applications running—make sure all Windows applications are closed.

- Start Designer or pre-3.0 Windows with the /n switch.

- Remove unwanted symbols from the files, even if they are in areas that don't display in the slide.

- Remove terminate-and-stay-resident (TSR) programs from memory.

- Change the buffers statement in your CONFIG.SYS file to BUFFERS = 20 or less, and the files statement to FILES = 5 or less (but don't do this unless you understand these DOS commands and their effect on other programs).

TRY IT YOURSELF

Producing a slide show is very easy, so why not try it? You can use the SAMPLE.SHW that Designer added to the SAMPLES subdirectory when you installed Designer, or PRECSION.SHW if you have Designer 3.1. Just follow this chapter—begin by using File | Open to open SAMPLE.SHW, and then follow the other instructions to add slides and modify the show. Before you view the show make sure you change the duration; Micrografx set the duration to 60 seconds for each of the slides in SAMPLE.DRW, which makes it rather slow.

WARNING
Don't run a slide while one of the slide files is open in Designer—
Windows may crash and you may have to reboot your computer.

A

Installing Designer

WHAT HARDWARE DO YOU NEED?

You need the following configuration to run Designer:

computer	An IBM 286, 386SX, 386, or 486 Personal Computer or compatible, or an IBM Personal System 2 computer. Slow machines, even slow 386s, may be very frustrating. If you use Designer in business, get the fastest 386 you can. Time is money, and you will spend a lot of time waiting for Designer if you use a slow machine.
memory	At least 512K RAM. Micrografx recommends 640K or more; much more is better. In fact, if you are using Windows/386 or Windows 3.0 you need 2Mb of memory to use the program's memory management capabilities.
disk drives	One hard-disk drive and at least one double-sided floppy-disk drive. You need at least 1 1/2 Mb free on the hard disk, more if you want to install TeleGrafx, outline fonts, some of the format translators, samples, and clip art.
graphics board	A Video Graphics Array (VGA) board, Enhanced Graphics Adapter (EGA) board, Color Graphics Adapter (CGA) board, Hercules Graphics Adapter (or compatible) board, or any other Windows-compatible graphics board
monitor	A monitor compatible with the graphics board
pointer	A mouse or other pointing device. Not strictly essential; you *can* use the keyboard for all of Designer's commands. But using the keyboard alone is frustrating and difficult—you need a pointing device to use Designer quickly and efficiently.
DOS	DOS 3.0 or higher.

Windows   Windows 3.0, or Windows/286 or Windows/386
                        (version 2.0 or higher). **Designer 3.1 runs only
                        under Windows 3.0.** If you bought one of the
                        early versions of Designer, you may also have taken
                        advantage of Micrografx's offer (no longer avail-
                        able) to send you a free *runtime* version of
                        windows.

Basically, the more RAM you have, and the better the version of Windows you are using, and the faster your computer, hard disk drive, and
video board, the faster Designer will run. And the faster Designer runs, the
easier it is to use.

MICROSOFT
WINDOWS AND DESIGNER

Designer runs under Microsoft Windows, a computer management
program that makes DOS easier to use and gives programs designed for it a
similar "look and feel." This makes learning new programs much easier,
because once you have learned one Windows application, you have learned
many of the skills you need to use all the others. It also lets you share data, to
copy text and pictures from one program running in Windows to another.
Designer 3.1 will run only under Windows 3.0, but pre 3.1 Designer
can run under several different versions of Windows:

- Windows 3.0

- Windows/386

- Windows/286

- Runtime Windows

The best Windows is 3.0. This is the latest version—it runs much faster
than earlier versions, and if you use Designer as a business or money-making
tool, you should upgrade, if not to Designer 3.1, at least to Windows 3.0.
You will find that the extra speed and ease of use will save you a lot of time.

If you use pre-3.1 Designer with earlier versions of Windows (Windows 286 and 386), you will find that Designer runs more slowly. In fact,

Designer has to take over the memory management functions of these programs to get the job done properly. If you don't have Windows, you may still be able to use a *runtime* version of Windows, a simplified version with enough of the Windows program to allow Designer to operate. Runtime versions used to be provided by many publishers of Windows applications in order to allow their clients to use their programs without buying Windows. But when Microsoft issued Windows 3.0 they said they would no longer support runtime Windows—and Micrografx no longer offers a runtime version.

INSTALLING AND STARTING DESIGNER

Installing Designer is a simple procedure: Micrografx has incorporated an installation program that leads you through the procedure. If you don't have Microsoft Windows you must install Designer's runtime Windows first. (Make sure you have the correct Windows installed. You can only use the versions of Windows listed previously; if you have an earlier release you must upgrade or use Designer's runtime version.)

Designer comes with either 3.5 inch disks or 5.25 inch disks; the box label states which. In these instructions I'm going to assume you are using disk drive A. Substitute drive B where necessary.

MAKING BACKUP DISKS

It is always a good idea to make backup copies of program disks before you load a new program. That way, if you accidentally damage a disk, you still have a copy. The following procedure will copy the disks:

1. Go to the DOS > prompt.

2. If you have two floppy-disk drives, type diskcopy a: b: and press ←┘. If you have only one floppy-disk drive, type diskcopy a: a: and press ←┘.

3. Your computer will give you the rest of the DISKCOPY instructions, telling you to put the SOURCE disk (the disk you want to copy) in drive A and telling you when and where to put the TARGET disk (the blank disk).

The disks don't need to be formatted before you use the DISKCOPY command; nor do they have to be blank. DISKCOPY will format the disk if necessary, and in the process will overwrite everything on the disk—so make sure it doesn't contain anything important.

You can also use a file-management program you may own (if you have Windows, use the Windows commands). But make sure you also copy the disk volume labels—if the backup copies don't have exactly the same volume labels as the originals the installation program will not recognize them, even if they contain all the correct files.

When you have copied the disks, put away the originals and use the copies.

SETTING THE FILES = NUMBER

Before you install Designer you should set the Files = number to 20 or more. This is a line in your CONFIG.SYS file (which is in your root directory) that tells DOS how many files may be open at one time. Open CONFIG.SYS with a word processor, such as Windows Notepad, and look for the Files = line. If the number after the equals sign is less than 20, replace it with 20. If it is more than 20, leave it as it is.

PREPARING TO INSTALL DESIGNER

Once you have installed Windows, you are *almost* ready to install Designer. Before starting, though, you should have some information ready:

- In which directory did you place the Windows files?

- Which printers or plotters do you want to use with Designer? Designer uses two types of drivers—those you installed during the Windows or runtime Windows installation procedure, and those to be installed during the Designer installation procedure. If you installed a device driver in Windows and you see it listed in Designer's installation procedure, Micrografx recommends that you install Designer's version of the drivers again to make sure you have the latest ones. If you don't see your device mentioned during the Designer installation, don't worry, Designer will use the ones you installed in the Windows or runtime installation.

- Which clip art files do you want to load? See Designer's reference guide for a pictorial directory of the art. Load at least the following files, because you will use them in this book's lessons: BKGRN10D.DRW, TRANS01D.DRW, and TRANS02D.DRW. Designer will put these in a subdirectory called CLIPART.

- Do you want Designer's sample art? These are examples of art produced for Micrografx. Some of these samples will be used in exercises in this book, so it is a good idea to load them now. (You can always delete them later if you want to.) Designer will load these in a subdirectory called SAMPLES.

- Do you want to import .DXF, .CGM, .GEM, or .PCT file formats? The installation procedure allows you to select these file-format translators. If you want to import .EPS, .PS, or .HP formats, you must load a PostScript or HPGL device driver, and Designer loads the translators automatically. All the other file-format translators are loaded automatically. You don't need to install any optional translators for the exercises in this book.

- Which fonts do you want to install? The fonts that come with Designer are displayed on this book's end papers.

- Do you want to use TeleGrafx, the utility used for transmitting Designer files across telephone lines to a print or slide imaging center?

INSTALLING DESIGNER 3.0, 3.01, 3.02

The following procedure assumes you are placing the disk in drive A:

1. Go to the DOS prompt. Install the disk labelled DESIGNER INSTALLATION DISK 1 into your floppy drive.

2. Type a:install and press ←.

3. The Install program displays an introductory screen; press ← when you see it.

4. A panel displays your hard-disk drive name, and asks if that is the drive on which you want to load Designer. Press ←.

5. A panel displays the name of a Windows directory on your hard drive; if you have installed Windows in a different path (for example, if you have more than one version loaded), type the path you want to use (for example, change it to \WIN386) and press ←.

6. Designer then tells you it is going to load the program files into a directory called DESIGNER, in the Windows directory you selected. Press ◄─┘ to accept this directory name.

7. Designer displays the Installation Main Menu (see Figure A.1). Press ◄─┘.

8. Designer leads you through the installation procedure, telling you when to change disks. On several occasions it allows you to choose what you want to load; you can choose which fonts, drivers, translators, samples, and clip art to load. In each case Designer tells you how much disk space all the choices would use, and how much space is available on your disk. Select the options you want to install.

9. When you have finished the procedure, Designer returns you to the main menu. With the highlight on the Quit option, press ◄─┘, type y, and press ◄─┘ again.

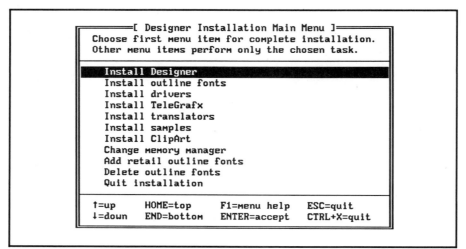

Figure A.1: The Installation Main Menu, pre-3.1 Designer

You have now finished the installation procedure. You can rerun installation any time you want to add or delete fonts, device drivers, file-format translators, the TeleGrafx files, sample art, and clip art. Just follow Steps 1 through 6 to get to the main menu, choose one of the options in the menu, and press ◄─┘. If you have Windows, don't use Windows' Control Panel to install Designer's fonts or drivers—you must use the installation program to do so.

Installation Problems

Problems may sometimes occur when you attempt to install Designer. You may find that the installation program ends abruptly, and takes you back to the DOS prompt. Or the program may tell you it cannot find the Windows directory. These problems may occur for the following reasons:

- You didn't install Windows first.

- The Windows WIN.INI file has been deleted somehow. Look in the Windows directory for this file. If you can't find it, reinstall Windows.

- The Windows directory is not in the DOS path statement. Go to the DOS prompt and type path c:\win and press ⏎ (substitute the correct disk drive and directory name). Then try to install Designer.

- You don't have enough space left on your disk drive. Remove unused files until you have at least 1.6Mb free, more if you need to load the optional fonts, samples, TeleGrafx, and so on.

- You are using a version of DOS that allows a large disk drive—one over 32Mb—to be installed. (Versions prior to 4.0 made you "divide" large disk drives into two or more virtual drives of no more than 32Mb each.) Sometimes the installation program gets "lost" on a large disk; try copying all the installation files into a directory on your hard disk and running the installation from there.

Building a Windows 3.0 Icon

If you are using Windows 3.0 you will want to build an icon in the Windows Applications window—you will then be able to open Designer by double-clicking on the icon.

1. Open Windows and open the Windows Applications window.

2. Select File | New, and the New Program Object dialog box appears.

3. Click on Program Item, and then on OK. The Program Item Properties dialog box appears.

4. Type designer in the Description text box.

5. Type c:\win\designer\designer.exe in the Command Line text box (substitute the correct disk drive and directories if necessary). Alternatively, click on Browse to open the Browse dialog box, use the list boxes to find the DESIGNER.EXE file, and double-click on the name.

6. Click on OK. The icon is added to the Window.

Follow the same procedure to add the TeleGrafx (TELEGRFX.EXE) and SlideShow (MGXSLIDE.EXE) icons.

3.1 INSTALLING DESIGNER 3.1

Designer 3.1 has a new Windows-based installation program. The following procedure assumes you are placing the installation disk in drive A:

1. Open Windows. If Windows is already open, close all other applications.

2. Install the disk labelled Installation Disk #1 into your floppy drive.

3. In the Program Manager window select File | Run. Type a:install and press ◄─┘.

4. An introductory dialog box appears; click on the Continue button.

5. The Main Menu appears (Figure A.2).

6. Click on Continue and the installation procedure begins. Designer leads you through the procedure, telling you when to change disks. On several occasions it allows you to choose which fonts, drivers, translators, samples, and clip art to load. In each case Designer tells you how much disk space all the choices would use, and how much space is available on your disk. Select the options you want to install.

7. The installation program also asks if you want it to create icons. If you tell it to do so it will create a Windows program group with up to six icons, depending on the options you selected earlier.

8. When the installation is complete the Main Menu is displayed again. Click on Quit to close the installation program.

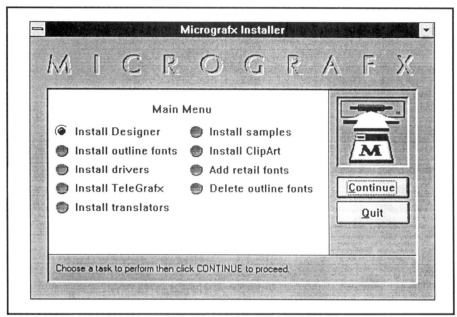

Figure A.2: The Designer 3.1 Installation Main Menu

You can rerun the installation program at any time you want to add or delete fonts, device drivers, file-format translators, the TeleGrafx files, sample art, and clip art. Just go to the Main Menu, select one of the options, and click on OK.

THE WINDOWS ICONS

If you told the installation program to add Windows icons, you now have a Micrografx program group in Program Manager, with up to six icons: Designer, Batch Print, SlideShow, TeleGrafx, MAGICorp, and Slidemasters. You can open any of the applications by selecting an icon and pressing ↵, or by double-clicking on the icon.

You can change some of the icons if you wish. There are 5 different Designer icons, 29 different SlideShow icons (most of which are the icons used in SlideShow's Preferences and Wipe dialog boxes), 3 different Tele-Grafx icons, and 5 different MAGICorp icons. To change an icon, follow this procedure:

1. Select the icon.

2. Select File | Properties from the Program Manager menu bar; the Program Item Properties dialog box appears.

3. Click on the Change Icon button; the Select Icon dialog box appears.

4. Click on the View Next button until you find the icon you want.

5. Click on OK in the Select Icon and Program Item Properties dialog boxes.

CREATING A TEMP DIRECTORY

Windows programs create temporary files while they are running. These files are stored in the TEMP directory, and are usually deleted when you close Windows. (You should never delete these files while Windows is running.) Occasionally, though, these files are not deleted; perhaps due to a faulty program or a power cut, Windows is closed and the files remain. Having these files in a special directory helps you to find files that were not removed, making it easier for you to delete them.

Windows 3.0 automatically makes a directory called TEMP. If you are using runtime Windows, or a version of Windows earlier than 3.0, *you* must make this directory. (If you don't create this directory, Designer may not be able to load the required device drivers when you try to print your art.)

Use Windows or DOS to create a new directory called TEMP. (To create one in DOS, get to the DOS > prompt, type c: and press ←. Then type mkdir c:\temp and press ←.) You must also change your AUTOEXEC.BAT file, the file that your computer looks at when it boots up. Using a text editor (such as Windows Notepad, for example) or the DOS EDLIN command, add the following lines to that file:

```
set temp = c:\temp
set tmp = c:\temp
```

CREATING AN ART DIRECTORY

You may also want to create a subdirectory in which to store your art. I have used a directory called ART to store the files created in the exercises in this book. Use the technique described above to create a subdirectory in the DESIGNER directory. For example, at the DOS prompt type mkdir c:\win\ designer\art and press ◄—┘.

DESIGNER'S READ ME FILES

It's a good idea to read Designers Read Me files. These include recent information about Designer, some of which is too recent to be included in any Designer documentation. Once you have started Designer and understand how to use Designer's menus (Chapter 2 describes how to start Designer and use the basic screen components), select Help | Read Me. Designer displays a small screen (expand it if you wish using the Windows maximize commands) with introductory text followed by a list of topics. Select a topic and press ◄—┘ to read more information about that topic. Appendix B fully describes Designer's online Help system.

DESIGNER'S MEMORY PROBLEMS

Designer uses a lot of memory. This can be very frustrating on slow machines and those with little RAM, or occasionally even on fast machines (when trying to translate large files from other formats, for example). Here are a few things you can do about it:

- Use the fastest computer possible.

- Upgrade to Windows 3.0.

- Add RAM—you need at least 2Mb to run Windows properly.

- If you are not using Windows 3.0, open Windows by typing /n after the windows command (win/n, for example). If using runtime Windows, open Designer by typing designer/n. This lets Designer take over Windows' memory management functions.

- Don't use any other applications while you are running Designer, even special Windows applications such as Calculator, Clipboard, or Control Panel.

- Unload local area network (LAN) drivers and drivers used for external disk drives if necessary.

- Don't open more than one Designer window at a time.

- Change the Windows Program Manager window (Windows 3.0) or MS-DOS Executive window (earlier versions) to an icon.

- Don't add text until you are almost finished with your drawing.

- If you have Windows 3.0, read the documentation's chapter on "Optimizing Windows" and follow the instructions.

- Empty the clipboard (see Chapter 12) to free some RAM.

- If you have pre-3.0 Windows, read your Windows documentation to learn about HIMEM.SYS and SMARTDrive.

You should also see the instructions for speeding up redraw in Chapter 11, and instructions for speeding up text in Chapter 8 (text slows down the system dramatically).

Also, you should save your work often—Designer's memory problems can sometimes cause it to lock up, so you should save before carrying out any operation that uses a lot of memory. Save before you import a file from another format, for example, or before you print, open TeleGrafx, open another Designer window, use SlideShow, enter large amounts of text, and so on. Saving is simple—press and hold Ctrl while you press *S*—and doesn't usually take long, and it's a good habit to get into for *all* the programs you use, not just Designer.

MEMORY MANAGEMENT WITH DESIGNER 3.01 AND 3.02

Designer 3.01 and 3.02 have three different "virtual memory managers" that control the use of expanded and extended memory. Only one of these files is loaded at a time; the files all have the same name, but can be distinguished by the size and date. You can view the files using a DOS DIR command, or in the Windows File Manager (Windows 3.0) or MS-DOS Executive window (pre-3.0 versions of Windows). The memory manager is stored in the DESIGNER directory.

- **MGXVM.EXE, 12840 bytes, 4-18-90**   Enhanced memory manager (LIM 4.0 specifications), automatically installed on 386s, 286s with extended memory that meet MS XMS 2.0 specifications, and 286s with neither expanded nor extended memory.

- **MGXVM.EXE, 8028 bytes, 4-22-90**   Standard memory manager (LIM 3.2 specifications), automatically installed on 286s with expanded memory.

- **MGXVM.EXE, 2667 bytes, 3-21-90**   Stub memory manager, a file that disables memory management.

Designer 3.0 had only the enhanced memory manager, but so many problems arose in 286s with expanded memory boards that Micrografx decided to add the other two memory managers to Designer 3.01.

The Designer 3.01 and 3.02 installation program has an option that allows you to change the memory manager. Load the installation program, then select the Change Memory Manager option, and Designer displays the screen shown in Figure A.3.

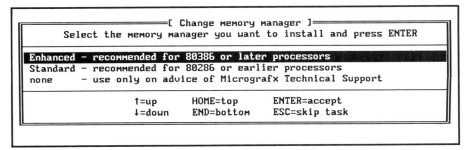

Figure A.3: The Change Memory Manager screen

You can experiment with your system by choosing one of the memory managers. It may be possible to use the enhanced memory manager with some good expanded-memory boards. Also, if you have an expanded memory manager board that lets you configure part of it as extended memory, you might try to do so. Configure all of it as extended if possible, but if you use applications that require expanded memory, decide how much you want to keep for those applications, and configure the rest as extended. Then select the enhanced memory manager.

Designer 3.1 handles memory in a different way, and has fewer problems.

INSTALLING DESIGNER ON A NETWORK

Personally, I don't like networks, and believe they are used in many situations where they are more trouble than they are worth—but if you really want to put Designer on a network you can. You may find problems when you print on a network printer. Your art may be garbled on the way to the printer, may take hours to arrive, or may never arrive at all. Of course this depends on all sorts of factors, such as the size and type of the network, the spooler size, the other software packages sending information to the printer, and so on. Networks are very complicated things to troubleshoot, and you may be forced to use a printer connected directly to your computer instead of one on the network. Also, Designer will probably run a little slower on a network than on your computer, which may make a slow computer unbearable.

Also, before installing on a network you need a license from Micrografx; each copy of Designer can be used on one computer at a time, so if you are making the program available to everyone on a network you must **3.1** make special arrangements with Micrografx. Designer 3.1 has automatic *network file locking,* which means that you can set it up so a file can be opened by only one person on the network at a time.

If you need to install Designer on a network, use the network drive and directory names when prompted for that information by the installation program. Then copy the WIN.INI file onto each user's hard drive. When you start Windows it searches the current directory and then all the directories in the DOS path statement until it finds WIN.INI. So if all the users have their own personal WIN.INI file, they can each customize Designer exactly as they want it. Just make sure that the WIN.INI file is in a directory that appears in the AUTOEXEC.BAT path statement before the network directory that has a WIN.INI file. (If Windows can't find a WIN.INI file anywhere, it uses a set of standard defaults.)

Designer 3.1 has automatic *network file locking,* which means that you can set it up so that a file can be opened by only one person on the network at a time.

B

Using Help

Designer has an extensive system of online help screens. These screens provide information about Designer's commands, and they are particularly valuable for finding information about configuring the devices on which you produce your art. For example, you can find detailed instructions on installing and using the Matrix film recorder.

These are the basic methods for using online help:

- Select the Help menu and select an option.

- Press F1.

- Select a tool and press F1.

- Select a menu option and (while the menu is still open) press F1.

- Select a tool from the toolbox or from the menus and press F1.

- Open a dialog box and press F1.

- Open a dialog box and select an option from the dialog box's Help menu.

THE HELP MENU

Selecting Help from the menu bar displays the Help menu. Selecting any of the options except Help | About displays the Help window. The content of the window depends on the option selected.

Index	Displays an index of help topics, in alphabetical order
Current Topic (F1)	Displays a help message related to the tool or dialog box in use. (If you haven't selected a tool or dialog box you will see a message explaining how to use Current Topic.)
Table of Contents	Displays a list of subjects. Selecting a topic displays a list of related topics.

Using Help (F1-F1)	Displays an explanation of how to use the online help system. Pressing F1 twice instead of selecting Help | Using Help also displays the Using Help window.
Getting Started	Displays a quick overview of setting up and working with Designer
Printing	Displays an explanation of how to prepare to print your work
Presentations	Displays a list of topics related to producing slides and onscreen presentations. These topics are also available through the Help | Index command, but Help | Presentations makes it a little easier to find them.
Read Me	Displays a list of Read Me files that contain information about Designer that is too recent to have been included in the Micrografx documentation.
About	Displays the About panel, not a Help window. The About panel shows the version number and date of the copy of Designer you are using, copyright notices, a list of authors, and information about the amount of random access memory you have available for use by Designer.

THE HELP WINDOW

Once you have selected one of the Help options you will see the Help window. Figure B.1 shows the window displayed after selecting Help | Index.

The Help window is an application, but with limitations. You can still work in Designer while the Help menu is displayed over the drawing area, but you cannot display the Designer window on top of the Help window. You can, however, move the Help window out of the way, and reduce it in size using the Control menu or the borders. If you maximize the window (using the Control commands or the maximize arrow in the top right corner), the window blocks out Designer; you cannot work in Designer,

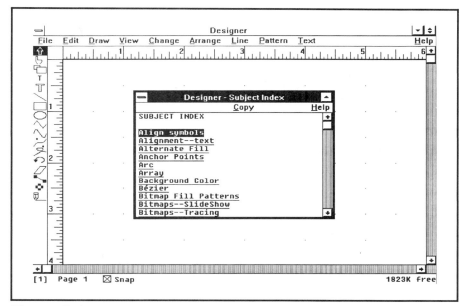

Figure B.1: The help index

because Windows won't allow you to use its commands to move to the
Designer window (though you can move to other applications).

The Help window has several menu options.

Index   Displays the index

Back   Displays the previous Help screen; you can move back
            16 screens

Next   Displays the next screen in the index sequence, or in a
            list-of-topics sequence

Copy   Copies the text displayed in the Help screen to the
            clipboard

Help (F1)   Displays the Using Help screen

Close the Help window by pressing Esc, by double-clicking on the
Control menu box in the top left of the window, or by selecting Close from
the Control menu.

PRINTING HELP SCREENS

You can enter the information from Help screens into a word processing program. Click on Copy in the menu bar and Designer puts the information from the displayed Help screen into the Windows clipboard. You can then export this information to another Windows application (such as Windows Write or a word processing program you are using in Windows), and save or print the information. (You can even import the information into Designer's drawing area—see Chapter 8.)

THE INDEX

The index (which you saw in Figure B.1) displays a list of all the help topics, in alphabetical order. You can scroll through the list using the scroll bars, and maximize the window so you can see more at one time. When you find a topic you are interested in, double-click on it, or click on it and press ◄─┘. (The double-click often "sticks" in the index—it is often easier to just click and press ◄─┘.) The list is actually in a "loop," so going up the list from the first entry takes you to the bottom of the list.

Using the Keyboard   Move the highlight down the index by pressing Tab or the right-arrow key—pressing and holding the key makes it move more quickly—or up the index by pressing Shift-Tab or the left-arrow key.

You can also scroll through by pressing PgUp, PgDn, End, and Home, but unfortunately these don't move the highlight—they just display a different part of the index—so you still need to use the Tab key to select the option. When you have selected an option, press ◄─┘. The table of contents also uses these keyboard commands.

Overlaying Another Help Window

You can display another Help window so that the index remains displayed while you view the contents of the message you selected from the index. Press Shift and double-click (or press ◄─┘) and Designer displays another window. You can display as many Help windows as you want, but be careful not to "lose" them. If you have the index maximized with a second Help window on top, clicking in the index again will move the second

window underneath the index window. In such a situation you need to minimize or close the index to get to the second window.

You can also use this method in the table of contents, or when you
select solid-underlined terms in the topic screens (explained in a moment).
Figure B.2 shows a second window on top of the table of contents.

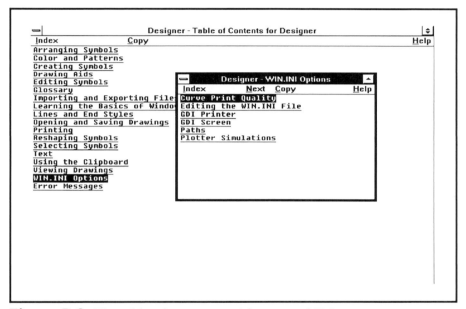

Figure B.2: The table of contents, with a second Help screen on top

THE TABLE OF CONTENTS

The table of contents is selected from the Help menu, or from the Table
of Contents entry in the index. The table of contents works in the same way
as the index. You can click on subjects you want displayed. The displayed
screen then shows another list of related topics from which you can select.
Figure B.2 shows the table of contents with the screen that is displayed if
you select WIN.INI options. Selecting one of *these* options then displays a
Topic screen.

DISPLAYING
INFORMATION ABOUT A TOPIC

Once you have selected a topic—from the table of contents, the index, or by selecting a tool or dialog box and pressing F1—Designer displays the appropriate Topic screen. Figure B.3 shows the screen displayed when you select Replace. You can scroll through the message if the scroll bars are displayed (they won't be if the message is only one screen long). Some messages include underlined terms. Double-click (or click and press ⬅) on a solid underline to see more information about that subject, or click once on a dashed line to see a definition of that term (click again to remove the definition). Figure B.3 shows a screen that has both solid and dashed lines, with a definition displayed.

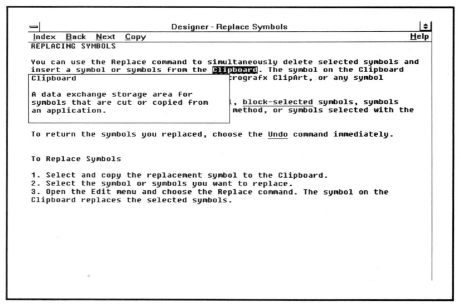

Figure B.3: The Replacing Symbols screen, with a definition box displayed

Using the Keyboard   To scroll through the Topic screen, use PgUp, PgDn, Home, and End. To move the highlight between underlined topics, press Tab or the right-arrow key (Shift-Tab or the left-arrow key to move in reverse). Press ← to select solid-underlined terms, or press the space bar quickly on a dashed-line term to make Designer display a definition box, and press Esc or ← to remove it. (Pressing and holding the space bar on a dashed line displays a definition just until you release it.)

USING THE GLOSSARY

Select Glossary from the index or from the table of contents to see the Glossary screen, shown in Figure B.4. Notice that each of the entries has a dashed underline, like the definition entries in the Topic screens. Move around in this screen using the same mouse and keyboard commands as those used in the index. When you have selected an option, display the definition in the same way you would in the Topic screens—by clicking once, pressing ←, or pressing the space bar.

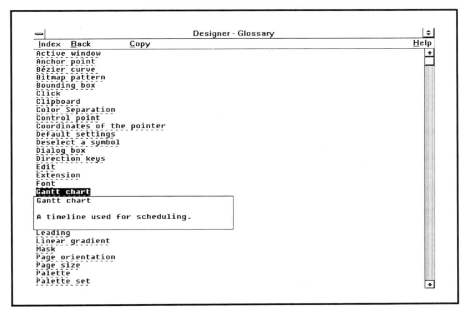

Figure B.4: The Glossary screen

USING THE
DIALOG-BOX HELP WINDOWS

Some of Designer's dialog boxes also have Help screens associated with them. For example, Figure B.5 shows the Index Help screen associated
with the HP ColorPro dialog box, and another selected Help window next
to it. (The HP ColorPro dialog box is displayed when you are exporting
images into HP Graphics Language—HPGL—format.) Actually, the Index
screens in the Help windows for the various devices are not really indexes—
they show a table of contents; selecting an option then displays a list of
related options.

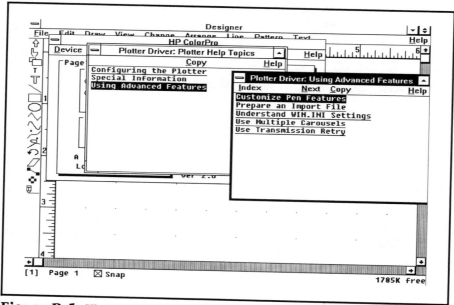

Figure B.5: The HP ColorPro Help screens

Several of the Export dialog boxes have online Help. These Help
screens have important information about preparing the file for export, so
you should read all the information before attempting an export. (It's not a
bad idea to copy all the screens into a word processing program using the
Copy command, and then print them out for future reference.)

Device-driver dialog boxes often have online help. For example, the Matrix film recorder has quite extensive online help that tells you how to avoid streaking your slides, how to prepare slides for a slide service, how to avoid text-kerning problems, how to use the menu options, and so on. If you are using an HP ColorPro plotter you can view the same Help menus you would see if you were exporting to HPGL format. The Micrografx PostScript driver also has online help.

NOTE

If you want to view information about the Toshiba driver, either select Help | Topics or select a menu, highlight an option, and press F1. The Help | Index command does not work in this driver.

Help is context-sensitive in most of the dialog boxes, so you can also view the Help window by displaying one of the menu options and pressing F1.

FINDING THE DESIGNER VERSION NUMBER

Use the Help | About command to view the About dialog box, which displays the version number and release date of the Designer package you are using. The dialog box displayed in Figure B.6 is from version 3.1. If you ever have to contact Micrografx's technical support, you need to make a note of the release number and date before calling. The telephone number is available via the rightmost icon—the telephone.

In Designer 3.0, the About dialog box also tells you how much conventional and expanded random access memory is presently available to Designer. In 3.1 you must use the Windows About box for this information.

VIEWING THE READ ME FILES

Many programs have Read Me files—files that you can read using the DOS TYPE command or a word processor. These files contain the latest

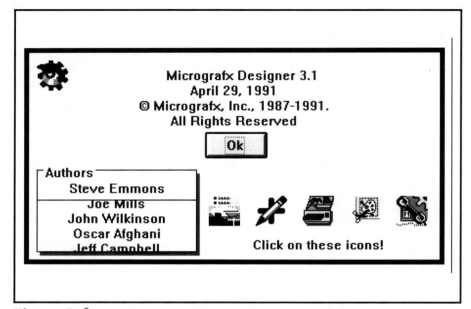

Figure B.6: The About box, Designer 3.1

information about the program, information that did not make it into the documentation.

Designer has made it easy to read these files by adding an option in the Help menu. Select Help | Read Me and you will see an introduction to the latest version followed by a list of topics. These include topics such as a list of changes to the software, features not included in the manuals, and general information about using fonts. It's a good idea to read the Read Me files when you first start Designer.

WINDOWS 3.0 HELP WINDOWS

If you are using Windows 3.0, the Control Panel and clipboard also have Help windows associated with them. These windows look quite different, but work in a similar manner. They have ''buttons'' at the top of the window. You can click on them or press the letter underlined in the button

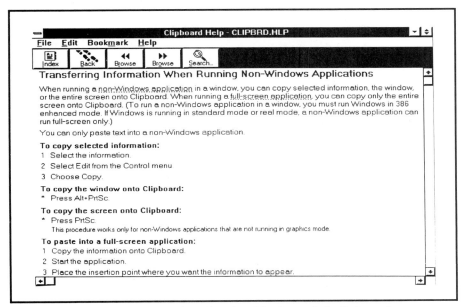

Figure B.7: The Help window for the Windows 3.0 clipboard

while you press and hold Alt. (For example, press Alt-I to see the index.) The clipboard's Help window is displayed in Figure B.7.

Above the buttons are menu options:

File	Lets you open another Windows 3.0 help file, print the information in the screen, or close the window
Edit	Lets you copy the contents of the screen into the clipboard, or add or delete your own notes
Bookmark	Lets you add a name to the displayed window; this name is then added to the Bookmark menu command, so you can quickly return to that screen at any time
Help	The same as Designer's Help menu option

The screens work in a manner similar to Designer's Help screens, with a few differences. You can still click on words underlined with a dashed line to see a definition of the word (hold down button 1), but you can't see the definition by pressing the space bar (use ↵ instead). Tab, Shift-Tab, and the PgUp, PgDn, Home, and End keys scroll through Windows' Help screens. The up and down arrow keys scroll through the window, but they don't move the highlight. (The right and left arrow keys don't do anything, except when you are selecting menu options.) Pressing Esc doesn't close the window—use the Control menu.

For more information on Windows' online help, see your Windows 3.0 documentation.

C

Customizing Designer

$\mathbf{T}$here are a number of things you can do to make Designer run just the way you want it—you can change mouse button 1 from the left button to the right, change the screen colors, add a warning beep, customize the toolbox, define the defaults for line and pattern styles, and so on.

You have already seen one way to customize Designer—using the Save checkboxes. For example, if you use the File | Open command, select a directory, select a file, click on the Save checkbox, and then click on OK, Designer opens the file and saves the directory setting; the next time you use Designer, selecting File | Open automatically displays that directory. However, as of this writing, not all of Designer's Save checkboxes are currently working. (The Save box in the Output File dialog box—the box displayed when you select Options | To File from the Print dialog box—does not work.) You have also learned, if you have read Chapter 13, how to make Designer open a color palette set other than the standard one.

Here's a summary of other ways to change Designer, and where to go to do so. It can be difficult to remember how to get to the dialog boxes that change these options, so use this as a memory jogger; the options are described in more detail later in this chapter.

- **AutoCAD Setup**   Change | Screen Color, Line | Color, Print | Reverse Black/White
- **Automatic Scroll**   View | Preferences
- **Border Width**   File | Print | Utilities | Control | Desktop icon
- **Color Palettes**   Color | File | Open (see Chapter 13)
- **Country Settings**   File | Print | Utilities | Controls | International icon
- **Cursor Blink**   File | Print | Utilities | Controls | Desktop icon
- **Double-Click**   File | Print | Utilities | Controls | Mouse icon
- **Drawing Area Color**   View | Screen Color and View | Preferences | Save
- **Font Sizing Units**   View | Preferences
- **Handle Size**   View | Preferences
- **Keyboard Speed**   File | Print | Utilities | Controls | Keyboard icon

- **Line Style**   Line | commands and View | Preferences | Save
- **Make Backups**   View | Preferences
- **Maximize Window**   View | Preferences
- **Mouse Button 1 (Change)**   File | Print | Utilities | Controls | Mouse icon
- **Mouse Button 2 (Add Command)**   Edit | Button 2 or Alt-Button2
- **Object-Background Color**   Change | Background Color and View | Preferences | Save
- **Opening Designer automatically**   Change Run = or Load = in WIN.INI
- **Pattern Styles**   Pattern | commands and View | Preferences | Save
- **Print Files**   Change the WIN.INI file
- **Save Current Settings**   View | Preferences | Save
- **Screen Colors**   File | Print | Utilities | Controls | Color icon. See Drawing Area Color, also.
- **Show Preview**   View | Preferences
- **Text Styles**   Text | commands and View | Preferences | Save
- **Time & Date**   File | Print | Utilities | Controls | Time/Date icon
- **Tool Box**   View | Tools
- **Warning Beep**   File | Print | Utilities | Controls | Sound icon

Most of these options are set using the Preferences dialog box or the Control Panel, so I've grouped the options accordingly.

USING THE PREFERENCES DIALOG BOX

Select View | Preferences to see the Preferences dialog box, as shown on Figure C.1. Selecting an item in this dialog box does not change the current session, it changes Designer's default settings that will be used the next

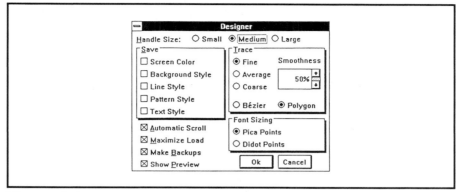

Figure C.1: The Preferences dialog box, Designer 3.1

time you open Designer. (You can also set the Trace options here—see Chapter 4 for more information.)

Handle Size	You can select Small, Medium, or Large handles. These are the black boxes that appear when you select an object.
Save	This is Save Settings. You can select which of the current settings you want used as the standard settings for the next time you open Designer. (The various options are discussed following this list.) For example, if you have changed the screen color (the drawing-area color) to blue and selected Screen Color in the Preferences dialog box, the next time you open Designer the drawing area will be blue.
Automatic Scroll	Automatic Scroll is the way the drawing area automatically moves when you move the pointer against the borders while dragging an object (holding button 1 down). If this is selected, the next time you open Designer Automatic Scroll will be working. This is especially important if you don't have a mouse, because it makes it easier to move around the drawing area using the keyboard.
Maximize Load	Selecting this option makes Designer display a full-screen (maximized) window when you open Designer.

Make Backups	If this option is selected Designer makes backups automatically each time you save a file (the Backup checkbox in the Save File dialog boxes will be selected automatically).
Show Preview	If this option is selected the Show Preview mode is on when you open Designer; that is, objects are displayed with all the detail included, rather than in "wireform" mode.
Font Sizing	This allows you to choose whether Designer will be working with *pica points* (0.0138 inches per point, used in the United States and the United Kingdom) or the slightly larger *didot points* (0.0148 inches per points, used in some other countries).

3.1

As soon as you close this dialog box the Save settings are written into the WIN.INI file, the Windows file that is used to save Designer's standard settings. If you then select other options—you pick a different Screen Color or a different Text Style, those changes are not written into WIN.INI, unless you use the Preferences dialog box again. There are five Save settings:

- **Screen Color**   The screen color selected with View | Screen Color

- **Background Style**   The object-background color selected with Change | Background Color.

- **Line Style**   The line type and color selected with Line | commands

- **Pattern Style**   The pattern and color selected with Pattern | commands

- **Text Style**   The font, size, features, and color selected with Text | commands

---

NOTE
There were some bugs in the Designer 3.0 Preference dialog box; some of the Save selection buttons did not seem to work, at least not consistently. The bugs were cleared in Designer 3.01.

THE CONTROL PANEL

The Control Panel (two versions are shown in Figures C.2 and C.3) is a Windows utility that Micrografx has also added to Designer, so even people with the runtime version of Windows can use it. If you already have Windows you probably know how to use the Control Panel; it can be opened by double-clicking on the Control Panel icon in the Main Program Manager window (in Windows 3.0), or by double-clicking on CONTROL.EXE in the MS-DOS Executive Window (in pre-3.0 versions of Windows).

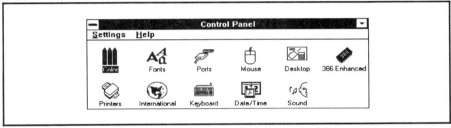

Figure C.2: The Windows 3.0 Control Panel

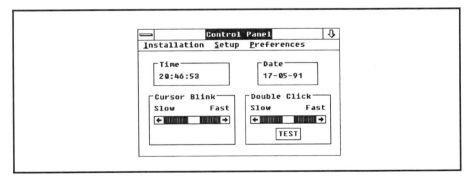

Figure C.3: The Pre-3.0 Windows Control Panel

IMPORTANT

Changing settings with Control Panel changes them for all Windows programs, not just for Designer. It also changes the system defaults; the next time you open Designer or Windows it will automatically use the settings you make in the Control Panel.

If you are using the runtime version you can access the Control Panel through a series of menu choices that constitutes almost a "hidden passage." Select File | Print | Utilities | Controls (File | Print selects the Print dialog box, and selecting the Controls command in that box's Utilities menu displays the Control Panel).

Notice that the Control Panel has no OK or Cancel command buttons. You make your changes and then close the panel by double-clicking on the Control-menu bar (in the top left corner), by pressing Alt-space and typing *C,* by using the Settings | Exit command (Windows 3.0), or by using the Installation | Exit command (pre-3.0 versions).

The Settings menu in the Windows 3.0 Control Panel duplicates the icons—for example, selecting Settings | Mouse is the same as double-clicking on the Mouse icon—and has an Exit option that closes the dialog box. The following description of the Control Panel explains the Windows 3.0 Control Panel, with notes describing how the pre-3.0 versions of Windows differ.

THE COLOR DIALOG BOX

Double-click on the Color icon to see the Color dialog box. Then click on the Color Palette command button to see the right side of the box (Figure C.4). This dialog box lets you change the colors of up to 13 different screen

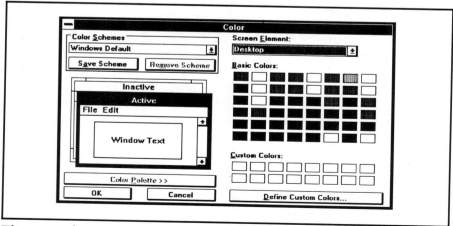

Figure C.4: The Color dialog box (Windows 3.0)

components. Windows has several color schemes you can select from (by clicking on the down arrow in the Color Schemes text box), but you can create your own by clicking on the down arrow in the Screen Element text box, selecting the element you want to change, and then clicking on one of the color boxes. You can even mix your own colors using the Define Custom Colors command button. Once you have added the colors you want, click on Save Scheme and Windows will ask you for a scheme name.

Note that within the sample box the Window Background is not the same as the Screen Color, even though it appears the same. Changing the Window Background color changes Designer's dialog boxes, rulers, toolbox, and status line, along with the window backgrounds of all the other Windows programs you may have, but Designer's drawing area remains unchanged. Changing the Application Workspace color changes the color of the area behind the drawing area, the area to the right of the drawing area when you select View | All Pages.

Pre-3.0 and Runtime Windows   As you can see from Figure C.5, the Color dialog box used by earlier versions of Windows was simpler. You select the item you want to change, use the scroll bars to change the colors, brightness, and hue, and see an example of what the colors will actually look like. The Reset command button changes the color settings back to the way they were when you entered the dialog box, and the OK button accepts the changes you have made.

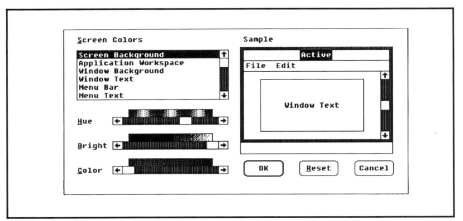

Figure C.5: The Pre-3.0 Windows Screen Colors dialog box

THE FONTS, PORTS, 386 ENHANCED, AND PRINTERS DIALOG BOXES

The Fonts dialog box is used to load Windows screen fonts, and is explained in Chapter 8. The Ports and Printers dialog boxes are used to provide Windows with information about the devices connected to your computer, and are explained in Chapter 10. The 386 Enhanced dialog box is used to tell Windows how to handle multitasking in 386 Enhanced mode—see your Windows documentation for more information.

THE MOUSE DIALOG BOX

The Mouse dialog box, displayed when you double-click on the Mouse icon, is shown in Figure C.6. Use the top scroll bar to adjust the Mouse "Tracking Speed." This changes the distance (not, strictly speaking, the speed) moved by the pointer when the mouse is moved. With the setting on high, the pointer moves about twice as far as it would with the low setting, even though you move the mouse the same distance.

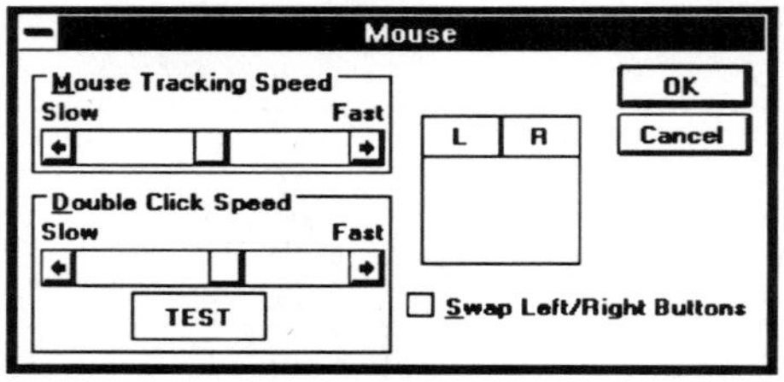

Figure C.6: The Mouse dialog box

Use the lower scroll bar to adjust the speed with which you must click mouse button 1 to effect a "double-click." Use the TEST box to experiment—the box changes from white to black when you click at the correct speed.

Use the Swap Left/Right Buttons checkbox to change the button 1 position (the button that is the "dominant" button, the one used most often) to the right button, something most left-handers find useful. You can even confirm the setting by pointing the mouse to a blank space in the dialog box and clicking; one of the boxes above the checkbox will flash; R flashes to indicate that you clicked the "right" button, and L flashes to indicate the "left" button.

Pre-3.0 and Runtime Windows   If you have a version of Windows earlier than 3.0 you will change mouse settings in two places. As you can see from Figure C.3 earlier in this appendix, you can set the double-click speed in the Control Panel itself. To change the other mouse settings, select Preferences | Mouse.

THE DESKTOP DIALOG BOX

Double-click on the Desktop icon to see the Desktop dialog box (Figure C.7). The Pattern and Wallpaper commands change the patterns displayed on the Windows desktop (the area underneath the windows), and the Icon Spacing and Granularity settings affect how icons are spaced; see your Windows documentation for more information on these commands.

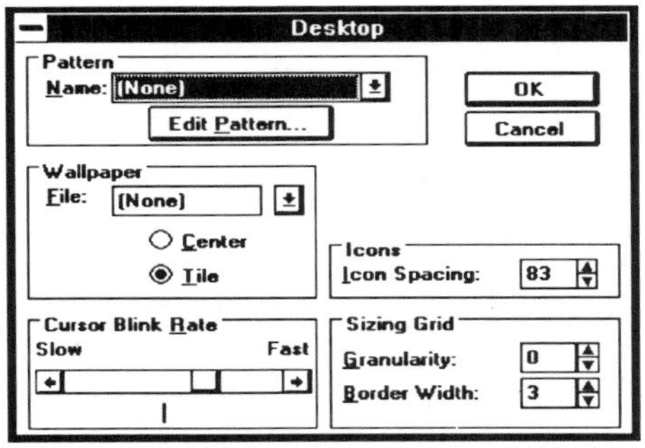

Figure C.7: The Desktop dialog box

The Cursor Blink scroll bar can be used to adjust the speed with which the text cursor blinks. Look at the cursor below the bar to see the current cursor blink; also, while the scroll bar is selected the scroll bar button flashes to indicate the blink rate.

The Border Width setting lets you adjust the size of the windows' borders, from almost too thin to see, to so thick it looks clunky.

Pre-3.0 and Runtime Windows   In pre-3.0 and runtime versions of Windows the Cursor Blink box appears in the Control Panel itself, and you can change the border width by selecting Preferences | Border Width.

THE INTERNATIONAL DIALOG BOX

Double-click on the International icon to see the International dialog box (Figure C.8). This dialog box lets you change time, date, number, and currency settings according to the country you are in. You can either select a country from the list (in which case the dialog box automatically changes to conform to that country's norms), or you can change the settings individually to customize your own settings (select Other Country at the bottom of the list first, so that you don't lose one of the country settings). The only setting that really affects Designer is the Keyboard Layout setting.

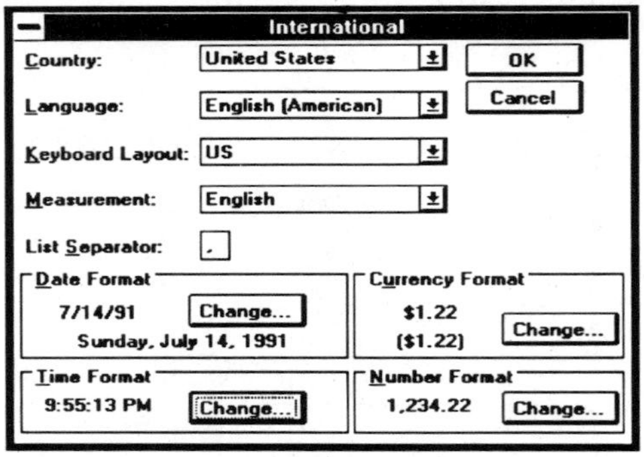

Figure C.8: The International dialog box

Pre-3.0 and Runtime Windows   If you are not using Windows 3.0, you can view the Country Settings dialog box by selecting Preferences | Country Settings in the Control Panel.

THE KEYBOARD DIALOG BOX

Double-click on the Keyboard icon to see the Keyboard dialog box (Figure C.9). This lets you change the keyboard repeat rate, the rate at which characters are repeated when you hold down a key. This is a very important setting if you don't have a mouse, because it affects how quickly the pointer is moved by the arrow keys. If you have a low setting, some operations are so slow as to be almost impossible; for example, copying or moving by ''dragging'' the item is almost impossible with a slow repeat rate, but easy with a fast one. The Keyboard dialog box has a scroll bar that lets you adjust the speed, and a text box where you can test the speed by holding down a character key.

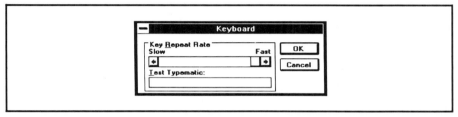

Figure C.9: The Keyboard dialog box

Pre-3.0 and Runtime Windows　　If you don't have Windows 3.0, select Preferences | Keyboard Speed to view the Keyboard Speed dialog box.

THE DATE & TIME DIALOG BOX

Double-click on the Date/Time icon to see the Date & Time dialog box (Figure C.10); click on the number you want to change and use the scroll arrows to change the number. This dialog box changes the time and date in DOS.

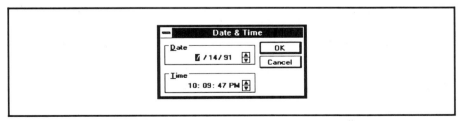

Figure C.10: The Date & Time dialog box

Pre-3.0 and Runtime Windows   In pre-3.0 and runtime versions of Windows the Time and Date boxes appear in the Control Panel itself; click on the number you want to change and a scroll bar appears to the right. Use the scroll bar to change the number.

THE SOUND DIALOG BOX

Click on the Sound icon to view the Sound dialog box (Figure C.11). You can choose to make your computer beep at you if you make an invalid keystroke or mouse click. For example, if Designer has locked up, perhaps due to a memory problem, your computer will beep when you try to select a menu or option (press Esc to clear it).

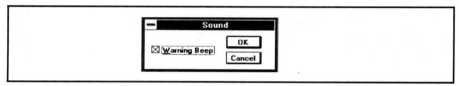

Figure C.11: The Sound dialog box

Pre-3.0 and Runtime Windows   If you don't have Windows 3.0, you can view the Warning Beep dialog box by selecting Preferences | Warning Beep from the Control Panel.

SETTING MOUSE BUTTON 2

Designer has a feature that allows you to assign any command to button 2 on your mouse. Select Edit | Button 2 (Keyboard Shortcut: Alt-button 2) to see the Set Button 2 dialog box (Figure C.12).

This is very easy to use. Just select a command from one of the menus; the dialog box disappears, and button 2 now activates the selected command. For example, if you selected Pattern | Color, each time you press button 2 the Select Pattern Color dialog box appears. The Home command button in the Set Button 2 dialog box removes the command from button 2, and if you select the Save checkbox, the command assigned to button 2 is saved when you close Designer, and is automatically assigned the next time you open Designer.

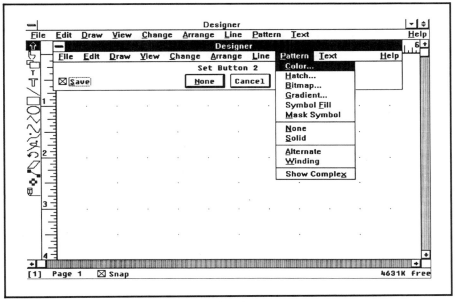

Figure C.12: The Set Button 2 dialog box

There is an even quicker way to assign a command to button 2. Point to a tool in the toolbox and press button 2. The command associated with that tool is now assigned to button 2.

NOTE

When you use the button 2 command, the pointer will not change shape to the type of pointer normally associated with that command. Also, the command assigned to button 2 does not work when you have selected the Trace tool.

CUSTOMIZING THE TOOLBOX

Designing lets you customize the toolbox using the View | Tools command. The Choose Tools dialog box (Figure C.13) allows you to turn the toolbox on and off (using the Show Tools checkbox), and save the toolbox

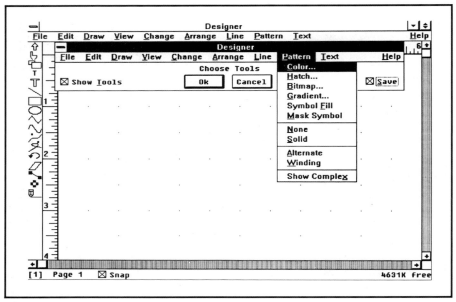

Figure C.13: The Choose Tools dialog box

settings for future Designer settings (using the Save checkbox).

   Add tools to the toolbox by selecting them from the menus in the dialog box. Tools already shown in the toolbox are indicated by a checkmark against the command name in the menu, and you can also remove tools from the box by selecting them from the menus. If you open a menu and point to a checkmarked command, the corresponding icon in the toolbox is highlighted—a quick way to identify icons you are not sure about. (Don't release the mouse button though, or the tool is removed from the box.) Once the toolbox is full, you cannot select any more tools. Any menu command can be added to the toolbox.

   If you assign a command to the toolbox, the toolbox icon acts just like the menu option. For example, if you add Change | Rotation to the toolbox, ROT is displayed. Whenever you want to use the Rotation dialog box, double-click on ROT.

SIMULATING AUTOCAD

   Some users may prefer to make Designer's screen drawings look more like CAD screens. Many CAD programs (such as AutoCAD) have a black background and white lines; if that's the way you want to use Designer, change the drawing-area color using View | Screen Color, change the line color to white using Line | Color, then select the Preferences dialog box (View | Preferences), click on the Screen Color and Line Style checkboxes, and click on OK. When you are ready to print your work, though, select File | Print and click on Reverse Black/White so that the art is printed correctly.

LOADING DESIGNER AUTOMATICALLY

You can make Windows automatically load Designer each time you open Windows. Earlier in this chapter I explained how to change the WIN.INI file; there are two lines in WIN.INI, near the top of the file, that allow you to load an application automatically.

The line ''Load = '' tells Windows to open Designer automatically, and to place it near the bottom of the screen as an icon. The line ''Run = '' tells Windows to actually display the Designer window as the active window. Simply type the drive and path name of DESIGNER.EXE, and save WIN.INI. For example, enter the following line, substituting the correct drive and pathname:

```
run = c:\windows\designer.exe
```

When you have used Designer for a while you will get ideas on how to streamline things; which tools to add to the toolbox, which command to use on button 2, and so on. Using the techniques in this appendix, you can customize Designer, making it easier and more efficient to use.

D

Importing and Exporting Art

Designer lets you use art from other graphics programs, and export art for use by other programs. Of the 18 different formats, you can import 14 and export 15. The translators are being updated constantly, so what I describe here may not be exactly what you have on your system; if you experiment a little, however, you should be able to figure out the differences.

FORMAT	IMPORT/ EXPORT	VECTOR/ BITMAT	DESCRIPTION
.AI	Both	Vector	Adobe Illustrator, the format used by Adobe Illustrator on the Macintosh and PC, and by Adobe Illustrator 88 on the Mac. You can also import Adobe Illustrator files that have .EPS extensions, using the .EPS translator.
.CGM	Both	Vector	Computer Graphics Metafile, an ANSI graphics format, used by PageMaker, Ventura Publisher, Harvard Graphics, Freelance.
.DRW	Both	Vector	MGX_DRAW, Micrografx Designer format. This format also used by Micrografx Draw Plus, Graph Plus, and Charisma. When exporting you have the option of saving in 3.0, 2.0, or 1.x format so that your images can be used in earlier versions of Designer.
.DXF	Both	Vector	Data Exachange Format, produced by Autodesk for Auto-CAD, and supported by many CADD programs.

.EPS (TIFF preview)	Export	Vector/ Bitmap	Encapsulated PostScript, used by Ventura Publisher, WordPerfect, PageMaker, and many Macintosh programs. This version includes the TIFF preview; that is, the graphic will be visible inside the application into which it is imported. This is a combination of vector and bitmap images. .EPS images can only be printed on PostScript printers, and before you can export a file in this format you must load the Micrografx PostScript printer driver.
.EPS (no TIFF preview)	Export	Vector/ Bitmap	The same as .EPS with TIFF preview, except this version has no TIFF preview; it will not be visible in the application into which you import it, though it will print when the document is printed. You can export this format if you have pre-3.1 versions of Designer, but you can only import the EPS file if you have Designer 3.1. These files use less memory than the .EPS with preview.
.EPS (Adobe Illustrator)	Import	Vector	Encapsulated PostScript files created by Adobe Illustrator. This format is exactly the same as the .AI format, the only difference being the extension. There is no .EPS (Adobe Illustrator) export translator; rather, you will use the .AI translator.

.GEM	Both	Vector	Graphics Environment Manager, produced by GEM Desktop for its GEM line of programs and used by many others, such as Ventura Publisher. Designer 3.1 lets you specify the export type: GEM Artline or GEM Draw.
.GRF	Import	Vector	Micrografx Graph file, produced by Graph Plus and Charisma. The .GRF file is very similar to a .DRW format, with a data file used to draw the graph, but Designer ignores the data.
.HP	Export	Vector	HP Graphics Language (HPGL), used by Hewlett-Packard plotters, Ventura Publisher, Microsoft Word, and WordPerfect.
.PCT	Both	Vector	Macintosh .PICT files. Used by Macintosh programs such as MacDraw, MacWrite, and PageMaker.
.PCX	Both	Bitmap	A common bitmap file format, produced by ZSoft for PC Paintbrush. Used by many other programs, such as Windows Paint and Microsoft Word, and produced by many scanners.
.PIC	Both	Vector	MGX_PICT, Micrografx Picture files; this format was used by earlier Micrografx programs such as In*a*Vision and Windows Draw, and even Designer for a very short time. Compatible with

			many desktop publishing and presentation programs. This is not the same as the Lotus .PIC format, nor the Macintosh .PICT format.
.PS	Export	Vector	PostScript, used by some PostScript-compatible applications (some, such as Page-Maker, use .EPS instead).
.TIF	Both	Bitmap	Tag Image File Format (TIFF), an industry-standard format. Produced by scanners and used by many programs, such as Microsoft Word, Ventura Publisher, and PageMaker.
.TXT	Import	Text	ANSI text files.
.WMF	Both	Vector/ Bitmap	Windows Metafile Format, developed for use in Micro-soft Windows applications such as PageMaker. This is a combination of text, vector, and bitmap.
.WPG	Both	Vector	WordPerfect Graphics, the format used by WordPerfect and DrawPerfect.

3.1

PREPARING YOUR SYSTEM

When you installed Designer most of the file translators were installed automatically; however, you must select the following translators if you intend to use them:

.AI   Adobe Illustrator

.CGM   Computer Graphics Metafile

.DXF   AutoCAD Data Exchange Format

.GEM   Graphics Environment Manager

.PCT   Macintosh PICT files

.WPG   WordPerfect Graphics

Note that the .AI and .WPG formats are only available if you have Designer 3.1. In addition, if you want to export .EPS or .PS files you must install the Micrografx PostScript printer driver, and if you want to export .HP files you must install the HPGL plotter driver.

Translating the vector images can take a lot of memory, so before doing so make sure that you have optimized memory management. You may have to unload memory resident applications such as network and external-drive drivers, and you should also make sure you have plenty of space on your hard disk. Designer also needs the TEMP directory, so the relevant lines must be in the AUTOEXEC.BAT file (see Appendix A). If you are using a version of Windows previous to 3.0, open windows using the /n switch. This gives Designer control of memory management. For example type win386 /n or win86 /n or win /n, depending on the version you are using. If you are using runtime Windows, start Designer using the /n switch—type designer /n. If you don't open the pre-3.0 Windows or runtime Designer using the /n switch some of the translators will be unusable, and others will be very slow. If you are using Windows 3.0, open it as you normally would.

Once in Windows, close any applications you are not using, including such accessories as the clock, Control Panel, calendar, and so on. Even with all these precautions, you may find some of the translations taking a very long time, especially on slow machines. Luckily Designer gives some indication that something is happening—either a dialog box displaying the percentage of the operation that has been completed, or a box showing the elapsed time (though of course this latter method doesn't tell you how much longer the operation will take). Some translations take just a few seconds, others take many minutes, especially if you have a slow processor with little memory.

TRANSLATING FILES

It is important to understand that the bitmap formats are not translated (converted) when you *import* them. They remain bitmaps, but can be manipulated within Designer; it may also be possible to convert them to

.DRW files using the Change | Trace command, depending on the complexity of the image. See Chapter 3 for more information.

Files *exported* in a bitmap format *are* converted of course, as are files exported in vector formats, or vector formats imported to Designer. However, conversions are not always perfect or complete. For example, although Designer 3.0 has Bézier curves, if you convert to Designer 1.x format those curves have to be converted to polylines, with a loss in accuracy. Some programs have features that Designer does not have. For example, importing a 3-D .DXF image doesn't work very well, because Designer doesn't use three-dimensional pictures. And some vector formats cannot be edited once you get them into Designer; they can be incorporated into your art, but you won't be able to modify the imported graphics directly.

Also, note that each format may have several different types; there are several different .TIF and .PCX formats, for example, and two different .AI formats. Make sure you are working with the type you need; you may have to experiment a little to get it right.

IMPORTING FILES

When you are ready to import a file, select File | Import. Designer displays the Import dialog box (Figure D.1).

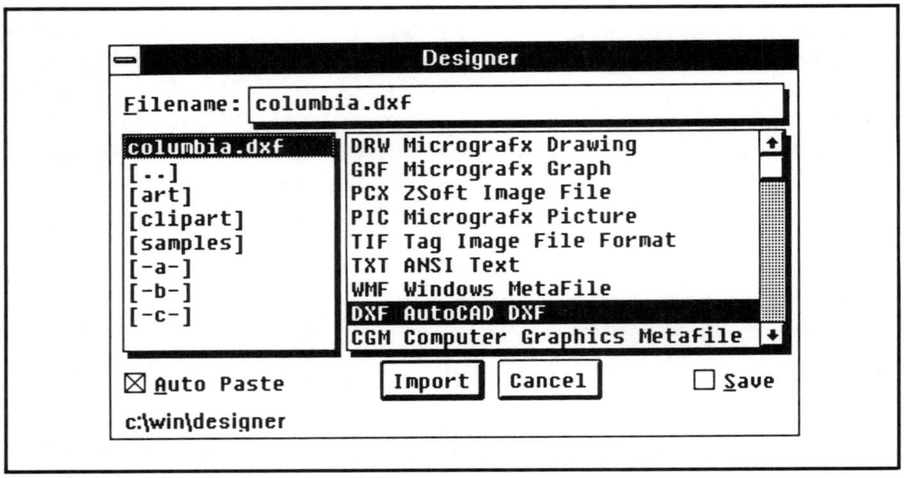

Figure D.1: The Import dialog box

Click in the right-hand list box to select the format of the file you are going to import, and the extension in the Filename box at the top of the dialog box changes to the appropriate one. Then select the file in the list box on the left of the dialog box.

Select the Auto Paste option you want to use. Using Auto Paste allows you to import files larger than the clipboard can handle. With Auto Paste on, the file will be pasted directly into the middle of the displayed drawing area. (If you import a lot of files at once you may find that Designer stops putting them in the area displayed; select View | All Pages to see where they went—probably to the top of the drawing area.) If you want to duplicate the imported image, turn Auto Paste off so that Designer puts the image into the clipboard; Designer automatically selects the Paste tool, so you can position the pointer and press button 1 to paste the imported file. Then move to the next position and paste the second image, and so on.

When everything is set as you want it, double-click on the filename, or click on OK. Designer begins importing the file, or, for some formats, displays a dialog box with options you must set (these are explained later in this appendix). Select the options you want and click on OK.

Designer then displays a status dialog box; this shows the percentage of the job that has been completed, or the elapsed time. When the translation is complete, Designer either pastes the file into the drawing area (if you had Auto Paste on), or puts it into the clipboard and automatically selects the Paste tool.

NOTE

Once the image has been imported to the clipboard, you don't have to paste it right away; you can select another tool to turn off Paste mode, and paste the image later. (Don't Edit | Cut or Edit | Copy anything else, though, or it will be written over the imported image.)

EXPORTING FILES

You can export a file, or just a portion of the file: if no object is selected the entire file is exported, otherwise only the selected objects are exported. When you are ready to export, select File | Export. Designer displays the Export dialog box, shown in Figure D.2.

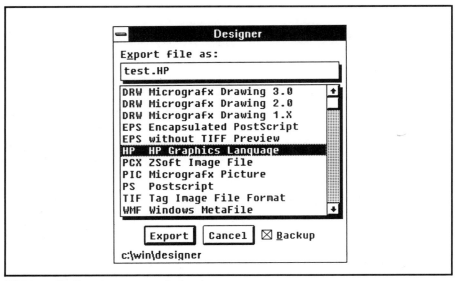

Figure D.2: The Export dialog box

Enter a path and file name in the text box at the top of the dialog box, and then select the format to which you want the file translated; when you select a format Designer adds the appropriate extension to the file name you entered. Then click on OK. Designer begins exporting the file, or, for some formats, displays a dialog box with options you must set (these are explained later in this appendix). Select the options you want and click on OK.

Designer then displays a status dialog box; this shows the percentage of the job that has been completed, or the elapsed time.

THE IMPORT/EXPORT FORMATS

Here, then, are the different formats, with information about importing and exporting each one.

3.1

.AI—Adobe Illustrator

When you import a .AI format file the file is brought in directly; you will not see a dialog box asking for information about the file. When you export a file to .AI format, though, you will see the AI Output dialog box (Figure D.3).

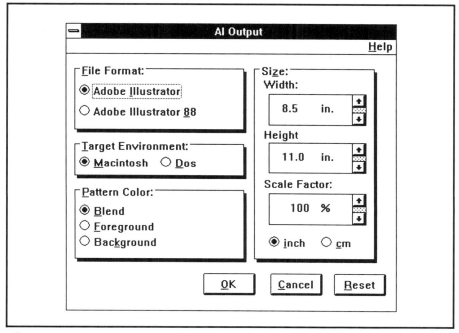

Figure D.3: The AI Output (Export) dialog box

You can specify what type of Adobe Illustrator file you want to create—a file for Adobe Illustrator or a file for Adobe Illustrator 88. If you select the first type you must also choose whether you want the file in the Macintosh or DOS format.

Adobe will not take Designer's bitmap or hatch patterns, so you must choose how to convert such patterns. You can select Blend to mix the colors to get an approximation of the pattern's color, or the Foreground color or Background color. Adobe Illustrator uses page-size limits, so you must tell Designer the size of the page that will be used; Designer will reduce the image to fit into the page size you define (the default is 8.5 inches by 11 inches). You can also adjust the scaling; for example, if you enter 50 percent the object is reduced to take up half of the page size. If you enter a scale value above 100 percent the image will be larger than the page size, which may be a problem when you try to manipulate the image in Adobe Illustrator.

Imported .AI files cannot be edited, nor can you add color or patterns. By the way, Micrografx also added an import translator named *.EPS (Adobe Illustrator)*; this is just the same as the .AI import translator, the only difference being that when the Import dialog box appears only files with the .EPS extension will be displayed in the list box. The .AI and .EPS translators can translate the same files.

.CGM—Computer Graphics Metafile

Importing in .CGM format displays the .CGM Input dialog box (Figure D.4).

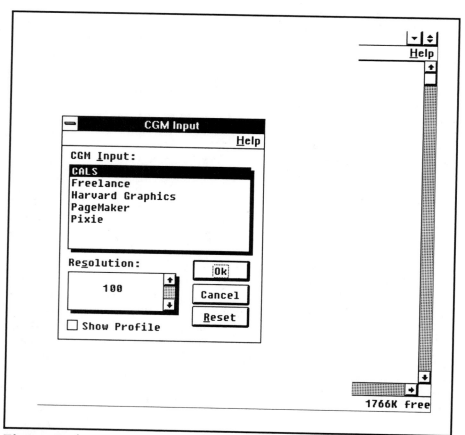

Figure D.4: The .CGM Input (Import) dialog box

There are several different .CGM formats; select the appropriate one in the list box (the one the file to be exported is intended for, or the format in which the file to be imported was originally created). Selecting the wrong format may lead to scaling and color-matching problems.

Select the resolution; selecting a larger number reduces the picture's size, and a smaller one increases the size.

When you export a .CGM file you see the .CGM Output dialog box (Figure D.5).

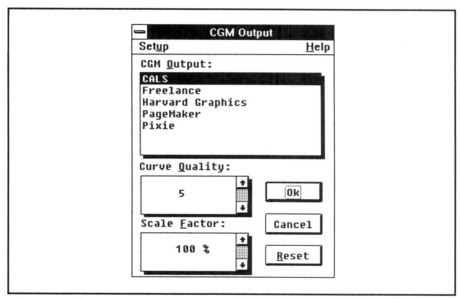

Figure D.5: The .CGM Output (Export) dialog box

.CGM files don't use Bézier curves, so when you are exporting a file you should select the Curve Quality; a high number creates smooth polylines with many points, while a low number produces polylines with fewer points. The higher the quality, the bigger the file will be. Some applications limit the numbers of points in an object, so high-quality objects will have points removed by those applications.

If you are exporting you can select a scale; a high number produces a large image, a small number a small one. The default size is 100.

The .CGM Output dialog box has a Setup menu, with the following options:

Add CGM Type	Lets you add a new CGM format to the list in the list box
Edit CGM Type	Lets you edit one of the formats in the list box
Delete CGM Type	Lets you remove one of the formats in the list box

Selecting Add or Edit CGM Type displays the CGM File Type dialog box (Figure D.6). You can set the following options (check the correct settings in the program's documentation, or call the program's technical support line):

Scaling Mode	Abstract (no defined page size, used by most .CGM programs) or Metric (sets the page size)
Color Specification Mode	Direct (red/green/blue—not all .CGM programs can use this) or Indexed (colors are indexed to a color table)
Include Color Table	Select this if you selected the Indexed Color Specification Mode
Coordinate Type	The coordinate system used by the program that will use the file

To Edit or delete a file format, select that format and then select the Setup menu option. This dialog box also has a Help menu. Use this to read further information.

.DRW—MGX_DRAW, Micrografx Designer

You can import .DRW files from any version of Designer. You might want to do this as a way to merge two files. You can also use the File | ClipArt command to import objects by Symbol ID from another Designer file, or open another Designer window using the Control menu's Add Window option and then copy objects through the clipboard (on slow systems, though, opening another window is impractical).

You can export Designer 3.0 files to earlier formats. However, because earlier formats didn't have all the features of 3.0, some distortion may

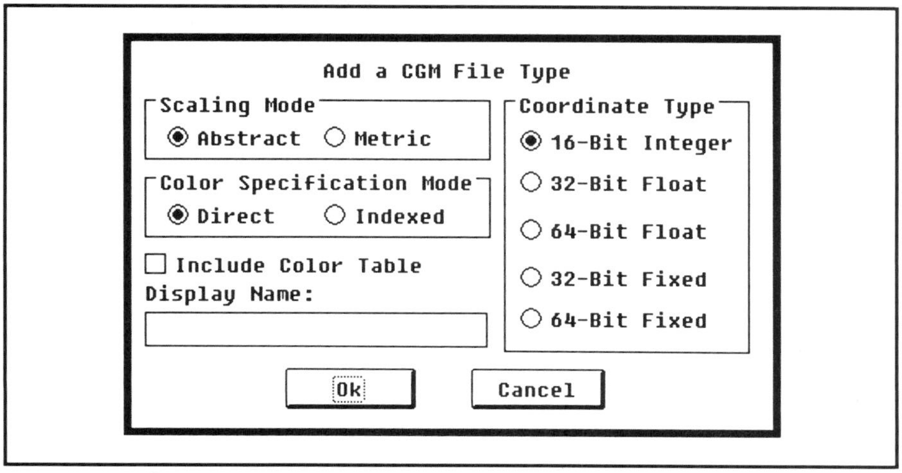

Figure D.6: The CGM File Type dialog box

occur. For example, when you export Bézier curves to .DRW 1.x format the curves are changed to polylines.

You can even export files to Designer 3.0 format. This is an easy way to duplicate the file; it is the same as using File | Save As to create a new file, and then opening the original file. But you can also use it to save selected portions of the file by selecting those objects and exporting them. You could use this technique to save parts of a file as templates for later use, for example, even selecting all the objects on one layer and exporting that layer to another file.

.DXF—Data Exchange Format

When you translate .DXF files Designer uses temporary files on your hard disk. If you don't have enough space (usually about half the size of the original file) Designer will not be able to complete the translation. Before importing a .DXF file use the AutoCAD Purge command to remove unwanted objects.

NOTE
Designer cannot import three-dimensional .DXF images

Because AutoCAD has a black background, it doesn't use black lines. Other programs' black lines are converted to white when you export to AutoCAD; to convert AutoCAD's white lines to black when you import, select Reverse Black/White in the DXF Input dialog box (Figure D.7). Colored lines are displayed in color, they don't require converting.

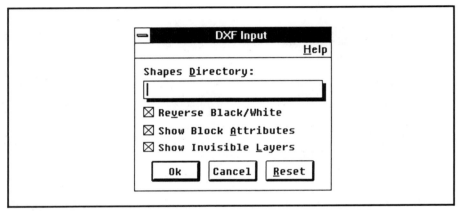

Figure D.7: The DXF Input (Import) dialog box

This dialog box lets you indicate the directory in which the AutoCAD *shape libraries* are kept. (The translation of shapes is explained in detail in the dialog box's Help menu (Help | Index | Translation).) You can also select these options:

Reverse Black/White	This converts AutoCAD's white lines to black.
Show Block Attributes	This retains the original file's block attributes. These are names given to blocks of objects in Auto-CAD. If you Show Block Attributes, Designer will convert the attribute names to text and place them next to the object in the drawing area.
Show Invisible Layers	If you don't select this, any layers frozen or hidden in the original file are not translated.

When you export a file in .DXF format you see the DXF Output dialog box, shown in Figure D.8.

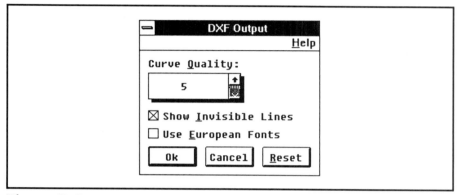

Figure D.8: The DXF Output (Export) dialog box

This box lets you define the Curve Quality—because .DXF files don't use Bézier curves, they must be translated into polylines. A low Curve Quality setting produces curves with few points, while a high setting makes smooth curves with many points. Show Invisible Lines includes invisible lines in the exported file, so that objects with invisible lines don't disappear. Use European Fonts converts European characters to their correct AutoCAD formats.

NOTE

If the file you are exporting has a text caret (^) Designer will not be able to translate the file. Remove the caret before exporting.

These dialog boxes have extensive online Help. Read the screens before trying to import or export. If you are having trouble importing a .DXF image into Designer, check to see if AutoCAD can import the same image; if AutoCAD can't use it, nor can Designer.

.EPS—Encapsulated PostScript

You can export .EPS files with or without a TIFF preview. A TIFF preview lets you see the object on the screen in the application into which you loaded it. If you load an .EPS file without TIFF preview into an application, you will see a box instead of the art, but you can still print the art on a PostScript printer. Files with the preview are larger than those without, and some programs may be unable to use the preview anyway. Make sure the Micrografx PostScript printer driver is installed before converting. You cannot import .EPS files, except—with Designer 3.1—those created by Adobe Illustrator.

.EPS—Adobe Illustrator Encapsulated PostScript Files

If you have Designer 3.1 you will see an import translator named .EPS (Adobe Illustrator EPS) in the Import dialog box; this translator is exactly the same as the one labelled .AI (Adobe Illustrator AI), except that when you use the .EPS translator only files with an .EPS extension are displayed in the Import dialog box. (When you use the .AI translator only files with an .AI extension appear.) The .AI (Adobe Illustrator AI) and .EPS (Adobe Illustrator EPS) translators can translate the same files.

.GEM—Graphics Environment Manager

When exporting to .GEM format, Designer creates translation files on your hard disk—you must have an area at least half the size of the original file available.

If you have a version of Designer earlier than 3.1 you see the GEM Output dialog box when you export to GEM format (Figure D.9).

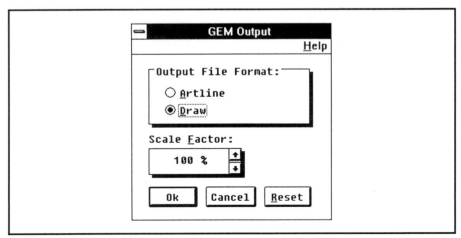

Figure D.9: The GEM Output dialog box

This dialog box lets you set the Scale Factor, from 0 to 100 percent. The higher the number, the larger the picture will be. Select the Draw selection button in the Output File Format area if you want to use the exported file in Ventura Publisher or GEM Draw; select Artline if you want to use it in GEM Artline. This dialog box has a Help menu—read it before exporting files. When you import GEM art, Designer can figure out the type of GEM format, so no dialog box is needed.

3.1

Instead of displaying a dialog box that asks you which GEM format you want to export to, Designer 3.1 has two .GEM entries in the Export dialog box: one labeled GEM DRI Draw GEM and one labeled GEM DRI Artline GEM. You don't see the GEM Output dialog box, so you cannot adjust the Scale Factor.

.GRF—Micrografx Graph file

You can import these graph files, but you cannot export in this format. The imported files, created in Micrografx's Graph Plus and Charisma, lose their links to the data used to create them.

.HP—HP Graphics Language (HPGL)

You can export in this format, but not import. Designer displays the HP ColorPro dialog box, the same dialog box used to configure an HP plotter if you have one connected to your system (Figure D.10). You use the dialog box to configure your export file in the same way you would configure a plotter to which you are going to send data.

This dialog box has extensive online Help. Read all the Help messages before attempting to export in HPGL format.

.PCT—Macintosh PICT Files

There are two versions of Macintosh PICT files: Version 1 (the original) and Version 2 (which has color). Designer converts a file from one format to another, but you also have to move that file from one piece of hardware to the other. You can transfer files from a PC to a Macintosh (or vice versa) in a number of ways; using translation software, a special disk drive, a special linked network, or by running DOS on the Macintosh.

When you export a file you see the PICT Output dialog box (Figure D.11).

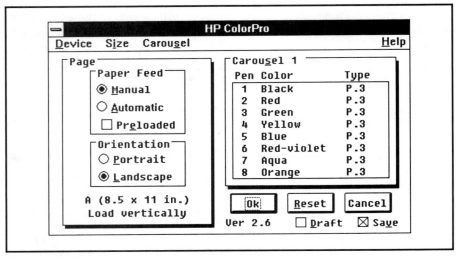

Figure D.10: The HP ColorPro dialog box

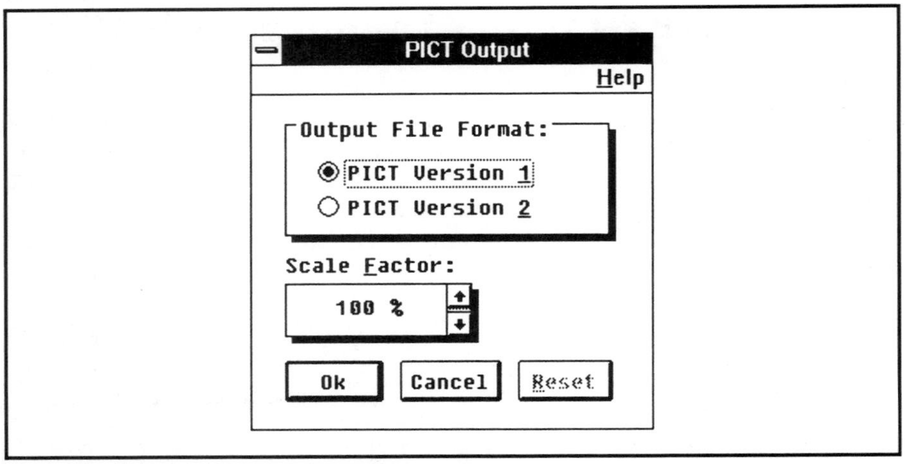

Figure D.11: The PICT Output dialog box

    Select the version in which you want to export the file, and set the Scale Factor—the larger the number the larger the exported file. Read this dialog box's Help messages before exporting.

.PCX—PC Paintbrush Bitmap

This is one of the most commonly used file formats. When you import a .PCX file you see the PCX Input dialog box (Figure D.12).

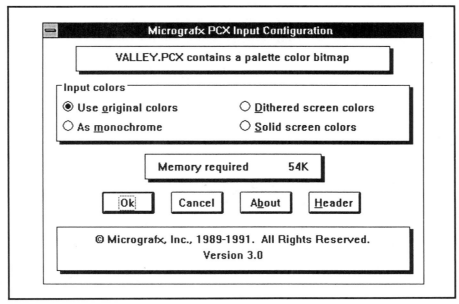

Figure D.12: The PCX Input (Import) dialog box

This dialog box tells you what the file contains—a color or monochrome image—and the amount of random access memory required to convert it. In some cases your computer may not have enough memory to import a large bitmap; if this is the case, you can either add memory or try using a bitmap program to break the file into smaller files.

Select the colors you want (if it's a monochrome bitmap, all options but As Monochrome are ghosted):

Use Original Colors	Imports the file with the original colors, if available on your system (otherwise, imports with dithered colors)

As Monochrome	Removes all colors (if any) and imports the file in black and white. Select this option if you want to change the bitmap's color (the other options won't allow you to do so).
Dithered Screen Colors	Replaces the original colors with dithered colors
Solid Screen Colors	Replaces dithered colors and colors that your screen cannot match with solid screen colors. Select this option if you want to trace the image.

You can view the header information by clicking on the Header command button. Figure D.13 shows an example of the Header Information dialog box.

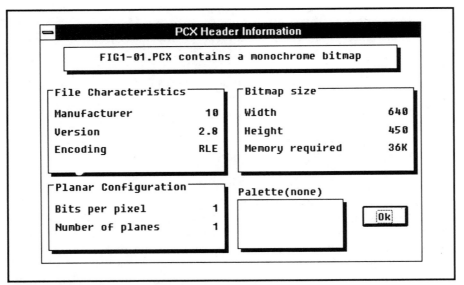

Figure D.13: The Header dialog box

When you click on OK, Designer begins importing, and displays a small dialog box (Figure D.14). If you click on Stop, Designer will stop importing the file, and place in the drawing area that part of the file already imported, letting you ''preview'' the file.

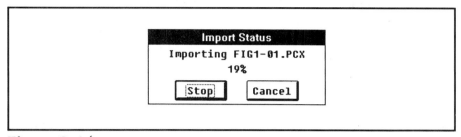

Figure D.14: The PCX Import Status dialog box

When you are exporting a file to .PCX format you see the PCX Output dialog box (Figure D.15).

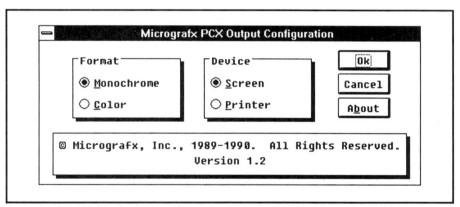

Figure D.15: The PCX Output (Export) dialog box

This dialog box lets you select the format in which to export the image—monochrome or color—and the resolution of the image. Select Screen to export it with the resolution that the image has on your computer's screen, or select Printer to use the resolution of the printer you have selected (in the Select Printer dialog box—File | Change Printer). If you select Screen, remember that the closer to the object the better the resolution; if, for example, several pages are displayed in the drawing area, you will get a low-resolution export. Use zoom to move in on the object and improve the resolution.

Selecting Printer creates a much larger file, with finer resolution. If you are not sure of the device on which the file will eventually be printed, you might select a printer with a high resolution to ensure that the file can be printed at high resolution later. (See Chapter 1 for an explanation of bitmap resolution.)

If you want to create a colored bitmap, you must select a color printer or None first; if you have selected a monochrome printer, the image will be monochrome, regardless of the color you select.

.PCX files are hard to work with, because the size of the exported or imported images is unpredictable; the image can vary in size tremendously from application to application, so you may find it easier to work with .TIF files, which remain the same size.

NOTE

Designer is not always able to import .PCX files directly from Windows 3.0 Paintbrush; Micrografx reports that Paintbrush saves its files in a nonstandard way. You can get around the problem, though, by saving the image in Paintbrush once, then reopening the file and saving it again. Now Designer will be able to import the image.

.PIC—MGX_PICT, Micrografx Picture Files

This is an early Micrografx format, used by In*a*Vision, Windows Draw, and Windows Graph. As these programs don't have all the features of Designer 3.0, some distortion will occur when exporting.

.PS—PostScript

The PostScript format is almost the same as the .EPS without TIFF preview, though the file header is different. If you load a .PS file into an application you will not be able to see the art on the screen—you will see a box instead—but you can still print it on a PostScript printer. This file format is the same as that created when you "print to file" with a PostScript printer loaded. In fact, you can use this .PS file as a print file. You can use the DOS COPY command to print it.

.TIF—Tag Image File Format (TIFF)

This is another common bitmap format. When you import a .TIF image you see the same dialog box displayed for .PCX files, and carry out the procedure in the same way. When you export a .TIF file you will see the TIFF Output dialog box, shown in Figure D.16.

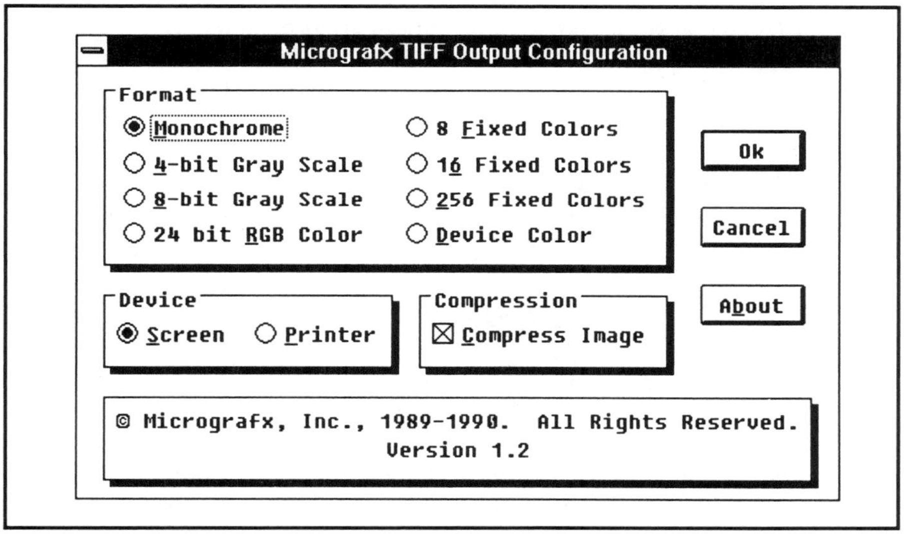

Figure D.16: The TIFF Output dialog box

The selection you make in the Format area of the dialog box determines the type of image exported:

Monochrome	Black and white
4-bit Gray Scale	16 greys
8-bit Gray Scale	256 greys
24-bit RGB Color	16.7 million colors
8 Fixed Colors	8 default Windows colors
16 Fixed Colors	2 shades of each of the 8 default Windows colors

256 Fixed
Colors   256 IBM-8514 display colors

Device Colors   The colors supported by the device selected at the
                     bottom of the dialog box

As with the .PCX images, if you want to create a colored bitmap, you must select a color printer or None first; if you have selected a monochrome printer, the image will be monochrome, regardless of the color you select.

The Device options, Screen and Printer, are the same as those for .PCX files. Compress Image builds a compressed TIFF file, which takes up less disk space. However, not all applications that work with TIFF can read compressed files.

You may find that thin lines disappear when you print TIFF images from other applications. You can fix the problem by changing the images' sizes slightly in the other application, or by redrawing with lines larger than the hairline size and re-exporting the image.

.TXT—ANSI Text Files

You can import ASCII and ANSI text files. While text is treated the same in ASCII and ANSI, ASCII special characters may not import correctly—see Chapter 8 for details.

You can also export text from Designer, but not using the Export dialog box. Instead, select the Text tool, press and hold Shift while you point to the text, and press button 1. When the text editor opens, select the text you want to export and select Edit | Copy. Then copy that text from the clipboard into the other application.

.WMF—Windows Metafile Format

This is a standard Windows graphics format, used to share graphics between different Windows applications. This is a very quick translation procedure.

.WMF files are a combination of vector and bitmap graphics, and the resolution of the exported image is determined by the resolution of the printer selected in the Select Printer dialog box (File | Change Printer).

Although Ventura Publisher uses .WMF, early versions do not accept Designer .WMF files; contact Xerox for a fix to correct the problem. And other .WMF files may not import or export in other situations, so you may need to try another format.

.WPG—WordPerfect Graphics

3.1

When you export in .WPG format you see the .WPG Output dialog box (Figure D.17). You can define the size of the exported image (from 5 percent to 9999 percent) and the quality of the curves on the final image. The .WPG format does not draw curves with the precision of Designer, so Designer has to decide how to reduce the points on the drawing. You can set a Curve Quality from 1 to 10, with 10 having the most points and so retaining the smoothest curves.

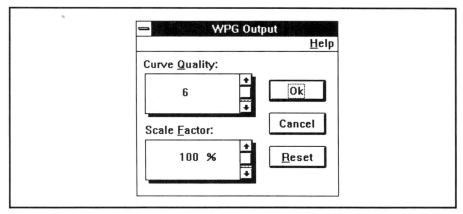

Figure D.17: The WPG Output (Export) dialog box

The PageMaker 4.0 Filter

PageMaker 4.0 has a special filter that uses Micrografx products to import .DRW files directly into PageMaker. You can create and save the image in Designer and then load it directly into PageMaker, and when you print a PageMaker file containing a .DRW image, the Micrografx product controls the printing, ensuring a high-quality output. You must have Designer 3.01 or later, Draw Plus 1.1, or Charisma 2.0 loaded on your computer when you load the image and print it, though the Micrografx application doesn't have to be running.

If you take the PageMaker file to a computer that doesn't have one of these applications loaded the .DRW image will still be in the file, but it will not have the same quality; it will be as if you had simply cut and pasted the image using the Windows clipboard. When you display using PageMaker's high resolution mode you will see a normal-resolution image, and when you print the file the image will not be printed with the high resolution that it would have had if one of the Micrografx products had been loaded on the computer.

INDEX

Note: Parentheses after command names indicate the "parent" menu or dialog box.

D

Selections from The SYBEX Library

DESKTOP PUBLISHING

The ABC's of the New Print Shop
Vivian Dubrovin
340pp. Ref. 640-4

This beginner's guide stresses fun, practicality and original ideas. Hands-on tutorials show how to create greeting cards, invitations, signs, flyers, letterheads, banners, and calendars.

The ABC's of Ventura
Robert Cowart
Steve Cummings
390pp. Ref. 537-9

Created especially for new desktop publishers, this is an easy introduction to a complex program. Cowart provides details on using the mouse, the Ventura side bar, and page layout, with careful explanations of publishing terminology. The new Ventura menus are all carefully explained. For Version 2.

Desktop Publishing with WordPerfect 5.1
Rita Belserene
418pp. Ref. 481-X

A practical guide to using the desktop publishing capabilities of versions 5.0 and 5.1. Topics include graphic design concepts, hardware necessities, installing and using fonts, columns, lines, and boxes, illustrations, multi-page layouts, Style Sheets, and integrating with other software.

Mastering CorelDRAW 2
Steve Rimmer
500pp. Ref. 814-9

This comprehensive tutorial and design guide features complete instruction in creating spectacular graphic effects with CorelDRAW 2. The book also offers a primer on commercial image and page design, including how to use printers and print-house facilities for optimum results.

Mastering Micrografx Designer
Peter Kent
400pp. Ref. 694-4

A complete guide to using this sophisticated illustration package. Readers begin by importing and modifying clip art, and progress to creating original drawings, working with text, printing and plotting, creating slide shows, producing color separations, and exporting art.

Mastering PageMaker 4 on the IBM PC
Rebecca Bridges Altman, with Rick Altman
509pp. Ref. 773-8

A step-by-step guide to the essentials of desktop publishing and graphic design. Tutorials and hands-on examples explore every aspect of working with text, graphics, styles, templates, and more, to design and produce a wide range of publications. Includes a publication "cookbook" and notes on using Windows 3.0.

Mastering Ventura for Windows (For Version 3.0)
Rick Altman
600pp, Ref. 758-4

This engaging, hands-on treatment is for the desktop publisher learning and using the Windows edition of Ventura. It covers everything from working with the Windows interface, to designing and printing sophisticated publications using Ventura's most advanced features. Understand and work with frames, graphics, fonts, tables and columns, and much more.

Mastering Ventura 3.0 Gem Edition
Matthew Holtz
650pp, Ref. 703-7

The complete hands-on guide to desktop publishing with Xerox Ventura Publisher—now in an up-to-date new edition featuring Ventura version 3.0, with the GEM windowing environment. Tutorials cover every aspect of the software, with examples ranging from correspondence and press releases, to newsletters, technical documents, and more.

Understanding Desktop Publishing
Robert W. Harris
300pp. Ref. 789-4

At last, a practical design handbook, written especially for PC users who are not design professionals, but who do have desktop publishing duties. How can publications be made attractive, understandable, persuasive, and memorable? Topics include type, graphics, and page design; technical and physiological aspects of creating and conveying a message.

Understanding PFS: First Publisher
Gerry Litton
463pp. Ref. 712-6

This new edition of the popular guide to First Publisher covers software features in a practical introduction to desktop publishing. Topics include text-handling, working with graphics, effective page design, and optimizing print quality. With examples of flyers, brochures, newsletters, and more.

Understanding PostScript Programming (Second Edition)
David A. Holzgang
472pp. Ref. 566-2

In-depth treatment of PostScript for programmers and advanced users working on custom desktop publishing tasks. Hands-on development of programs for font creation, integrating graphics, printer implementations and more.

Up & Running with CorelDRAW 2
Len Gilbert
140pp; Ref. 887-4

Learn CorelDRAW 2 in record time. This 20-step tutorial is perfect for computer-literate users who are new to CorelDRAW or upgrading from an earlier version. Each concise step takes no more than 15 minutes to an hour to complete, and provides needed skills without unnecessary detail.

Up & Running with PageMaker 4 on the PC
Marvin Bryan
140pp. Ref. 781-9

An overview of PageMaker 4.0 in just 20 steps. Perfect for evaluating the software before purchase—or for newcomers who are impatient to get to work. Topics include installation, adding typefaces, text and drawing tools, graphics, reusing layouts, using layers, working in color, printing, and more.

Your HP LaserJet Handbook
Alan R. Neibauer
564pp. Ref. 618-9

Get the most from your printer with this step-by-step instruction book for using LaserJet text and graphics features such as cartridge and soft fonts, type selection, memory and processor enhancements, PCL programming, and PostScript solutions. This hands-on guide provides specific instructions for working with a variety of software.

SYBEX

FREE BROCHURE!

Complete this form today, and we'll send you a full-color brochure of Sybex bestsellers.

Please supply the name of the Sybex book purchased.

_____

How would you rate it?

_____ Excellent   _____ Very Good   _____ Average   _____ Poor

Why did you select this particular book?

_____ Recommended to me by a friend
_____ Recommended to me by store personnel
_____ Saw an advertisement in _____
_____ Author's reputation
_____ Saw in Sybex catalog
_____ Required textbook
_____ Sybex reputation
_____ Read book review in _____
_____ In-store display
_____ Other _____

Where did you buy it?

_____ Bookstore
_____ Computer Store or Software Store
_____ Catalog (name: _____)
_____ Direct from Sybex
_____ Other: _____

Did you buy this book with your personal funds?

_____ Yes   _____ No

About how many computer books do you buy each year?

_____ 1-3   _____ 3-5   _____ 5-7   _____ 7-9   _____ 10+

About how many Sybex books do you own?

_____ 1-3   _____ 3-5   _____ 5-7   _____ 7-9   _____ 10+

Please indicate your level of experience with the software covered in this book:

_____ Beginner   _____ Intermediate   _____ Advanced

Which types of software packages do you use regularly?

_____ Accounting	_____ Databases	_____ Networks
_____ Amiga	_____ Desktop Publishing	_____ Operating Systems
_____ Apple/Mac	_____ File Utilities	_____ Spreadsheets
_____ CAD	_____ Money Management	_____ Word Processing
_____ Communications	_____ Languages	_____ Other _____
		(please specify)

Which of the following best describes your job title?

_____ Administrative/Secretarial _____ President/CEO

_____ Director _____ Manager/Supervisor

_____ Engineer/Technician _____ Other _____
(please specify)

Comments on the weaknesses/strengths of this book: _____

_____

_____

_____

_____

Name _____

Street _____

City/State/Zip _____

Phone _____

PLEASE FOLD, SEAL, AND MAIL TO SYBEX

SYBEX, INC.
Department M
2021 CHALLENGER DR.
ALAMEDA, CALIFORNIA USA
94501

SYBEX

SEAL

FONTS PROVIDED WITH DESIGNER

BITSTREAM FONTS

Cheltenham, Stubserif 205
Cheltenham Bold, Stubserif 205
Cheltenham Italic, Stubserif 205
Cheltenham Bold Italic, Stubserif 205
Courier 10 Pitch SWA, Fixed Pitch 810
Courier 10 Pitch SWA Bold, Fixed Pitch 810
Courier 10 Pitch SWA Italic, Fixed Pitch 810
Courier 10 Pitch SWA Bold Italic, Fixed Pitch 810
Dutch 801 Roman SWA
Dutch 801 Bold SWA
Dutch 801 Italic SWA
Dutch 801 Bold Italic SWA
Geometric 415 Medium
Geometric 415 Medium Italic
Geometric 415 Medium Black
Geometric 415 Medium Black Italic
Italian Garamond, Aldine 525
Italian Garamond Bold, Aldine 525
Italian Garamond Italic, Aldine 525
Swiss 721 SWA
Swiss 721 SWA Bold
Swiss 721 SWA Italic
Swiss 721 SWA Bold Italic
Swiss 721 Narrow SWA
Swiss 721 Narrow Italic SWA
Swiss 721 Narrow Bold SWA
Swiss 721 Narrow Bold Italic SWA